PENGUIN BOOKS

I HEAR AMERICA COOKING

Betty Fussell is a Californian who now makes her home in New York City. She holds a doctorate in English Literature, and she has lectured widely on food history and has written regularly for publications ranging from *The New York Times* to *Vogue* to *The Journal of Gastronomy* and *Country Journal*. She is the author of *Home Bistro, Crazy for Corn, The Story of Corn, Home Plates, Food in Good Season, Eating In*, and *Masters of American Cookery*.

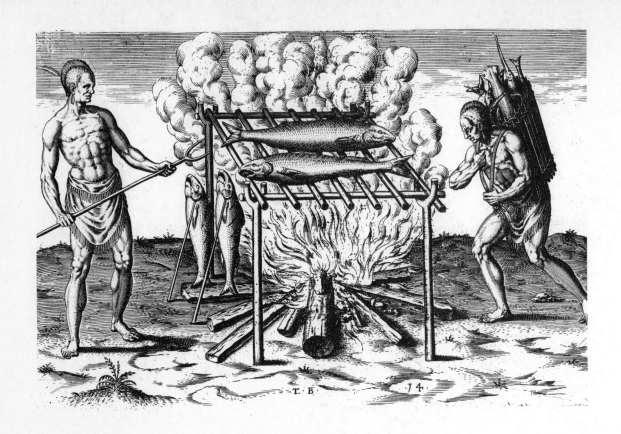

Fter they haue taken ſtore of fiſhe, they gett them vnto a place ſitt to dreſs yt.
Ther they ſticke vpp in the grownde 4. ſtakes in a ſquare roome, and lay 4 potes
vppon them, and others ouer thwart theſame like vnto an hurdle, of ſufficient
heigthe. and layinge their fiſhe vppon this hurdle, they make a fyre vnderneathe
to broile the ſame, not after the manner of the people of Florida, which doe but
ſchorte, and harden their meate in the ſmoke onlye to Reſerue theſame duringe
all the winter. For this people reſeruinge nothinge for ſtore, thei do broile, and ſpend away all att
once and when they haue further neede, they roſte or ſeethe freſh, as wee ſhall ſee heraffter. And
when as the hurdle can not holde all the fiſhes, they hange the Reſt by the fyrres on ſticks ſett vpp
in the grounde a gainſt the fyre, and than they finiſhe the reſt of their cookerye. They take good
heede that they bee not burntt. When the firſt are broyled they lay others on, that weare
newlye broughte, continuinge the dreſſinge of their meate in this ſorte,
vntill they thincke they haue ſufficient.

BETTY FUSSELL

I Hear America Cooking

THE COOKS AND RECIPES OF AMERICAN REGIONAL CUISINE

PENGUIN BOOKS

PENGUIN BOOKS
Published by the Penguin Group
Penguin Books USA Inc., 375 Hudson Street,
New York, New York 10014, U.S.A.
Penguin Books Ltd, 27 Wrights Lane, London W8 5TZ, England
Penguin Books Australia Ltd, Ringwood, Victoria, Australia
Penguin Books Canada Ltd, 10 Alcorn Avenue, Toronto, Ontario, Canada M4V 3B2
Penguin Books (N.Z.) Ltd, 182–190 Wairau Road, Auckland 10, New Zealand

Penguin Books Ltd, Registered Offices:
Harmondsworth, Middlesex, England

First published in the United States of America
by Viking Penguin Inc. 1986
Published in Penguin Books 1997

1 3 5 7 9 10 8 6 4 2

Grateful acknowledgment is made for permission to reprint the following copyrighted material:

Excerpt from "Rice Pudding" from *When We Were Very Young*, by A. A. Milne.
Copyright 1924 by E. P. Dutton, renewed 1952 by A. A. Milne. Reprinted by permission
of the publisher, E. P. Dutton, a division of New American Library.

Excerpt from The People of 'Ksan, *Gathering What the Great Nature Provided*.
Published by the University of Washington Press, 1980.

Excerpt from "Kitchen Man" by Andy Razaf and Alex Bellenda. © Copyright 1929 by MCA Music
Publishing, a division of MCA Inc., New York, N.Y. Copyright renewed. Used by permission.
All rights reserved.

The frontispiece is John White's depiction of the American barbecue for Theodor de Bry's edition of
Thomas Harriot's *A Briefe And True Report of the New Found Land of Virginia* (1590). In explaining that the
Algonkians of Roanoke Island do not smoke their fish to preserve it but broil it over a hot flame, Harriot
gives the first native American recipe in the English language.

THE LIBRARY OF CONGRESS HAS CATALOGUED THE HARDCOVER AS FOLLOWS:
Fussell, Betty Harper.
I hear America cooking.
"Elisabeth Sifton Books."
Includes index.
ISBN 0-670-81241-2 (hc.)
ISBN 0 14 02.6332 2 (pbk.)
1. Cookery, American.   I. Title.
TX715.F978   1986   641.5973   85–41085

Printed in the United States of America
Set in Caslon

For Brother Bob

"Strange people, strange people, these Americans!"
—Comment of the Zuni chiefs
Palowahtiwa, Waihusiwa, and Heluta,
visiting Boston in 1886

Acknowledgments

Among the many hundred strangers and friends who helped me on my way, I would like to thank a few whose names do not appear in the text. Some hunted out recipes, others books, still others people and places, but all shared their special knowledge with generosity. Howard and Janet Adams, Ronda Allen, James Baird, Alfred Bush, Cordelia Cannon, Elizabeth Carter, Rita Chaipel, Phyllis Dennery, Linda Donelson, Jeannie Driver, Chris Dubbs, Margaret Eagle, Walter Edgar, Marilyn Einhorn, Meryle Evans, Rita and John Finger, Laura Flannery, Sara Gillespie, Martha and Jack Hall, Mary Hansen, Stanley Hearst, Mina Kempton, Gary Knowles, Jan Longone, Frances Lowenstein, Lawrence Maxwell, Virginia Meynard, Rosetta Miller, Jacqueline Newman, Alfonso Ortiz, Louise Searing, Lydia Shire, Florence Snider, Frederick Turner, Thomas and Lois Watson, Nahum Waxman, Lloyd Wescott, Jasper White.

For help with the specifics of this book, thanks to Melinda Corey, Gloria Loomis, Glenna Putt, Elisabeth Sifton.

Thanks finally to the staffs of the Charleston Museum, Cooper-Hewitt Museum Library, Firestone Library of Princeton University, Louisiana State Museum, Louisiana Office of Tourism, Milwaukee County Historical Society, Milwaukee Public Library, Museum of the American Indian, Oregon Historical Society, Prints and Photographs Division of the Library of Congress, Rare Books and Manuscripts Division of the New York Public Library, Smithsonian Institution National Anthropological Archives, South Carolina Historical Society, South Caroliniana Library of the University of South Carolina, State Historical Society of Wisconsin, Washington State Historical Society.

Contents

List of Illustrations

Frontispiece: John White's depiction of the American barbecue for Thomas Harriot's *A Briefe and True Report of the New Found Land of Virginia*, 1590. *From the collections of the Library of Congress.*

Introduction

Hitting the Corn-Pone Trail

You tell me whar a man gits his corn pone, en I'll tell you what his 'pinions is.

—Mark Twain, "Corn Pone Opinions,"
Europe and Elsewhere, 1925

In the sleepy California town where I grew up during the Depression, I never heard of corn pone but I heard plenty of opinions, mostly about the wickedness of caffeine and Roosevelt and the virtues of Postum and Landon. My parents thought they had left corn pone behind them on the farms of Edgerton, Kansas, when they packed up their opinions and brought them intact to the orange groves of Riverside, halfway between Los Angeles and Palm Springs and, in my folks' view, halfway to heaven. In my view Riverside was the dullest cornball town on earth. It was the kind of place where even the swear words were corny. My mother said, "Good governor!" and my father said, "Oh, shucks!"

In my ignorance I thought I could escape. I didn't know that I was literally a corn-fed, corn-bred child, which made me different from a child in Canton or Amsterdam or Moscow or Bombay. It made me an American child. For breakfast I had a bowl of cornflakes with sugar and cold milk, for lunch a pack of potato chips crisped in corn oil, which also furnished the mayonnaise for my tuna-salad sandwich. The margarine I colored yellow to look like butter owed its life not to cows but to corn. My jelly beans and gum drops, despite their rainbow colors, were sugared starch made from corn. The same starch that made our chocolate puddings and lemon meringue pies made the sauces for our chop sueys and chow meins. Syrup made of corn was the key to a whole tooth-decaying Sunday of taffies and butterscotch, caramels and fondant.

I was a literalist and recognized corn only in its obvious forms: a fresh ear, boiled and buttered; cut kernels mixed with limas for succotash or pickled in vinegar for relish or bathed in their own milk for creamed corn; corn turned into white hominy to eat with butter and sometimes milk and sugar; or ground into meal to mix with eggs and baking powder for pancakes or muffins or cornbread proper in a pan; or boiled into mush, then sliced and fried in butter and drowned in maple syrup.

It never occurred to me when I fed dried corn to the chickens we kept in the backyard under the loquats that chickens too were made of corn, condensed into eggs and flesh, like a slice of bacon or a pork chop or a beef steak or a glass of milk. In a family of teetotalers, I would never have guessed that beer and bourbon came from devil corn. Nor did I dream that corn infiltrated the most common objects of our daily lives: the soap we washed our hands with, the polish we shined our shoes with, the glue my brother used on his model airplanes, the fabric that made my rayon dress.

In the eternal now of California, I didn't know that cornbread had a history rather like our own. I didn't know that the batter I baked in a pan in a gas oven was really a dandified pone, which earlier had been baked on a shingle or a hoe beside a campfire. Nor did I know that the corn we kids loved most, the dried kernels we shook in a covered pan until they popped, then soaked with butter and salt and put in a wooden bowl to eat in the parlor while we listened to Jack Armstrong, the All-American Boy, was the most American corn of all, the original seed of life for an ancient civilization mistakenly called Indian in a world mistakenly called New.

When I ate my bag of buttered popcorn at a Saturday matinee in the Fox Riverside Theater, I was eating 5000 years of American history and 80,000 years of prehistory. *Zea Mays,* "the life-giver grain," is a hybrid name given by a Swiss botanist to a hybrid of wild grasses that gave life to the natives of Peru long before the Druids were eating acorns or the Israelites locusts and wild honey. My movie-time popcorn was a direct descendant of the popcorn Chief Massasoit brought to the spread laid out by Governor Bradford of Massachusetts in 1621 and a devious descendant of the Lilliputian pod-popcorn cobs, no bigger than the tip of a baby's thumb, which were found in 1948 in Bat Cave, New Mexico, said to be 5600 years old.

In rootless California, I knew as little of people roots as I knew of food roots. We were all migrants; it was just a question of when. We Bible Belt migrants of the 1920s snubbed the Okie migrants of the 1930s and were snubbed in turn by the Hispanic migrants who had claimed the land and founded the missions a century before. The Chinese, in our local Chinatown, snubbed the late-coming Japanese. Blacks from Los Angeles snubbed the Wetbacks (or pachukos, as we called them) from Tijuana. And all of us migrants, without exception, not so much snubbed as ignored the only people whose roots were truly in this land. The natives of California we sequestered in a philanthropic Sherman Institute at the far end of town and on a reservation near the San Andreas Fault in Palm Canyon.

Certainly I did not connect the inhabitants of these charitable ghettoes with my buttered popcorn. If the Indians ate corn in any form, we didn't know it. I'm sure they were fed cornflakes at the Institute and I imagined they ate roasted lizards in the canyon. If we had any sense of a local use of corn, related to a particular people, it concerned the Mexicans' tamales and tortillas. Since their opinions were at the bottom of the social pecking order, their corn pones were at the bottom of the culinary scale. My parents never soiled their lips with a tortilla, not to mention a hot pepper sauce.

After the Second World War, when I married and lived in Boston, having migrated backward to the East, I ate my first Indian pudding and thought it had been invented by S. S. Pierce of Boston because it came in a can from that store. I thought it quaintly typical of a people who pronounced "heart" "hat" and thought "the West" began on the far side of Boylston Street. On my first trip south, I ate grits in Williamsburg but was far more impressed with the eccentricity of a people who said to perfect strangers, "Y'all come back now, y' hear?" Not until I went to Europe in the 1950s, looking for cultural roots, did I come across food roots shockingly different from my own and, country by country, different from each other. Only then did I discover the intimate connection between opinions and pones, in Europe and Elsewhere. And because I was a prodigal daughter, I was ashamed of my own corn-pone past. Now I didn't eat corn on the cob but *maïs frais au naturel.* I didn't eat cornmush but polenta. I adopted the European view of Americans and their food—that it was one barbaric yawp from the time the first explorers found the vexed Bermoothes inhabited by cannibals and anthropophagi. I can only say in my defense that there is no snobbery as intense as food snobbery and I had lots of company.

Amerigo Vespucci had set the tone in 1504 when he explained *Mundus Novus* to fellow Florentines and told them what to expect when they visited Brazil. "And I likewise remained twenty-seven days in a certain city where I saw salted human flesh suspended from beams between the houses, just as with us it is the custom to hang bacon and pork. I say further: They themselves wonder why we do not eat our enemies and do not use as food their flesh which they say is most savory."

Over the centuries travelers from the Old World were seldom pleased even with more conventional New World foods. Thus Sarah Kemble Knight, traveling between Boston and New York in 1704, described a dish of pork and cabbage served at an inn: "The sause was of a deep Purple, wch I th't was boil'd in her dye Kettle; the bread was Indian, and . . . I being hungry, gott a little down; but my stomach was soon cloy'd, and what cabbage I swallowed serv'd me for a Cudd the whole day after." Thus Joseph Conrad, in the early twentieth century, who attributed the ferocity of American Indians to the bad cooking of their wives: "The Seven Nations around the Great Lake and the Horse tribes of the plains were but one vast prey to raging dyspepsia." Thus even today the latest French chef scorns upstart America's claims for a national cuisine: "Since there is very little past, there *is* no American cuisine."

From his opinions, I knew where the French chef got his corn pone. He got it, he says, from five centuries of French culinary tradition, which is also five centuries of French provincialism that called corn *blé de Turquie*. English opinions have been no less contemptuous of the new. John Gerard in his sixteenth-century *Herball* allowed that Turkie or Guinea Wheat was okay for New World Indians because "the barbarous Indians, which know no better, are constrained to make a vertue of necessitie." But civilized Englishmen would "easily judge that it nourisheth but little, and is of hard and evil digestion, a more convenient food for swine than for man."

I began to see that opinions about pones had political consequences and that if Revolutionary America had gone to war over tea it had more importantly gone to war over corn. At the time of the Stamp Act in 1766, when the London *Gazetteer* sneered that rebellious Yanks would have to import English tea in order to choke down their indigestible breakfasts of Indian corn, Benjamin Franklin replied, "Johnny or hoe-cake hot from the fire is better than a Yorkshire muffin." Ben quickly made an alliance with France.

There was nothing new about turning a *batterie de cuisine* into a weaponry of nationalism. When Hannah Glasse wrote *The Art of Cookery Made Plain and Easy* in 1747, she expressed a century of Anglo-French antagonism that opposed honest Beefeaters to foppish Sauce-eaters. "So much is the blind folly of this age," she wrote, "that they would rather be imposed on by a *French* booby, than give encouragement to a good *English* cook!" Americans, in turn, defended New World innocence from the depravities of English, French, and Italian boobies. Thus spoke the anonymous author of *The Cook Not Mad, or Rational Cookery* (1830): "Still further would the impropriety be carried were we to introduce into a work intended for the *American Publick* such *English, French* and *Italian* methods of rendering things indigestible, which are of themselves innocent, or of distorting and disguising the most loathsome objects to render them sufferable to already vitiated tastes."

The Cook Not Mad was in the Twain tradition inherited by humorists like Russell Baker, Calvin Trillin, and Roy Blount, Jr., all of whom pose, from time to time, as corn-fed chauvinist pigs. "There is here and there an American who will say he can remember rising from a European table d'hôte perfectly satisfied," Twain wrote in *A Tramp Abroad,* "but we must not overlook the fact that there is also here and there an American who will lie."

After tramping much abroad, I too began to hunger for home and the comfort of hot cornmeal mush. I began to see that Europeans missed the point of American food because they missed the joke. The joke of American food, voiced often by Twain, is the joke of comic excess. What Europeans condemn in American food is that it is too hot, too cold, too sweet, too sour, too rushed, too standardized, too bland, too much. But their corn-pone opinions are scaled to the dimensions of their own turf. America is simply too big, too wild, and too varied for the maps they project on our culinary territory. A nineteenth-century Englishwoman, Mrs. Frances Trollope, looked for English manners in domestic America and found barbarians swilling at the trough. A pair of modern Frenchmen, Gault and Millau, look for *haute, bourgeoise,* and *régionale* categories in anarchic America and find only Television Cuisine spewing out "gastronomic pornography." But Gault and Millau got America wrong from the start by identifying a continent with a city: "Beautiful and hideous, tender and violent, generous and mean, fascinating and horrifying, New York is the image of the entire continent." Is Paris the image of the entire continent of Europe or Tokyo of the entire continent of Asia?

But if American cooking is not a plastic pornography *"du ketchup au cake mix, du Jell-O au peanut butter, du Coke à l'orangeade sans orange,"* what is it? What it is *not* is regional cooking in the European sense of local products native to a place with strong local traditions. Back in 1926, H. L. Mencken found American restaurant food "as rigidly standardized as the parts of a flivver," so that "one hunts in vain in Boston for a decent plate of beans, and in Baltimore for a decent mess of steamed hard crabs, and in St. Louis for a decent rasher of catfish." Instead, he found dishes for men hurrying to catch trains—"tasteless roasts, banal beefsteaks, cremated chops, fish drenched in unintelligible sauces, greasy potatoes, and a long repertoire of vegetables with no more taste than baled shavings." Imagine what he would say about today's dishes for men hurrying to catch planes and space shuttles.

Restaurants are in themselves as foreign to the American temper as the syntax of a French menu or the boy apprenticeship of a French chef. It was the French who invented restaurants in the late eighteenth century to employ chefs put out of work by the national mania for applying cleavers to heads. It was the French who invented international cuisine by creating draconian standards for a new "profession" of cuisiniers. It was the French who invented Cartesian categories to distinguish international from regional, professional from domestic, erudite from "silent" cuisine. And it was a Frenchman who concluded that "silent," not erudite, cuisine was the way to separate countries where the eating was good from those where it was bad.

"Silent" means the "silent majority" of ordinary people cooking daily at home. This is the cooking that few Europeans ever experience in depth in a continent as large as all the countries of Europe put together. For the same reason, few Americans experience it either. It is not the cooking that appears on television or in gourmet magazines or posh restaurant guides, because its purpose is neither showbiz nor celebrityhood nor fashion. It is not designed to streamline bodies or delay cardiac arrest. This is cooking for the pleasure of cooking and eating. And because it does not make money or news in a money-making media-blitzed culture, it is unusually "silent."

To hear the voices of America's silent cooks is to hear so many voices that foreign interpreters are deafened by babel or white sound. The Britisher Jane Grigson, who finely interprets her own language, hears in the language of American cook books only nostalgic recollections of immigrants or melting-pot anthologies "Bedding down Koenigsberger Klops with sweetcorn and elk, gremolata with raccoon, Sally Lunns with Johnnycake—a mammoth enterprise." "Mammoth" is the word, like Melville's whale or Whitman's enterprise—"my elbows rest in sea-gaps . . . my palms cover continents."

I had covered continents abroad but not at home. Now, if I wanted to hear the silent voices of America cooking, I would have to hit the road and look and listen for myself.

I knew from the start that "authentic" was a buzzword like "regional." Authentic to what? I agreed with Elizabeth David that even French Provincial cooking, born and bred of local products and strong traditions, is authentic only *in* that locale, and often not even then. I have had—as who has not?—ghastly bouillabaisses in Marseille, unspeakable salades niçoises in Nice, inedible London broils in London. It's not the name of a dish, the cook, the ingredients, or the methods that make a dish seem authentic to a particular place, but the whole enchilada—the soil, the climate, the rhythms of the place, the sound of the language, the feel of the air, the smell of the kitchen, the shape of the pots—everything that makes a place unique. Cooking authentic to a particular region is a particularly French idea because France was founded on provinces that were staked out by Rome, developed by dukes, organized by kings, and reorganized by republicans, but that never lost their native character. America, on the other hand, was founded on colonies that, as transplants, were wholly inauthentic to the land. "The uniqueness of America," Daniel Boorstin writes in *The Americans,* "would prove to be its ability to erase

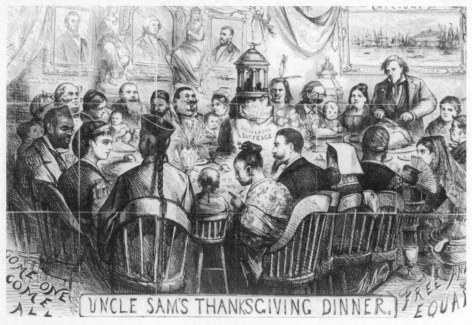

uniqueness." From the start, colonists, pioneers, and then industrial entrepreneurs labored to annihilate seasons, distances, and the particularity of places in order to make food portable over long periods of time. The mammoth enterprise of American cooking was to produce food-in-motion for a people constantly on the move. Go-getters condensed food into cubes and biscuits, bottles and tins, dry powders and frozen granules. The enterprise demanded that they deny the local, the particular, the traditional, the in-born, the inbred. We were going to start over and make ourselves up from scratch.

Forget Roman logic, French reason, British tradition. America's places would be as muddled as the faces, races, and cultures that mixed and moved on. American cooking is unique in the world's cuisines because it is hybrid cooking for a nation of hybrids. An *authentic* American hamburger is named for a German city, splashed with British ketchup, and served with fries called French. An *authentic* Louisiana gumbo gets its name from African Bantu, its sauce from a French roux, its hot pepper from the West Indies, and its sassafras from Choctaw Indians. So much for authentic regionalism or ethnic purity.

Now that America has bred its first generation of native-born chefs, it wants to establish an "authentic" American voice, but it keeps looking to French models. Yet the best of the New American cooking is as muddled and

---

OPPOSITE, ABOVE: In this 1876 lithograph, published by Schumacher and Ettlinger, Uncle Sam celebrates his first centennial with a little dinner party at which Mistress Columbia serves, the Black Boy cooks, and each Regional Child provides rice, corn, or fish balls to help feed the World. The bill of fare, designed to advertise the capacities of the "Uncle Sam" range, reveals mainstream American attitudes toward the ethnic diversity depicted amiably by Thomas Nast in the happy Thanksgiving family dinner (OPPOSITE, BELOW), at which Uncle Sam carves and nobody serves. The bill of fare (ABOVE) amusingly identifies England with Roast Beef and Plum Puddings; Germany with Sausages, Pretzels, and Sour Cream; France with Saddle de Horse, Curried Frogs, Snails, and Donkey à la Mode; Ireland with Potatoes—Fried, Boiled, Stewed, Roasted, Baked, Mashed, and Raw; China with Birds' Nests, Boiled Grasshoppers, and Rats Fricasseed with Watermelon Seeds; Italy with Macaroni, Roasted Chestnuts, and Sardines; Russia with Tallow Candles, Seal's Blubber, Train Oil, and White Bear; Turkey with Pistachio Nuts and Olive Oil. Through hyperbole, the artist exhibits both the strength and the dilemma of America's polyglot cuisine, solved here by the alchemy of technological progress embodied in a cast-iron stove.

as shifty as the old. The pace setter of California's new style is Alice Waters, born in New Jersey, ravished by Provence, and married to the communes of Berkeley, where she dishes up Pacific-Provençale in a Monterey-styled house called Chez Panisse. The embodiment of Louisiana's Cajun style is Paul Prudhomme, who was born in the swamps but who by the very act of bringing country food to the city has spawned a brood of Instant Cajun from Portland to Kalamazoo. The spokesman for Manhattan's new all-American style is Lawrence Forgione, who flies in "native" American ingredients to Madison Avenue as if a morel from Michigan would make a place American and a French *morelle* would not. To hear the sound of "silent" cooking, I would have to avoid restaurant noise, even when the noise was American and not French. I would have to avoid American fast-food noise even if the Musak was "authentic." I would have to look for other models than French or commercial ones. I found them in three overlapping native languages: the language of corn, the language of slapstick, and the language of jazz. Together they spelled out the vernacular of American cooking, which is as unique to America as blue corn, white custard pies, and red hot tomatoes.

If Americans were hybrids, so the grain that gave them life was hybrid and multiploid. The name *Zea Mays,* or "life grain," was a hybrid of West Indian *mahiz* and a Greek additive, *Zea.* The vocabulary of corn cooking was hybrid, transliterating multiple Indian dialects into Americanized English. Even before they could consume this new grain, explorers and settlers had to invent words to comprehend it. When they heard Algonquins and Lenapes and Narragansets explain their cooked mush as *apan, suppan, nasaump, rockahominie, tackhummin,* the foreigners translated the words to "pone," "samp," "hominy." When John Josselyn wrote *An Account of Two Voyages to New England* in 1674, he had to translate the new colonial language into the King's English to explain how they "make a kind of loblolly to eat with Milk, which they call Sampe; they beat corn in a Mortar and sift the Flower out of it; the remainder they call Homminey, which they put into a Pot of two or three Gallons with Water, and boyl it upon a Gentle Fire till it be like a Hasty Pudden."

They improvised language as they improvised survival, combining what they knew with what they found. "Pone" they retranslated into "ashcakes," like those baked of barley, rye, and wheat, in the ashes of their English hearths. They retranslated pone into "spoon breads" when they shaped their corn cakes on chips or shingles of wood called "spoons," and into "hoecakes" when the man in the field improvised an iron griddle from a hoe.

What could be more appropriate to the cooking of a hybrid people than a grain that was a hybrid of the hard flint of the North with the gourdseed of the South and that multiplied best not by inbreeding but by crossbreeding? What could be more productive of growth and national enterprise than a plant capable of varying its product endlessly in a "wonderful copulation" of half-breeds? What would better suit an improvised nation than a grain of such unpredictable genetic elements that its genes were called "jumping genes"? At the same time, what would be more self-reliant than an ear of corn, sporting both male tassel and female silk, a rugged individual in its own husk, an embodiment of "E Pluribus Unum" in its separate but equal seeds united in a single cob?

Spontaneous, improvised, impromptu, potluck cooking—that was the American vernacular of corn that united the tamales of New Mexico to the johnnycakes of Rhode Island and joined the succotashes, gallimaufries, olla podridas, chow meins, and slumgullions in a shifting ethnic mix. American cooking was the French gastronome Curnonsky's *Cuisine Improvisée,* thrown together "on a potluck basis, with whatever comes to hand . . . shrimps caught on the spot, fish from the nearby stream, milk from a farm close by, the best parts of a hare just decapitated by a speeding car." American cooking was road food in every sense, and when people got together for a moment in their rush to someplace else, they cooked out of doors: a clambake in Cape Cod, a fais-dodo in a Cajun swamp, a chili cookout at a Texas ranch, a salmon roast on the Olympic Peninsula. They used whatever came to hand or foot, like Charlie's tramp in *The Gold Rush,* who dines on *rôti de boote garni avec lacets italiennes.*

As an American child I had teethed on the vernacular of comic American movies as much as on the vernacular of corn, and I now discovered that they shared a grammar beyond jokes called corny and acting called ham. Chaplin, a Cockney transplant become the all-American Tramp, spoke in his silent comedies the language of America's silent cooking because they had jokes in common. Bananas were eaten for the sake of the peel. Pies were made to push in a face. The excesses of parody and burlesque linked the hyperbole of the American language to the hyperbole of American gesture in our characteristic style of slapstick, where the Tramp strikes a blow for democracy every time he whacks a pompous backside. The language of American food in name and substance parodies the high-falutin' airs of haute cuisine, calling salt pork "overland trout," onions "skunk eggs," sheep testicles "Rocky Moun-

Comic hyperbole links the American language to American food, as in this tall-tale post-card devised by Ed Burden in 1956 to recall the joke cards popular between 1905 and 1915, when boosterism was at its height. Excessive abundance in an outsized continent engendered whoppers that parodied truth: "The fish here even top the lies for size."

tain oysters," puddings and pies "slumps and grunts," chipped beef on toast "shit on a shingle," codfish balls "sleeve buttons," ham and beans "stars and stripes," buffalo turds "prairie pancakes."

When America got pompous about cuisine and gourmandise, there was always a Huck Finn to tell how "Jim he got some corn-dodgers and butter-milk, and pork and cabbage and greens—there ain't nothing in the world so good when it's cooked right." When America went ape over the international cuisine mediated by Craig Claiborne, there was always a Russell Baker to outsnob the snobs: "Wine being absolutely de rigueur with cheese, I chose a 1974 Muscatel, followed with a maraschino cherry, and afterward cleared my palate with three pickled martini olives." Or a Calvin Trillin to treat Alice to Frozen Duck à l'Orange Soda Pop in La Maison de la Casa House. Or a Roy Blount, Jr., to praise "My Mother's Macaroni and Cheese": "I wish that I / Were up to my knees / In my mother's mac- / Aroni and cheese." America's cooking is parody cooking and it speaks loudest and clearest in street cries, folk rhymes, and the whole subverting voice, rhythm, and structure of American jazz. Europe kept high life high and low life low, but America turned them upside down and messed them musically in a slumgullion of opera, brass bands, minstrel songs, and the drumbeats of Congo Square. Jazz, too, was vernacular rather than regional, and it was not limited to New Or-leans or Chicago any more than it was limited to black, Creole, or white. It was a hybrid and a crossbreed, like the food from which performers took their names. "Daddy" Rice sang the songs of "Cornmeal." "Jelly Roll" Morton (born Ferdinand Joseph La Menthe) was backed by his "Red Hot Peppers."

America cooked road food as it played road music—ragging the beat, improvising, exaggerating, fantasizing—a pick-up band of traveling folk who took potluck with the music. Jazz started with street bands who blared fare-well to the flesh at "Carne Vale" and funeral bands who trumpeted "letting the body go." When they played inside, they played in a church they called Funky Butt Hall. America made joke music the way it made joke food, and it liked to mess the two together in songs like Bessie Smith's "Kitchen Man."

> I love his cabbage, gravy, hash
> Daffy 'bout his succotash
> I can't do without my kitchen man.

Even more than "dirty rags," it was the syntax of jazz that clued me in to the syntax of American cooking. The potluck nature of a jazz ensemble was the opposite of a melting pot in which separate ingredients were homogenized. In jazz every musical voice was separate and distinct even in the chorus. The paradox of jazz was the paradox of harmony out of anarchy. "Everybody go his own way, everybody play for hisself" means the solo riffs are over, now everybody play at once. That, I decided, was the only way to explain the structured chaos of both American cooking and American social structure.

"There are no distinct classes, as in aristocratic lands, whose bounds are protected by distinct and impassible lines," Catharine Beecher wrote in *A Treatise on Domestic Economy* (1841), "but all are thrown into promiscuous masses." "Promiscuous" was a word to hold on to, like the unpredictable jumping genes of American corn. When Frenchmen come to Louisiana they expect to find vestiges of colonial France, baguettes, and *truite bleue,* a Cajun folklorist told me, but what they find instead are French-speaking cowboys who love beer and fried chicken. In a culture of promiscuous masses, only the unexpected is predictable. Distinct tables like distinct classes dissolve in the swamps and the prairies, in the Canyons called Grand and Divides called Great. The homesteader Elinor Pruitt Stewart, an "ex-washlady" in Burnt Fork, Wyoming, described in 1914 the promiscuous mass served by a cowpuncher from his bean hole, which contained meat, beans, potatoes, bread, and apricot pie. "I ate a good deal of ashes with my roast beef," she wrote, "but fastidiousness about food is a good thing to get rid of when you come West to camp." Ways of cooking and of eating mutate when the conventional invitation to dine is the Texan one of "Sit up, stranger, and take some fry."

America was always looking west but, as a Westerner, I had to reverse direction and look east to find my food roots along the corn-pone trail. Because American cooking, like the American continent, was a fantasy of extremes as wacky and contradictory as the baked ice-cream cake originally called "Alaska-Florida" before it became Baked Alaska, I looked for frontiers of confrontation. I wanted extreme borderlands, where land confronted water, to show the drama of America's polarities: man against the wilderness, European against Indian, successive waves of immigrants in a cacophony of voices, unintelligible to each other that yet, against all reason, play most together when "everybody play for hisself."

On my culinary map, I circled six regions around the borders of the country, moving counterclockwise, west to east. These were ports of entry where culture contacts were extreme and voices still distinct. These were pockets of vernacular cooking which would stand for larger regions: the Southwest of New Mexico, the Delta South of Louisiana, the Southeast of the Carolinas, the Northeast of New England, the northern Midwest of Wisconsin, the Pacific Northwest of Washington and Oregon. Only the Southwest was not bordered by water, but there the desert continuous with Mexico stood in for the sea. I touched only the perimeter, circling what Joel Garreau in *The Nine Nations of North America* calls the Breadbasket and the Empty Quarter. The fat middle of America was more homogeneous in its ethnic roots and therefore in its cooking roots, so I left it alone. As a port, each chosen region had a history of ethnic roots important to the history of American cooking. In the Southwest, Indians confronted conquistadors to found the hybrid desert cooking of Mexamerica. In Louisiana a mixture of Spanish, Caribbeans, Acadian French, and homeland French founded Cajun cooking in the swamps and prairies and Creole cooking in the city of New Orleans. In the Carolinas British and French confronted Africans as planters and slaves to found the plantation cooking of Dixie. In New England successive English seafarers followed by settlers founded the cod and clam cooking of the Northeast coast. In Wisconsin Germanic tribes became milkers and trappers to found cheese-and-beer cooking in the pastures around the Great Lakes. In the Pacific Northwest Indians, Chinese, and Japanese confronted Anglo-Saxons, Scandinavians, and Estonians to produce the fresh-market cooking of the ecotopian Northwest.

Each place had a communal rite and tribal dish typical of its own vernacular and of the crossbred culture of its tribal gods. The Southwest held Indian corn dances and ate *posole,* honoring both Christ and the corn gods. Louisiana staged Carnival and ate gumbos, presided over by the spirits of Evangeline and Mardi Gras Rex. The Carolinas parodied their high-table buffets with soul-food barbecues, doubling Scarlett O'Hara with Brer Rabbit. New England dug its clambakes and ate chowders in an uneasy accommodation of Captain Ahab and Hester Prynne. Wisconsin held Oktoberfests and fish boils, honoring both Hiawatha and *der Bier König*. The Northwest offered Indian salmon and tofu, yoking the Fish-Maiden and Paul Bunyan to Sleeping Buddha.

Each regional city cooked foods typical of its ecology, which gave each a distinct flavor and smell and feel. Santa Fe paraded blue corn, green chili and red chili, tortillas, and wild herbs. New Orleans and New Iberia mingled crayfish and shrimp, sugar cane and rice, sassafras and *boudin,* and hot cayenne. Charleston and Greensboro displayed grits and greens, country hams and angel biscuits, syllabubs and sesame soups. Boston and Cape Cod celebrated blueberries, cranberries, lobsters and quahogs, maple syrup, and beans. Milwaukee boasted wild mushrooms and wild rice, fresh cheeses, pickled meats and cabbages, bratwursts, fresh perch, and tortes. Seattle and Portland flaunted smoked salmons and geoducks, Dungeness crabs, tofus and fiddleheads, wild berries and sourdough breads. Each, too, downed its typical drink, rooted in native plants: tequila, rum, bourbon, cider, beer, and wine.

It was hard to grasp such mammoth abundance, such immense variety of materials and methods, originating in so many elsewheres, crossbreeding so many hybrids. To make a culinary geography, I divided the food map of America into three belts and two panels: a chili belt across the South, a grain belt in the middle, a dairy belt across the North, banded East and West by a seafood panel. To search out the characteristic taste of American food, that triple combination of salt, sweet, *and* crisp that the French deplore, I looked for its roots in our most ancient ways of preserving food in an untamed wild. Desert Indians preserved foods by drying them in the sun. Indians in the wet climates of the Deep South and Northwest preserved foods by smoking and seasoning: hot peppers in the South and sea salt in the North. Dried and smoked foods were crisp foods: venison jerky, barbecued salmon strips, pumpkin slices. Honey, the sap of maples, and the natural sugars of wild berries also preserved foods by sweetening them. When the white man came, he brought with him cane sugar and refined salt; but long before he came and long after he came, the need to annihilate time and distance established the American taste for smoky, hot, salt, sweet, crisp—all at once and plenty of it.

When I tried to condense this macrocosm into my miniature kitchen and the markets of New York City, I faltered. Out of context any dish will taste different, but since cooking is a way of knowing, I felt others could know what I had found by a kind of stove-side traveling. Through cook books I have traveled to modern Morocco and Georgian England and Louis XVI's France. By the same token, anybody can travel around America without leaving his own kitchen, if he is willing to be a tourist in his own land.

But there had to be some travel rules. I've tried to limit the recipes here to those anybody can cook in any kitchen near a market big enough to have a fish counter, meat counter, and produce counter. To give the character of a place, I've also included recipes intended for reading rather than making, unless you have a ready source of crayfish from the South or geoduck from Washington or dove from North Carolina. Every recipe in the book I've made in my own place, limited by my own equipment and skills, whether that meant smoking salmon in the fireplace or washing chitterlings in the bathtub. These are translations, hybrid results, variations on major themes, authentic to my place, my corn pone, my opinions, in the American tradition of making it new and doing it oneself.

Sometimes I talked to chefs when their own roots were in the land, but mostly I talked to people who love food because they know that food is a matter of life and death and family and sex and worship and guilt and ancestors and all the hungers that shape our lives. In my travels I heard the voices of men who hunted turtle and alligator and pressed on me their recipes for shark tempura and barbecued coon. I heard the voices of women whose shelves were lined with Aunt Sarah's pickled peaches and whose kitchens smelled of Mandy's kush-kush. I heard children laugh when they dug into a box of Aplets and Cotlets and grandparents weep when they made the San Marco bread they made once in Croatia.

There were many voices not heard. I was looking for the earliest roots, the sources, in the American family of foods, so I went for the earliest immigrants, beginning with the first Asiatics to cross the Bering Strait and found our first civilization. In that time frame, I had to ignore major immigrants of the late-nineteenth and twentieth centuries: Italians, Portuguese, Irish, Poles, Hungarians, Puerto Ricans, Russians, Vietnamese, Iranians, Koreans. Mine is but a sampling—a matter of luck and circumstance endemic to road travel—of the voices I might have heard were there but world enough and time.

Because I wanted voices rooted in the past, I also listened to the rich literature of the past: Amelia Simmons, Eliza Leslie, Mary Randolph, Lafcadio Hearn, Sarah Rutledge, Catherine Beecher, Mary Lincoln, Fannie Farmer, Maria Parloa, Lizzie Kander, Irma Rombauer, Frank Hamilton Cushing, Juliet Corson, to mention but a few of the voices that shaped our cooking lives in the last century. I heard again the voices of Twain and Whitman and Thoreau, men who tried to catch the wildness of the land and its immensity, which kept men wanderers and adventurers, rootless and on the road.

I heard at last the silent voices of the Indians, whose roots in this land were as ancient as the Sumerians and their language as untranslatable. When Frank Hamilton Cushing took a trio of Zuni chieftains to Manchester-by-the-sea in Massachusetts in 1886 to see the Ocean of Sunrise, the Indians had trouble understanding the corn pone and opinions of the white tribes of Boston and Wellesley. Here were a people who had plenty of seeds to eat and water to drink and still they wandered, rootless, and when they ate they did not share a common bowl but ate from separate dishes, each with his own spoon. "Strange people, strange people, these Americans!" the Zunis said.

Wandering, in search of roots that would help me find my own, I had tasted many strange dishes and seen many strange people and heard many strange voices, from Finland to Ceylon. But none was stranger than the voices of Americans talking food to a hungry stranger. Nobody offered me the fried mush of my childhood, but I heard America cooking and I knew I was home.

I Hear America
Cooking

PART I

Indians and Conquistadors

THE MEXAMERICAN DESERT

ILLUSTRATION FACING PART TITLE PAGE:
A Pueblo dwelling,
by Rudolf Cronau, 1891.

RECIPES IN PART I

*The West of which I speak is but another name for the Wild; and
... in Wildness is the preservation of the World.*

—Henry Thoreau, *Walking,* 1862

I was a child of the West but not the Wild, and in New Mexico I found a kind of wildness that Thoreau, who never got west of Minnesota, had not imagined. On the hottest day of August I was in the middle of a desert, stuffing myself with Sno-Kones and Indian fry bread and popcorn and soda pop while I watched an Indian corn dance at the pueblo of Santo Domingo, halfway between Albuquerque and Santa Fe, 7000 feet above sea level. It wasn't the altitude that made me dizzy. It was the time warp.

I was caught in a crossfire between amplified country-rock from the carnival rides by St. Dominic's church and the beat and moan of Indian drums and chants by the kiva. I was watching Indians in Adidas and Return-of-the-Jedi T-shirts watch Indians in feathers and furs, some painted ocher and some blue and some black and white all over, with their hair tufted on top like corn silk. Some five hundred members of the clan, who yesterday were dentists and schoolteachers and mechanics, today were Squash People and Turquoise People, beating with their feet the patterns of rain and lightning in dances older than the Governor's Palace at Santa Fe, older than the ruins of the Anasazi at Chaco Canyon, as old probably as the pods of Bat Cave. For a tourist it was like being zapped back to some Hamitic dance among the Pyramids; only this was 1984 and in an American village sprouting television sets as well as corn.

Even without a corn dance, the 360-degree horizon, with the sun blazing away on one side and black thunderheads piling up on the other, is enough to put a crick in your neck. You begin to welcome the thunder that booms every afternoon above Taos and the Sangre de Cristo Mountains because the desert

LEFT: At Santo Domingo Pueblo, New Mexico, 1899, two Kersahi Indians reveal in their dress the same hybridization of Spanish and native traditions revealed in their food. The man on the right wears the black and white paint, the pine boughs, and the tufted hairdo of cornhusks and feathers of the clowns, or *koshare*, who oversee the annual Corn Dance on the feast day of Saint Dominic.

BELOW: At Santa Clara Pueblo, New Mexico, 1911, Tewan Corn Dancers in embroidered white kilts and parrot feathers, moccasins and sleigh bells, shake down the waters of the sky with the rhythm of their stamping feet, droning chants, and rattling gourds. Behind, a row of women wear wooden tablitas painted with symbols of thunder and lightning. The dances yoke the kivas of the Indians and the chapels of the conquistadors in a ritual of fertility as old as the cultivation of corn and as current as T-shirts and jeans.

reorders priorities and rain comes first. Wild or cultivated, southwestern food is sun food, as primary as the four elements: corn, beans, squash, and chili. In this wildness, preservation depends literally on food dried in the sun, so that every sunbaked adobe will have ears of corn and spikes of blood-red chili peppers hanging from the porch beams. And while these primary foods typify the whole Mexamerican region, New Mexico is special in that here the corn is blue and the chili green. Blue corn has a particular fragrance and delicacy, just as the native hybrid chili pepper Big Jim has a particular mildness and sweetness. The result, in a dish like blue-corn enchiladas with green sauce, is unexpectedly subtle and refined.

In New Mexico, it is hard to figure what is wild and what is civilized, since the Anasazi ancestors of the Pueblo Indians tamed the desert through irrigation and "waffle" gardens during their Classic Pueblo period about the time the Normans tamed the Saxons. In the desert, time gets skewed. Ever since Francisco Vásquez de Coronado crossed the Rio Grande four hundred years ago in search of the Seven Cities of Cibola and found instead the land of blue corn, the Indians have lived in two worlds, two languages, two time frames, and to enter their territory is to suffer culture shock.

Tony Garcia, a Tewa Indian born in San Juan Pueblo, on the main road from Santa Fe to Taos, helped me get my bearings. "We are seed people, the children of corn, which is the seed of seeds," Tony explained over Ritz crackers and a glass of Indian tea made from the yellow-blossomed *cota,* which weavers use as a dye. Tony is his Spanish name, the one he used as a music student at Denver University, as a Second World War army cook, and as a French cook at a dude ranch. In this world Tony is a child of Christ and Mother Mary. In the Tewa world he is a child of Father Sky and the Great Corn Mothers, the Blue Corn Woman of summer and the White Corn Maiden of winter, who live with the other immortals beneath the Lake of Emergence from which man came and to which he will return. The difference between mortals and immortals is food, Tony explains, for the name for mortals is the Dry Food People.

When Tony says that "corn is the lifeline of the Tewas," he is not referring to my childhood mush. The Indians grow six colors of corn—red, white, yellow, black, speckled, and blue—which mark the six corners of the world, east, west, north, south, zenith, and nadir. Of all these corn colors, blue is the

In Taos, New Mexico, 1939, a Pueblo woman removes loaves of wheat bread from the adobe beehive oven, or *horno,* which Indians call the bread's "home." She has preheated the oven with a wood fire, swept out the ashes with straw or cedar leaves, sealed the opening shut before baking, and now retrieves the loaves with a hand-carved paddle of pine.

most sacred because it is the color of water, without which the Seed People and their brothers and sisters, the multicolored Corn, would die. Tony's mother ground corn in the ancient way, between stones, the hollowed-out volcanic stone *metate*, and the stone in the hand, the *mano*. And when she baked her corn in the form of bread, by either burying it in a heated pit or sealing it in an adobe oven, she sent the corn "home."

Tony grinds his chili in a blender, sends his corn over to the mill at Rancho Casados, and bakes his bread in a gas oven. But he collects old *metates* as I might collect antique butter churns. They stand in his kitchen garden like

In the Hano Pueblo of a Hopi mesa, 1892, two Tewa women grind corn in the stone metate (left) and make piki bread on the smooth piki stone, fired from beneath (right). Today, piki baking is almost a lost art, since the baker must smooth the blue-corn batter with a single swipe of her hand on the red-hot stone to make a wafer transparent as smoke.

tombstones in a churchyard. All the pueblos grow some blue corn, mostly for ceremonies, Tony says, but nobody outside the Hopi and Navajo makes *piki* bread anymore. *Piki* is a blue-gray "paper-bread" translucent as smoke, which is rolled like tissue paper and tastes a bit like Kleenex.

"We can't make *piki* here, no *piki* house, no *piki* stones," says Bea Tioux, the daughter of Ignacia Duran. We sit in Ignacia's modern kitchen built by Bea's husband, Paul, a Sioux Indian reared in Princeton, New Jersey. Bea lives where she was born, in the pueblo of Tesuque, just north of the Santa Fe Opera house, and she is making tuna-salad sandwiches for her daughters, Apple Blossom and Aspen. I ask Bea and Ignacia what they cooked for their annual feast day on November 12. "First we bought a cow," says Ignacia, a tiny bright-eyed woman, "and a fifty-pound sack of flour." They stewed a hundred pounds of beef and baked fifty loaves of bread. "We stewed the beef with dried corn and chick peas in the big iron pot outside and made a big pot of green chili and a big pot of red chili." There were also potato salads and boiled yams for filler. And for sweets, little pies of dried apples, sugar cookies (*bischotinos*), *sopa* (bread pudding with cheese and raisins), and Jell-O. And coffee and Kool-Aid to drink.

They baked their bread in a new adobe oven, which took nearly a year to

A Luiseno Indian woman in Pachenga, California, 1934, pounding acorns in a stone mortar with a stone pestle in order to make flour. The California acorn is larger and more bitter than the dwarf variety of the Southwest desert and must be leached with water to remove excess tannin. Acorn flour may thicken stews or be mixed with corn and wheat flours for bread.

cure. "In the old days," Ignacia says, "the kitchen was the hearth, but stooping over all day was hard work, not like turning on an Anglo stove." We might be sitting in a suburban kitchen as Bea shows me how to make sweet blue-corn balls wrapped in corn husks or blue-corn cakes called *chacella,* which are spread with butter and jam, or blue porridge called *atole,* which is eaten with milk and butter and sometimes sugar. Ignacia does not miss hearth stooping, but she does miss foraging for wild plants: young sprouting tumbleweed to steam with chili and onions, wild spinach and purslane, cattails and yucca roots and chokecherry. Nearly every day, she still makes flour and corn tortillas by hand, and she still dries strips of pumpkin, slices of apple, pumpkin seeds and piñon nuts, beef and venison jerky. She hangs strips of venison and little bunches of *cota* on laundry lines strung by her water heater. Bea wants to revive more of the old ways. "Paul has promised to make me a *piki* stone," Bea says, "which must be as smooth as Teflon."

Cooking in the Southwest combines the food roots of two cultures. Before the Spaniards, the Indians used chili instead of salt, corn instead of wheat, bear's grease instead of suet or lard, ground seeds and nuts instead of butter, venison and rabbit and wild birds instead of beef, pork, and chicken. Most importantly, they leavened their bread with wood ashes instead of yeast. But what was "authentic" Indian corn pone? The food roots were as mixed as the name Mexamerica, as anomalous as Cortez' men of iron, pointing their thundersticks at Montezuma's men of feathers, bearing maize cakes the color of gold.

Although Southwest Indians are trilingual, their own traditions are largely oral, which helps keep them alive even as the elements and implements change. A pioneer ethnographer from Pennsylvania, Frank Hamilton Cushing, was the first to write down systematically Indian recipes in English, in his *Zuni Breadstuff* of 1884. The language problem is clear from his opening question to the Zuni woman kneeling over her *metate* by the hearth to make what Cushing called "hoe-cakes."

> "How do you make them?" I inquired. *"Sa-k'o, o'-lut-si-na ta k'ia-kok-shi, hi-ni-na hâ i'-ya si; tem kwi'l-ip-nan, hâ ko-la ma-we ta i'-sha-nan wo-lu . . . a'ya-naie!"* replied the old woman.

To translate was as "hard as Zuni milling," Cushing said, but he would "try to grind it into English":

Meal, soft corn-flour and good water, equally I mix; then stirring, red-pepper, salt, and suet, I put in, into husks I roll this, into an oven all place shutting the hole; time passed, I take them out. Now then, for eating they are ready.

There's a formulaic ring here, echoed by an unusual cook book, *Traditional Navajo Foods and Cooking,* put out in 1983 by the students of Pine Hill High School, New Mexico. Photographs as well as text show how to butcher a sheep, clean the intestines, bake the head, make sausages from the blood, and roast the heart and lungs—that sort of thing. We also learn how to make kneel-down bread, which is surely an aboriginal corn pone. "Get the fresh corn on the field," the recipe begins, build a fire in a pit, and cut the kernels from the cob. "Get out your grinding stones and place them on a clean sheep or goat skin," it continues, and after you've shaped the ground mash into cakes, laid them between corn husks, and buried them under the ashes, "wait for an hour and then remove all the ashes and husks off the bread and then you have finished your kneel-down bread." Getting the grinding stones and sheepskin didn't sound easy, but I was perfectly willing to try.

In Taos, New Mexico, 1939, a Spanish-American mother cooks in a typically hybrid kitchen. She rolls out wheat-flour tortillas with a ribbed rolling pin and bakes them on her Anglo enameled-iron stove.

1
Indian Corn

The Raw, the Cooked, and the Rotten

In Bea Tioux's house, as in every house in the pueblo, a bunch of dried corn of many colors hangs in the kitchen to bless and protect the house. Corn is to the Indian what bread and wine are to the Christian: an incarnation of body and blood, flesh and spirit. But unlike the industrialized Western world, the Indian world is still centered on the cycles of nature, on the annual sprouting, ripening, harvesting, and burial of the seed. Corn in its many transformations from raw kernel to cooked porridge to fermented mast never loses its sacredness because it is man's kin. "Europeans can't understand that," Tony Garcia says, laughing. "They think corn is for animals."

To understand southwestern cooking you must become intimate with Indian corn. You have to understand why Aztec girls who once danced before the Goddess of Green Corn, Xilomen, let down their hair so that the green corn would let down its silk. You have to understand why Zuni makers of *piki* bread would talk to the *piki* stone and ask it "to not be lazy and to work well." You have to understand why Indians talk to their budding corn as if to their own children and think good thoughts in order to help both children grow. You have to follow each corn transformation from green youth to parched age, aided by man's preserving, processing, milling, and cooking arts.

To find our corn roots, we have to begin at the beginning with the most ancient form of corn, the pod, which enclosed each kernel in a separate husk. Today's ear of corn is a giant seedpod hiding within outer husk and inner silk

Corn Terms

Hominy: Anglicized Algonquin term for dried corn soaked or boiled with an alkali (unslaked lime, caustic soda, or lye leached from hardwood ashes) to remove the hulls.

Big hominy: southern vernacular for whole-kernel hominy.

Grits or small hominy: southern vernacular for hominy ground into coarse meal.

Samp: Anglicized Narraganset term for dried corn pounded coarsely into meal.

Posole: Mexican term for dried hominy kernels and for the soup-stew made from them.

Nixtamal: Mexican term for wet hominy kernels ready to be ground finely into meal for tortillas and tamales.

Masa: Mexican term for the meal freshly ground from wet hominy.

Masa harina: the same meal dried and packaged commercially, often mixed with some wheat flour.

Chicos: Mexican term for dried unhulled whole-corn kernels.

Parched corn: whole ripe kernels toasted or roasted rather than dried.

Chaquegue: Mexican term for toasted white corn ground into meal.

Atole: toasted blue-corn meal ground very fine.

Pinole: toasted white or yellow cornmeal, ground fine, spiced and sweetened to make a thick drink.

Corn Milling

Metate: a concave stone for grinding corn with a small hand-held stone called a *mano.*

Hominy block or *samp mill:* a wooden basin and pestle for pounding corn into meal; the basin was often a hollowed tree stump and the pestle a block of wood.

Quern: a rotation stone grinder composed of a stationary bottom stone and a rotating cap stone, turned by human hand or by animal, wind, or water power.

Wet milling: modern term for commercial milling in which corn is soaked, then crushed between rolling mills with steel disks, after which the germ is removed for oil and the gluten separated for further processing into starches, sugars, and syrups.

Dry milling: commercial milling that crushes the kernel without previous soaking, then removes the germ and the hull to produce a meal halfway between grits and corn flour, with prolonged shelf life from the removal of the germ.

A word about cornmeal colors and taste. Except for that of blue corn, the taste of cornmeal lies not primarily in corn color, since any of our five basic kinds of corn can have yellow pigmentation or white, but in the method of grinding. Corn milling, like that of wheat, changed radically after the Civil War, when metal rollers and disks replaced stone querns. Standardized supermarket cornmeal, yellow or white, is denuded of the germ that gives grain life and thus lacks the character and nutty sweetness of stone-ground whole corn. Among our two chief commercial brands, Indian Head is to Quaker what Heckers is to General Mills, but the product of local grist mills is in another league entirely, and such mills should be encouraged to survive. Quaker does put out a good grade of *masa harina* and of quick or instant grits, but at the sacrifice of genuine freshness. If you can get freshly ground whole meal, store it in the refrigerator to retain freshness.

many seeds, formed in even-numbered rows of identical twins. Each seed in turn has an outer skin and an inner flesh or endosperm, surrounding a germ or embryo. The corn's endosperm determines its flavor and texture.

We have five kinds of native Indian corn from which our multitudinous hybrid corn family has sprung: pop, flint, dent, flour, and sweet. Popcorn pops because it has a high ratio of protein to starch, which holds in the moisture until heat vaporizes it, explodes the skin, and turns the flesh inside out. Flint, the hardest corn, is high in protein and has a hard starch. Dent is softer because its starch is waxy, which makes the dried kernel easier for men and other animals to eat. (According to Henry A. Wallace, dent is a hybrid of North American flint and South American gourdseed.) Flour corn contains a high proportion of starch and sweet corn a high proportion of sugar. What we call "Indian corn" today is flour and flint corn, variegated in color because of different skin pigments.

Unlike other staple grains, corn we can eat raw as well as cooked. Today we have so hybridized sweet corn that the mature ear is as tender and sweet as a youthful one. Until the 1920s, however, the corn to eat on the cob was "green," that is, immature corn of any species. Nineteenth-century recipes using fresh corn kernels meant green corn kernels, as in the Navajo kneel-down bread, which Anglos would have called green corn pudding.

Today, a typical Pueblo way of eating corn on the cob is to roast the corn in its husk for flavor as well as protection. As soon as he picks ears from his garden, Tony soaks them in their husks in cold water for a couple of hours before grilling them over a hot fire until the husks are burnt. He then strips off husk and silk to reveal taffy-colored kernels inside. A slight burnt flavor lingers, the way it does in roasted peppers, to bring out sweetness.

Because summer is short and winter long, most corn was not harvested in its youth but left on the stalk to mature, its sweetness replaced by the starchiness of age. Southwesterners often roast or parch mature kernels in an iron skillet, then salt them to eat as a snack the way Southeasterners eat salted peanuts. They also hang ears of corn to dry in the sun and to mix later with meats, game, pumpkins, squash, or beans in any liquid that will return moisture to the kernels as they stew.

If nature blessed the Indian with corn, the Indian blessed corn cooking with ash. Wood ash (or ground limestone, where available) was the key to the Indian diet of corn because the alkaline in ash acted as a food supplement to balance the amino acids in which corn is deficient. With ash, corn was a life-sustaining, well-balanced meal in itself. The staple tortilla was made of corn processed by ash, or a similar alkaline, to remove the hull; ash was often added to cornmeal to sweeten and slightly leaven the dough for other kinds of breads. A contemporary Navajo recipe for blue-corn bread begins, "Burn green part of juniper until you get ½ cup of ashes." Cushing called ash or lime flour "Indian Yeast," because the alkaline combined with the natural acids in corn to form carbon dioxide. When we add baking powder to our cornbreads today, we add a powdered leavening that evolved from Indian wood ash, refined successively into potash, saleratus, baking soda, and today's commercial "double-acting" powders of soda and acid salts such as cream of tartar and sodium aluminum sulfate.

Cushing discovered that among the Zunis the most prized leaven was *sa'-k'o-we* or, as Cushing called it, "chewed samp," made by chewing cornmeal, then mixing it with ash or lime and salt, and letting it ferment by the hearth. This was a form of rotten or fermented corn that Champlain found in the North and José de Acosta in the South. The Aztecs called it *chica;* José wrote in 1589, "The Indians believe that, for the best leavening, it must be masticated by repulsive old women, which makes you sick even to hear of it." Such corn mast or mash was transformed yet again, through the white man's alembic, into beer, moonshine, and bourbon.

Even before chili or salt, ash took the place of salt in the Indian diet. Chemically it supplied minerals such as potassium, magnesium, and sodium, which corn lacks. Ash also supplied flavor according to the kind of wood and its relative greenness or dryness. Juniper, cedar, the desert saltbush called *chamisa*—each lent a different flavor, as notable as the difference between cinnamon, nutmeg, and clove. Finally, ash was essential to the cooking of blue corn because without it blue cornmeal will turn like litmus paper from blue to pink; the alkaline of ash or baking soda stabilizes the blue in blue cornmeal and prevents it from turning pink when heated. If you want your blue-corn tortillas to stay blue, add baking soda.

The milling of the grain is more important to corn cooking than to wheat, oat, or barley cooking because the range is wider between whole kernel and finely ground powder. By A.D. 1000, the Indians had set up milling "factories" where women would grind corn communally on a series of three *metates,* each designed to grind more finely than the one before. Coarse, medium, and fine grinds were used separately and mixed together for different dishes. The coarsest would correspond to what we now call "grits" and the finest to corn flour.

Today, to find out how Bea and Tony grind their corn, I had to go to the

Spanish *molino* at Rancho Casados near San Juan Pueblo on the Rio Grande. The ranch is not easy to find in the long strip of green shaded by cottonwoods that separates river from desert. Nor is the mill easy to find at the ranch amid symmetrical rows of green corn and green chili. Young Orlando, grandson of the founding Casados, opens a shed door, and the sweet smell of corn overwhelms: corn drying on tiers of trays, roasting in small ovens, being ground into meal in an electrically powered grinder, the *molino*. Another shed zaps the senses with the equally sweet smell of chili and spices—oregano, cumin, cilantro, manzanilla—all that one needs for a tortilla, salsa, a cup of tea.

I move from the mill to a tortilla factory in Sante Fe—Josie's Best Tortilleria on Agua Fria. In this factory, the size of a ranch-house living room, a young couple, the Montoyas, work the counter out front, while in the back an old man flours Ping-Pong–sized balls of dough and a young girl feeds each one into a flattening machine. The Spanish furnished the first mechanized flatteners when they designed a wooden press in the eighteenth century to help non-Indian cooks slap the crumbly cornmeal dough into thin wafers between the palms of their hands. The Montoyas make tortillas of white corn, blue corn, white flour, whole wheat flour. They also turn tortillas into tacos, burritos, tamales, tostadas, and blue-corn tortilla chips. Josie's is the Mexamerican equivalent of a French bakery; few housewives outside the pueblos make at home nowadays what they can so easily buy freshly made at bakery or grocery.

For all today's variety of corn cookery, it is less than yesterday's, when corn was appetizer, soup, salad, main dish, dessert, and beverage. In *Zuni Breadstuff*, Cushing describes boiled breads or dumplings called "water balls," which date back to the time when Indians cooked gruel by dropping hot stones into earthen pots filled with water. He describes "salty buried bread" made of white cornmeal flavored with dried flowers, licorice root, or wild honey, buried in a pit dug in the hearth and sealed with mud to bake overnight. He describes a sweet pudding of yellow cornmeal masticated, fermented, and wrapped in green corn leaves shaped into crescents for a wedding. He describes batter cakes of corn flour and lime-yeast pasted over smooth baking stones greased with sheep brains. He describes the special delicacy of corn smut, that black truffle-smelling fungus which attacks ripening corn and is eaten today in Mexico as *cuitlacoche*. He describes the universal traveling food of the Indian, "moistening flour," carried in a small leather pouch, much as granola in a backpack today. Moistening flour was made from corn kernels boiled with ashes, then thrice toasted and thrice ground to reduce a bushel to a few quarts of finest flour. The flour would last indefinitely and a teaspoon in a pint of water would make a meal.

In choosing recipes typical of the Southwest, I've included a few using blue corn because you can now buy blue cornmeal through mail-order sources and specialty stores. I've also included a few recipes for *posole* because you can buy hominy, yellow or white, in cans. I've avoided the current fads of Tico-Taco snackeries and combination-plate glopperies because these have less to do with food than with margarita slush in goblets the size of Jacuzzis. I'm all for the booze, but this is a cook book.

A Note on Ingredients

Butter always means unsalted butter.
Salt always means sea salt.
Black pepper always means freshly ground, unless peppercorns are specified.

INDIAN POPPED CORN

If you think about how many thousands of years American Indians have been popping corn, you'll know that corn popping requires only heat and a cover to keep the kernels from exploding in your face. Specialized poppers are fun but they take up space, and I prefer a simple heavy cast-iron skillet with a lid. To avoid unpopped kernels, fill the skillet with but a single layer of kernels, and heat the oil before you add the corn. One quarter cup of kernels is plenty for a nine-inch skillet; a fourteen-inch skillet can take one-half cup, which will make about one quart of popped corn.

> 1 tablespoon corn oil
> ¼–½ cup corn kernels
> ¼–½ teaspoon salt
> 2–4 tablespoons butter
> ½–1 teaspoon pure ground chili

Heat oil in a skillet over high heat until a test kernel pops. Shake in the kernels, cover with a lid, and when you hear the kernels begin to pop, turn down heat and shake pan gently back and forth to keep the kernels moving. When popping sounds cease, the corn is done.

Pour the corn into a large bowl and sprinkle with salt. Melt the butter with the chili and pour over the corn. Mix it with your hands.

Makes 2 to 4 cups.

PARCHED SWEET CORN

Once upon a time, dried seed corn, parched in oil or butter and salted, was a snack as popular as salted nuts. A Californian named Albert Holloway began packaging "cornnuts" to sell to bars when Prohibition ended, and his sons carry on the business today with a hybrid corn based on a giant type still grown by the Indians of Peru, the original home of corn. Today the Holloways grow this giant-kerneled corn in valleys as different as the Salinas in California and the Mad River in Ohio. I am so addicted to these parched salted kernels that I wanted to make my own, and I found a recipe for them in *The Corn Cook Book* (1918; war edition), by Elizabeth Hiller, principal of the Chicago Domestic Science Training School. This is the kind of rerouting that makes hash of "regionalism" in American cooking but that also reveals the links between an Inca in Peru and a domestic science principal in Chicago.

      2 cups sweet seed corn (dried kernels of sweet corn)
      4 tablespoons butter or olive oil
         salt to taste

Put corn kernels in a large sieve, pour boiling water over them, and drain them on paper towels. Melt butter in a large cast-iron skillet (or "iron spider"), add corn, and stir constantly until each kernel is slightly puffed and browned. Sprinkle with salt. Corn will brown more evenly if you parch it a cup at a time.

Makes 2 cups.

INDIAN CORN ROAST

Roasting fresh sweet corn on the cob and in the husk gives a very different flavor from boiling it. Nature has prepackaged the rows of tender seeds within their own wrapper, better than plastic or foil, because the wrapper sweetens while it protects. *The Corn Cook Book* (1918) advises the cook to keep the husks on, after removing the inner silk, whenever boiling or steaming "green corn on the cobs." But when you roast corn on a grill, or under a broiler, you needn't remove even the silk because you can easily strip it off with the burned husk when the corn is done. The Indian method is to give the husks a good soaking in cold water before you put the ears on the fire, which helps to steam the kernels as they roast to a golden brown and absorb the flavor of the charred husks. If you're not in a hurry, you can bury the husks directly in hot ashes and let the corn bake for an hour (or less, depending on the heat of the ash). On a hot grill the corn will roast in fifteen or twenty minutes.

    8 ears sweet corn in the husk
    ¼ pound (1 stick) butter
    ½ teaspoon each salt, black pepper, and pure ground chili

Soak the ears in cold water for 2 to 3 hours before grilling. Place on a hot grill (or about 5 inches below a broiler) for about 15 minutes, turning the ears to roast them on all sides.

Test for doneness by stripping back husk and silk and nibbling a kernel or two. The point is to heat the kernels, but the longer you cook them after they are hot (3 minutes for boiled corn), the tougher they get as sugar converts to starch.

Melt the butter with the seasonings and put in a sauce bowl. The easiest way to butter corn is to pour some seasoned butter on your plate, strip your ear, and roll the naked ear in the butter as you eat.

Serves 4 picky corn eaters, 2 devotees.

NAVAJO KNEEL-DOWN BREAD

This is less a bread than a fresh-corn pudding, in which the pulped kernels bake slowly, enclosed in fresh corn husks. The recipe in *Traditional Navajo Foods and Cooking* calls for shaping the pulp into small cakes, two inches by five inches, before placing them between husks split open and flattened. The husks keep the corn both sweet and moist in the baking. But just as most of us are not going to follow tradition and grind our kernels on a *metate* or catch the mash on a clean goat skin, I find it easier not to make individual cakes but one large cake from the mash. The mash does not require husks for baking in a casserole in a modern oven after the corn has been puréed, but husks make an attractive package in addition to providing flavor. I've added some cooked jalapeño peppers and sour cream because I like the extra bite and creamy texture, but these are simply my small modern variations on one of America's oldest cornbreads.

8 ears fresh sweet corn in the husk
¼–½ cup canned jalapeño peppers, drained and minced
    salt to taste
1 cup sour cream
    pure ground chili pepper to taste

Chop a slice from the bottom of each ear with a cleaver so that you can remove the husks easily and stand the ears upright for cutting off the kernels. Remove husks and save. Discard silk. Place cob upright, cut end down, on a cutting board or wide soup plate and cut kernels straight down with a sharp knife. Purée kernels in a food processor, grinder, or blender to make a slightly chunky pulp.

Tear ends of husks slightly to help uncurl them. In a shallow casserole, overlap husks to make a solid layer. Mix corn pulp with the peppers and add salt if desired. Spread pulp 1-inch thick on the husks and cover with a top layer of husks. Seal top of dish with aluminum foil. Bake at 350° for 1 hour.

Remove foil and top layer of husks. Ladle sour cream in a mound in the center of the dish and sprinkle with chili before spooning out portions.

Serves 4.

HOMEMADE HOMINY AND MASA

In the Southwest, you can buy hominy in several forms: fresh, dried, canned, and frozen. In the rest of the country, the Goya brand of yellow or white canned hominy is usually available where there are large numbers of Hispanics. It is good to know, however, how to make hominy from scratch. Indian recipes usually call for a specific kind of wood to burn for ash, such as juniper, cedar, or *chamisa*. Spanish recipes usually call for powdered unslaked lime (two heaping tablespoons to two quarts water and one quart dried corn). Juanita Tiger Kavena, a Creek Indian who married a Hopi, advises in her *Hopi Cookery* (1981) that baking soda can substitute for the alkaline but it lacks the nutrition and flavoring of wood ash (two tablespoons soda to two quarts water and two cups corn).

To turn cooked hominy into fresh dough (or *masa*) for tortillas or tamales, you simply grind the hulled kernels in a *metate,* food grinder, or processor.

> 1 cup real wood ashes (*no* chemical firelogs)
> 2 quarts water
> 3 cups dried white corn kernels

Boil ashes in 1 quart water, then strain to get ash broth. Cover kernels with broth and remaining water in a deep pot, cover pot, and boil until hulls are well loosened, 2 to 3 hours. Drain in sieve or colander under cold running water to get rid of the ash and rub off the loosened hulls with your hands. Be sure to remove the tough skin at the base of the kernel, called the "eye." For fresh *masa,* grind the kernels fine at this stage. For later use, dry or freeze the kernels.

To use kernels whole, cover the rinsed kernels with fresh water, add salt to taste, and simmer until kernels begin to burst or "blossom," 1½ to 2½ hours. A pressure cooker will reduce cooking time to 35 or 45 minutes.

Makes 6 cups hominy.

FRESH CORN-DOUGH TORTILLAS

Tortillas, meaning "little cakes," the major breadstuff of the New World, are a unique form of bread because they are made from precooked dough: first the corn is cooked to make the dough, then the dough is cooked to preserve the shape of a flat round pone or cake. The best tortillas are made of freshly boiled hominy, drained and ground fine. Fresh corn dough is tricky to shape because the dough must be wet enough to stick together but not so wet that it will disintegrate when you transfer the flattened cake from your hand to the pan or griddle.

The meal from wet hominy (fresh or canned) produces a paper-white round, lightly flecked with brown from the skillet, delicate and yet intense in its taste of corn. These will be moister and less chewy than supermarket tortillas, made usually from dehydrated hominy, which does not have the same taste or texture as fresh. You don't need special equipment, but you do need patience, a compelling need, and, if possible, a skilled teacher. The trick is to keep the cake small enough and thick enough to handle. I can manage a three-inch cake about an eighth of an inch thick, but not a standard six-inch round of that thickness. You cook the cakes quickly, like pancakes, in a hot ungreased skillet or griddle (a *comal*, in Spanish) until they stiffen, about two minutes a side.

Because of their moistness, these cakes do not dry out as quickly as commercial tortillas, and they keep well, plastic wrapped, in the refrigerator or freezer. Cut in quarters and deep fried, they also make delicious tostados. Try them once, anyway, because they are much closer to the little cakes that Montezuma ate than those made from dried hominy flour or, that modern aberration, from bleached white wheat flour.

> 2 cups hominy, well drained
> salt to taste

Grind the hominy as fine as possible in a processor or food mill. Taste for salt (homemade hominy may be flavored enough with ash or lime; canned hominy may have been packed in salted water), but add as little as possible. Shape dough into balls 1 to 2 inches in diameter. Cover them with an inverted bowl to keep them moist while working.

Place the dough on a square of heavy plastic wrap (like a freezer bag) and cover with another square of plastic. Press the ball flat with the palm of your hand, a heavy smooth-bottomed pan, or a rolling pin, to make a cake ⅛ inch thick.

Peel off the top plastic carefully, invert the cake onto the hot skillet or griddle, and quickly remove the remaining plastic.

Cook 2 minutes on one side, turn, and cook 2 minutes on the other. The cake will stiffen and show a few uneven flecks of brown. Repeat with each ball of dough. Keep the cooked tortillas hot in a low oven or wrap them in foil as you go.

Makes about 12 tortillas.

VARIATION: To make 4- to 5-inch rounds with a chewier texture.

> 1 cup hominy
> 1 cup *masa harina*
> ⅔ cup boiling water
> salt to taste

Grind hominy, then add the *masa harina* and water, and process all together. Add salt to taste. If dough seems too dry and crumbly, add a bit more water. Shape into 2½-inch balls and proceed as above.

Makes about 12 tortillas.

FRITOS

Fritos is both a trademark and a common name for thin corn pone cut in strips and fried. The name and use as a finger-food snack or scoop for guacamole or hot chili sauce suggest its Mexamerican origins, but the corn crisp was everywhere in American corn-pone cooking. An easy recipe for Corn Meal Crisps comes from *The Corn Cook Book* (1918), easy because you just spread the cornmeal batter on an inverted baking pan and cut it into strips once it is cooked. Elizabeth Hiller specifies strips "the size of Saratoga wafers," but we might say "the size of large Fritos corn chips."

> 1 cup yellow or white cornmeal, stone-ground if possible
> 1 cup boiling water
> 4 tablespoons butter, melted
> ½ teaspoon salt
> vegetable oil for frying

Stir meal gradually into the water, and when perfectly smooth add butter and salt. Spread dough evenly on an inverted buttered 9-by-14-inch baking pan no more than ⅛ inch thick, and bake at 350° about 30 minutes. Immediately cut into strips about ½ inch by 3 inches and remove them carefully to a rack with a spatula.

Heat vegetable oil 2 inches deep in a wok or skillet until hot but not smoking. Add strips, a few at a time, and cook until crisp. Remove with slotted spoon and drain on paper towels. Salt to taste.

Makes about 30 strips.

TOSTADOS

Tostados, those crisp wedge-shaped wafers that are to a bowl of salsa as pepper is to salt, originated in the need to use up all those left-over tortillas at the end of the day. Of course today you can buy tostados in bags almost as easily as Fritos, but freshly made tostados taste better and keep their freshness so well that they are worth the small trouble they take to prepare. Any store-bought tortillas will taste better when tostadoed, so this is a good way to use up tortillas that were flaccid the first time around.

> 12 yellow or white corn tortillas
> vegetable oil for frying
> salt to taste

Cut tortillas in quarters or sixths with a pair of kitchen scissors. Heat oil at least 2 inches deep in a wok or heavy skillet and, when oil is hot but not smoking, add quarters a few at a time and fry until they turn crisp and light brown. They like to stick together, so fork them apart as they fry. Drain on paper towels and salt them to taste.

Makes 48 to 72 tostados.

BLUE-CORN GRIDDLE CAKES

Blue corn makes the best and the worst of cornmeals—the best because it has a desert fragrance and sweetness all its own; the worst because it is harder to work with than white or yellow corn, loses its freshness faster, and crumbles more easily. But like other rare and exotic things, difficulty increases its charm.

If white-corn tortillas are difficult, blue-corn are impossible and are best left to Josie's Best Tortilleria or similar purveyors. You can, however, experience the pleasures of this strange blue meal by mixing it with a little wheat flour to make crepe-like tortillas or with other cornmeals to make breads and corn cakes. Juanita Kavena, in her *Hopi Cookery,* gives a number of such mixtures, as do many southwestern Indian recipe books, so the tourist cook need not feel he is desecrating the true blue. I have supplied a recipe for unmixed Blue Chips (see page 29) for determined *aficionados,* but the mix here is as easy to make as any pancake batter. Use these cakes as you would any tortillas, though they are designed specifically for Green Chili Enchiladas (see page 42).

¾ cup blue-corn meal
¼ cup all-purpose flour
 1 teaspoon baking powder
¼ teaspoon salt
 1 egg
⅔ cup milk, plus more if needed
 2 tablespoons butter or lard, melted

Place ingredients, in order, in processor or blender, blend, and then let sit for an hour. Heat griddle or heavy skillet, brush with cooking oil, and pour in a couple tablespoons of batter to make a 4- to 6-inch griddle cake. Add milk if the batter seems too thick. Brown quickly 1 to 2 minutes on each side.

Makes about 10 cakes.

BLUE CHIPS

These small round tostados are the result of my final admission of defeat in making blue-corn tortillas. But I will not admit defeat without the compensation of these unique and delectable blue chips, about two inches round—thin, crisp, and almost worth the large challenge of their making if you are as stubborn and greedy about blue corn as I am. These are fun-time tostados the way margaritas are fun-time cocktails, not for everyday unless you have a live-in slave with nothing much to do.

> 1 cup blue cornmeal, ground fine
> ¼ teaspoon baking soda
> ½ teaspoon salt
> ¼ cup lard or shortening
> ½ cup boiling water
>   vegetable oil for frying

Mix meal with soda and salt and work in lard with fingertips as in pie-crust dough. Add water, mix well, and refrigerate dough in plastic wrap for 2 to 3 hours.

Cover a baking sheet with plastic wrap. Shape a quarter of the dough into ½-inch balls (about 12) and place them with space between on the plastic. Cover with another sheet of plastic and flatten each ball with the bottom of a saucer or tumbler to make a thin 2-inch round. Place baking sheet in the freezer and repeat with more baking sheets until all the dough is used. Let dough freeze for 1 hour.

Heat a large cast-iron skillet or griddle. Strip top layer of plastic from one sheet of the chilled rounds. Lift the entire bottom sheet of plastic and flip it over so that you can now strip the remaining plastic sheet from the dough. Quickly lift the chips, one by one, with a spatula and flip each chip into the skillet without crowding. Let the chips brown 2 or 3 minutes before you try to turn them or they will crumble. Brown them on the other side and repeat. (If dough warms up, put the sheet back in the freezer.)

When all the chips are cooked, fill skillet with 2 inches of cooking oil and deep fry the chips until crisp. Drain on paper towels, and salt to taste.

Makes about 48 rounds.

LAMB AND CHILI STEW
WITH BLUE BALLS

The ancestor of these blue dumplings was described by Frank Hamilton Cushing in his *Zuni Breadstuff* (1884). Today, when made with blue corn-meal, they are sometimes called "blue marbles" or "blue balls." Blue dump-lings by any name are commonly steamed on top of a meat or vegetable stew, particularly for festive occasions. The red chilies here show off the blue balls and turn a humble one-dish meal of meat, vegetables, and bread into the colors of a Zuni desert.

Lamb and Chili Stew
        1 large onion, chopped
        1 tablespoon lard, bacon fat, or shortening
        1 pound boneless lamb, cubed
        2 cups diced potatoes
        ½ cup chopped celery tops
        ⅓ cup red chili pulp (see page 38), or 2 tablespoons pure ground
            chili
        3 fresh tomatoes, chopped, or 1 cup canned tomatoes, drained
            and chopped
        3 cups hot beef stock
          salt to taste

Blue Balls
        1 cup finely ground blue cornmeal
        2 teaspoons baking powder
        1 teaspoon salt
        1 teaspoon lard or bacon fat
        ⅓ cup milk

In a large, wide-mouthed pot like a Dutch oven, sauté onion in lard. Add lamb and sear quickly, then add remaining ingredients. Bring to a simmer and stew gently for about 30 minutes. Meantime, make the dumplings.

Mix together meal, baking powder, and salt. Work in lard with your fin-gertips and add milk. Roll into balls 1½ inches in diameter, drop on top of stew, cover the stewpot, and steam for 20 to 25 minutes without lifting the lid. The dumplings do not expand but stay mealy.

Makes 8 dumplings. The stew and dumplings serve 4.

VARIATION: You can make a good meatless stew by substituting for the lamb a cup of cubed zucchini and a cup of green beans or cooked pinto beans, and by substituting any good vegetable broth for the beef stock.

INDIAN BLUE CORNBREAD

Blue corn for cornbread is as traditional for the Pueblo Indians as yellow corn is for the rest of us. Pork cracklings are often added, as are chili and cheese. Sometimes the cornmeal is sweetened with raisins and minced onions. Usually the meal is leavened with baking powder, which also retains the blue color, and is mixed with wheat flour. The addition of eggs makes for a still lighter bread, which is capable, like cornmeal mush, of folding an entire meal within its nourishing embrace. A seasoned frying pan is convenient for baking, but you can of course use any kind of greased pan, round or square.

1 small onion, minced
2 tablespoons lard or bacon fat
1 cup blue cornmeal (or white or yellow)
1 cup unbleached flour
1 teaspoon salt
1 tablespoon baking powder
1 cup milk
2 eggs, beaten
1 cup pork cracklings, or ½ cup crumbled cooked bacon
¼ cup minced jalapeño
⅓ cup grated or cubed goat, Monterey Jack, or Muenster cheese

Sauté onion in the lard in a frying pan. Mix together meal, flour, salt, and baking powder in a bowl. Add onion and remaining ingredients and pour the mixture into the hot frying pan. Bake in a 450° oven for 20 to 25 minutes. Cut into wedges.

Serves 8.

PORK AND HOMINY
POSOLE

As someone said of Mexican cooking, so also Mexamerican cooking is Aztec cooking plus pigs. The Spaniards brought pigs to the American Southwest after Hernando de Soto landed the first pigs in eastern Florida in 1542. The hog and hominy belt stretches like the chili belt across the southern United States from coast to coast, but different places give different names and different spices to these hog and hominy stews. In the Southwest, *posole* refers to not only Spanish hominy but also a fine and festive one-dish meal traditional on Christmas Eve and New Year's Eve, when friends gather to thank Christian or corn gods for another year's survival.

Posole is so traditional that nobody agrees on the details of its making. An Anglo friend from Ohio who now lives in Santa Fe insists that no *posole* is true *posole* without dried hominy. Tony at San Juan Pueblo insists that the best *posole* is made with canned hominy. "It's easier, cleaner, and tenderer," says Tony. "Anglos always ask for the secret of my hominy," and the secret is a can opener, a little onion, a little oregano, and *lots* of bone. Pork bone is what gives this soup-stew its savor, and while some use pig's feet, Tony adds spareribs. "I put a big tomato in it, too, even though that isn't kosher for Indians because we didn't start using tomatoes until about sixty-five years ago, when I was young." The only ingredients that don't vary are hog, hominy, and chili, the more the better. The longer they simmer together, the better the taste. Best is to make the dish ahead and reheat a couple of days later when the ingredients have met and married.

> 4 tablespoons lard or rendered pork fat
> 1 pound pork ribs or back or neck bones
> 2 pounds boneless pork, cut into 2-inch cubes
> 2 large onions, chopped
> 4 cloves garlic, minced
> 1 or 2 pig's feet, split
> 1 large tomato, chopped
> 2 teaspoons salt
> 1 teaspoon oregano

1 cup red chili pulp (see page 38), or ⅓–½ cup pure ground chili
2 cups canned hominy or dried hominy parboiled
    water or meat stock

Heat the lard in a heavy skillet and brown pork bones and boneless pork. Then transfer to a large stewpot or casserole. Sauté onions and garlic in the skillet and add to the meat.

Add remaining ingredients, with cold water or meat stock to cover, bring stew slowly to a boil, and remove any scum. Taste for seasoning and adjust salt and chili.

Simmer gently until meat is fork tender, 1½ to 2 hours.

Let cool; then remove any excess fat, cut meat off the ribs and pig's feet, and return meat to the stew before reheating.

Serves 6 to 8.

TRIPE AND HOMINY
MENUDO

One of those revealing distinctions between Indian and Anglo worlds is that Anglos call a cow's stomach lining "tripe," which has come to mean rubbish or trash, while Indians call the same lining, from the way its folds resemble the pages of a book, "the Indian Bible." Every part of an animal's body is treated with the respect due one's own: since the animal has been good enough to give up his life to sustain man's, no part is wasted. One of the happy results of this kinship is the second great soup-stew of the Southwest. During a winter visit to Sante Fe, I was once snowed in for a week and lived entirely on a single large pot of *menudo,* which improved with each reheating.

2 pounds honeycomb tripe
1 calf's foot, veal knuckle, or pig's foot
     water or meat stock, as needed
2 onions, chopped
4 cloves garlic, chopped
2 teaspoons salt
½ cup red chili pulp (see page 38), or 3–4 tablespoons pure
     ground chili
2 teaspoons oregano
1 tablespoon minced fresh coriander (cilantro)
1½ cups canned hominy or dried hominy parboiled

Cut tripe into narrow strips about 2 inches long and put into a deep pot with the calf's foot. Add cold water or meat stock to cover, bring slowly to a boil, and remove the scum.

Add remaining ingredients except for the hominy and simmer gently, covered, until tripe is barely tender, about 2 hours. Remove knuckle, add hominy, and simmer gently, covered, for another hour. Taste and adjust seasoning, as the tripe will absorb a lot of seasoning.

Serves 6 to 8.

2
Chilies

An English traveler's complaint in the eighteenth century that the fiery fruit of the Indians was "so very acrid as to cause an extraordinary great Pain in the mouth and Throat of such Persons as are not accustom'd to eat of it" has not prevented chili pepper from becoming the world's most popular spice, more of it being eaten in greater quantity than any other seasoning in the world, including black pepper. Like corn, chili crossbreeds like crazy, so that today there are nearly two hundred varieties of *Capsicum frutescens* and *annuum*, ranging from sweet and fruity chilies like the ones used in Hungarian paprika to hellishly hot ones like the wild *chiltepins* that Mexicans were eating in 7000 B.C. and are eating still.

Because the chili belt encircles the globe, it's hard to believe that it all began in the Americas and that chili was probably cultivated as early as corn. The Spanish, who called it *ají*, explained to the wondering folk at home that "*ají*, after maize, holds the first place as the plant most common and of greatest esteem among the Indians." As usual, Europeans mistook the unknown for the known and confused matters with their labels. A German botanist, who assumed Columbus had at least reached India, named the new pod with more fancy than science, "Calcutta pepper." Although chili is a member of the nightshade family, which covers tomatoes, potatoes, eggplants, and tobacco, and is wholly unrelated to the pepper vine of India, the English tongue has its reasons which science knows nothing of and so chili *pepper* it remains.

Chili pepper spread rapidly not only to the Old World but to its fabled origin in the Far East. So next time you have a hot Indian curry or a Szechuan hot and spicy shrimp, you can thank the savages of the New World for their taste and cunning.

Columbus and later explorers were puzzled by how little Indians used salt even when, as in the Carib islands, they were surrounded by salt seas. Since they got sodium from green plants and the ashes of plants, they didn't need salt. They had chili instead, rich in vitamins, with a palatal range from hot to sweet.

What makes a chili hot is the capsaicin that is concentrated in the seeds and white "veins," actually the placenta, to which they are attached. You can reduce or intensify a pod's heat by the number of seeds you discard or include. To many conservative Anglos, however, even the mildest chili can seem as rude as a dinner-table belch. Not for them the rapid bite at the back of the throat, the slow take along the tongue and the eye-watering ascent to the scalp. Hot chili is without question a stimulant that gives a high, which no doubt accounts for its popularity in less inhibited cultures. In the medical lore of the Southwest, it is said to protect against disease, aid digestion, clarify the blood, and stimulate flagging virility.

Those who think of Texas as the chili capital of Mexamerica probably also think of chili mostly as a dried powder, premixed with black pepper, cumin, oregano, and garlic. There's a reason for this, since a German named William Gebhardt, operating a cafe in New Braunfels, Texas, began the Mexamerican food industry in the States by packaging a chili blend in 1896 under the label Eagle Brand. Gebhardt's was the chili I grew up on in southern California, so I was startled to discover in New Mexico the joys of fresh chili and of pure dried chili from their native types, which are as sweet as they are hot.

Chili even more than corn is a sun food because it records the sun's rays in its color changes. All chilies begin life green (or sometimes yellow) and all turn red as they ripen. Dried, they will turn mahogany red to brown or black. Color has not to do with hotness but with age. On the hotness scale, forget red and green and look for the chili type. New Mexico's major native types are Colorado and Big Jim, much like California's Anaheim, remarkably sweet and mild. More typical Mexamerican chilies are the small, slightly pointed *serrano*, the somewhat larger and rounder jalapeño, and the longer and thinner *poblano*. *Poblano* is a problem because it keeps changing its name. When the green *poblano* is dried, it is called *ancho* in Mexico, *pasilla* in California, and *pisado* in Texas. The hottest chilies, generally, are the long, pencil-thin curved ones like cayenne, the Chinese *yunk ko,* or the short Japanese *takanotsume.*

Hotness, to put it mildly, is a matter of taste. To increase the range, agriculturists at the State University of New Mexico at Las Cruces have over the last decade made this border town the experimental chili capital of the world. As the Rio Grande widens under the Organ Mountains, so do some 15,000 acres of chili peppers, like a green sea in August. Here the latest hybrid, "a New Mexican green with just a little kick," is named NuMex R. Naky, after its developer, Roy Nakayama. This should tell us something about the mixed roots of American food.

Within a given type, there is just no telling how hot an individual pepper may be without registering it cautiously on the tongue. I like the unpredictability of chili pepper. It makes chili cooking not only stimulating but adventurous, which is just what Herr Gebhardt wanted to save the housewife from. The great pleasure of chili cooking in New Mexico is the unexpected variety of chili flavors and textures, with fresh pods, red and green, and dried pods soaked to a pulp or ground coarse or fine. Fresh chili you roast and skin for the fullest flavor. Dried pods you toast before soaking or grinding. Ground pepper you should put in the freezer or refrigerator to keep the flavor fresh.

When I opened the door of Tony Garcia's refrigerator, I opened a world of chili. Here were bags of chili fresh and bags of chili dried, some ground coarsely with seeds and some without, some ground medium and some fine as powder. "I don't like my chili hot," Tony explains, "so I mix it in various ways, usually with browned flour and garlic—my mother said the more garlic the less hot—and sometimes a little sugar." These are the kind of niceties that fuel the Great Chili Wars waged by the Chili Appreciation Society, International, headquartered in Terlinga, Texas. But Tony is an Indian, not a Texan, and is appalled at the barbarous heat of a typical Texan bowl of red.

Dried Red Chilies for Pulp

To turn dried chili pods into pulp, first wash them, then toast them lightly in a skillet or in a 250° oven for about 10 minutes. Under running cold water, remove their stems and all seeds. Cover the pods with boiling water and let them soak for 30 minutes. Drain them, reserving the water, and put them into a blender with a little of the liquid; then blend until smooth. (After handling the pods, wash your hands and fingernails carefully with salt water to avoid transferring any capsaicin oil in the seeds to your face or eyes.)

For 1 cup pulp, you will need 8 to 10 large dried New Mexican chili pods.

Dried Red Chilies for Powder

To turn dried chili pods into powder, first wash them, then toast them lightly in a skillet or a 250° oven for about 10 minutes. When pods are cool enough to handle, remove stems, break the pods in pieces, and put in a blender or spice grinder. To make the hottest powder, include the seeds. To make medium-hot powder, remove three-fourths of the seeds. To make mild powder, remove all the seeds. Grind in small quantities to retain freshness. If you make more than you need, store in the refrigerator. In recipes, 1 tablespoon chili powder equals roughly 1 dried chili pod.

Substitutes for Red Chili Pulp

Where dried red chilies are unavailable, substitute fresh sweet red bell peppers, roasted, skinned, and seeded (see page 39). To make 1 cup pulp, use 2 large bell peppers. To increase hotness and flavor, add pure ground chili powder, available commercially, in degrees of mild, medium, and hot. Use 1 tablespoon mild chili powder to equal 1 dried chili pod, or ½ cup mild chili powder for 1 cup chili pulp. Where pure ground chili powder is unavailable, substitute cayenne pepper, hot pepper flakes, or minced fresh or canned hot green peppers like jalapeño or *serrano*. Add these hot peppers to taste, beginning with 1/16 teaspoon for cayenne, or 1/2 teaspoon for minced whole peppers. Remember that cooking will temper a chili's heat.

To Prepare Fresh Chili Peppers, Sweet or Hot

To bring out the flavor of any chili pepper, including bell peppers, roast the pepper directly over a gas flame or electric unit, holding the pepper with tongs or a long toasting fork, or under a broiler or over a charcoal grill. Char the skin evenly by turning the pods until the skin is blackened and puffed on all sides. Put the peppers in a paper bag for 10 minutes to loosen their skins while they cool. Remove the charred skins under cold running water. Cut off the stems and squeeze out all the seeds. The peppers are now ready to be chopped by hand or pulped. To freeze roasted peppers, leave them intact, skins on, because thawing helps remove the skins.

To Make Chili Less Hot

In a fresh sauce, add fresh chopped tomatoes and/or roasted and peeled sweet green or red bell peppers, chopped or puréed. For a cooked sauce, add 1 to 2 tablespoons flour browned in a skillet or 1 to 2 cloves garlic, mashed, or 1 teaspoon sugar.

To Make Chili Hotter

For a fresh or cooked sauce, add chili seeds or cayenne powder. Or mince hot green or red, fresh or canned, whole chilies and add.

To Cool a Chili-Heated Mouth or Throat

Don't drink water, which distributes the capsaicin oil, but instead absorb the heat with a spoonful of sugar or a slice of bread.

FRESH GREEN CHILI SAUCE

In New Mexican restaurants, you are asked whether you want your chili sauce green or red, and New Mexicans opt for green. "Green means summer and red means winter," my Indian friend Bea Tioux explains. Green chili is picked while young, therefore green, and it retains a fresh delicate flavor even when it is frozen or canned. Chilies are roasted to remove their tough outer skins so that even in a basic fresh chili sauce like this one, a *salsa cruda,* the chili has been precooked. If fresh green New Mexican or California chilies are unavailable, you can improvise the sweet-and-hot combo by substituting green bell peppers and adding some fresh or canned hot green chili like jalapeño.

This kind of uncooked sauce is good as a dip for corn chips; or as a garnish or sauce for tortillas, enchiladas, and tacos; or in fresh salads, guacamoles, and gazpachos. To intensify the greenness of a *salsa verde,* use green tomatillos (husked and parboiled three minutes) instead of red tomatoes. Purists will omit tomatoes entirely as a decadent incursion from Texas.

> 10–12 fresh green chilies, or 3–4 green bell peppers plus 1 jalapeño pepper
> ¼ cup minced onion or green onions
> 2 cloves garlic, minced
> 3 medium tomatoes, seeded and chopped
> ½ teaspoon salt
> black pepper to taste
> 4 sprigs fresh coriander (cilantro)

Roast the chilies over a gas flame or under a broiler. Steam 10 minutes in a paper bag to loosen skins, then peel them and remove stems. Discard seeds and veins if you want mild chili. Chop chilies coarsely and mix with the other vegetables and seasonings. Taste.

Makes 3 to 4 cups.

VARIATION: COOKED CHILI SAUCE Sauté vegetables lightly in 1 tablespoon of lard or vegetable oil. Thicken with ¼ cup toasted and ground sunflower or pumpkin seeds, or with 1 tablespoon cornstarch. Add a liquid such as ½ cup beef broth mixed with ½ cup tomato purée or tomato sauce. Simmer about 5 minutes.

RED CHILI SAUCE

Red chili sauces are made from mature pods that are dried and turned into pulp, coarse flakes, or fine powder. In New Mexico such sauces are based on red chili pulp rather than on tomatoes, as in Texas. Spices vary widely but usually center on the southwestern trio of cumin, oregano, and fresh coriander (cilantro). This sauce is a particularly rich and spicy one, sometimes called "chili Caribe," which adds to the spices of the West Indies the cinnamon and clove of East India. The combination is familiar to us through ketchups and barbecue sauces, which preserve flavor by vinegar or salt, but these dried chili sauces reconstitute flavor by liquid and have a fresh sharp bite that is quickly lost. The best way to keep left-over sauce is to freeze it. The sauce can be used hot or cold as a dip for corn chips, a sauce for main dishes, or an enrichment for a salad dressing, soup, or stew.

8–12 dried red chili pods, or 2–4 red bell peppers plus 1 fresh
      jalapeño pepper
1 tablespoon lard, bacon fat, or oil
2 cloves garlic, mashed
½ teaspoon each salt and oregano
¼ teaspoon each cumin, cinnamon, and black pepper
⅛ teaspoon cloves
1 cup chicken or beef stock

Toast, soak, and purée the dried chilies with a cup of their liquid (see page 38). Melt the lard in a skillet, stir in the garlic and remaining seasonings, and heat 2 to 3 minutes. Add the chili and blend to a smooth purée.

In a saucepan combine the meat stock and chili purée and simmer 5 to 10 minutes to blend flavors. Use reserved chili liquid if needed to thin your sauce.

Makes about 2 cups.

VARIATION: CHILI SAUCE WITH TOMATOES Roast 2 large tomatoes, charring their skin under a broiler or on a grill as you would a fresh pepper. Pulverize the tomatoes, skin and all, in a blender and add to the other ingredients. You can substitute for fresh tomatoes 1 cup canned Italian plum tomatoes, drained and puréed.

GREEN CHILI ENCHILADAS

New Mexico likes its chili green, its tortillas blue, and its enchiladas stacked instead of rolled. A stacked enchilada, layered with red chili sauce, green chili sauce, grated cheese, and raw onion, creates a southwestern form of the club sandwich, dripping sour cream instead of mayonnaise. It may be that New Mexico gets the stacked or open-faced tortilla from an old Zuni dish described by Cushing as "stone-cakes": The Zunis spread tortilla dough on corn husks laid flat on square thin stones; they then stacked the stones and buried them in the hearth to bake. (This is one way to solve the problems of making blue-corn tortillas on the griddle.)

While blue corn is traditional to Santa Fe's enchiladas, yellow or white tortillas will do. If you can get a goat cheese like the southwestern *ranchero seco,* use it. If not, a Greek feta cheese gives something of the same salty bite.

> 12 corn tortillas
>
> **Green Sauce**
>> 2 medium onions, chopped fine
>> 2 tablespoons lard or oil
>> 2 cups cooked thick tomato pulp (see page 41)
>> 2 cups chopped green chilies, fresh roasted or canned
>> 1½ cups sour cream
>> ¾ cup grated Monterey Jack or Muenster cheese
>> ½ cup crumbled white goat cheese (*ranchero seco* or feta)
>> 2 tablespoons white or red wine vinegar
>> 1 teaspoon oregano
>>
>> 2 cups Red Chili Sauce (see page 41)
>> 1½ cups grated sharp Cheddar cheese
>> 1 cup finely chopped onions

Wrap tortillas in foil and heat them at 300° while preparing the sauce.

For the green sauce, sauté the 2 onions in lard until soft, remove from heat, and add the tomato pulp, chopped chilies, sour cream, the cheeses, vinegar, and oregano.

Dip 4 tortillas in the red chili sauce and place them in a single layer in the bottom of a baking dish. Cover them with a third of the green sauce and repeat with the final 2 layers of tortillas. Cover top layer with 1 cup red chili sauce and ½ cup Cheddar cheese. Bake at 350° until the mixture is thoroughly hot and the cheese melted, 15 to 20 minutes. Serve with bowls of extra red chili sauce, the remaining Cheddar cheese, and the chopped onions. Serves 4.

GREEN CHILI FRY

In midsummer, when green chili ripens in alternating rows with red tomatoes and yellow corn, it's time for a garden stir-fry. In her *Pueblo Indian Cookbook* (1972) Phyllis Hughes suggests a number of summer skillet dishes, depending on what your garden grows—squashes, onions, green beans. Southwestern flavor is in the spicing—cumin, oregano, coriander, and, of course, the heat of chili pepper. Canned green chilies work well if you can't get fresh ones, or use sweet bell peppers jazzed with cayenne.

> 8 fresh green chilies, or 4 bell peppers plus cayenne
> 1 onion, chopped fine
> 1 tablespoon lard or vegetable oil
> 3 ears fresh corn, kernels cut off
> 3 fresh tomatoes, seeded and chopped
> ¼ teaspoon each cumin and oregano
> 4 sprigs fresh coriander (cilantro) or parsley
>   salt and black pepper to taste

Roast chilies or bell peppers; peel and chop coarsely.

Sauté onion 2 to 3 minutes in a wok or large skillet. Add the chilies, corn kernels, tomatoes, and seasonings, mix well, and turn into a serving dish. Corn and tomatoes should be very crisp. Can be served hot, warm, or cold. Serves 4.

GREEN CHILIES WITH CHEESE
RELLENOS

The marriage of chili to cheese comes close, in an imperfect world, to an ideal coupling of the wild and the tame. Such coupling was not possible until the conquistadors brought milk animals—sheep, goats, and cows—to the New

World. While stuffing pepper pods with cheese seems simple, hiding the pods in a soufflé batter puffed in deep fat is not. Avoid chilies *rellenos con queso* in any but the best restaurants because they require care in the making, the kind of care you can give them in your own kitchen. Of all Mexamerican dishes, they are my favorite because they are like Chinese boxes, each layer concealing another within, the whole embraced in a creamy red sauce.

> 6 large green chilies, preferably fresh
> ⅔ pound Monterey Jack, Muenster, or mozzarella cheese, or any mixture of them, grated

Tomato Sauce

> 4 large fresh tomatoes, or 2 cups canned (and drained) Italian tomatoes
> 2 cloves garlic
> ½ onion, chopped
> ½ teaspoon oregano
> 3 tablespoons lard or vegetable oil
> 1 cup chicken or beef stock
> salt and pepper to taste

Batter

> 3 eggs, separated
> 1 tablespoon flour
> ½ teaspoon salt
> vegetable oil for frying

Garnish

> 1 cup sour cream
> 1 tablespoon chopped fresh coriander (cilantro)

Roast the chilies under the broiler, steam them 10 minutes in a paper bag, and remove skins without removing stems. Slit the side of each pod to remove seeds and veins. Stuff each pod with grated cheese.

For the tomato sauce, broil fresh tomatoes and garlic until their skins are charred (if using canned tomatoes, drain before measuring). Remove garlic skins and purée the peeled garlic with the tomatoes, skins and all, in a blender. Add the onion and oregano and blend until smooth. Melt lard in a skillet and cook the tomato purée over high heat for 4 to 5 minutes, stirring constantly.

Add the stock and simmer over low heat about 10 minutes. Taste for seasoning and add salt and pepper as wanted. Keep sauce warm.

For the batter, beat the egg yolks with the flour until thick; beat whites separately with the salt until stiff, then fold them into the yolks.

In a wok or heavy skillet heat oil at least 2 inches deep until hot but not smoking. Dry each chili well so that the batter will stick to it. Dip each chili in the batter, put it on a saucer, and slide the chili from the saucer into the oil to fry until golden brown. (With a spoon you can add a little more batter to the topside of the chili while it fries.) Turn the chilies at least once with tongs or a pair of spoons to brown both sides. Drain well on paper towels.

Cover the bottom of a large warm serving platter with the prepared tomato sauce. Arrange the chilies on top and serve. Pass separately a bowl of sour cream sprinkled with fresh coriander.

Serves 3 to 6, depending on the size of the chilies.

CHILI WITH MEAT
CHILI CON CARNE

Chili con carne, disclaimed by Mexicans as "a detestable food with a false Mexican title," is nevertheless a true Mexamerican child of the border. It originated in towns like San Antonio, where poor Mexican families made a little meat go a long way with lots of chili. J. C. Clopper first described the dish in 1828 as "a kind of hash with nearly as many peppers as there are pieces of meat." In the 1880s, however, the dish became fashionable when sporting ladies known as "chili queens" dished out chili from open-air stalls around Alamo Plaza at night for San Antonians on the prowl for a hot dish. The Texas fashion went national when Texas set up a state chili booth at the 1893 Columbian Exposition in Chicago and when Gebhardt exploited the new taste in 1908 by canning the stuff.

Ever since then, prize-winning recipes at the annual Chili Cookoffs in rival Tropico, California, and Terlingua, Texas, rely heavily on canned tomatoes and premixed commercial chili powder. New Mexicans, on the other hand, insist on freshly made chili pulp or at least pure ground chili.

To get back to a good honest hash of peppers and meat, try this New Mexamerican version that appeared in Erna Fergusson's *Mexican Cookbook* published in Albuquerque in 1934. She uses mutton, of which there was plenty in the 1930s. Now you have to eat with the Navajos to find it, so I've used here the more usual beef and pork.

2 pounds beef chuck
1 pound boneless pork
3 tablespoons rendered beef suet, lard, or bacon fat
3 medium onions, chopped
4 cloves garlic, minced
4 cups fresh tomato pulp, or 2 cups canned Italian plum tomatoes
1 cup chili pulp (from 8–10 dried chilies; see page 38), or ½ cup
    mild pure ground chili
1 tablespoon oregano
1 teaspoon cumin
2 bay leaves, crushed
    salt and pepper to taste
    tomato juice or beef broth, if needed
    optional: cayenne pepper, Tabasco, or minced jalapeño pepper

Cut meat in ½-inch cubes and sear it quickly in the fat over high heat. Lower heat and sauté onions and garlic along with the meat until they are golden. Add the tomato and chili pulp and remaining seasonings. Simmer uncovered over very low heat for 2 hours or more until meat is fork tender and pulp is reduced to a thick sauce. If sauce becomes too thick, add tomato juice or beef broth. To make sauce hotter, add cayenne pepper, Tabasco, or minced jalapeño pepper.

Serves 6 to 8.

HOT PEPPER PORK
CARNE ADOBADA

In the Southwest, the meat in *carne adobada* usually means pork and the sauce means chilies spiked with citrus juice or vinegar to preserve the meat as well as flavor it. In the pueblos, women still cure pork by marinating it in a chili sauce and drying it, in strips, in the sun. The result is a spiced pork jerky, which is then pounded and roasted or fried. Even without a preserving function, the chili marinade has an affinity with pork and deliciously penetrates the meat with its spices and aromatics.

1 cup chili pulp (from 8–10 dried chilies; see page 38), or 2–4
    sweet red bell peppers plus cayenne
1-inch cinnamon stick or ½ teaspoon ground cinnamon
3 whole cloves
4 cloves garlic, mashed
¼ teaspoon each oregano and cumin seeds
¼ cup fresh orange juice
1 tablespoon lemon juice
3 pounds boneless pork
¼ cup rendered pork fat or vegetable oil
1 medium onion, sliced

Add to the chili pulp the seasonings and citrus juices and blend to make a thick purée.

Cut pork into 1-inch cubes or 2-inch strips. Put with the marinade into a nonmetallic bowl or a plastic bag and refrigerate for 24 hours.

Remove meat from the marinade and sear it quickly in the hot fat over high heat. Lower heat, add marinade, and simmer gently until meat is tender, 15 to 30 minutes. Make this dish ahead because the flavor improves with reheating. When ready to serve, strew the sliced onion over the meat.

Serves 6.

TAMALES

At her restaurant, Maria's, in Santa Fe, Priscilla Hoback makes tamales in her own kitchen rather than buying them at Rose's Tamale Factory off Cerrillos Road. Rose's tamales are good, and there is always a cluster of trucks outside and a line inside to prove it. But Priscilla is first a potter, then a cook, and she finds that making tamales is like making pots: the container conditions the thing contained.

Corn husks have an edge over modern metal or ceramic containers because they flavor what they hold. The distinction of the tamale, in its long heritage from the Aztec *tamalli,* lies not only in its rich dough but in the sweetness the corn husk lends as it cooks. (In the Southwest sweet tamales are as frequent as hot tamales, and the best combine sweet and hot with surprising delicacy. The Indian tamale, in fact, is to a stuffed tortilla what cake is to bread. Montezuma's Indians wrapped their dough-like husks around flowers, nuts, and seeds, sweetening them with fermented corn yeast, adding shredded meats, chilies, and quantities of dried chopped fruits.) Today the richness of the corn dough, the *tamal*, comes from whipping in lard rather than bear's grease or nut butter. Vegetable shortening, however, is a poor substitute for lard because it has no taste. If you can't get lard, use butter. As for corn husks, you can of course substitute aluminum foil but why bother? If you can't get corn husks, don't make tamales.

Traditionally, tamale dough is made from wet hominy, freshly ground, just as tortillas are. Commercial tamales are more often made with dried hominy flour, *masa harina*, but I like to combine three hominy types: canned hominy for flavor, *masa harina* for adhesiveness, and instant grits for texture.

Traditional fillings can make your head spin: cheeses with jalapeño peppers, refried beans, sausages, shredded pork, chicken and beef, shredded coconut, candied pumpkin and orange, chopped almonds and pecans, apricots and dates. Whatever delicious nuggets you tuck inside the dough, make sure that the seasoning is intense because the dough will absorb flavors the way a dumpling dough will. In the filling below, I've combined meat and fruit with nuts, chili, and cumin.

Wrapping each packet of dough in a corn husk is a bit difficult, but fun. To make dried corn husks malleable, you must soak them for several hours or overnight in warm water to cover. When you are ready to assemble your tamales, drain the husks and keep them moist with a wet towel.

Filling

    2 cups shredded cooked pork or chicken

    ½ cup dried apricots, soaked until soft and chopped

    ⅓ cup piñon nuts or walnuts

    ⅓ cup pure ground chili

    ¼ cup cumin

    salt and pepper to taste

Dough

    1 cup instant grits

    1 cup *masa harina*

    2 cups canned (and drained) hominy

    2 teaspoons salt

1 tablespoon baking powder
1 cup lard or butter, room temperature
1 cup boiling chicken broth
48 dried corn husks, soaked

Make the filling by mixing all ingredients together, and set aside while you prepare the dough.

Grind the instant grits as fine as possible in a blender or processor and mix them with the *masa harina*. Process the canned hominy with the salt and baking powder to make a smooth purée and add to the *masa*. Whip the lard separately until it is light and fluffy. Add to the hominy mixture and beat well. Gradually add the chicken broth until the liquid is all absorbed.

Flatten a corn husk (6 by 9 inches is an ideal size). Spread 2 tablespoons of the dough in a square in the middle, leaving about 2 inches at the top and bottom of the husk and an inch at each side. Place a tablespoon of filling on the dough and enclose it by rolling one edge of the husk over the other. Fold the pointed end of the husk down over the middle and fold the broader end up to cover it. Tie the husk around the middle with a narrow strip shredded from a large corn husk. Continue until you have used up the dough and filling.

Line the top of a steamer (or similar lidded pan into which you can fit a rack) with half of the remaining corn husks and stack the tamales upright if possible. Cover with the rest of the corn husks and a small kitchen towel. Cover pan with a lid and steam 2 to 3 hours.

Serve hot with a sauce like Fresh Green Chili Sauce or Red Chili Sauce (see pages 40 and 41), in which to dip the tamales once they are unwrapped. You can freeze leftover tamales in their husks and reheat them, wrapped in foil, at 350° for about 30 minutes.

Makes 36 tamales about 3 inches long.

X-LNT TAMALE PIE

A visitor to southern California in 1893 described the tamale as "a curious and dubious combination of chicken hash, meal, olives, red pepper, and I know not what, enclosed in a corn-husk." Enclosing meal in husks is as old as the Aztecs' *tamalli*, but the olives are a California addition. Californian also is the device of turning a Mexican tamale into a Mexamerican shepherd's pie by enclosing meat and olives between layers of cornmeal mush. I grew up on this kind of tamale pie in the Depression, which has given the dish its current low repute, so low that even Helen Brown scorns it in her *West Coast Cook Book* (1952) as an ersatz American dish unworthy the true tamale. For me, however, the ersatz pie was every bit as delicious as the fat corn-husked tamales sold in grocery stores then under the label "X-LNT." These were far hotter than Mother's bland version but they lacked a crucial ingredient—the California olive. To get the best of both worlds, use a good textured *tamal* dough of grits, but don't hold the olives.

> ¼ pound lard or butter
> 3 cups instant grits
> 3 cups boiling chicken or beef stock

Filling

> 1 large onion, chopped
> 2 cloves garlic, minced
> 1 green bell pepper, chopped
> 3 tablespoons lard, butter, or vegetable oil
> 4 cups cooked meat (shredded chicken, pork, or beef)
> 2 pimientoes, chopped
> 1½ cups pitted olives, black and green
> ⅓–½ cup pure ground chili, or more to taste
> salt and pepper to taste

Whip the ¼ pound lard or butter until soft and light. Beat in the grits and gradually add the boiling stock until mixture is smooth. Cover and set aside while you make the filling.

Sauté onion, garlic, and bell pepper in the lard until soft, about 5 minutes. Stir in remaining ingredients and mix well. Taste and add more chili if wanted, because the mush will absorb much of the chili's heat.

Spread half the prepared mush in a 9-inch-square baking pan. Cover with the meat mixture and smooth remaining mush over the top. Bake at 350° until mush is crusty on top and the filling is heated through, about 30 minutes.

Serves 6 to 8.

3
Beans and Squashes

"New Mexico cooking is corn, beans, and squash—with a lot of chili thrown in," says Tony Garcia, standing in the middle of his garden in San Juan Pueblo, as he might have stood 5000 years ago in Old Mexico, surrounded by the ancestors of these same plants. The cultivation of pumpkin, squash (genus *Cucurbita*), and both lima and common bean (genus *Phaseolus*) is older than corn and chili. The natives of Mexico, Central America, and Peru (which named its capital for the bean) have rooted these nutritious and beneficent plants in their gardens for at least 9000 years. And while it is odd to think that the fiery dishes of India, Malaysia, and southern China are indebted to New World chili, it is even odder to realize that the whole world of winter and summer squashes, from "British" vegetable marrow to "Italian" zucchini, along with a world of beans, from "French" haricots to "Tuscan" cannellini, all spring from the same New World cradle of civilization.

The only bean Europe knew before the Spanish explorers returned from South America with seeds in their pockets was the broad or fava bean. The only squash Europe knew was the cucumber. But so quickly did Europe domesticate the many species of the bean and squash families that only an occasional name revealed an exotic origin. The Aztec word *ayacotl* remains in the French *haricot*. The American word "pumpkin" derives from the puzzlement of English explorers over what to call these *pompions* (from Greek *pépon* for large melon) so different from their own "native" squash.

As everyone knows today, corn, beans, and squash formed a complete and balanced food chain of proteins, vitamins, and minerals many thousand years before the modern science of nutrition developed names and labels. The Indians expressed the symbolic interrelation of these foods, so essential to their lives, by dancing. Today, as yesterday, Indians of the Southwest link their lives to nature's seasonal cycles by bean dances and squash dances. Among the Hopi, at the kachina ceremony of Páchavu, or Plant Life, Bean Maidens dressed in white, with giant headdresses of green bean sprouts twined with cornmeal molded into the shape of scarlet runner beans, confront the Warrior Mother, in black. She wears a hideous mask—teeth bared, scarlet tongue lolling—as she appears on Pumpkin Seed Point to be defeated, once again, by spring. Among the pueblos, the clowns called *koshari* mark the turn from winter to spring, at the vernal equinox, by reversing sexual roles to become comic and obscene transvestites in their squash dances.

Beans and squash were particularly valuable to these desert people because they could so easily preserve them. "We planted everything that we could preserve by drying," Tony says. "In summer we eat our squash green, but in the fall we let it turn yellow and then we use it for puddings and pies. Later we dry it, along with melons and apples and plums. My mother would peel a melon, then cut it in half and scoop out the seeds in order to dry them separately. Then she'd peel each half of the melon in a single strip and hang it over a wooden fencepost to dry."

Beans and squash, like corn, are edible at every stage of their growing. In spring, green and tender bean pods are eaten whole. In winter, the dried seeds of pods are eaten as legumes or ground into meal and flour. In spring, squash blossoms are an important garden staple. In winter, squash, pumpkin, and melons, all dried in spiral strips (or nowadays often frozen), are reborn in stews, puddings, and pies. All year long the dried seeds of pumpkins, melons, and sunflowers are an important source of protein and oil. Where once they were ground in a *metate,* today they are ground in a blender to make rich and delicious sauces.

We call that typical American mix of corn and lima beans succotash, after a Narraganset Indian word, *misickquatash,* or maybe *sukquttahash* (there are several candidates). The Southwest completes the Indian triad and adds squash or pumpkin to its succotash. Where the Northeast will add cream or milk and salt pork, the Southwest will add tomatoes or lamb broth or sunflower seeds. Corn, beans, and squash go together in the same southwestern pot because they still grow together in the fields, in their mutual stretch toward the sun.

The people triad—Indians, Hispanics, and Anglos—is less mutual. Priscilla Hoback, who grew up in her mother's restaurant, Rosalie Murphy's The Pink Adobe, and who now runs her own restaurant, Maria's, grounded me when I enthused over the cultural mix: "How long have you been here?" "Two weeks," I answered. Priscilla laughed. I searched out Priscilla because Tony in his garden and Bea at her mother's adobe oven are only one side of the southwestern triangle; Priscilla and her Texan husband, Peter Gould, are another. Priscilla is Scotch-Irish–Russian–Portuguese and "a little bit of everything else." Priscilla pots while raising Arabian horses, pumpkins, and fruit trees on their farm in Galisteo, just south of Santa Fe. Peter, having made money in Texas, now makes chairs.

They live in a 135-year-old adobe on Quarter Mill ranch, given as a land grant to the Ortiz family by the king of Spain two hundred years ago. The seed stock for their fruit orchards was brought in by Bishop Lamy, the hero of Willa Cather's *Death Comes for the Archbishop*. Beyond the orchards is the Bosky, a two-acre dell of cottonwoods and Navajo willows, where Priscilla raises peacocks, holds pottery workshops, and now and then barbecues a few steers over apple and pear wood.

When Priscilla and Peter talk about old cooking traditions, they don't mean New Mexican. "New Mexico is only three hundred fifty years old," Priscilla says. "I'm talking about traditional pottery cooking, which is several thousand years old." She is talking about the way pots create cooking as much as cooking creates pots. When she began to pot she made bowls in order to use them, then she began to supply restaurants, and now when she wonders what to serve she thinks first of the pot. "I potted thirty-five Irish-coffee cups for an Australian film crew last week," she says, "and then had to find some Mexican coffee to put in the Irish cups." When Priscilla looked at her field of ripening pumpkins in September, she saw a field of orange pots and threw together a delicious stew of chicken, chilies, and tomatoes to put in them. Priscilla knew that if women were growing pumpkins 9000 years ago in their gardens they were also growing pots.

FRIED BEAN PURÉE
FRIJOLES REFRITOS

Indians begin with sun-dried beans, which they spread on stretched canvas until the beans dry to the color of dark bricks. Tony Garcia remembers the way his mother made beans, with a big cut-up onion and meat bones and sometimes fried bacon and garlic and more onions—"Oh, so very *very* good." When beans are cooked good to begin with, they can't fail to be very *very* good when recooked, especially when turned into a purée smoothed with lard. *Frijoles refritos* now appear on every combination plate of Mexamerican tacos, tamales, enchiladas, and rice, but they are too often an unsavory purple paste used as filler. Rightly done, however, they can be as unctuous as pâté. Because of the lard, the purée is best when hot or warm. With added hot peppers, it makes a good bean dip for tostados.

> 1½ cups fresh dried pinto beans
> 1 onion, chopped
> 2 cloves garlic, mashed
> 2 thick slices bacon, cut up
> 2 bay leaves, crumbled
> 1 hot green pepper (jalapeño or *serrano*), minced
> 1 teaspoon salt
> ¼ cup lard
> ¼ cup white cheese, Monterey Jack, Muenster, or feta

In a pot, cover beans with cold water at least an inch above the beans. Bring to a boil, boil 1 minute, remove from heat, cover the pot, and let sit for an hour. Add the onion, garlic, bacon, bay leaves, pepper, and salt to the beans, bring to a simmer, and simmer, covered, until beans are tender, 45 to 60 minutes. Add water if needed during the cooking.

Whip or process the beans into a smooth purée. Beat in the lard and taste for seasoning.

Pour the beans into a hot ungreased skillet and fry, stirring, until the liquid evaporates and the purée clings together so that it can be turned out like an omelet, 10 to 15 minutes. Sprinkle the top with grated cheese.

Serves 4 to 6.

DEEP-FRIED SQUASH BLOSSOMS

Sometimes the Indians mash squash blossoms to make a pudding with the scraped kernels of young corn. Sometimes they use squash blossoms instead of corn husks to wrap a nugget of blue-corn meal. But the prettiest use of the blossom retains the shape of the flower by dipping it in batter and frying it until crisp. The problem for nongardeners is to find fresh squash blossoms for a recipe which begins, "Pick blossoms early in the morning before they close." Since Italians are fond of fried zucchini blossoms, however, nongardeners can search out Italian markets for a supply of blossoms in the spring.

>   ¼ pound fresh squash blossoms (20–30)
>   3 eggs
>   ⅓ cup milk
>   1 teaspoon pure ground chili
>   salt to taste
>   1½ cups fine cornmeal or *masa harina*
>   oil for deep frying

Wash blossoms gently and pat dry. Beat together the eggs, milk, and seasonings. Dip each blossom in the mixture, roll it evenly in the cornmeal, put on a cookie sheet, and refrigerate for 10 minutes before frying.

Heat oil in a wok or heavy skillet and fry the blossoms a few at a time until crisp and golden brown, about 3 minutes. You'll need tongs or a pair of spoons to turn them over. Drain on paper towels and serve immediately.

Serves 6.

VARIATION: BEER BATTER   Instead of egg and cornmeal, use a beer batter for dipping. In a blender combine 2 egg yolks (save the whites), ½ cup flour, ½ cup beer, 1 tablespoon vegetable oil, 1 teaspoon salt, and ⅛ teaspoon chili powder. Beat the 2 egg whites until stiff but not dry and fold into the batter.

ZUNI SUMMER SUCCOTASH

Succotash is Indian for "hodgepodge," "gallimaufry," *olla podrida,* meaning whatever you have on hand, depending on the season. Eliza Leslie, in her *New Receipts for Cooking* (1852), used dried shelled beans and hard corn for Winter Saccatash to accompany pickled pork. A typical southwestern Indian succotash retains this meaning in a stew of fresh spring or summer vegetables enriched with spring lamb. This is the sort of stew that might be sweetened by squash blossoms or thickened, as here, with crushed sunflower seeds.

How much tastes change while ingredients remain the same is illustrated in Cushing's *Zuni Breadstuff* (1884), where he praises a succotash for its melting-pot homogeneity: "The delicacy of the year was the far-famed succotash, made by scraping the milky kernels from the ears, mingling them with little round beans, which had now come to be domesticated, and with bits of fresh meat, the whole being seasoned with salt, thickened with sunflower-seeds . . . or piñon-nut meal, and boiled until reduced to an almost homogeneous stew."

1 pound boneless lamb, cubed
3 cups hot beef stock
1 clove garlic, mashed
4 mint leaves, crushed
½ teaspoon salt
¼ teaspoon black pepper
2 cups green beans
2 summer squash (zucchini, yellow summer, or white pattypan)
3 ears fresh sweet corn
4 green onions, with tops
¼ cup shelled and crushed sunflower seeds

Gently simmer the lamb in the stock, together with garlic, mint, salt and pepper, until it is tender, 30 to 40 minutes.

Meanwhile prepare vegetables. Remove the ends of the green beans and cut each in two. Cut squash into small cubes. Cut kernels from the corn cobs. Chop onions and their tops. Add vegetables to the meat and simmer until vegetables are tender but still crisp, 5 to 8 minutes. Stir in the sunflower seeds to thicken the broth.

Serves 6.

VARIATION: Add 6 squash blossoms to the vegetables, either whole or chopped. Add 2 green chilies, roasted, seeded, and chopped.

INDIAN SQUASH AND GREEN CHILI

Tony Garcia grows all kinds of squash in his garden, but what he calls "Tewa" squash is the green-and-white-striped cushaw, one of the oldest of Indian squashes, the seeds of which have been found in excavated sites such as Chaco Canyon. But any garden squash is good, fresh and green, sautéed with a little onion, and made greener yet with the addition of green chili.

> 1 large onion, chopped
> 3 tablespoons lard, butter, or olive oil
> 6 cushaw squash or zucchini, diced
> 1½ teaspoons salt, or to taste
> ½ teaspoon oregano
> 2 ears fresh corn
> 1 cup chopped fresh or canned green chilies
> 1 cup grated Monterey Jack, Muenster, or sharp Cheddar cheese

Sauté onion in the lard in a large skillet. Add the squash, salt, and oregano, cover, and steam 5 to 10 minutes.

Cut corn kernels from the cob and add with the chili; cook 3 to 5 minutes more. Remove from heat, sprinkle with cheese, and cover pan tightly until the cheese is melted. Serve hot from the skillet.

Serves 6.

PUMPKIN SHELL STEW

The original American casserole was surely an orange pumpkin shell, just as our original wrapping paper was a corn husk. Filling a pumpkin shell with chopped vegetables and meats to bake in a modern oven is but a step or two away from filling a pumpkin to bake in the earth in a stone-heated pit. "Peter, Peter, Pumpkin Eater" understood the usefulness of pumpkin shells, but one wonders about the size of his wife. Today's best eating pumpkins, like small sugar or Cheyenne bush, are a bit small (two to four pounds) to act as a casserole. And the large field pumpkins like Big Max are bred for jack-o-lanterns, not for taste. I find the best solution for serving pumpkin in its own pot is to buy two pumpkins, one for flesh and one for shell. (An exception is the red Caribbean pumpkin, *calabaza,* which is both large and firm fleshed.)

The recipe below can be varied endlessly in its ingredients, but I adapted this one from Priscilla Hoback, who in turn had adapted a South American recipe. She uses salted peanuts, but to keep it southwestern I've specified salted pumpkin seeds.

1 large field pumpkin (10–12 pounds)
1 small sugar pumpkin (2–3 pounds)
8 chicken legs or thighs
2 tablespoons each olive oil and butter
3 cups sliced onions
2 cloves garlic, minced
3 cups hot chicken broth
½ teaspoon thyme
  pinch of saffron
1 tablespoon pure ground chili
  salt and black pepper
4 large ripe tomatoes, peeled, seeded, and chopped
1 cup pumpkin seeds, roasted and salted
4 ears fresh corn, kernels cut off
2 cups sour cream

Cut top from the large pumpkin, about a third of the way down. Scoop out the seeds and stringy fibers, put pumpkin on a sturdy oven-proof platter, and warm it slowly in a 250° oven. Cut the small pumpkin into quarters; remove seeds and stringy fiber. Peel off outer rind with a sharp knife and cut pumpkin meat into 1-inch cubes.

In a large casserole, brown chicken pieces in hot oil and butter. Lower heat and add onions and garlic, cooking them until golden. Add hot chicken broth and seasonings. Bring to a simmer and barely simmer for 15 minutes.

Add pumpkin, tomatoes, and pumpkin seeds and simmer 15 minutes more.

Add corn and ladle the stew into the heated pumpkin shell. Bake 15 minutes at 350°. Serve stew from the shell with a sauceboat of sour cream.

Serves 6 to 8.

4

Game and Fowl

Because Pueblo Indians were gardeners and gatherers rather than nomadic hunters of the plains, they were more bean eaters than buffalo eaters. But long before the Spanish enriched their stews with domestic animals and fowls, the Indians savored the animals of the wild: jackrabbits, wild turkeys, bear, rodents, quail, and, above all, deer.

Once the deer hunt was communal in the pueblo of Cochiti, where the hunters, led by Cougar Man, would sprinkle red ocher on the eyes of the ancient Stone Lions that crouch still, among the ruins of Potrero de las Vacas, waiting to pounce. Even today a deer hunter seldom hunts alone because a successful hunt means a communal feast. When the men bring home a deer from the Jemez Mountains, they choose a woman to be the Mother of the Deer. She is the "Giant," who will take charge of preparing the deer feast.

"Almost every night in November, in deer season, we sit on the floor around two or three big bowls of deer stew and eat communally," explains Laverne Garcia, whose ancestors were all Cochiti-born. "We must share the deer feast so the deer will be plentiful next year."

Laverne when I met her had recently left the pueblo for the first time, as a young bride, to accompany her husband, who had won an Ivy League scholarship in the East. Laverne and her husband, Robert, would learn of events in the pueblo by the packages that arrived in the East, two weeks later, full of food—spoiled, of course, but sent to be shared. "Here were all these boxes of rotten food and I would groan," said Robert, "because I knew what they had been before."

One thing that did not spoil was dried venison, which Laverne's mother makes in the time-honored way of cutting the flesh in a circular motion to produce long, thin, spiraling strips. Instead of simply drying the strips in the sun, she prepares a dry-cure mixture of salt, cinnamon, black pepper, and allspice to rub into the strips before threading them on strings to hang in a dry cool place like the screened porch of her adobe. Nearly three thousand miles away, her daughter resuscitates the deer by softening the strips in water to make the soup-stew of a feast celebrated in a graduate dorm at Princeton University instead of a pueblo adobe near Santa Fe. Since the Indians had originally devised jerky as traveling food, there was no reason it shouldn't travel as well by U.S. mail as by horse or foot.

Traveling myself by air one time from California to Santa Fe, I had a seatmate who also spoke of venison. She was a handsome white-haired tawny woman, flying with her grandson back to her home in Peralto, near Albuquerque. Ruth Sedillo, retired from her career as a social worker, looked forward to the opening of deer season. Ruth was the kind of cook who raised all her own food on the family ranch called Bosky Farms. She slaughtered her own pigs, she made her own tortillas every day for her large family, and soon she would skin and carve the deer. "That your husband will bring home?" I asked. "Oh no, I'm the deer hunter," she said. "I'm the best shot."

VENISON AND CORN STEW

At their seasonal deer feasts in the pueblo of Cochiti, Laverne Garcia told me, they eat only venison stew, with Indian fry bread. But there are problems if you want to celebrate the feast in a place as remote as Princeton, New Jersey. As a New Englander trying to celebrate Thanksgiving in the Congo might remark, the natives may well have frozen butterball turkeys but where are the cranberries? Laverne found frozen venison roasts at her local supermarket, but where were the deer bones? "You don't eat bones with deer," said the butcher. "Indians do," said Laverne. Because they are close to their food roots, Indians know that bone is more important to flavor than flesh is. Venison tastes most itself not as a costly loin roast but as chopped shoulder, neck, and shank, in a mix of meat and bone.

The dried corn kernels called *chicos* are traditional in the deer feast stew, and dried corn has its own character just as a dried bean does. Sometimes the kernels are cracked and sometimes cooked whole, but they act to thicken a stew as well as flavor it, so they are a favored ingredient for winter stews just as *posole* is. Dried corn is available wherever there are Spanish markets, but if you must substitute, whole hominy works better than fresh or frozen corn kernels, which will toughen with long cooking.

        1 cup dried corn kernels
        ½ cup chopped beef suet
        3 pounds venison stew meat (shoulder, neck, shank, rump)
        2 pounds deer (or beef soup) bones
        3 large onions, chopped
        3 cloves garlic, minced
        4 green chilies, roasted, seeded, and chopped
          salt and cayenne pepper to taste
        4 cups beef stock, or as needed

Cover corn with 2 cups water, bring to a boil, boil 1 minute, and remove from heat. Cover pot and let sit for an hour.

Cut meat into 1-inch cubes. Heat the suet in a heavy cast-iron pot. Sear the meat along with the bones, and when they are browned, remove and put aside. Sauté onions and garlic in the same pot until onions are translucent. Add the chilies and remaining seasonings.

Return the meat and bones to the stew pot. Add the corn with its liquid. Add beef stock to cover. Bring mixture slowly to a simmer and simmer gently until meat and corn are both tender, 1½ to 2 hours. Remove bones and serve. Serves 6.

BAKED RABBIT WITH PEANUT SAUCE

In the spring and fall in Cochiti Pueblo, there are still communal rabbit hunts in which women and children join. If a girl beats out a boy running for the same rabbit, the boy must exchange clothes and wear her dress until he kills his own rabbit. If two women claim a rabbit at the same time and argue over the prize, a third may take it by crying like a wolf. Such are the rules of rabbit hunting before the game is brought back to the village for the feast.

Because jackrabbits are tough, they are usually stewed, sometimes with hominy or corn, usually with chilies or chili powder, sometimes with ground nuts or seeds for thickening. A fine thickening sauce can be made from peanuts, that strange underground pod which the conquistadors brought north from Mexico and its native Peru. While peanuts were not cultivated in the Southwest as they were in the Southeast, their accessibility and robust flavor make them one of the best nuts to use in Indian ways new to Anglos accustomed to spreading nuts on bread.

1 2½- or 3-pound rabbit
¼ cup lard or vegetable oil
2 tablespoons pure ground chili
½ teaspoon cumin
2 large onions, chopped
1 clove garlic, minced
2–4 sweet red or green bell peppers, seeded and chopped
1 cup roasted peanuts, ground fine
2 cups hot chicken stock
2 tablespoons white wine vinegar
salt and black pepper to taste

Cut rabbit into serving pieces. Heat lard in large casserole with chili and cumin, and toast the spices by stirring them in the oil 2 or 3 minutes. Add rabbit pieces and sear quickly, remove them, and set aside.

Add onions, garlic, and peppers to the casserole and sauté lightly. Return rabbit to the casserole; add peanuts, stock, vinegar, and seasonings and mix together well. Taste for seasoning. Bring to the simmer, cover casserole, and bake at 325° until meat is fork tender, 1½ to 2 hours. Meat should barely simmer, not boil.

Serves 4 to 6.

CHICKEN WITH
PUMPKIN SEED SAUCE

If the Indians of the Americas gave Spain its first turkey, Spain gave the Indians their first domesticated chicken. The results of such culinary crossing are birds of both kinds simmered in rich sauces called *mole*. The word means a mixture of any kind, and one of the best mixtures is made of Indian squash or pumpkin seeds to flavor Spanish chicken. The sauce below would be called a green *mole,* or *mole verde,* because it has everything green about it: green pumpkin seeds, green chilies, green Mexican tomatillos, and even radish and romaine greens. The flavor is as gentle and unusual as the color.

> 1 4-pound roasting chicken
> 4 cups hot chicken stock, or more if needed
> ¾ cup pumpkin seeds
> 8 black peppercorns
> ⅛ teaspoon cumin seeds
> 6 tomatillos or 2 to 3 green tomatoes
> 2–4 hot green chilies (jalapeño or *serrano*), roasted, peeled, and seeded
> 4 green onions, with tops
> 2 cloves garlic, mashed
> 2 tablespoons chicken fat or lard
> 1 bunch young radish leaves or mustard greens
> 2 large romaine lettuce leaves
> 4 sprigs fresh coriander (cilantro)

Put whole chicken in a casserole, cover with the stock, and bring to a simmer. Cover pot and poach chicken just below the simmering point over very low heat or in a very low oven (275°) for 1 hour. Remove chicken from stock and let it cool enough to carve it.

Toast the pumpkin seeds together with the peppercorns and cumin in a hot ungreased skillet about 5 minutes, stirring constantly to prevent scorching. Put into a blender and grind fine.

Remove outer husks from the tomatillos, put them in a pan with cold water to cover, and bring to a simmer. Simmer 10 minutes, drain, then add them to the blender with ½ cup of their liquid and blend to a smooth thick purée. Chop all the remaining ingredients and add them to the blender. Add chicken stock, if needed, to thin the purée. Pour sauce into the skillet and simmer about 10 minutes to evaporate some of the liquid.

Carve chicken in 4 or more pieces and add to the sauce, coating the pieces well. If possible, let chicken sit overnight in the sauce so that the seasoning permeates and the hotness of the chili diminishes. Reheat gently so that sauce does not boil. Serve hot or at room temperature.

Serves 4.

TURKEY WITH CHILI AND BITTER CHOCOLATE
MOLE

Xocolatl, or "bitter water," is what the Aztecs called it. "Chocolate" is how the Spanish translated it when Montezuma toasted Cortez with a cup of the bitter brew. The Aztecs liked to mix their roasted and ground cocoa beans with red chilies, cooled sometimes by snow. It was the Spanish who turned the bitter sweet, by adding sugar, when they took the powder home to Spain. But the true taste of the cocoa bean remained in a concoction, or *mole,* in which the seasonings of the New World combined with the Old to produce that exotic black sauce we call "turkey *mole."* The Spanish added garlic, saffron, cinnamon, and cloves to the black-brown Mexican chilies called *mulato* and *negro.* If you can find these black beauties, use them, but they are not necessary to a sauce that finds its distinctive character in the bitter water of the cocoa bean.

             4 cloves garlic
            12 hazelnuts, with skins
            12 almonds, with skins
             2 tablespoons pine nuts
            ½-inch cinnamon stick
             4 whole cloves
            ¼ teaspoon aniseed
            ½ teaspoon saffron
             1 square (1 ounce) bitter chocolate, preferably Mexican, grated
             2 cups chicken broth
         8–12 dried chilies
                optional: 6 *mulato* or *negro* chilies

             1 7- or 8-pound turkey
            ½ cup lard or vegetable oil
             1 large onion, chopped
             6 fresh tomatoes, peeled, seeded, and chopped

In a skillet, roast the garlic cloves over medium-high heat until their skins are brown and can be removed. Toast the nuts in the same skillet for 5 minutes, stirring so they don't burn. Put them in a blender with the garlic. Toast the cinnamon, cloves, aniseed, and saffron in the same skillet to bring out their flavor. Add them to the blender with grated chocolate and 1 cup of the chicken broth.

Prepare chili pulp by toasting, soaking, and puréeing the chilies with a little of their liquid until smooth (see page 38). Add to the chocolate mixture.

Cut the turkey into serving pieces, heat the lard in a large casserole, and brown quickly in the lard. Lower heat and add the onion. Sauté until soft. Add tomatoes and the remaining cup chicken broth, cover, and braise in a 325° oven 40 to 60 minutes, depending on size of turkey. Remove turkey and set aside while finishing the sauce.

Purée the sauce in which the turkey has braised, and mix with the chili-chocolate mixture, keeping the sauce relatively thick. Return turkey pieces to the casserole, pour the sauce over them, cover, and return to the oven to cook until meat is tender and flavors blended, 20 to 40 minutes more.

Serves 8 to 10.

5
Wild Things

One man's wilderness is another man's larder, just as one man's weed is another man's salad. Before Columbus, the Indians of America made use of some two thousand plants for food, most of them wild by European standards of cultivation. But here the abundance of land turned a whole continent into a salad bowl for those who knew where to look and how to transform root, stalk, leaf, pod, fruit, blossom, seed, nut, berry, and pollen into foods raw and cooked, into flour, syrups, preserves, wines, stews, as well as into cleansers and medicines and bright-colored dyes.

Here among roots and pods wholly unknown to European explorers were wild cognates of what Europe had tamed: wild onions, garlic, celery, plums, the lily bulb Europeans named "Indian cucumber," nasturtiums they named "Indian cress." Here known plants were given strange uses. Cattail and bulrush pollen were made into flour, along with acorns and the roots of bracken and fern. Here unknown plants like the sunflower were made familiar by grinding their seeds for meal or boiling them for oil.

Among Indians, the Pueblos were the craftiest gatherers and gardeners because their larder was the desert. It was the Pueblos who learned to pick out the tender green sprouts of the tumbleweed, to drop the flowers of the yucca into soup, to disarm the fruits of the prickly pear and turn them to jelly.

Harvesting cactus in the spring was a major communal undertaking. In June, the Pima and Papago Indians of Arizona would move into the forests of giant cacti called saguaro to gorge on the sugary fruits. They would dry the seeds and grind them into flour while turning the pulp into juice and cactus wine. In the same way, the Hopi and Apache would gather the crowns of the

Toasted Piñon Nuts and Pumpkin Seeds

Piñon picking was once the occasion for an outing for whole villages in the pine-covered forests west of Taos, west of Rio Grande, on the other side of the river, *la otra banda*. Villagers would camp out for days in the fall and early winter, gathering cones as they fell to the ground or pulling them down with rakes, spreading them in the sun to dry, then threshing them with sticks or trampling feet. Sometimes a picker would be lucky and come on a cache of nuts gathered by wood mice and hidden in a hole in the ground carefully marked by a pile of cactus pads or thorns.

For the city dweller piñon nuts (pine nuts or pignoli) are expensive because they must be picked from the piñon pine by mouse or human hand. For the Indians the nuts are one of the oldest staples because they *could* be picked by hand. But if piñon nuts are expensive, their counterpart staples—the seeds of sunflowers, pumpkin, and other squash—are cheap. Shelled, toasted, and salted, in the manner of Laverne Garcia of Cochiti Pueblo, they are the best foods to nibble on. "Their saltiness," says Laverne, "is like being splashed with a margarita."

Skillet Roasting
for Shelled Nuts and Seeds

All nuts and seeds can be dry roasted by heating them in an ungreased heavy skillet for 5 to 10 minutes, stirring constantly so they will not burn. For snacks, sunflower, pumpkin, and other squash seeds will taste better if they are toasted in a little oil, 1 tablespoon

agave, or mescal, baking them in pits and then eating their edible hearts like artichokes or fermenting the pulp to make the fiercely intoxicating *pulque*.

Today, Anglos know of the agave only as it is liquefied and distilled into tequila and cocktailed into margaritas. Similarly they know of mesquite only as per cup of seeds. Sprinkle with salt to taste, or try Laverne's method of sprinkling nuts or seeds with brine while they are still in the skillet, so that the water evaporates to leave a thin salty coating. For 1 cup, use ½ teaspoon salt dissolved in ¼ cup water. You can also roast shelled nuts and seeds in the oven at 350° about 15 to 20 minutes, but stir often to prevent burning. Another method for salting nuts and seeds is to soak them in salted water (salt to taste) for 8 hours, drain on paper towels, and roast at 350° in a shallow baking pan for 15 to 20 minutes. For long storage, refrigerate or freeze roasted nuts and seeds because the oil that makes them rich and tasty quickly goes rancid.

Oven Roasting
for Unshelled Nuts and Seeds

Roast in a single layer in a baking pan in a low (250°) oven for 1 hour, stirring occasionally. To shell, place nuts or seeds between a pair of dampened dishtowels and push a rolling pin over the top of them.

Chili-Flavored Nuts and Seeds

Piñon nuts are so delicate in their buttery taste that they need nothing but toasting and salting to bring out their flavor. Various seeds, however, are complemented by the colorful accent of pure ground chili. Toast 1 cup of shelled seeds in 1 tablespoon of oil in a heavy skillet. Shake in ½ teaspoon salt and ½ teaspoon mild chili powder, or to taste.

a fashionable fuel for grilling steaks and fish. But the beans of mesquite were long a staple of desert tribes of the Southwest because they could be ground into meal for bread or turned into broth for soup, gruel, or fermented punch.

While most of us will have difficulty finding the ingredients for such intriguingly named dishes as Baked Shad with Wild Leeks and Nannyberries, or Milkweed Pods Vinaigrette, cited by the ethnobotanist Barrie Kavasch in his *Native Harvests* (1979), we can cull from city supermarkets nuts and seeds for toasting or mesquite for grilling. And in our own unweeded backyards we can often find poke and purslane for salads, if we would but do as the Indians do and look to the wilderness for our larder.

SUNFLOWER AND PIÑON CAKES

Until late in the nineteenth century, a cake in America did not connote a sweet treat but referred to a molded shape—as in hotcake, hoecake, johnny-cake. As the Indians molded corn into shapes we sometimes called "cakes" and sometimes "breads," so they molded nuts and seeds into delicious nuggets that, unsweetened, we would now call cocktail biscuits and, sweetened, cookies. The unsweetened form below is a kind Laverne Garcia makes according to the time-honored ways of her Cochiti grandmothers. But whereas they would have wrapped the cakes in fresh leaves or husks, we wrap them in envelopes of foil to keep the nuts from scorching.

1 cup shelled sunflower seeds, untoasted
1 cup shelled piñon nuts, untoasted
2 tablespoons chicken broth
1 teaspoon salt

Pulverize seeds and nuts in a blender or processor. Add liquid and salt and shape them into 1-inch balls. Line a 14-by-17-inch cookie sheet with foil. Place balls on the foil and flatten them with the heel of your hand to make small rounds. Cover them with another sheet of foil and seal the edges all around to make a large packet. Bake at 275° until lightly browned, 15 to 20 minutes. When foil is cool enough to handle, unseal and let cool. Remove rounds very gently with a spatula—they crumble easily.

Makes about 30 cakes.

PIGWEED AND PURSLANE SALAD

Pigweed, otherwise known as lamb's quarters, goosefoot, or wild spinach, is one of our oldest and most prolific wild greens, used not only for its spear-shaped leaves but for its small black seeds. Equally venerable as a culinary weed is the pink-stemmed purslane, a cousin of the bright-flowered but inedible portulaca. At their youngest, in the first breath of spring, the leaves of both pigweed and purslane are delicious raw. As they grow into adolescence, both need only a quick parboiling to restore tenderness but maintain crispness. If other wild things are near at hand, like leafing poke sprouts, the leaves of dandelions, or the blossoms and leaves of budding nasturtiums, use them, too, with sunflower seed dressing.

> 4 cups each purslane and pigweed leaves
> 4 green onions, with tops, chopped
> ¼ cup toasted sunflower seeds
> ½ cup olive oil
> 3 tablespoons wine vinegar, or more as needed
> salt and pepper to taste

Wash the purslane plants and the pigweed leaves separately. If the purslane is large, chop into 2-inch lengths. Put the purslane in a saucepan, cover with water, and boil 3 to 5 minutes. Drain and set aside. Put the wet pigweed leaves and green onions in a skillet, cover tightly, and steam 3 to 5 minutes, depending on size and age of leaf. Drain and mix with the purslane in a salad bowl.

Put the sunflower seeds in a blender with the oil and pulverize until chunky. Add the vinegar and season to taste. If dressing is too thick, thin with more vinegar. Pour the dressing over the salad greens.

Serves 4 to 6.

CACTUS EGGS

Nondesert tribes may not know that cacti have many edible parts once the eater has outmaneuvered the prickly spines. There are buds, blossoms, and fruits to turn into juice, jelly, and preserves. There are also seeds and sometimes pads, when the cactus grows by disk-like joints instead of stalks. Almost everything about the prickly pear cactus is edible, from its purplish fruits called, confusingly, "tunas," to its prickly pads, or *nopales*.

I find the pads more interesting than jelly or juice and, fortunately, you no longer have to go armed with tongs and asbestos gloves to stalk the wild pads in their lair. Nor do you have to devote hours to scraping the pads clean of their stickers and hair-fine thorns. Now you can buy *nopales* fresh and cleaned in markets which carry exotic fruits and vegetables and you can also buy *nopales* cooked and canned. Canned is easiest, but fresh is best.

½–¾ cup diced cooked *nopales,* or 1–2 fresh *nopales*
½ cup finely chopped onion
4 tablespoons butter or oil
½ cup Red Chili Sauce (see page 41)
8 eggs
salt and pepper

If using fresh pads, trim around the edges with a pair of scissors or a sharp knife to remove the base of the thorns. Wash well and examine each pad to make sure all tiny thorns are removed. Cut each pad into dice, cover with salted water in a saucepan, and simmer gently until tender, 5 to 10 minutes. Drain in a sieve and rinse under cold water to rid pads of their sticky, okra-like juice.

In a large skillet, sauté the onion in butter until soft. Add the *nopales* and Red Chili Sauce and mix well. Break the eggs gently on top of the mixture, cover tightly, and steam until the egg whites are set, 5 to 10 minutes. Season to taste with salt and pepper and serve directly from the frying pan.

Serves 4.

VARIATION: Instead of cooking the eggs whole, scramble them, stirring them into the onion-*nopal*-chili sauce and continuing to stir until the eggs are cooked but still moist. Add ½ cup chopped cooked bacon for a richer dish.

HOT GUACAMOLE SOUP

Forty years ago, guacamole was almost as rare north of the Mexamerican borderlands as the avocado of which it is made. Today, mashed avocado seasoned with chili and spiked with lemon or lime is as common as crackers. Guacamole means literally "avocado sauce" (*guaca* from the Aztec *ahuacatl* for "testicle" and the similarly shaped fruit; and *mole* from Mexican-Spanish for "sauce" or "mixture," as in "turkey *mole*"). The only way to go wrong with any avocado sauce or mixture is to start with an unripe and tasteless avocado. Otherwise anything goes. (You can hasten the ripening of an avocado by putting it in a closed plastic bag with a banana peel.) I've included here an unusual use of the mixture in a hot avocado soup. If you have any leftover guacamole, you can preserve its good flavors and green color by puréeing it with a green lettuce leaf or two and simmering it in enough liquid to turn it into soup. Here I've started from scratch.

> 1 ripe avocado
> 2 large leaves romaine (or other) lettuce
> ¼ cup chopped green onions, with tops
> 1 clove garlic, mashed
> 2 tablespoons lime or lemon juice
> 1–2 tablespoons pure ground chili
> 4 sprigs fresh coriander (cilantro)
> 4 cups chicken stock

Cut avocado into quarters, remove pit and peel, and put the flesh in a blender or processor. Tear the romaine leaves into pieces and add to blender. Add remaining ingredients, together with half the stock, and purée until smooth. Combine with remaining stock in a pan and simmer, covered, 10 minutes.
Serves 4.

JÍCAMA SALAD

Only yesterday the large brown-wrapped crisp tuber called jícama was as exotic in American produce stores as the kiwi was the day before that. Thanks to adventurers like Frieda Caplan of Frieda's Finest in California, who introduced both strangers into our kitchens, we can now savor in Oshkosh and Kalamazoo fruits and vegetables once restricted to native wilds. The jícama of Mexamerica is one of the best of these newcomers because it is as crisp as a fresh waterchestnut, as sweet as a white turnip, and keeps as well as a carrot.

Jícama makes an excellent base for a salad because its sweetness complements tart fruits like oranges and reinforces sweet vegetables like carrots. The only disadvantage with jícama is that it turns brown once it is peeled so that you need to squeeze citrus juice, like lime or lemon, over its cut surfaces as you would do with an avocado. Here I've used orange juice because one of the best traditional salads is of jícama and orange segments.

> 1 large jícama (to make 2–3 cups diced or julienned)
> 1 cup orange juice
> 2 navel oranges
> 6 tomatillos, or 2–3 green tomatoes
> 2 carrots, grated
> 1 large bunch arugula, rinsed
> 1 egg yolk
> 2 tablespoons lemon juice
> ½ cup olive oil
>   salt and black and cayenne pepper

Peel brown skin from jícama and julienne the flesh in a food processor or dice it. Mix with the orange juice and set aside.

Peel and segment the oranges, removing membranes and pith. Remove husks from the tomatillos and slice very thin. Grate carrots.

Drain the jícama, reserving the orange juice. Arrange vegetables by color on a bed of arugula. Put carrots in the center, surround with the white jícama, then the orange segments, and finally the tomatillos.

Make a thin mayonnaise by mixing the yolk with the lemon juice, and beating in the oil slowly. Thin with reserved orange juice. Season to taste.

Serves 4 to 6.

6

Sweet Nibbles

The discovery of America, as Waverley Root has said, revolutionized the history of sugar. Before Columbus planted sugarcane in the West Indies on his second voyage there, Indians were as deprived of processed sugar as they were of dentistry. For sweetenings, they had to rely on the honeybee, on the sticky sap of maples and pines, on wild berries and flowers and the sugars of pumpkin and corn. As late as the nineteenth century, the Zunis were still sweetening their batters for puddings and breads with a corn paste masticated and fermented to convert cornstarch to sugar.

Cortez and his conquistadors had stimulated the taste for cane sugar, however, early in the sixteenth century as they converted soldiers to sugar merchants for their planted fields of cane. The Southwest still uses a form of relatively unrefined dark-brown sugar, which has a rich fudgelike flavor and is shaped into old-fashioned cones instead of granules. The Spanish call it *piloncillo*.

Along with sugar, the Spanish introduced wheat, so that in the Southwest the sweetened loaf of wheat bread got a head start on the rest of the country. Unfortunately, the round loaves of adobe bread baked to a nice crust in the earthen ovens of the pueblos today and sold at tourist prices are as vapid inside as a white man's loaf of white flour and white sugar. "It will take time for the reverse snobbery of 'peasant bread' to hit the pueblos," Priscilla Hoback warned, and I know what she meant. A far more interesting form of sweetened wheat is the pudding-porridge of sprouted wheat and brown sugar the Southwest calls *panocha*. A more problematic form is the ubiquitous Indian fry bread, with its Spanish name *sopaipilla*, which can be ghastly or delicious, depending on the quality of the cook and the cooking oil. It is less a bread than a giant doughnut, like a beignet, sprinkled while hot with powdered sugar or a dripping of honey or honey butter.

I suppose wild plants like the Navajos' yucca bananas, which they bake, grind, and shape into balls of dough to dry, might count as a native dessert, but more common today are apricots dried to strips of "leather," pumpkins boiled and sweetened to make candied chips, quinces or apples condensed to "butter." Jelly is made of green chili or jalapeños, of pyracantha berries or prickly pears. But the most typical desserts are either Spanish custards and bread puddings with raisins and cheese, or Spanish pastries like the little fruit pies folded like *empanadas.* My own taste runs to nibbles like the aniseed cookies called *biscochitos,* little nut cakes made of piñon nuts, or piñon-nut candy. Best are sun-ripened fruits like apricots, peaches, and melons, which the padres planted in mission gardens to make the desert bloom. The best thirst quencher is the watermelon, and one of my fondest memories of the Indian Southwest is the image of a group of black and white clowns, the *koshari* of the corn dance, sitting in a row in the shade of an adobe and like country boys anywhere spitting out watermelon seeds.

NAVAJO FRY BREAD

While Hispanics say *sopaipillas* to describe squares of fried dough puffed like little pillows, Indians say "fry bread" to describe circles of fried dough puffed like giant doughnuts with a hole in the middle. The dough is basically the same and is a puffy variant on the dough for a flour tortilla, consisting of wheat flour, shortening, salt, and water, leavened sometimes by baking powder and sometimes by yeast. Flavored with anise and lightened by eggs, the same dough makes the sweet fritters called *buñuelos,* which are usually dunked in a thick sticky syrup.

Every fiesta has its stalls of fry bread vying with Sno-Kones and spun-sugar candy. The pleasure of fried bread is not only in the mouth but in the eye, in watching the women pinch off a ball of dough, roll it into a circle with a cut-off broom handle, poke a hole in the middle, drop it into a vat of boiling oil to puff and crisp, and then fork it onto a paper plate to sprinkle with powdered sugar or drizzle with honey. Like fast food anywhere, however, fry bread is subject to abuse if the oil is rancid. Let your nose be your guide.

    2 cups all-purpose flour
    1 tablespoon baking powder
    1 teaspoon salt
    1 tablespoon vegetable oil
    ¾ cup warm water
      oil for frying

Mix the dry ingredients together, then stir in oil and water and mix until smooth (a processor will do this in a minute). Knead lightly for a minute until dough is elastic but don't work it too hard or it won't roll out. Shape dough in a ball, put it in a plastic bag, and refrigerate for an hour.

Pinch off 12 balls of dough, flatten them with your hand, and roll them into 3- to 4-inch circles. Roll again to make circles as thin as possible, 7 to 8 inches in diameter. The thinner they are, the better they puff in the oil. Poke a hole in the center with your finger.

Dust the tops lightly with flour while the oil heats in a wok or deep skillet to 375°. Slip rounds one at a time into the oil to brown about 1 minute per side, turning them with tongs or a slotted spatula. Drain on paper towels and sprinkle with powdered sugar. Or drip honey over the top or spread with honey butter.

Makes 12 circles of bread.

HONEY BUTTER

Fry bread with honey butter is a specialty of New Mexico. At her restaurant in Santa Fe, Priscilla Hoback makes a yeasted sourdough fry bread and serves it with pots of a honey butter that is good enough to eat straight. The honey is countered by lemon juice to make a three-part harmony of the sweet, the tart, and the creamy.

½ pound (2 sticks) butter
¼ cup strong dark honey
2 teaspoons lemon juice, or to taste

Soften butter by leaving it at room temperature or by cutting it into pieces and whipping it in a food processor. Beat the honey and lemon juice into the butter. Taste and adjust lemon juice or honey to find the balance you like. Refrigerate in a covered container, where it will keep better than regular butter.

Makes 1 cup.

PUMPKIN-PIÑON BREAD

While pumpkin meat can be made into a delicious unsweetened yeast bread, the typical pumpkin bread of the Pueblos uses baking powder to leaven a dark rich cakelike bread, flavored by pumpkin and studded with piñon nuts. Such breads can be made year round from pumpkin slices dried in the sun or, nowadays, from pumpkin cooked and frozen. Canned pumpkin tastes canned, no matter what you do to spike it up, so when pumpkins are in season, it's worth puréeing the meat and freezing it for future stews, pies, and breads.

2 cups cooked pumpkin meat (from a 3- or 4-pound pumpkin)
¼ pound (1 stick) butter
1½ cups dark brown sugar
3 eggs
3 cups unbleached white flour
1 tablespoon baking powder
1 teaspoon each salt and cinnamon
½ teaspoon each white pepper and freshly ground nutmeg
2 cups piñon nuts, lightly toasted

To cook a pumpkin, prick its skin in 4 or 5 places, put it in a pan containing ½ inch boiling water, and bake it at 350° for 1 to 1½ hours. When the pumpkin is cool enough to handle, cut it in two, discard the seeds and stringy pulp, then scrape the meat into a bowl. Mash it with a fork or purée it.

Cream the butter, add sugar gradually, and beat until fluffy. Beat in the eggs and add the mixture to the pumpkin purée.

Mix together the flour, baking powder, and seasonings, then add the toasted whole piñon nuts. Add to the pumpkin purée, mix well, and spoon the batter into 2 buttered 9-by-4-by-4-inch loaf pans. Push batter into the corners of the pans to help the loaves rise more evenly.

Bake at 350° until a straw inserted in the middle of a loaf comes out clean, about 1 hour. Remove bread from the pans and cool the loaves on a rack. To preserve, keep bread in refrigerator or wrap in foil and freeze.

Makes 2 loaves.

To Prepare Sprouted Wheat Flour

Spread wet dishtowels on 2 cookie sheets. Sprinkle the towels with 8 cups hard wheat berries. Cover with wet dishtowels and put in a warm dark place. At least once a day, sprinkle water over the top towels as they dry in order to keep them damp. The berries will start to sprout in 2 or 3 days. They are ready to dry when the sprout is as long as the berry. Remove sprouted berries from the towels, put them on the cookie sheets, and dry them thoroughly in a low (250°) oven for 3 to 4 hours. Grind in a blender, spice grinder, or processor.

SPROUTED WHEAT PUDDING
PANOCHA

"*Panocha* was our special Easter dessert," said Tony at San Juan Pueblo. "We would dampen the wheat, put it in sacks behind the stove and leave it a few days until it sprouted. Then we would dry it and grind it for flour." While it is still special for Tony, it is everyday for Ignacia Duran, at Tesuque Pueblo, who keeps a large jar of it in her refrigerator to spoon out for hankering grandchildren. This most typical southwestern sweet is halfway between a pudding and a jam, but its flavor is unique because of the special sweetness of sprouted wheat flour. In New Mexico you can buy the flour ready-prepared in your neighborhood grocery, but you can also, like Tony, sprout it at home with little trouble and much pleasure in watching it grow.

> 4 cups *panocha* (sprouted wheat flour)
> 2 cups all-purpose flour
> 3 quarts boiling water
> 1 cup white sugar
> ¼ pound (1 stick) butter
> 2 cups brown sugar
> ¼ teaspoon each cinnamon and cloves
> 1 tablespoon vanilla extract
>   optional: 1 cup heavy cream

Mix the 2 flours together and stir in half the boiling water (6 cups).

Caramelize the white sugar over low heat in a heavy skillet, stirring until it is golden brown. Add remaining boiling water to sugar (beware of possible spattering) and boil 1 minute at high heat. Add butter, brown sugar, and spices and stir until brown sugar dissolves.

Combine with the flour in an oven-ware pot and boil over medium heat 15 minutes, stirring constantly. Add vanilla, cover pot, and bake at 400° until pudding is dark brown and very thick, about 1½ hours. Serve at room temperature or chilled with a bowl of heavy whipped cream.

Makes 16 to 20 servings.

VARIATION: Add 1 cup each brandy-soaked raisins and piñon nuts when you add the vanilla to the flour mixture.

PUMPKIN CANDY

A uniquely American sweet is one made from fresh pumpkin chips. The Indians would cut a pumpkin or squash into two-by-four-inch strips, then soften the strips in a bath of woodashes or lye. Finally, they would boil the strips in sugary syrup, sometimes flavored with cilantro, until the syrup was clear and the chips brittle. Easier probably for the city cook is a device recommended by Eliza Leslie in her *Directions for Cookery* (1837), in which lemon juice helps to soften the chips and counteract the sweetness of the sugar.

    1½ pounds uncooked pumpkin meat (from a 3- or 4-pound
        pumpkin)
    2 cups sugar
      thinly pared rind of 3 lemons
    1 cup fresh lemon juice

Cut meat into uniform strips, 4 by 2 inches and ¼ inch thick. Put the strips in a bowl and sprinkle with the sugar.

Cut the lemon rind into narrow strips. Add to the pumpkin and pour lemon juice over all. Let the mixture stand at least 12 hours or overnight.

Put the mixture in a covered saucepan, bring to a simmer, and simmer gently until the pumpkin becomes translucent but is still firm, about 1 hour.

Remove strips with a slotted spoon and drain on paper towels. Let them dry for 12 hours or overnight. Roll them in granulated sugar or eat them plain. You can also cover them with the syrup and store, refrigerated, where they will keep several weeks.

Makes 3 cups.

CREAMY CUSTARD
NATILLAS

"Pumpkin pie or *natillas?*" the waitress asked me at Rancho Chimayo, on the high mountain road between Taos and Santa Fe. I had just finished a wholly American traditional Thanksgiving dinner of turkey and dressing with the usual trimmings, and now it was time for dessert. No New Mexican dinner, at any season or for any occasion, is complete without a soft creamy custard that the Southwest calls *natillas,* the French call *île flottante,* and the English "floating island." The Southwest variant uses cinnamon and simplifies the beaten egg whites by folding them into the custard instead of poaching them and "floating" them on top. Recipes vary in richness: this one is moderately rich with the addition of heavy cream.

> 1 teaspoon cornstarch
> 1 cup heavy cream
> 1 cup milk
> ½ cup sugar
> 2 teaspoons vanilla extract
> 4 eggs, separated
> pinch of salt
> garnish: nutmeg and cinnamon

Dissolve cornstarch in a small amount of the cream and beat in the remaining cream. Add milk and sugar. Bring to a simmer, stirring constantly. Add a little hot liquid to the egg yolks to warm them, then stir into the remaining mixture and cook over low heat, stirring constantly, until the custard just begins to thicken. Add vanilla and cool to room temperature.

Beat egg whites with salt until stiff but not dry and fold into the custard mixture until well mixed. Sprinkle top heavily with grated nutmeg and cinnamon.

Serves 4.

ANISEED COOKIES
BISCOCHITOS

Traditionally, these are Christmas cookies, enlivened with brandy or bourbon and shortened with lard to make a crisp sugar cookie shaped in a royal fleur-de-lis. The dough is soft and wonderful for rolling and cookie cutting, but a good old-fashioned way is to roll out the dough in a single thin sheet on a baking pan and then cut the baked dough into diamonds as soon as it comes from the oven. (As it cools the dough becomes too brittle to cut without breaking.) Anise is one of the ancient Mediterranean spices Mexico inherited from Spain, just as Spain inherited it from conquering Romans and invading Moors.

  ½ pound (2 sticks) butter
  1 cup sugar
  2 teaspoons aniseed
  1 egg, beaten
  ¼ cup bourbon or brandy
  3 cups all-purpose flour
  1 teaspoon baking powder
  ½ teaspoon salt
  ¼ cup sugar mixed with 2 teaspoons cinnamon

Cream butter with 1 cup sugar until fluffy; add aniseed, egg, and bourbon and mix well. Mix flour, baking powder, and salt and stir into the egg butter to make a soft dough. Lightly grease a baking sheet and roll dough about ⅛ inch thick over the sheet. Sprinkle with the sugar and cinnamon mixture. Bake in upper third of a 375° oven for 10–15 minutes. Immediately cut baked dough on the diagonal in one direction and then the other to make diamonds. Lift with a spatula onto a plate.

Makes about 36 diamonds.

LITTLE FRUIT PIES
PASTELITOS

On feast days, Pueblo tables will be loaded with platters of little fruit pies made of dried fruit layered between sheets of pastry and cut into squares or rounds, folded over, and crimped like *empanadas*. If you are asked into a house, you will not be allowed to leave without a handful, or bagful, of pies, to nibble like the cookies they resemble, Fig Newtons. Any kind of dried fruit in any combination will be good—apples, peaches, raisins, prunes, apricots, plums. Particularly good are the wild plums of Arizona and New Mexico, but I have used dried apricots here because they are nonseasonal.

Filling

    2 cups dried apricots
    ½ cup brown sugar
    ½ cup sultana raisins
    ½ cup piñon nuts or chopped pecans
    ⅓ cup white sugar mixed with ½ teaspoon cinnamon

Dough

    2 cups all-purpose flour
    1 teaspoon baking powder
    ¾ teaspoon salt
    ¼ pound (1 stick) butter
    5 tablespoons lard or shortening
    ¼ cup ice water

Put apricots with cold water to cover in a pan and simmer gently until fruit is soft, about 30 minutes. Drain and purée. Add brown sugar and cook until purée is very thick. Remove from heat, add raisins and nuts, and let cool.

Make pastry by mixing together the flour, baking powder, and salt. Cut in the butter and lard until butter is pea-sized. Add just enough ice water to make the flour stick together. Shape into a flattened ball, put in a plastic bag, and refrigerate 30 minutes.

Roll out half the pastry directly on a greased baking sheet. Spread fruit mixture on top. Roll out remaining pastry to cover the mixture. Press edges together all around. Sprinkle with mixture of white sugar and cinnamon. With the blunt edge of a table knife, mark the pastry into small squares and prick each square with a fork.

Bake at 400° until pastry is lightly browned, about 20 minutes. Cool and cut into the marked squares.

Makes about 30 small squares.

BAMBOULA

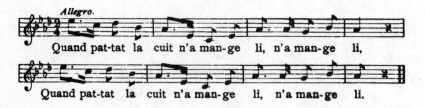

Quand pat-tat la cuit n'a man-ge li, n'a man-ge li,

Quand pat-tat la cuit n'a man-ge li, n'a man-ge li.

PART II

Cajuns and Creoles

THE DELTA SOUTH

Recipes in Part II

Pinch my tail, suck my head, eat me.

—Motto on the official Crawfish Festival
T-shirt of Breaux Bridge,
"Crawfish Capital of the World"

I was with Ruth the Swamp Woman at Henderson the night Pat Huval got re-elected mayor. Henderson is near Breaux Bridge on the main road west of Baton Rouge that links New Orleans to Lafayette and Creole to Cajun. There are three crawfish restaurants on Bayou Amy, which is mostly all Henderson is, and two of them are Pat's and the other one is Robin's. There's The Original Pat's "Where It All Began," before his big dance hall burned down and ended the Sunday afternoon fais-dodo's, which is Cajun baby-talk for "make sleep-sleep," which you hope the kids will do while you go off and dance. And there's The New Pat's, which Pat built after he split with his wife, and there's Robin's, which Robin built after he split from Pat and decided to run against him for mayor. Henderson is a very small town.

I had just had the Original Pat's regular crawfish dinner for $12.95, not the super one for $14.50, which begins with crawfish bisque and proceeds to crawfish boiled, fried, smothered, stuffed into green peppers, rolled into patties, all washed down with ice cold beer in frosted mugs. Ruth ate a large beer tray of boiled crawfish, followed by gumbo and then soft-shell crabs stuffed and deep fried. I call Ruth the Swamp Woman because she was born in the swamps around Krotz Springs to a big family that was Irish, French, Spanish, Indian, Baptist, "you name it." Later she married a Portuguese from British Honduras whose construction work took him to Singapore and Saudi Arabia. "I never thought this little swamp girl was going to live 'round the world," says Ruth, back at Krotz Springs with her children grown and gone.

When we left Pat's, we walked into a clearing surrounded by pickup trucks with loudspeakers amplifying a zydeco trio for fifty or so people, everybody in town, who were mostly sloshed from the beer poured out at long trestle tables—free. In Louisiana bars never close, not even for elections, and now folks were waiting, Cajun style, for the returns. A man staggered past with blood streaming down his face, yelling obscenities. Two grade-school couples danced cheek to chest, the girls so much taller than the boys that the

Cajuns steaming crawfish by the billion at the annual Crawfish Festival in Breaux Bridge, Louisiana, "Crawfish Capital of the World."

girls didn't have to remove their cigarettes to dance. In the middle a teenage mongoloid slowly lifted one knee, then the other, kicked and whirled in time to the music.

My day had begun with zydeco music at ten o'clock on a Saturday morning, at Fred's Lounge in Mamou, northwest of Lafayette near Opelousas. On the way to Fred's I had passed signs like "Cold Beer + Hot Boudin = Good Company" and Belle's Seafood, "If it swims, I got it," so I knew I was in heavy eating country, but still I wasn't prepared for Fred's. With Cajun you translate twice, first from pig-French into French and then into English, like zydeco, which comes from *les haricots,* which means green beans. Cajun is dialect music—two fiddles, an accordion, and two electric guitars— and here were a bunch of old old-timers doing their weekly broadcast for KNEV-Radio while other old-timers knocked back Wild Turkey and beer between dances. Cajuns don't dance, they glide, with incredible smoothness, beer belly to beer belly, as if they'd been doing this all their lives, which they have. Next to me a guy was nursing a beer, so I knew he wasn't Cajun. He was an accordion player from Norway who runs a Cajun band in Oslo and was on his first trip to the States. When Fred closes, he says, they'll all move across the street to Manuel's.

My day ended, after Henderson, at Mulato's in Breaux Bridge, where Dennis McGee was playing. Ruth learned that Pat Huval had won yet again, but the band was just packing up. The boys had been playing since eleven this morning and it was now nine at night and they wanted to take a breather before they started again tomorrow. Ruth and I had another Dixie beer while she told me about her father, who died at the age of ninety—a trapper, hunter, and fisherman who did all the cooking, especially barbecued alligator. He'd cut up the tail in little squares, she says, and sauce them good.

Just to be in Cajun country is to be welcomed as family, and family means talk about food. I never heard anyone talk about food the way Louisianans talk about food, and I never saw folk eat the way they eat. Paul Prudhomme was an Opelousas boy and he once weighed in at four hundred pounds. Cajun cooking is family cooking, Paul tells me, in his now-famous K-Paul's Louisiana Kitchen café in New Orleans. There were thirteen in Paul's family, and when they had one of their special Sunday get-togethers there'd be a big iron pot for whatever the men had caught hunting and fishing. His dad would barbecue half a calf, a couple of goats, and a three-hundred-pound garfish. The women would bring the "made" dishes—pork chops, *boudins*, fried chicken, meat pies, black-eyed peas, sweet potatoes, dirty rice, bread puddings, pecan cakes and pies. And there was Dixie beer, homemade apple-jack, fig brandy, dandelion wine, and lemonade for the kids. Everybody cooked and everybody ate. The men ate first, then the children, then the women. "And everything we ate we'd either caught or grown," Paul says. The men did the field garden for canning, the women the house garden for everyday. "Everything the family used we had a couple rows of, that's the way families lived and that's what makes food good."

Paul is the link between Cajun and Creole because he brought this back-woods bayou food into the city of New Orleans to cook first at The Commander's Palace and then to create with his wife, Kay Hinrichs (the K of K-Paul's), a storefront family café in the Creole heart of the French Quarter. Cajun and Creole are dialects of the same swamp language, one in country style and the other in city style. If the Southwest is sun cooking born of the desert, the Delta South is wet cooking born of swamp mud and air. Its elements breed in the wet: rice, sugarcane, hot peppers, and mud crawlers. It's the kind of wet that turns air soft and gray and mud green, that stains oil slicks with color and beards trees with moss that looks "like the matted dirt," as Jonathan Raban says, "inside the bags of vacuum cleaners." As the desert is a wild of sage and piñon and tumbleweed, this is a wild of rotting cypress stumps, mangroves on giant claws, marshes of alligator weed and bull tongue, of water moccasins and things that go bump in the night.

"Swamp food is sexy food," Barry Ancelet says, "spicy, wet food, animal life in its natural state, hot food that makes your tongue move and vibrate." Barry is a handsome Cajun who heads the Folklore Program at the University of Southern Louisiana at Lafayette, and he claims he won his wife by seducing her with shrimp creole. Cajun men cook as much as women do, says Barry,

---

In Akers, Louisiana, 1938, a Cajun family returns in their pirogue to their home on the bayou after early-morning fishing and an even earlier morning wash. If they are lucky, they have caught some redfish, speckled trout, croaker, catfish, garfish, maybe an eel, maybe even a turtle.

only with men it's a matter of performance—at a barbecue, a crawfish boil, a catfish fry—like a rooster strutting his feathers.

To talk food is to talk family and Barry's family were latecomers. They came from France in 1840 and settled in the upland prairies instead of the wetlands on the gulf. Their corner of Lafayette and Acadia parishes was "a haven for smugglers, ruffians, bootleggers, a wasteland with no trees and no water and no way to scratch a living" and boasted a sign at the far edge of the Vermillion River, "This is where the West begins."

If the West is a state of mind, Cajun is even more so, says Alex Patout, who runs a family restaurant in New Iberia on the Bayou Teche at the crossroads of wetlands and prairies, seafood Cajun and land Cajun. Alex's family also came from France, in 1825, with a land grant from Louis XVIII to start a vineyard. It was too hot and too wet for grapes but not for cane, so they set up a sugar mill which still turns out cane syrup and molasses. New Iberia is a nineteenth-century country town built of small family businesses that grow out of the land and water. "Everything that comes in my back door," Alex says, "has come from less than a thirty-mile radius. Blue crabs and redfish from the 'Cajun Riviera' at Cypremont Point on Vermillion Bay; crawfish at Bon Creole gleaned from dozens of local ponds; rice from Konriki Rice Mill; hot sauce from McIlhenny's Tabasco factory on Avery Island fifteen minutes away; *boudin* and other sausages from Robichaux's meat market; cane syrup from the family sugar mill." "I'm not a great chef," he finishes, "but a great provider."

The bottom of Louisiana is a confluence of ecologies as rare and strange as the confluence of races and cultures that has hybridized Cajuns and Creoles. Parallel to the "big ditch" of the Mississippi is the little ditch of the Atchafalaya (pronounced *Chuflya*) River, which debouches into a basin of the same name on the gulf, where the mix of fresh and salt water creates, despite proliferating oil wells, one of America's last great wetland wildernesses.

Listening to Alex recite the products of these waters is like listening to Achilles number the hosts of the Argive plain: crawfish, oysters, crabs, shrimp, redfish, speckled trout, croaker, catfish, sac-a-lait, red snapper, pompano, sheepshead, Spanish mackerel, cobia, black drum, mullet, garfish, turtles, frogs, eels, alligators, and miscellaneous unnamed fish caught by the best fisher in Cypremont Point that they name for her, "Ladyfish." The products

A carnival float celebrating the peanut at the New Orleans Mardi Gras, 1949, incarnates local and national chauvinism in the style of parody and burlesque, a style that links Mark Twain to Paul Prudhomme.

———————————

of the land are no less: pigs for sausages like *boudin* and *andouille;* free-ranging ducks, chickens, and geese; wildfowl like teal, mallard, pintail ducks, wood-cocks, snipes, bobwhite quail, partridge, bobolink, coot, mourning dove; game like armadillo, rabbit, 'coon, 'possum, squirrel, and black bear; plants like okra, eggplants, yams, peaches, pecans, figs, and mirlitons, which others call "chayotes."

"God put these stupid Cajuns in the middle of it all, and made them French and poor, and that's their salvation," Alex concludes. Home-style cooking once meant poor folks' cooking. Until a few years ago everyone de-

At the docks in New Orleans, 1938, men unload sacks of wild oysters from the packet-boat *Majestic* to supply innumerable oyster bars such as the Acme and restaurants such as Antoine's and Gallatoire's.

———————

spised crawfish as dirty mudbugs, the poor man's shrimp. Gumbos and jambalayas were pot cooking to stretch what you had for company. The luscious white sausage *boudin* was a way of using up pork liver from your slaughtered hog. Hot pepper was a way of making tasty whatever alligator tail or turtle leg you ate to survive.

Hot pepper was also a way of surviving the tropics. Baton Rouge, Calvin Trillin reminds us, is not southern United States but northern Costa Rica. The closer you get to the Equator, Barry Ancelet says of the Chili Belt, the hotter the food because it makes you sweat and cools you off. Communal visiting became a tradition, Paul Prudhomme says, "because it was just so damn hot—no air conditioners or fans—so everybody goes out because who wants to stay home and smolder?"

Hot pepper is what makes Paul's restaurant "Totally Hot," as the hand-drawn cartoon of a cayenne pepper in his window advertises. Paul's cooking is based on pepper cooking that is "rounded" and complex from its variety of peppers—black, white, red, and cayenne—hitting all the bases in the mouth separately: the black first at the front of the mouth, the white at the back of the throat when you chew, the reds after you swallow. "I like food to have an afterglow," he says, "because that's what gives satisfaction." That discovery changed his life, on his first trip to Europe, when he ate in the finest restaurants and found, like Twain, that nothing satisfied: "I realized at that moment that I was as good a cook as anybody else in the world . . . and it was one of the freeing-est things in my life because I hadn't gone to any cooking school or European training program but had learned from my mother, my family, and I could get the best ingredients in the world here in America, which has technologies nobody else in the world has."

Chauvinism is big in this part of the world and passions run high, bayou by bayou, kitchen by kitchen. Paul's sister Enola says he does his roux and vegetables wrong—too fast. She holds to the traditional "smothered" cooking that appears in the word *étouffée*. Alex's mother explains that her eggplant dressing is better than Alex's because she uses tomatoes, and his father says his is best because he starts with ground meat. "In southern Louisiana," Trillin explains, "it is customary for a serious cook to assume the pre-eminence of his version of anything—as in, 'You ever taste our shrimp étouffée? You taste our étouffée, you'll throw rocks at other people's étouffée.' "

Creole cooking, fed from the same source, sharing the same étouffée parody of continental French, differs from Cajun only in degree. Where Cajun rapes, Creole seduces; where Cajun explodes the palate, Creole titillates it. Creole built America's finest traditional public cooking with names as resonant as Galatoire's, Arnaud's, Antoine's, Brennan's, Commander's Palace. Creole also built a traditional body of cook-book literature in Lafcadio Hearn's *La Cuisine Creole* (1885), *The Picayune's Creole Cook Book* (1900), the Junior League's *River Road Recipes* (1959), now in its fifty-sixth printing. Creole suggests black cooks named Celestine or Tante Zoe ruling the kitchen of *"femme de l'intérieure,"* as the *Picayune* calls her, "queen of hearth and home," and not disposed in 1906 to solve "the many vexing questions of woman suffrage and woman's rights that agitate the minds of many of the sex of our day."

Creole was composed of "Gombo French," as Hearn called it, a hybrid

Tabasco Sauce

In theory the world's best-known hot sauce is no more than pickled peppers, the sort Peter picked a peck of, provided the peppers are hot ones of the species *Capsicum frutescens* and are pickled with salt and vinegar. Mrs. N. K. M. Lee, "a Boston Housekeeper," supplied a recipe "To Pickle Capsicums" for *The Cook's Own Book* (1832), which calls for green pods to be soaked in strong brine for three days, then boiled in vinegar, and finally spiced with mace and nutmeg. Doubtless Mrs. Lee's peppers were *Capsicum annuum,* which includes the sweet bell pepper a Bostonian might have grown in her garden in 1832. The small, fiercely hot *frutescens* was not grown in the United States until veterans of the Mexican-American War of 1846–48 returned to Texas and New Orleans with seeds in their pockets and an Indian name on their lips. Tabasco, which meant "damp earth," was the name of a river near Vera Cruz that a New Orleans banker, Edmund McIlhenny, liked the sound of when he came to name his hot pepper sauce.

Tabasco sauce consists of red capsicum pods that are ground with salt and placed in white-oak barrels. The peppers ferment for several months the way brined cabbage ferments to make sauer-

of the French, Spanish, West Indies, and American South that produced proverbs like *"Jadin loin, gombo gâté:* When the garden is far, the gombo is spoiled," meaning, "If you want a thing done well, do it yourself." Gombo was the language of Congo Square crossed with Paris and Madrid and the Choctaw Indians who came twice a week from Bayou Lacombe to the French Market in New Orleans to sell their dried and pounded sassafras leaves.

Both gumbos and jambalayas wore their histories in their names. "Gumbo" is African Bantu for okra. "Jamba" is French *jambon* or Spanish kraut. Flavor develops from their long, three-year cure in the barrels before strong vinegar is added the last month. What makes Tabasco sauce unique is Avery Island and its salt. In 1862 John Marsh Avery discovered that beneath the brine springs that supplied the Confederate Army with salt was a deposit of solid rock salt, the first known on the North American continent, and of a size equal to Mount Everest. After the Civil War, when McIlhenny married Mary Eliza Avery, he wed a handful of migrant peppers to Avery salt and produced in 1868 the first 350 samples of a sauce he put up in used cologne bottles and sealed with green wax.

More than forty years ago, the McIlhennys won the Tabasco War when they battled it out with the Trappeys, who wanted to use the name for their own hot sauce. "Not quite like the Hatfields and McCoys," says Alex Patout, but in this part of the world local hot sauces—Bruce's, Landry, Cajun Chef, Durkee-Frank's, Evangeline, Crystal—are disputed as hotly as gumbos and roux. What has made Tabasco nearly generic for the rest of the world, however, is the marketing sense of the McIlhennys, still a tightly knit clan, who dispense millions of bottles of a New World product as singular as their small Tabasco-red and green factory set in the midst of a wildlife refuge for egrets and alligators.

jamon for ham, "ala" for French "in the manner of," and "ya" both an African word for rice and an expletive. The best translation of jambalaya is probably "Ham with rice, yeah-yeah," just as the gumbo ya-ya, served today at Commander's Palace, translates as "Gumbo cha-cha." If jambalaya is a kind of parody paella, gumbo is a parody bouillabaisse, both of them catchall dishes, "handed down from generation to generation by the old negro cooks," the *Picayune* writes, "and preserved in all their delightful combinations by their white Creole mistresses."

A white Creole family in New Orleans, 1895, served by their Tante Zoe, at a table replete with French wines and an American pumpkin.

———————

There are no rules for gumbo as there are no rules for roux. Anything that flies, creeps, crawls, or lies as still as an oyster may end up in the gumbo pot. Escoffier laid down rules for roux, that traditional French thickening of flour and fat—use only clarified butter, do not cook it rapidly and never darker than a "fine light brown." But look what happens in Louisiana. Always use lard, says Prudhomme, and cook it hot, fast, and black. Creoles cook it "blanc," "blond," or "brun." Cajuns like Prudhomme cook it caramel brown for dark foods and Hershey-bar black for light foods. But no roux goes undisputed among Cajuns. Alex's mother makes her roux in seconds in a microwave. Barry's mother demands slow cooking and constant attention: "Your eyes should be riveted to the inside of the pot the whole time." Seasoning is the most inflammatory subject of all. "His mild is our *hot*," says Mitch, Alex's brother, of Paul Prudhomme's peppery meals. "That's *his* kind of cooking, but I tell you I was drinking water, man, like it was running out."

"Anybody who came down here who wasn't *from* here, we'd call them 'Americans,' " Ruth the Swamp Woman says. To an "American" like myself, Cajuns and Creoles share more than they differ. They share the garnish of chopped onions, green bell peppers, and celery, "the holy trinity" they call it, as essential as chili sauce to Mexamerica. They share the religious language of "trinity" because they share roots in a Catholic past of four centuries, beginning with Spanish explorers in the sixteenth century and enforced by French colonists like Pierre le Moyne, Sieur d'Iberville, who celebrated the first Mardi Gras on March 3, 1699. They share a feeling for Emmeline Labiche, renamed Evangeline, after her flight from Acadia in Nova Scotia in the middle of the eighteenth century. They share the destiny of French aristocrats fleeing the revolution of the Jacobites, of French West Indian planters fleeing the revolts of their slaves, and of French pirates like Jean Laffite fleeing arrest. Jefferson and the "Americans" were no better than foreign absentee landlords when they bought the property of Louisiana in 1803 for a mere $15 million.

They share too the radio voice of Sister Gloria Ann, who spoke when I was hopelessly lost driving along Bayou Queue de Tortue. "This is your regular missionary and prophetess, Gloria Ann, born gifted of God, inspirited by the Holy Ghost to help folks in all walks of life, and I want to help you." And they share the voice of my New Orleans taxi driver, who explained the virtues of pickled pork while we threaded Basin Street, "We wuz poor but we ate good."

7
Rice

The staple of Louisiana's swamplands is rice. Rice was not introduced here until 1718, by a company romantically named Company of the West, nearly a century after the British attempted to grow rice in Virginia. The crop failed in Virginia but succeeded in South Carolina, where black slaves working for French Huguenots produced "Carolina gold." Today, rice is Louisiana gold, since the state is America's largest producer of rice.

You can visit the country's oldest rice mill, Konriki, in New Iberia. With the sweet, musty smell of rice dust in the air, you can see rice being husked, skinned, polished, and bagged. You can discover new varieties of rice, both in the breed and in the processing: long grain and short grain, white and brown, and a new hybrid, "wild pecan."

Rice in Louisiana restaurants is among the best I've had anywhere, including the fine long-grain Persian rice of Iran and the fat round-grain Arborio of Italy. The *Picayune* called the rice fields of Louisiana "the wonder and admiration of tourists" and instructed them how to boil rice properly so that "every grain will be . . . soft, snowy white and perfectly dry." Their method was typical of nineteenth-century rice boiling: first wash the rice to remove excess flour, then cook it in large quantities of boiling water (a quart of water to a cup of rice) and test for doneness by squeezing a grain between the fingers. Drain the rice, then fluff it in a warm oven about ten minutes to "sweat" it.

Today, methods differ as much as cooks. Prudhomme prefers for wet dishes like gumbos and jambalayas the parboiled and extra-processed rice known as "converted rice." His method is to put nearly equal volumes of rice and water (two cups rice to two and a half cups water) in a baking pan sealed tightly with aluminum foil, and to bake it for a lengthy seventy minutes. If you like converted rice but want a speedier result, you can boil it on top of the stove, covered, about fifteen minutes, and then let it fluff, off heat and still covered, for five. If you like grains snowy white, Alex Patout suggests adding a little vinegar to the water.

Since rice replaced both corn and wheat as its central carbohydrate, Louisiana specialized in rice uses that seem unusual today. Old cook books abound in recipes for rice waffles and griddle cakes, dumplings and croquettes, and the New Orleans fritter called *calas*, eaten with *café au lait* the way beignets are today. Then there were the famed "snowballs," or *boulettes à la neige*, made of rice cooked with milk and egg whites, flavored with lemon juice, formed into balls, and covered with a stiff meringue. Since southern slaves were less apt to encounter snow than snowballs, perhaps this local sweet inspired the song, "Why do they call me Snowball/When Snowball ain't my name?"

Instead of popcorn, Creoles in the old days ate parched rice. According to the *Picayune*, refugees from Santo Domingo introduced the dish after "the great insurrection" in the West Indies. Parched rice blossoms into a beautiful popped-open grain, says the *Picayune*, to be eaten with salt or sugar. In the early nineteenth century, rice-parching parties were as fashionable among Creole youth as chestnut roasts in New England.

BUSTER'S RED BEANS AND RICE

Anyone in New Orleans knows that red beans and rice is a Monday dish, to soak up the Saturday night hangover, to use up the Sunday noon ham bone, and to spare the Monday washday cook who has spent the day over a hot tub and has no inclination to spend it over a hot stove as well. Anyone in New Orleans also knows that the place to eat red beans and rice is Buster Holmes' watering hole on the corner of Orleans and Burgundy in the French Quarter.

Buster was born in Pointe a la Hache, where his daddy was a farmer, trapper, and fisherman and his mama cooked what he caught. Buster cooked red beans and rice from his red wagon at Congo Square when the jazz bands were playing there, and it was the jazz boys who made him famous, boys like Louis "Satchmo" Armstrong, George "Kid Sheik" Colar, and Alcide "Slow Drag" Pavageau. Buster used to travel around the world with the Preservation Hall Jazz Band "as a kind of court chef," Trillin says, who puts Buster right up there with Arthur Bryant of Kansas City.

When Buster opened his present café-bar in 1960, a plate of red beans and rice cost twenty-six cents. The price has gone up to seventy-five cents, but it is still one of the best meals in town. The rice is fluffy, the beans creamy, and the beer cold. Beans and rice is a po'man's dish, too low-down to make it into *The Picayune's Creole Cook Book,* but today's reverse chic has put it into Brennan's *Commander's Palace Cookbook,* upscaling it with poached eggs on rice fritters and spiced beans and calling it "Eggs Basin Street."

> 1 pound red kidney beans
> 1 pound smoked ham hocks
> 1 large onion, chopped
> 1 green bell pepper, chopped
> 2 cloves garlic, mashed
> 1 bay leaf, crushed
>   a few drops Tabasco sauce
>   black pepper to taste
> 4 tablespoons butter
> 1 teaspoon salt
> 1 quart water
> 1 cup long-grain rice

"Pick through beans to remove any rocks," Buster advises. Cover with cold water, bring to a boil, boil 1 minute, remove from heat, cover, and let rest for 1 hour. Add ham, onion, bell pepper, garlic, and seasonings, with water to cover, and simmer until beans are tender, 1 to 2 hours. Add butter and cook 10 minutes more.

Half an hour before serving, prepare the rice. Bring salted water to a rapid boil, add rice, and stir once. Taste for doneness in about 12 minutes. Drain in a colander and return rice to the pot. Cover and put in a low (225°) oven 10 to 20 minutes. Fluff it with a fork before serving.

Heap rice in the center of a serving plate and surround with the beans. Place a ham hock at either end.

Makes 3 to 3½ cups rice. With beans, serves 4 to 8.

COWPEAS AND RICE: HOPPIN' JOHN

The dish is simple but the names for it are not. Cowpeas are not botanical peas at all but a type of bean, a low legume that was fed to cattle and slaves in eighteenth-century America and named for the more valued animal. Brought to the West Indies from Africa, cowpeas crept north to Georgia in the 1730s and multiplied so rapidly that they became both the common "field pea," as they are often called, and the decorative "black-eyed pea" that Jefferson planted at Monticello. Creoles called the peas "congri," echoing Congo Square. And when they mixed the peas with rice and threw in pickled pork, they called the dish "jambalaya au congri."

The combination of cowpeas and rice also got known as "hoppin' John" for reasons lost in the mists of popular naming. One lexicographer suggests the name may have been a corruption of *pois à pigeon,* since pigeon peas were common in the Caribbean. Another suggests that the name originated in a children's game played on New Year's Day, since the dish and the game were thought to bring good luck, beans carrying with them the magic of voodoo. The name certainly springs from the same joking matrix that calls red beans and rice "limpin' Susan" and black beans and rice "Moors and Christians."

Like its cousin limpin' Susan, hoppin' John is a useful dish because it absorbs the flavors of pickled pork, pig's tails, or hog's jowls, with plenty of vinegar or hot pepper to spice it up. As with red beans and rice, the rice keeps its character best if it is cooked separately and then mounded on a platter surrounded by the beans.

1 pound dried cowpeas (black-eyed peas)
½ pound salt pork, cubed
1 large onion, chopped
2 cloves garlic, minced
½ pound cooked ham, cubed
1 ham bone or pig's foot
black pepper to taste
¼ teaspoon red pepper flakes
dash Tabasco sauce

Pick over peas for stones, rinse, and cover peas with cold water. Bring to a boil, boil 1 minute, remove, and cover pan. Let sit for 1 hour.

Sauté salt pork until golden brown to release fat, add onion and garlic, and sauté until onion is somewhat softened.

Add the pork and onion mixture to the peas, along with the ham, ham bone, and seasonings, adding enough water to cover. Bring to a simmer, cover, and simmer gently until peas are tender but not mushed, 1 to 2 hours. Taste for seasoning and adjust.

Cook rice separately. Mound rice on a platter and surround with peas. Serves 6 to 8.

CAJUN DIRTY RICE

Clean rice is as white as a hound's tooth. Just as "dirty rags" was a name for jazz, so "dirty rice" is a name for what happens to rice when you jazz it and color it with chicken gizzards and livers and a little ground pork. Even though rice so dirtied is a funky Cajun dish, it got into the Junior League's *River Road Recipes* and it gets served with roast quail at Commander's Palace. I find it too hefty for an accompaniment and prefer to eat it, like an Italian risotto, as a main dish. You can, however, easily make it lighter by increasing the amount of rice here to two and a half cups and the chicken broth to five cups.

¾ pound chicken gizzards
3½ cups hot chicken or beef broth
2 tablespoons chicken, pork, or bacon fat
4 tablespoons butter
½ pound ground pork
½ cup each chopped onions, celery, green bell pepper, and green
    onion tops
2 cloves garlic, minced
2 teaspoons salt
1 teaspoon each black pepper and paprika
½ teaspoon cayenne pepper, or dash Tabasco sauce
1½ cups long-grain rice
½ pound chicken livers, minced

Simmer gizzards in broth for 20 to 30 minutes, remove with slotted spoon, and grind or chop fine. Heat fat and half the butter (2 tablespoons) in a heavy casserole. Sauté the pork and gizzards over high heat until browned. Lower heat, add vegetables and seasonings, and cook until vegetables are wilted, about 5 minutes. Add rice and reserved broth, bring rapidly to a boil, stir once, cover, and lower heat. Simmer 15 minutes.

Sauté minced chicken livers in remaining butter for only 2 to 3 minutes (they should still be faintly pink). Toss with the rice, taste for seasoning, and adjust. Cover and let rice fluff in a low (225°) oven for 10 minutes (the rice becomes very moist with the addition of the vegetables).

Serves 4 to 6 as a main dish.

JAMBALAYA ALA EVERYTHING

The Spanish Cajun town of Gonzales calls itself the "Jambalaya Capital of the World," and at its annual Jambalaya Competition contestants compete with a classic chicken jambalaya. The chicken should be caught preferably during Cajun Mardi Gras, when cowboys racing from village to village on horseback are pelted by farmers' wives with live chickens that must then be lassoed, plucked, cleaned, and hurled into the communal bubbling jambalaya pot.

Celestine Eustis, in *Cooking in Old Creole Days* (1904), claims jambalaya as "a Spanish Creole dish" whose three essentials were chicken, rice, and tomatoes. On the other hand, Madame Eustis says, oysters, shrimp, and sausages are also "very nice." The blood sausage called *chaurice,* which the *Picayune* decided was the hottest and therefore the "very nicest and most highly flavored" of all Creole sausages, was a favorite because of its pepper content: sweet red (paprika), black, cayenne, and "very hot" chili.

In the jambalaya here, I've combined the works and have added to the chicken some "very nice" smoked sausages, smoked ham, shrimp, and oysters, in a mix long familiar through paella. The dish will have a richer flavor if you use chicken fat or a meat fat instead of vegetable oil. The texture will have a good crunch if you save some of the "holy trinity" vegetables to use as a garnish at the last. Cajun cooks use the locally smoked ham called *tasso,* but a Smithfield or even some prosciutto works well. When fresh tomatoes are unavailable, sun-dried tomatoes left whole, or chopped, give a nice jolt to the palate. A clever Creole addition is a bit of lemon rind, but season as you will. Any ingredient for a jambalaya should be qualified by the Shakespearean subtitle *Or What You Will.*

    2 tablespoons chicken, pork, or beef fat
    1 3½-pound chicken, cut into serving pieces
    ¼ pound smoked ham, cubed
    1 pound smoked sausage (Polish, garlic, French), sliced
    2 cups chopped onions
    1 cup each chopped celery and sweet bell pepper
    2 cloves garlic, minced
    2 cups long-grain rice
    1 teaspoon each salt, black pepper, and paprika
    1½ teaspoons each hot red pepper flakes and thyme
    2 bay leaves, crushed
    ¼ teaspoon allspice
    1 pint shucked oysters
    3 cups hot chicken, beef, or fish broth

1 pound ripe tomatoes, peeled, seeded, and chopped
½ pound shelled shrimp
rind of 1 lemon

Heat fat in heavy skillet and fry chicken pieces until well browned. Remove and let cool, then cut meat from the bones into 2-inch cubes.

Fry ham and sliced sausages in the same fat. Remove and set aside. Mix the onions, celery, bell pepper, and garlic together, save ¾ cup for garnish, and sauté the remainder in the fat until wilted, about 5 minutes.

Stir in the rice and seasonings and sauté 3 to 4 minutes to coat the grains with oil.

Drain oysters and add their liquid to the rice. Add hot broth, stir rice well with a fork, cover pan, and simmer over low heat until rice and chicken are barely tender.

Fold in tomatoes, shrimp, oysters, remaining vegetable garnish, and lemon rind, bring to a simmer, cover, and let stand off heat about 10 minutes, or until the seafood is cooked but the shrimp still crunchy.

Serves 6 to 10.

RICE FRITTERS
CREOLE *CALAS*

"Belle Cala! Tout chaud!" was the cry of the Cala Woman in the French Quarter during the nineteenth century, as she roused cooks to their doors to buy hot rice fritters for the morning *café au lait* of their masters and mistresses. Or so the *Picayune* described the Cala Woman, "in quaint bandana tignon, guinea blue dress, and white apron," on her head a cloth-covered bowl filled with "the dainty and hot Calas."

While Tante Zoe has gone the way of Aunt Jemima, rice fritters are still around New Orleans in abbreviated form, served usually as a garnish like hushpuppies instead of morning fritters. Seasoned with hot pepper, they make an unusual and delicious hors d'oeuvre. But here I've chosen the traditional sugar and spice to make a cookie alternative. The rice can be leavened with baking powder instead of yeast, but I like the old-fashioned way of letting the rice dough rise slowly for a few hours to develop flavor.

½ cup long-grain rice
1 teaspoon salt
3 cups boiling water
1 package dry yeast
½ cup very warm (110°–115°) water
3 eggs
¼ cup sugar
½ cup all-purpose flour
½ teaspoon freshly grated nutmeg
¼ teaspoon each cinnamon and mace
oil for frying
powdered sugar

Boil rice in salted water until soft and mushy (about 30 minutes). Dissolve yeast in warm water and, when rice is cool, beat the yeast into the rice by hand or food processor. Cover the bowl and let rice ripen in a warm place 4 hours or more.

Beat eggs with the sugar until light and fold into the rice. Mix flour with the seasonings and add to the rice mixture. Let mixture rise again about 30 minutes.

Heat oil to 375° and drop batter by large spoonfuls into the oil until they are golden brown. Drain on a paper towel–lined baking sheet in a low (200°) oven, to keep the cooked fritters warm while you cook more. Sprinkle with powdered sugar and serve hot.

Makes about 24.

8
Wetland Foods

The foundation of swamp cooking is foursquare—crawfish, oysters, shrimp, and crab—and of these four, the crawfish is king. So fecund are the creatures in the waters of the delta that there are scarcely nets enough to catch them or mouths to eat them. The brackish bayous and marshes are also ideal for oysters, wild or farmed, and more of them are produced and eaten in Louisiana than in any other state. Because the oysters are half the size of their northern cousins, you have to eat them in quantity. There are still a number of oyster bars in New Orleans where you stand at a marble counter, sauce them up, and slurp them down as fast as your man can shuck them. In more innocent days saloon bars were heaped with oysters raw and pickled, boiled crawfish and shrimp, red snappers and roast beef, all for free. Only plenitude can account for the number of oyster dishes named by New Orleans restaurant cooks desperate to distinguish their bivalves from the po' boy oyster loaves of the bars by adding watercress and Pernod to make oysters Rockefeller; mushrooms and cream for oysters Bienville; shrimp, mushrooms, and garlic for oysters Rossignac.

Half of the country's shrimp is caught by the shrimp fleets of Louisiana in the gulf ports of Delcambre, Morgan City, and Houma. The advantage of eating fresh shrimp here is that cooks leave the shrimp's head intact and in the head is the tomalley that, like lobster tomalley, distills its seafood essence. Louisianans show the same respect to crab fat, the creamy white goo inside the top shell and body cavities of their multitudinous blue crabs. Crab fat, plus crab liver and coral eggs, is essential, locals say, to Creole gumbo, where even the shells are crushed to extract flavor.

Louisiana mud breeds crawfish the way a Louisiana bayou breeds mosquitoes. After a heavy rain, says Alex Patout, your backyard sprouts mud chimneys six inches high, the breathing holes of a yard full of mud bugs. Louisiana produces 95 percent of America's crawfish, but it also consumes 95 percent of what it produces, says Randy Montegut, the young owner of Bon Creole crawfish processors in New Iberia. His "factory" is a shed surrounded by fields now flooded for crawfish farming that were once farmed for rice or soybeans. In the shed a couple dozen Laotian women stand at long tables and peel mountains of crawfish, separating head from tail, peeling the meat from the shell and reserving the fat in the head. "Out of state," Randy says, as if this were a separate country, "they want peeled meat, but it may take one hundred fifty to two hundred tails to make a pound of live weight, so you're talking a lot of costly peeling."

There are two reasons crawfish do not export easily. First is the small proportion of meat to total shell: about 10 to 15 percent for crawfish in comparison to 40 to 50 percent for shrimp. Second is the brief shelf life of crawfish fat. The heart and soul of a crawfish, any self-respecting Cajun will tell you, is in the yellow fat concealed inside the head (it is actually the liverpancreas of the critter). The oil content makes the fat go rancid quickly, even if it's frozen. "They can open Cajun restaurants all they want in New York," says Alex Patout, "but it won't be the same as down here where we will lie, cheat, and steal to get the fat." But even down here crawfish was shame food in the world of silent cooking until Henry Guidry at Henderson went public with the mud bug in a restaurant in 1935. Now the Guidry family processes up to 15,000 pounds of crawfish a day from 1000-acre crawfish farms and can barely keep up with local demand.

Another swamp food much in demand locally is turtle. Turtles were one of the first exotic delicacies to be exported in quantity to the banquet tables of Europe after seventeenth-century explorers returned with tales and soon the living bodies of these creatures of the West Indies and surrounding gulfs. By the middle of the eighteenth century, turtle soup was de rigueur for wealthy middle-class families of any pretension to swank, and turtle soup is still the featured dish at the Lord Mayor of London's annual banquet, which requires 500 pounds of turtle meat.

In the colonies of America, turtles were so popular that they were barbecued, stewed, and souped in turtle-soup houses the length of the Atlantic seaboard, especially in Philadelphia and Baltimore. By the end of the nineteenth century, turtles were in danger of extinction until conservationists called a halt and merchants took to turtle farming. But in Louisiana the wild turtle tradition is still strong, the favorite being the diamondback terrapin of the marshes, named from the Algonquin word *torope*. Only slightly less popular are the green sea turtle of the Gulf of Mexico and the freshwater snapping turtles called "cowan" and "turkle."

Turtle is not the easiest food for a home cook to prepare. For its numerous Soupes à la Tortue, the *Picayune* suggests that the cook begin with a method typically French: "First cut off the head." To do this it advises hanging the turtle upside down and warns that the body will quiver for several hours afterward, which gave rise to the "darky tradition" that a turtle never dies. For the modern cook, Howard Mitcham, in *Creole Gumbo and All That Jazz* (1982), begins with the sensible suggestion that the cook first sharpen his ax, then turn the turtle on its back and wait for the beast's curiosity to overcome its prudence. Once beheaded, the turtle should be plunged into cold water, parboiled to remove the shell, then skinned and the legs denailed. Liver and small intestine are cooked like chitterlings, the bones and shell are chopped for stock, and the calipash and calipee, like crawfish fat, are turned into sauce. Calipash is a greenish goo under the upper shell and calipee a yellowish goo over the lower, and it is the flavor of these that lets a connoisseur know he is eating true turtle soup rather than beef or lamb or some other "mock."

Frogs also abound in the bayous, so much so that the *Picayune* made a frog its mascot and emblem, inspiring recipes like Picayune Frog Lemonade. Cajuns call frogs *ouaouaran,* in onomatopoeic imitation of croaking bullfrogs, like the ancient Greeks' *brekekekex.* "Frog gigging," as they call it, is still a favorite springtime sport, where froggers work in pairs, one to mesmerize the frogs on the riverbanks with a spotlight attached to the front of the pirogue, or canoe, the other to catch the frog by his legs before he leaps.

A local delicacy I did not get to sample was alligator. "Truly delicious," Marjorie Kinnan Rawlings calls alligator meat in her *Cross Creek Cookery* (1942). I believed her from Buster Holmes' recipe in his *Restaurant Cookbook,* subtitled *New Orleans Handmade Cookin',* in which he calls for a three-foot-long alligator, plus lemon, oil, butter, flour and, if you're feeling fancy, a bouquet garni. Marinate the tail meat (skinned and cut into strips) in lemon and oil, dust it with flour, and sear it in butter before simmering very slowly in stock. Next time I go south, I will head straight for Buster's alligator.

CRAWFISH BOIL

A crawfish boil, like a New England clambake, is a community affair numbering several hundred eaters and several thousand pounds of crawfish. I do not exaggerate. With my own eyes I watched the Ragin' Cajun Boil and Beer Festival held annually at the season's final football game at Southwestern Louisiana University, better known as SLU. While the team played its heart out, spectators deserted the bleachers to engulf 10,000 pounds of freshly boiled pepper-hot crawfish ladled from tank-sized tubs and washed down with tank-truck kegs of beer.

For even a small local party of eight to twelve, Howard Mitcham recommends a forty-pound sack of crawfish to boil in a thirty-gallon garbage can. I've found that a mere ten to twenty pounds will do for ten people up North, provided it's only a first course and you've got other food coming. The only problem with cooking crawfish is cleaning the beasts. They're muddy inside and out, so you have to purge them in salted cold water, which makes them splutter and crawl up the side of your kitchen sink or bathtub to escape. Not once do you rinse them, but you do so two, three, or four times, until the water is no longer muddy but clear. If you are squeamish about crawling creatures, get a friend to do this job for you, preferably outside with a big washtub and a garden hose.

Besides crawfish, the only other essential ingredient for a boil is a quantity of powdered crab- or shrimp-boil seasoning, or a peppery-seasoned oil like Zatarain's to make a courtbouillon so spicy that the flavor will seep through the shells and into the meat. The bouillon then makes a good liquid to boil new potatoes in as ballast for the shellfish.

The best way to serve crawfish is on newspapers or large paper plates with bags at the ready for shells. According to the experts, the best way to eat crawfish is to turn a fellow on its back and break it in two to separate the large head from the small tail. With your thumbnail split open the underside of the tail shell and push out the meat. If the dark vein is very prominent, as in some shrimps, discard it. Otherwise ignore it. Now lift off the back of the head, insert your index or little finger into the head's cavity, and remove the yellowish fat. If you're Cajun, you'll go on to the claws and crack them with your teeth to suck out the tender flecks of meat. "A true crawfish connoisseur can keep it up for a couple of hours," Mitcham claims, "and eat ten or fifteen pounds— which after all is only a pound or two of pure meats." Basically, the method is that described succinctly by the Breaux Bridge Crawfish Festival T-shirt, "Pinch my tail, suck my head, eat me."

        10 pounds live crawfish
         3 large onions, chopped
       3–4 celery stalks, with tops, chopped
         3 lemons, sliced
        ½ bunch parsley, chopped
        ½ bunch green onions, with tops, chopped
         1 pound (1½ cups) salt
         3 3-ounce packages crab- or shrimp-boil seasonings
         4 bay leaves, crushed
         6 sprigs fresh thyme, or 1–2 tablespoons dried thyme
         2 cloves garlic, mashed
         1 tablespoon each black and cayenne pepper
        20 small new potatoes

Purge crayfish by soaking them in salted cold water about 15 minutes. Drain, rinse well, and repeat until the water runs clear. Discard any dead crawfish.

In your largest stockpot, bring 6 to 7 quarts of water to a boil with the chopped vegetables and seasonings and boil 20 minutes to mingle flavors. Add crawfish and potatoes, cover pot with a lid, and bring rapidly back to the boil. Boil gently about 10 minutes. Remove from heat, add a cup of cold water to reduce heat, and let steep, covered, for an additional 10 minutes.

Drain and serve them hot, warm, or cold. Excellent with Creolaise Sauce (see page 126) or Hot Mustard Mayonnaise (see page 119) to dip the tails in and spread on the boiled potatoes.

Serves 1 to 10.

PAUL'S CAJUN POPCORN

Paul Prudhomme is as cagey with names as with cast-iron skillets. By calling deep-fried crawfish tails "Cajun popcorn" instead of their traditional name, fried crawdaddies, he has made a regional dish national. Fresh peeled crawfish tails are of course best, but you can use the same hot-pepper seasoning and crisp corn-flour coating to make small shrimps or bay scallops into Cajun popcorn. At his K-Paul's Louisiana Kitchen, Paul serves this finger food with what he calls a Cajun martini, which is simply our usual martini spiced with a hot pickled green tomato or onion and served in a Mason jar.

There are many things that Prudhomme uses that are not my taste, including sugar, onion powder, and garlic powder. He likes to balance the hot with the sweet, and doesn't like the afterglow of live onion and garlic, but I don't like the chemical taste of these powdered seasoners and prefer to omit them in my batter. One trick that Southerners have is to mix corn flour (not cornstarch but cornmeal finely ground) with regular flour to give deep-frying batters an extra crunch and flavor. This is another way to use the *masa harina* of the Southwest.

> 1 cup milk (or half-and-half)
> 2 eggs
> ½ cup each corn flour and all-purpose flour
> 1 green onion, diced
> 1 clove garlic, mashed
> 1 teaspoon salt
> ½ teaspoon each black, white, and cayenne pepper and thyme
> 2 pounds peeled crawfish tails, small shrimp, or bay scallops
>   lard or oil for deep frying

Make batter by putting all ingredients but the seafood and lard, in order, in a blender and blending until smooth.

Put the seafood in the batter and let it marinate for an hour.

Heat lard or oil 2 inches deep in a wok or skillet until hot but not smoking, about 370°. Fry the seafood in small batches so that it will turn golden brown as fast as possible.

Drain on paper towels and serve with lemon quarters or Hot Mustard Mayonnaise (see below).

Serves 4 to 8.

HOT MUSTARD MAYONNAISE

For a good dipping sauce for shellfish, one Cajun-Creole trick is to add a bit of the shellfish itself to the oil and lemon to give it body and flavor. Creole mustard generally is hotter than Dijon mustard because it uses whole mustard seeds, but you can adjust the heat of the sauce by adjusting the amount of Tabasco sauce.

    1 egg
    1 tablespoon Creole (whole-seed) or Dijon mustard
    1 tablespoon lemon juice, or more as needed
    ½ teaspoon salt
    ¼ teaspoon white pepper
       dash Tabasco sauce
    ¼ cup cooked crawfish tails, shrimp, or shrimp butter
    1 cup corn or peanut oil

Put egg in blender or processor with mustard, lemon juice, and seasonings and blend. Add seafood and purée until fairly smooth. Add oil slowly, with machine running, until oil-egg mixture thickens. Taste for seasoning. Thin with lemon juice if desired.

Makes about 1½ cups.

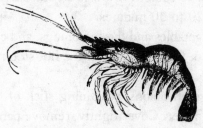

CAJUN CRAWFISH
ÉTOUFFÉE

"The key to good *étouffée*," says Barry Ancelet's mother, Maude, "is letting the butter and crawfish have their say." Hand-lettered signs in front of roadside shacks in Cajun country spell it "A-2-FAY" and it means suffocated or smothered. (When Creoles smother crawfish, they do it in a white or blond roux and call it "écrevisses gratinées.") Cajuns smother theirs in a chocolate-black roux to thicken the courtbouillon (pronounced Cajun-style "coo-byong"), smoothed out with quantities of butter. Smothering doesn't mean mushing. In a good *étouffée*, the crawfish flesh will be sweetly firm in its pools of black butter. For the real thing, you need crawfish fat. But even without it, and even without crawfish, you can substitute shrimp and still have a good *étouffée*. If you can get whole shrimp, use the shrimp fat in the heads.

½ pound (2 sticks) butter
½ cup all-purpose flour
½ cup each chopped onion, celery, and sweet bell pepper
2 cloves garlic, minced
1 teaspoon each salt and cayenne pepper
½ teaspoon each white and black pepper
¼ teaspoon thyme
2 cups hot fish stock
2 pounds peeled crawfish tails (plus crawfish fat if possible)
1 cup chopped green onions, with tops
¼ cup brandy

Make a roux of 1 stick butter and flour by melting butter in a heavy skillet, stirring in the flour to cook over low heat, and stirring constantly until the flour is dark brown, 20 to 30 minutes.

Add the chopped vegetables and the seasonings, and cook until the vegetables are slightly softened. Gradually stir in the hot stock and let simmer 15 minutes to thicken.

Add the crawfish, green onions, remaining stick of butter, and brandy and bring gently to the simmer. Cover tightly, remove pan from heat, and let sit 15 minutes. Unless the crawfish are unusually large, the heat of the sauce will cook them through. If they are not firm or if you have made the dish in advance, reheat very gently and serve in heated soup bowls or deep plates around a mound of rice.

Serves 4 to 6.

ALEX'S CRAWFISH BISQUE

Bisque is a classy French name for a rich soup intense in seafood flavor. When made with crawfish, the *Picayune* calls it "Potage à la Bisque d'Écrevisse." The dish consumes a lot of time, as well as crawfish fat, which is stuffed into the crawfish heads that garnish the thick broth, so you may prefer reading to cooking. It helps to have a family as large as Alex Patout's if you want to feature a crawfish bisque at a big family reunion. Seven hundred members of Familie Patout showed up at their last reunion, but that also meant 1400 hands to separate crawfish heads from tails, scoop out the fat, and chop the tails up fine. It also helps to have a cooking father and mother like Eugene and Ann Patout, who have cooked together most of their lives in restaurants and at home, and who trace the family recipes back four generations on each side.

Most of all it helps to have a source for extra fat. "Beg, borrow, steal, cheat, kill—but get that fat," slim, bespectacled, mild-mannered Alex warns, as his voice turns to steel. "Guys will work in teams," he says of the locals, "so one guy will call the crawfish dealer over while the other cleans out the fat in his refrigerator. As we say around here, the fat belongs legitimately to anyone's got guts enough to take it." You need that fat to make the superb forcemeat of crayfish, vegetables, and bread crumbs with which you stuff the empty heads.

The dish demands four stages: cleaning, boiling, and peeling the crawfish; making the stuffing for the heads; making the soup base; putting it all together. Here I've reduced the usual big-family recipes to one that will serve eight to ten people, which means about twenty pounds of live crawfish to get two to three pounds of peeled crawfish tail meat. You will have to supplement the crawfish fat to get a total of two to three cups. This is not a first-course soup but a super-filling one-dish meal.

    20 pounds live crawfish
    ½ pound (2 sticks) butter
     3 cups chopped onions
     2 cups each chopped sweet bell peppers and celery
     2 teaspoons salt
     1 teaspoon cayenne pepper
    ½ teaspoon each black and white pepper
        dash Tabasco sauce
    ½ cup chopped green onions, with tops
    ½ cup minced parsley
     1 cup toasted bread crumbs
    ½ cup all-purpose flour, plus more as needed

Purge crawfish in salted cold water 15 minutes, rinse well, and repeat until water is clear and not muddy. Put crawfish in a deep pot and cover with boiling water. When water returns to the boil, cook 1 minute, drain crawfish through colander set over another pot, reserving the liquid, and cool.

When crawfish are cool enough to handle, break tails from heads and snap tail shell lengthwise to peel. Save shells in a pot. Remove the yellow fat from the heads (without bursting the mud sack behind the fat) and save. Clean the black mud sacks from the heads, snap off the claws and legs, rinse them well, and add to the pot, saving out 30 heads for stuffing. Cover shells with the reserved crawfish liquid and boil until reduced to 2 quarts. Strain and stir all but ½ cup of the crab fat into the stock.

Melt 1 stick butter in a skillet, add 2 cups chopped onions and 1 cup each bell peppers and celery, and cook until tender. Chop half the crayfish tails very fine by hand or in a food processor. Add to the vegetables with the remaining crab fat and half the seasonings and simmer gently 2 to 3 minutes. Add half the green onions and parsley and all the bread crumbs. Taste and adjust seasoning. Stuff the reserved heads with this dressing, roll them in extra flour, and bake on a greased baking sheet at 300° about 30 minutes to brown them.

Make a roux of the remaining 1 stick butter and ½ cup flour in a heavy skillet. Cook slowly, stirring constantly, until sauce turns the color of peanut butter. Add remaining onions, bell peppers, and celery and cook until tender. Put mixture into a large pot, add reserved stock slowly, and then the remaining seasonings. Simmer until sauce thickens, about 30 minutes.

Add baked heads to the bisque and simmer 8 minutes, then add the remaining crawfish tails and simmer 2 minutes. Add remaining green onions and parsley for garnish and serve over separately cooked white rice or with a side bowl of rice.

Serves 8 to 10.

PO' BOY OYSTER LOAF WITH GARLIC BUTTER

The acme of downtown New Orleans oyster bars is the one called Acme, at Iberville and Bourbon in the French Quarter, where on a normal day they open 5700 oysters at the marble bar. You stand at the bar with a frosted glass of beer and toss together your own sauce from the large bottles of ketchup, Tabasco, and oil, and bowls of freshly grated horseradish on the counter. If your eyes water and your head explodes, as mine did, it's your own damn fault, but be assured that the oyster shucker will not break stride or look up even if you pour beer on your hair to quench the flames.

Uptown are oyster houses like Casamento's, on Magazine Street, where fried oysters are tossed into Italian bread loaves to make the oyster version of a po' boy. A po' boy can also mean roast beef and gravy, but not in an oyster house. "Make a pirogue of it," the *Picayune* instructs the sandwich maker: hollow out the insides of a long crusty loaf until it looks like a wooden canoe plying the bayou. The *Picayune* claims that the loaf was called "la mediatrice," when men were men and women easily pacified, but I wouldn't try it today. Today the couple who drink together make a po' boy together and call it "la détente."

48 oysters, shucked
1 cup corn flour (or *masa harina*)
1 teaspoon each salt and white pepper
½ teaspoon cayenne pepper
1 loaf Italian or French bread (about 18 inches long)
¼ pound (1 stick) butter
2 cloves garlic, minced
lard or oil for frying

Drain oysters well; if you like, save their liquor for another use. Mix flour with seasonings in a paper bag, add oysters, and shake well to coat them on all sides.

Split the loaf of bread in half lengthwise. With a sharp spoon, scoop out the insides, top and bottom, leaving a ½-inch-thick shell. Melt butter with the garlic and brush on the inside, top, and bottom of the loaf. Toast the buttered sides under a broiler until golden brown.

Heat lard or oil in a wok or skillet until hot but not smoking and add the oysters a few at a time to brown quickly, 2 to 3 minutes. Remove with a slotted spoon and place them in the bottom crust until all are cooked.

Cover with top crust and present as a loaf. To serve, remove top crust, spoon out the oysters, and cut slices of the crust to go with them.

Serves 4.

PEANUT AND OYSTER SOUP

An exemplary hybrid of a French method applied to an American ingredient appears in Celestine Eustis' recipe in *Cooking in Old Creole Days* for a peanut and oyster soup thickened with a French roux. We can shortcut the roux, however, and make a lighter soup for today's tastes by following the American Indian method of thickening liquids with nut butters. This soup is as quick and easy to make as it is rich and satisfying to taste, and with a crusty loaf of bread it makes a meal.

½ cup peanut butter

4 cups chicken broth

1½ pints oysters, shucked, 1 cup oyster liquid reserved and
strained

1 teaspoon salt

½ teaspoon each black and cayenne pepper

Put peanut butter with 2 cups chicken broth in a blender and liquefy until fairly smooth (you may like your peanut butter crunchy).

Pour into a saucepan and add remaining broth and oyster liquid. Add seasonings and heat soup gently, stirring, until liquid is hot. Add oysters and let simmer just until the edges of the oysters begin to curl, 2 to 4 minutes.

Serves 4 to 6.

STUFFED SOFT-SHELL CRABS
WITH CREOLAISE SAUCE

"Busters," they call them in the spring when the blue Atlantic crab, like spring itself, busts out all over. When the crab shucks its hard shell, the crab inside expands one third of its size, like a woman shucking her corset. Because crabs are so plentiful along the gulf shores, Cajun-Creole variants are many. Instead of the classic dish of soft-shell crabs fried in butter and splashed with lemon, Chez Marcelle, in Broussard, stuffs them Cajun fashion with a crab-shrimp stuffing and serves them with a hot mustard hollandaise they call "Creolaise." The stuffing is a bit of work, but it beautifully plumps the flesh and complements its tenderness.

A soft-shell crab is easier to clean than it looks, and it will taste best if you clean it just before you cook it. So buy it live, always, and clean it yourself when you are ready to cook. You want to get rid of four parts: tear off the apron flap on the underside of the crab; lift up each side of the soft top "shell" and remove the spongy white gills that reach up from the sides like "dead men's fingers"; clip off the eyes and small mouth parts with a pair of scissors; push out the small sand bag in the center, just behind the eyes, by pressing the "shell" in front of the legs on each side. The creamy yellow stuff inside is crab fat and is the best part of the crab.

Stuffing

½ cup white wine
2 tablespoons butter
4 green onions, with tops, chopped
1 clove garlic, minced
¼ pound mushrooms, chopped
¼ pound raw shrimp, peeled and ground fine
¼ pound lump crab meat
½ teaspoon each salt and cayenne pepper
¼ teaspoon each white and black pepper
1 cup fresh bread crumbs

12 live soft-shell crabs
2 eggs, beaten
1 cup buttermilk
1½ cups corn flour (or *masa harina*)
salt and pepper to taste
lard or oil for frying

Creolaise Sauce

4 egg yolks
4 tablespoons Creole (whole-seed) mustard
several dashes Tabasco sauce
1 tablespoon fresh lemon juice
½ pound (2 sticks) butter

To make the stuffing, heat the wine and butter in a saucepan. Add the vegetables, shrimp, and lump crab meat, together with the seasonings, and sauté until shrimp is just cooked, 2 to 3 minutes. Add bread crumbs, mix well, and taste for seasoning. Chill for an hour.

Clean the crabs and stuff them by lifting the soft top "shell" on each side and packing in the mixture. Beat the eggs with the buttermilk and dip each crab in the egg mix before rolling each in corn flour. Salt and pepper lightly.

Heat lard or oil until hot but not smoking, 365°, in a wok or deep skillet. Cook crabs 2 or 3 at a time so as not to crowd them, until they are golden brown and crisp. The shells will turn faintly red on top. Drain them well on paper towels on a baking sheet in a warm oven until all are fried.

To make the sauce in a blender or processor, beat egg yolks with the mustard, Tabasco, and lemon juice. Heat butter in a skillet until it bubbles and froths. Remove the froth and, while butter is still bubbling, pour it in a slow trickle through the opening in the lid of a whirring blender or processor. Discard the milky residue in the bottom of the butter pan. Keep the sauce warm over hot water or in a warm place until ready to serve with the crabs.

Makes about 1½ cups sauce to serve 6.

PEPPER SHRIMP

The Italian connection is strong enough in New Orleans to have developed an Italian-Creole variant on the sandwich and seafood themes. "Muffuletta" is the local hero, submarine, or hoagie sandwich, piled with the usual Italian charcuterie meats but topped with a chopped olive-and-garlic salad that smothers the whole. Barbecued shrimp is the local Italian seafood dish made famous by Pascal Manale's restaurant on Napoleon Avenue. "Barbecued" is a misnomer for Manale's shrimp, because there is no grill or sweet-hot sauce in sight, only shrimp baked in a sea of butter and reefs of black pepper. It's a dish for family and friends who will take the plunge and dip fingers and hot French bread into the butter to fish for shrimps in the shell. Howard Mitcham, in *Creole Gumbo and All That Jazz,* claims to have secured Manale's recipe from an ex-Manale chef, but there are no secret ingredients here. The one essential is totally fresh shrimp, preferably with the heads on.

> 5 pounds large shrimp (7 pounds with heads on)
> 1 pound (4 sticks) butter
> ½ cup freshly ground black pepper

Rinse and drain shrimp and place them in a single layer in a large shallow baking pan. Cut each stick of butter in two to make eight pieces and place on top of the shrimp. Grind peppercorns in a spice grinder or blender to make ½ cup and sprinkle the pepper evenly over the shrimp. Bake at 350° for 45 minutes, turning the shrimp at least twice to absorb the pepper-butter on all sides.

Serve directly from the pan with a loaf of sliced French bread so that guests can peel the shrimp as they go and sop up the sauce with hunks of bread. It's not a bad idea to provide a platter of hot washcloths, Japanese style.

Serves 4 to 8.

GREEN TURTLE SOUP

Turtle soup, one of the great traditional European dishes derived from a New World product, should be reclaimed from the English and French and restored to its native land. Cajun-Creole cooking thickens the liquid with a roux; flavors it with tomatoes, onions, garlic, and bell peppers; enriches it with butter; garnishes it with lemon, parsley, and hard-cooked eggs; and tops it up with quantities of sherry. "Fit for a king," says the *Picayune,* of soup made from fresh snappers and cowans and diamondbacks and loggerheads. Outside of the bayous you're not apt to get fresh turtle meat, but in many places you can get it frozen, and almost everywhere you can get it canned. Turtle soups, like gumbos, express the whim of the cook, who may add spinach like Paul Prudhomme or Worcestershire sauce like Buster Holmes or calipash and calipee like Howard Mitcham, who would deny that turtle "fat" is whim. If you are lucky enough to begin with a whole fresh turtle, chop up the shell to flavor your stock; otherwise use a good beef broth.

    2 pounds boneless turtle meat
    1¾ cups all-purpose flour
    2 teaspoons salt
    1 teaspoon each black and cayenne pepper
    lard or oil for frying
    ½ pound (2 sticks) butter
    2 cups chopped onions
    1 cup chopped celery
    2 cloves garlic, minced
    2 cups tomato purée (from fresh or canned Italian plum
        tomatoes)
    ½ teaspoon each thyme and oregano
    ¼ teaspoon allspice or cloves
    6 cups good meat stock
    ½ cup good dry sherry
    ½ lemon, seeded and chopped
    3 hard-cooked eggs, chopped fine
    ½ cup minced parsley

Cut turtle meat into ½-inch cubes. Mix 1 cup flour with ½ teaspoon each salt and black and cayenne pepper in a paper bag and add turtle cubes, shaking bag to coat the meat with flour. Heat lard or oil until hot but not smoking and quickly fry turtle meat until golden brown. Drain on paper towels.

Make a roux in a heavy skillet by melting the butter and adding the remaining ¾ cup flour. Cook, stirring constantly, until roux turns a dark reddish brown, about 20 minutes.

Add onions, celery, and garlic and cook until softened, about 5 minutes. Add tomato purée, remaining salt and peppers, and other seasonings and cook 10 minutes. Add stock and turtle meat and simmer, uncovered, until liquid has thickened, 30 to 50 minutes.

Just before serving, add sherry to the soup, taste, and adjust seasoning. Ladle soup into hot soup bowls and garnish each with a mixture of chopped lemon, egg, and parsley.

Serves 8 to 10.

FRIED FROGS

"Frog gigging" (transfixing a frog with a spotlight in order to catch him by the legs) is no longer the major source of supply of fresh frog legs, now that bullfrog farms have increased in the South. But frog legs are still a seasonal delicacy, as favored today as they were when the *Picayune* waxed lyrical in recipes like Picayune Frogs à la Creole, or my favorite, Fried Frogs.

Should you go a-frogging and end up with frog legs fresh from the wild, you must skin them first, then parboil three minutes in water to which lemon has been added for bleach (a half cup lemon juice to two cups water). Old recipe books argue about battering, flouring, or crumbing, but all agree that the best oil for frog frying is lard. To make a frog fancy, the *Picayune* suggests serving the legs on a "snow-white folded napkin in a dish," or on a bed of fried parsley garnished with red radishes and sliced lemons.

16 small or 8 large pairs frog legs
1 cup buttermilk
1 cup corn flour (or *masa harina*)
½ teaspoon salt
¼ teaspoon each black and cayenne pepper
   lard or oil for frying
1 bunch parsley, washed and dried
2 lemons, quartered
1 bunch radishes, trimmed

Prepare legs by cutting off backbone (if any remains) with a pair of poultry shears or strong kitchen scissors. Cut legs in two where they join. If they are fresh, parboil 3 minutes in acidulated water (1 portion lemon juice to 4 portions water), drain, and pat dry. Soak for an hour in the buttermilk. Mix flour with seasonings in a paper bag, add legs, and shake to coat them.

Heat lard or oil until hot but not smoking, 375°, and fry legs a few at a time until golden brown, 2 or 3 minutes. Fry parsley about 1 minute, drain on paper towels, and serve with the frog legs, lemon quarters, and radishes. Serves 4.

VARIATION: Instead of deep frying the legs, sauté them in ¼ to ½ pound butter until brown. Remove and add to the butter the juice of one lemon, stir, and pour over the legs.

BLACKENED REDFISH WITH LEMON BUTTER

Redfish is as native to Louisiana as white cod to New England. Actually redfish is but a local name for a type of common drum fish, only down there they call big ones (which may reach eighty pounds) "bull reds" and small ones (under fifteen pounds) "red rats." The *Picayune* called them "poisson rouge" for their reddish-bronze scales and remarked that "the old Creole darkies" believe that the pair of distinctive black spots near the base of the fish's tail are "de marks ob de Lord's hands" when He performed the miracle of the loaves and fishes with a redfish.

On Creole menus, redfish appears in every form—baked, poached, grilled, or garnished with shrimp, crab, and oysters à la Galatoire—but the classic dish is a redfish courtbouillon in a tomato broth. It led Thackeray to praise the bouillabaise of New Orleans above that of Marseilles. More recently, Prudhomme has popularized redfish by grilling it in a skillet so red hot that it turns the fish black. You can apply the same excessively hot grill to any firm-fleshed meat, such as tilefish, sea trout, or striped bass, to get the effect of barbecued fish.

> 4 ½-pound redfish fillets, ½ inch thick
> 2 teaspoons salt
> 1 tablespoon paprika
> ½ teaspoon each black, white, and cayenne pepper
> 1 teaspoon each thyme and oregano
> ¼ cup olive oil or corn oil
>
> 1 whole lemon
> ¼ pound (1 stick) butter
> 2 green onions, with tops, chopped fine
> 1 clove garlic, minced

Mix the dry seasonings and rub well into each side of the fish fillets. Coat fillets with a little oil and set aside while you heat the skillet and make the sauce. Heat a heavy cast-iron ungreased skillet until it is ashen hot, about 10 minutes.

For the lemon-butter sauce, grate the lemon zest and reserve. Cut off all the white pith from the lemon and discard. Cut lemon into quarters, remove seeds, and purée lemon pulp in a blender. Remove any remaining membranes. Melt butter and pour it, bubbling, into a whirring blender containing the lemon.

Add the fillets, 1 or 2 at a time, to the heated skillet and char on each side, about 2 minutes a side.

Place on a serving platter, sprinkle with the green onions, garlic, and lemon zest and pour the lemon butter over the top.

Serves 4.

RED SNAPPER WITH ORANGES

Red snapper, the queen of Campeche, is cloaked in a peppery tomato sauce when served "à la Creole" or "Vera Cruz." But before the Spaniards brought tomatoes north from south of the border, they had brought from Seville the bitter oranges we now associate with marmalade. From their seeds wild oranges proliferated along the gulf coast from Louisiana to Florida, so much so that by the time William Bartram traveled in the South in 1789 he found the Seminoles steaming red snapper with wild oranges as they had once done with wild grapes, wrapping the fish in grapeleaves to steam over the coals.

Because the beauty of a snapper is in its color and classic fish shape, it's best to serve it whole, steamed in grapeleaves or banana leaves, if you can get them, but if not, use foil. An orange-pecan rice stuffing will plump out the fish and intensify the orange juice and orange slices in which you poach the flesh. To duplicate the bitter oranges of Seville, difficult to obtain in this country, add lemon juice to regular oranges.

Stuffing

```
     4 tablespoons butter
   ¼ cup finely chopped onion
     1 cup long-grain rice
 1½ cups boiling water
   ¼ cup lemon juice
   ½ teaspoon each salt and black and cayenne pepper
       grated rind of 1 orange
   ½ cup chopped pecans

     1 4-pound red snapper (or 2 small snappers), cleaned and with
       tail and head on
       salt and black and cayenne pepper to taste
     4 tablespoons butter, melted
   ¼ cup fresh orange juice
     2 tablespoons fresh lemon juice
     2 tablespoons dry vermouth
       garnish: 2 whole oranges
```

For the stuffing, melt butter in heavy saucepan, sauté onion until wilted, 5 minutes, and add rice. When the kernels have puffed and turned white, 3 to 5 minutes, add boiling water, lemon juice, and seasonings. Stir rice once with a fork, cover, and bake at 350° for 45 minutes. Add orange rind and nuts. Take out 1 cup of the rice mixture for stuffing and keep the rest warm until fish is cooked.

Season the fish inside and out with salt and pepper and dip it in the melted butter to coat both sides. Stuff fish with the reserved rice mixture, place it in the middle of a large piece of heavy-duty foil, and bring up the sides before pouring in the orange and lemon juices and vermouth. Slice oranges thin and arrange over the top of the fish like fish scales. Close the foil and seal well. Put foil package on a baking sheet and place another baking sheet on top to conduct heat to the upper half of the fish.

Bake on top rack of oven at 350° for 20 to 25 minutes, turning the fish upside down between the pair of baking sheets after 15 minutes. Test for doneness by opening foil and poking fish with a fork at its thickest point to see whether the flesh flakes easily.

To serve, place foil on a serving platter and open it at the table. Fillet the meat by cutting down the middle and along both sides, cutting crosswise at tail and below the gills to make 2 fillets per side.

Pass separately a dish of the orange-pecan rice stuffing.
Serves 4.

POMPANO IN A SALT CRUST

The Choctaws did it with Mississippi mud. They smeared a freshly caught fish from the salt waters of the gulf or the fresh waters of Lake Pontchartrain with a thick layer of clay and baked it whole—head, tail, guts, and all—in hot coals. Once baked, the mud was split open, the fish removed, and its innards stripped out in one piece.

We can do a similar thing with a salt crust, since salt is easier to find in most kitchens than Mississippi mud. Antoine's restaurant does it in parchment paper, adopting the French trick of wrapping lamb or other meat in paper to oven-poach it. Jules Alciatore of Antoine's supposedly invented *pompano en papillote* back in 1901 to honor a Brazilian balloonist, but in fact Jules merely gave a French trick a fish twist. The Spaniards dubbed the fish *pámpano* because its silver-green color reminded them of a grapeleaf. Mark Twain called the pompano "as delicious as the less criminal forms of sin," but in these inflated times, we should probably change "less" to "more."

> 6–8 leaves romaine lettuce
> 1 1½- or 2-pound pompano, cleaned and with head and tail on
> salt and pepper to taste
> small bunch parsley or other fresh herbs
> 1 3-pound box kosher salt
> ¼ pound (1 stick) butter
> ½ teaspoon cumin
> 2–3 sprigs fresh coriander (cilantro), chopped
> 1 lemon, quartered

Blanch romaine leaves in boiling water for 30 seconds to soften them. Drain, rinse in cold water, drain, and pat dry.

Season fish lightly inside and out. Stuff cavity with parsley or herbs. Wrap fish entirely in the romaine leaves. Place a thick layer of salt in a deep baking dish. Add the fish and cover with salt, at least an inch deep on top. Sprinkle salt lightly with cold water to help the salt solidify while baking. Bake at 400° for 40 to 50 minutes.

Crack the crust, remove fish from salt, and then from its green wrapper. Remove fillets from the backbone, top and bottom, and place on a serving platter. Melt butter with cumin and coriander and pour over the fillets. Serve with lemon quarters.

Serves 2.

9
Prairie Foods

Upcountry is hog country. While hogs are raised in many parts of America and sausages made from them, only in Cajun country can you find the sausages with an ancient French lineage. Hogs fatten on the prairies north and west of Lafayette, and Cajuns fatten on the whole hog—innards, intestines, head, feet, and blood, transformed into *boudin blanc, boudin rouge, andouille* and *chaurice*.

In 1906 when the *Picayune* put out its *Creole Cookbook, boudin* meant blood sausage, or *boudin rouge*. "Take a pound of hog or beef blood and mix it with hog fat and seasonings" was their formula for blood sausage. *Boudin blanc*, on the other hand, was a more ladylike version, made without blood and often with added white chicken meat, cream, and egg yolks to refine the ground pork. *Andouilles*, in this part of the world, were called "chitterlings" because they included the lining of the hog's stomach and its intestines, packed with pork meat into long lengths of intestines before smoking. Tied into small sausages, they were called *andouillettes*.

The premium sausage, however, was the *belle chaurice*, thick with chunks of pork, lean and fat, and heavily spiced with onions, garlic, cayenne and black pepper, thyme, parsley, bay leaf, and allspice. The *Picayune* says that Creoles stuffed the filling into sheep rather than hog entrails and fried the sausages in boiling lard for breakfast, "always having sufficient to have the sausage swim in it."

Today *boudin* has developed a local form that combines rice and ground pork with pork liver, seasoned with green onion tops, parsley, and of course cayenne. "I normally down *boudin* while standing in the parking lot of some Cajun grocery store," Trillin writes, "that has managed to snatch me off the road by displaying in its window a hand-lettered sign that says 'Hot Boudin Today.'" Some butcher or grocer makes hot *boudin* every day, so the lucky Cajun housewife doesn't have to turn her hand to it any more than a Parisian housewife turns out her own luncheon charcuterie.

The Robichauxes in New Iberia make hot *boudin* every day in time for breakfast, and usually three times a day. Mr. Robichaux has been making it for thirty years and his ancestors for three centuries, ever since the first Robichaux butcher arrived from France in 1689. "When everyone did his own butchering in the backyard," Robichaux says, "to make *boudin* was a way of using up all that pork liver." There's good *boudin* and bad *boudin,* Alex tells me, and the bad comes from a disproportionate amount of liver, which overwhelms the palate instead of providing a melting texture so delicious that Cajuns eat *boudins* the way others eat bananas. In warm weather, Robichaux makes 300 pounds of *boudin* a day, in cold weather 500 pounds. He was once deluded into thinking he should retire from the *boudin* business, after twenty years in nearby Opelousas, but *boudins* were his destiny. "We opened up the Bible," his wife explains, "and God showed us the passage about the man with the talents and when God gives you a talent you shouldn't misuse it, whether it's selling cars or bags of peanuts, and God led us to New Iberia to stay in the meat business, praise the Lord."

Many hereabouts praise the Lord by raising not only their own hogs but also their own chickens and rabbits so that they taste, as once all such barnyard fowl or furred game did, of something more flavorful than dried pellets. Backyards also produce a rich array of farm vegetables, tasting of the black earth and humid air. Creole tomatoes, they claim, are sweeter and less acidic than the tomatoes up North, deprived as they are of Mississippi delta mud rich in salts and minerals. The land also abounds with sweet and hot peppers, with eggplants to be stuffed with seafood or vegetables, and with the West Indian mirlitons (chayotes). The fashion for crisp vegetables has made few inroads here except among innovators like Paul Prudhomme, but smothering vegetables by long, slow cooking produces a flavor and texture as soothing as the creamed corn they call *maquechoux,* the mush they call *kush-kush* or *chou-chou,* or the soft yam celebrated annually at the Opelousas Yambilee Festival.

SMOTHERED CORN
MAQUECHOUX

Just as every Cajun believes that his roux is the only roux, so he believes that his *maquechoux* is the only *choux*. All agree, however, that you must begin with fresh corn kernels. Some make a kind of succotash, cooking the mixture quickly in butter and milk. Others smother it with slow cooking and heavy cream. Prudhomme likes to thicken his sauce with evaporated milk and beat in an egg for "a rich frothy texture." I don't claim to have made a true *choux* here, but it is one of the best creamed corns I can imagine.

        8 ears fresh corn (to make 4 cups kernels)
        4 tablespoons butter
        ¾ cup chopped onions
        ½ cup chopped green bell pepper
        4 green onions, with tops, chopped
        1 tablespoon sugar
        ½ teaspoon each salt and white pepper
        ¼ teaspoon cayenne pepper
        1 cup heavy cream
        1 egg, beaten

With a sharp knife, cut kernels straight down from the cob. With the back of the knife, press the cut rows of the cob to strip them of as much corn "milk" as possible.

In a skillet heat butter and sauté kernels with chopped vegetables and seasonings for 3 to 4 minutes. Add all but 2 tablespoons of the cream, cover, and simmer gently 20 to 30 minutes. Uncover for the last 5 minutes to allow mixture to thicken slightly.

Just before serving, beat the remaining cream to a froth with the egg and add to the corn.

Serves 4 to 6.

SAUSAGE AND SEAFOOD GUMBO

Land Cajun and sea Cajun join in the big black gumbo pot. If you're cooking Cajun, you emphasize the dark, smoky taste of a black roux, heightened by the peppery smoked ham they call *tasso,* and thickened by gluey okra. If you're cooking Creole, you keep the roux blond and thicken it with the powdered sassafras called "filé." What you put in the pot is what you have in your hand. The *Picayune* is rather conservative in listing among its gumbos Turkey Gumbo, Squirrel or Rabbit Gumbo, Okra Gumbo, Crab Gumbo, Oyster Gumbo, Shrimp Gumbo, Cabbage Gumbo, and Herb Gumbo. Howard Mitcham is more typical in his Seafood-Sausage-Chicken Gumbo Filé. Paul Prudhomme gussies up the pot with Egg and Dried Shrimp Gumbo and Guinea Hen and Andouille Gumbo.

The recipe below is merely one gumbo scenario, which you can thin with fish broth or thicken with a tablespoon or two of filé powder. One warning about filé is to not let it cook or it will turn your liquid gummy. Just add the powder to the hot liquid, remove from the heat, cover the pot, and let it sit five minutes.

A fish stock for your gumbo is quick to make. When you buy the shellfish, buy also three or four fishheads or whole cheap fish like porgies, remove their gills, cover the fish with water and white wine, and add celery tops, parsley, thyme, bay leaf, peppercorns, and salt. Then simmer twenty minutes and strain.

> 2 cups chopped onions
> 1 cup each chopped sweet bell peppers and celery
> 1½ pounds okra, sliced into ¼-inch rounds
> 2 tablespoons minced parsley
> 1 tablespoon salt
> 2 bay leaves, crushed
> 1 clove garlic, mashed
> 1½ teaspoons cayenne pepper
> 1 teaspoon each black and white pepper
> ½ teaspoon thyme

¾ cup lard or vegetable oil
¾ cup all-purpose flour
1 pound smoked sausage, sliced into ¼-inch rounds
2 quarts hot fish stock

1 pound medium shrimp, peeled
1 pint oysters, shucked
¾ pound lump crab meat
½ cup chopped green-onion tops
   optional: Tabasco sauce
4 cups cooked white rice (1⅓ cups raw)

Mix the vegetables with the seasonings.

To make the roux, heat lard or oil in a heavy cast-iron pot like a Dutch oven, add flour, and cook over medium heat, stirring constantly, until flour turns the color of dark chocolate, about 30 minutes. Immediately add the seasoned vegetables and cook 2 to 3 minutes, stirring them so they don't scorch. Add sausage, then add stock gradually, stirring all the while, bring to the boil, and simmer gently until gumbo is somewhat thickened and vegetables are soft, about an hour.

Add shrimp, oysters, crab meat, and green onions, return barely to the simmer, and remove from heat. Cover tightly and let sit 10 minutes to cook the shellfish. Taste for seasoning and add Tabasco if wanted.

Place a scoop of rice in each soup bowl and add a cup or more of gumbo; or serve with the rice in a small bowl on the side.

Serves 8 to 10.

PICKLED PORK

Food snobs say *petit salé,* but down South the term is "pickled pork," and nobody is too poor to be a connoisseur of it. The New Orleans taxi driver who told me, "We wuz poor but we ate good," explained how it was they ate good: "We used to go to the store and say, Lemme see your pickled meat, and only if it wuz nice and lean you'd say, Cut me off a inch piece." The taxi man had just had a long discussion with his wife about "how come poke chops today don't taste like my mama's mama's chops. We got the same skillet, one of those heavy cast-iron fellas," he says, "and we got the same seasonings but the poke ain't juicy, it's tough. By golly, I realize, we don got the same poke. My mama's mama killed her own hogs and put the meat in the pan. Now we got to go to the superstore and you don know how long it's been frozen or thawed but you know there ain't no juice to be just oozin out so's you can dip your bread in it."

Even though few of us raise our own hogs to put in the pan, we can recapture some of the country taste of pork by the centuries-old method of brining it instead of freezing it. Time was when almost everybody's mama had a barrel of pickled pork on hand for her gumbos and jambalayas and the taste of salted or cured pork was entirely different from slowly smoked and aged ham. The *Picayune* favored pork shoulder as the best cut for pickling, "about twenty hours after killing," and if made in small batches of three or four pounds, the meat would keep in the pickle barrel for a year.

The Cajuns called pickling salt "Turks Island salt," after the Caribbean island where it was once produced. They were as particular about their salt as about their pork. Any pure salt will do, but table salt will not do because of its iodized additives. The salt draws out the meat juices to create a brine that both preserves and flavors the meat.

> 1 fresh picnic shoulder or shoulder butt (about 5 pounds after
>   boning)
> 1 pound pickling or kosher salt
> 2 tablespoons brown sugar
> 2 bay leaves, crushed
> 1 teaspoon each thyme and black pepper

2 cloves, mashed

½ teaspoon allspice

optional: 1 teaspoon saltpeter*

Remove bone from the shoulder and cut meat into 1-pound hunks. Mix ¾ cup pickling salt with the remaining seasonings. Rub the spiced salt into the meat on all sides.

Put a layer of salt in the bottom of a stoneware crock or plastic bucket, pack the meat into the salt, and cover with a thick layer of salt. Place a weighted board or plate on top to press the meat down. Leave in a cool place (38° is ideal) for a minimum of 10 days (2 days per pound of meat). Once cured, the meat can remain in the brine at least a couple of months. You can use home-cured pork wherever you would use ham, ham hocks, pig's feet, or fatback.

Serves 6 to 8 as a main dish.

BOUDIN PIE

I have never believed that a sausage-stuffing attachment to a food grinder was necessary in my kitchen, but neither do I want to stuff a pig's casing by hand. I would rather buy my *boudin* freshly made by Mr. Robichaux, but when that is not possible I can still savor the delicious, melting stuffing of a *boudin* by improvising another kind of wrapper than pig intestine. Cabbage leaves make a good wrapper, either by stuffing a whole cabbage or by blanching large leaves and making individual packets to steam. Or you can do as I've done here: enclose the creamy rice and pork in a pie crust. Classic French recipes

---

*Saltpeter is a nitrate salt that has been used since the sixteenth century to help preserve color, flavor, and texture in cured meats. It dropped out of general use when commercial curing, with pure nitrites, replaced home curing. If you wish to preserve a pink color in the pork, which will otherwise turn gray, and if you don't wish to use a nitrate in any form, you can substitute for the saltpeter ½ teaspoon ascorbic acid.

for *boudins blancs de Paris* usually add white chicken meat to the pork and egg to the cream, but this recipe is more rustic, using puréed pork liver and cream.

¼ pound pork liver
1 pound fresh pork, half lean and half fat
½ cup finely chopped onion
1 clove garlic, minced
½ cup heavy cream
1 tablespoon salt
1 teaspoon each black and cayenne pepper
½ teaspoon each sage and thyme
¼ teaspoon mace
⅛ teaspoon allspice
1 bay leaf, crushed
2 cups cooked white rice (⅔ cup raw)
¼ cup minced parsley
3 green onions, with tops, chopped
1 egg, beaten, as needed
top and bottom crust for a 9-inch deep-dish pie, 2 inches deep

Freeze the pork liver for 30 minutes to firm it before cutting it into small cubes and purée in a processor or blender. Cut meat into 1-inch cubes and grind them in a meat grinder. (Freeze the cubes for 10 to 15 minutes if you use a food processor for grinding.)

Put ground pork meat and fat in a skillet with the onion and garlic and sauté lightly 2 to 3 minutes without browning. Add puréed pork liver, cream, and seasonings to the skillet and simmer, stirring constantly, until liver is barely cooked and still pinkish. Add rice, parsley, and green onions and beat together off heat. If the mixture doesn't hold together, add a beaten whole egg.

Line a deep-dish pie pan (or a standard 9-inch cake pan) with crust and fill it with the *boudin* mixture. Cover with a top crust, seal the edges, cut some vents for steam in the top, and bake at 400° until crust is browned, about 30 minutes.

Serves 4 to 6.

VARIATION: TO MAKE SAUSAGES Cut pig casings into 4 12-inch lengths, stuff them with the mixture, and tie at both ends. Put the sausages in just enough simmering water to cover the bottom of a pan, cover tightly, and steam 20 to 30 minutes.

GUMBO Z'HERBES

For vegetarians, this traditional Lenten meal should prick the appetite and win, according to local legend, as many friends as you put in greens. "z'herbes" in Cajun means *les herbes,* or greens, the way "z'aricots" or zydeco means *les haricots* or green beans. The more greens the better, according to the *Picayune,* which adds equal parts of the leaves of radish, turnip, mustard, spinach, watercress, parsley, young cabbage, and green-onion tops. Other greens you might consider are celery or carrot tops, Swiss chard or collard or beet greens. For nonvegetarians or non-Lentenites, a veal brisket or ham bone would not be amiss.

   8 packed cups mixed greens
   1 large onion, chopped
  1½ teaspoons salt
   ½ teaspoon each black and cayenne pepper, thyme, and oregano
   2 bay leaves, crushed
   2 whole cloves
   6 whole allspice
   ⅔ cup vegetable oil
   ⅔ cup all-purpose flour
   8 cups hot beef, chicken, or vegetable broth
   8 cups cooked rice (2⅔ cups raw)

Wash greens well and parboil them about 5 minutes in water barely to cover. Drain in a colander over a pot to catch the liquid. When the greens are cool enough to handle, chop them fine.

Mix onion with the seasonings before you make the roux. Make the roux by heating oil and adding flour, stirring constantly, until it is golden brown, 15 to 20 minutes. Add the onions and gradually stir in the liquid. Bring to a boil, lower heat, and simmer 1 hour. Serve with or over rice.

Serves 8 to 10.

VARIATIONS: For additional flavors, add a garnish of crumbled bacon, diced ham, or cooked and chopped chicken gizzards.

EGGPLANT WITH EGGPLANT DRESSING

Because eggplants grow as thickly as tomatoes and peppers in Louisiana, recipes for eggplant (called "aubergine") abound in Creole cook books. One Cajun method is to stuff the eggplant to resemble a stuffed pirogue, the bayou canoe. Another is to smother the eggplant in eggplant dressing, which is a mashed purée flavored with shellfish. When the dressing is served over slices of fried eggplant, as Alex Patout makes it, it is a main dish as richly complex as the Eggplant Parmigiana of the Italians. I like the contrast of firm slices and smothered dressing, but if you don't want the bother of slicing and frying, you can simply cut the eggplant in half, scoop out the inside pulp, cook it, and return it to the shell to bake ten minutes.

1 pound shrimp in the shell
¾ pound (3 sticks) butter
2 onions, chopped fine
1 green bell pepper, chopped fine
1 large stalk celery, chopped fine
1 teaspoon salt
¼ teaspoon each black, white, and cayenne pepper
⅛ teaspoon each thyme, oregano, and basil
3–4 dashes Tabasco sauce

4 medium eggplants
½ pound lump crab meat
¼ cup each chopped green-onion tops and parsley
   oil for frying
   corn flour seasoned with salt and pepper for dipping

Peel shrimp and make a fish stock of the shells by boiling them in water to cover and then reducing liquid to ½ cup.

Heat ½ pound (2 sticks) butter in a skillet. Add onions, pepper, celery and seasonings and sauté slowly until softened, about 10 minutes. Add shrimp and cook until shrimp are firm and pink, 4 to 5 minutes. Remove the cooked shrimp from the vegetables to use as garnish.

Bake 2 of the eggplants whole at 350° for 45 minutes. Split them, scoop out the flesh, and mash with a fork or purée in a food processor. Mix the eggplant purée with the strained shrimp stock and cooked vegetables and simmer about 15 minutes to mingle flavors. Add crab meat, green-onion tops, and parsley and heat through.

Prepare remaining 2 eggplants by slicing them, skin on, into ½-inch-thick slices. Dip each slice in the corn flour and fry in hot oil a few slices at a time. Drain well.

Arrange slices on a serving platter, heap the eggplant dressing on top, and decorate with the shrimp.

Serves 8.

SHRIMP-STUFFED MIRLITONS

Native to Central America and the Caribbean, the chayote takes its name from Nahuatl, *chayotli*. In Louisiana it is called "mirliton," a name the French give to a toy musical pipe and to a Rouen pastry. Either mirliton or chayote is a far prettier word than the prosaic "vegetable pear" that most of the world calls this squash. Once cooked, the delicate but firm pale green flesh (which conceals a flat but edible seed) is good in cold salads. I once made a dazzling salad by alternating orange papaya slices and sweet red pepper strips with the pastel green mirliton on a bed of dandelion greens. But the Cajun-Creole way is to stuff the vegetables with seafood and deep fry them. Prudhomme stuffs his mirliton "pirogues" with crawfish and *andouille* and serves them with an oyster-flavored hollandaise. Any seafood will make a good stuffing, such as crab, scallops, or oysters. If you don't want to deep fry your stuffed mirlitons, you can simply bake them at 400° for ten to fifteen minutes to brown the topping of crumbs. Deep frying, however, makes the vegetable crisper.

> 3 large mirlitons (chayotes or vegetable pears)
> 4 tablespoons butter
> 1 pound fresh shrimp, peeled and chopped
> ½ cup chopped smoked ham
> 2 teaspoons salt
> 1 teaspoon each dry mustard and thyme
> ½ teaspoon each black, white, and cayenne pepper
> ¼ cup minced parsley
> ½ cup milk
> 1 egg, beaten
> ½ cup corn flour for dredging
> 1 cup fine bread crumbs
>   oil for frying

Cook mirlitons in an inch or two of simmering salted water in a covered pot until tender, about 20 minutes. When they are cool enough, cut each in half and remove outside rind. Scoop out some of the pulp with a spoon but leave a shell ½ inch thick. Dice the pulp.

Meantime, heat the butter in a skillet and quickly sauté the shrimp and ham with half the seasonings. Remove from heat and stir in the parsley and cubed mirliton pulp. Cover and keep mixture warm.

Beat together the milk and egg. Roll mirliton shells in the remaining seasonings, dredge with flour, dip in the milk-egg mixture, and finally cover with bread crumbs. Heat oil in a wok or deep skillet to 350° and deep fry the mirliton shells 1 to 2 minutes on each side. Drain on paper towels.

Fill each half with the shrimp stuffing and serve with Lemon Butter (see page 131) or Hot Mustard Mayonnaise (see page 119) or what you will.

Serves 6.

YAM YEAST BREAD

Sweet potatoes in two colors grew in Peru, Central America, and the West Indies when Columbus came, tasted, and approved. One was pale yellow and the other dark orange. The Arawakan Indians called these tubers *batatas* and Columbus was happy to transport tuber and name back to the Old World to the eternal confusion of botanists and cooks. The Old World already knew of another exotic tuber, this one native to Asia and Africa, which was also sweet in taste, varied in color, and elephantine in size. So substantial was this family of tubers (*Dioscorea bulbifera*) that West Africans called it by their verbs "to eat"—*njam, nyami, djambi*—and so yam came to mean any nutritious sweet-tasting root. Botanically, sweet potatoes and yams are as unrelated as apples and oranges, but we are eaters first and the language of eaters continues to call the New World sweet potato "yam," as it has for four centuries.

Such linguistic niceties do not encumber the annual Yambilee Festival at Opelousas, which awards prizes to the year's best yam recipes. Heavy favorites are yams turned into a sweetened purée, then souffléed or baked in a crust, a cake, or a quick bread like biscuits or pone. The yam bread tradition goes back to the *Picayune*, which calls *pain de patates* "a delicious Creole bread," only this one leavens yam purée with yeast to produce a beautiful saffron-colored loaf, unsweetened with any sugar but its own. The easiest way to make yam purée is to bake yams with their skins on until they are soft (an hour at 400°); when they cool, peel them and mash the flesh with a fork or purée in a processor.

      2 packages dry yeast
  1½ cups very warm (110°–115°) water
  5–6 cups unbleached white flour
      1 tablespoon salt
      1 teaspoon white pepper
  ⅛ teaspoon each allspice and mace
      2 tablespoons butter, softened
      1 cup cooked yam purée (from 1–2 yams)
      1 egg for glaze

Dissolve the yeast in the warm water in a large bowl. Mix 5 cups flour with the seasonings and stir into the yeast mixture. Add butter, the yam purée, and additional flour, if necessary, to make a moist but kneadable dough. Knead until dough is elastic—10 to 15 minutes by hand or 5 minutes in an electric mixer with doughhook. Then put in a buttered bowl, cover with plastic and a towel or plate, and let rise in a warm (75°–80°) place until doubled.

Punch dough down and let rise again about 45 minutes. Punch down and shape into one large round loaf or divide between 2 buttered standard bread pans (9 by 5 by 3 inches). Let rise once more for another 45 minutes.

Beat egg with a teaspoon of water and use as glaze for top of bread. Bake at 425° until the bottom of the loaf sounds hollow when rapped with the knuckles, 30 to 40 minutes. Cool on a rack at least an hour before slicing.

Makes 1 large round loaf or 2 smaller ones.

CREOLE CORN MUSH
KUSH-KUSH

Sometimes spelled *couche-couche,* this is a Cajun-Creole way of turning mush into a potion so soothing that it puts young and old to bed, as in *coucher.* In a delightful 1929 cook book called *Mandy's Favorite Louisiana Recipes,* devised by Natalie Scott to honor all the cooking Mandys (whose names were sometimes Pearl, Mammy Lou, and Prosine and sometimes Tante Celeste and Tante Felicie), Mandy is quoted as saying her *kush-kush* is "good on de tongue en' easy on de stumick, da's how to cook fo' chilluns."

> ½ cup hot water
> 2 cups stone-ground white or yellow cornmeal
> 1 cup milk
> 1 egg, beaten
> 1 teaspoon baking powder
> 1 teaspoon sugar or cane syrup
> 1 teaspoon salt
> 4 tablespoons butter
> warm milk or half and half

Stir hot water into the cornmeal, then gradually add the milk. Beat in the egg, baking powder, sugar, and salt. Melt the butter in a skillet and when it bubbles, pour in the corn batter. Lower heat and let the bottom crust over without stirring. As the crust forms, scrape it into the rest of the mush and continue until most of the mush is browned. Serve with a pitcher of warm milk or half and half.

Serves 4.

10
Cane and Molasses

Only America's hottest, wettest states—Louisiana, Mississippi, Alabama, Florida, and Georgia—attempted to compete with the West Indies in growing "these honeyed reeds called sugar." Columbus had brought cane shoots with him in 1494 to plant in the Caribbean and reported that they germinated within a week and "succeeded very well." As the world well knows, this Asian cane succeeded so very well in the New World that it revolutionized the tables and politics of the Old, enslaving palates to sugar and men to sugar mills. Sugar took Europe by storm and Europe squabbled for the next two centuries over the Sugar Islands of the New World while planters killed off the native Indians through slave labor and imported some 10 million replacements from Africa.

In the United States, only Louisiana has hung on to its cane and to the family mills that turn honeyed reeds into molasses, syrup, and crystallized granules by a process discovered at the end of the eighteenth century by a Frenchman, Jean Étienne Boré. Syrup and molasses represent different degrees of concentrated cane juice, from which more and more crystallized sugar is extracted by boiling. At the bottom of the commercial scale is blackstrap molasses, which has the least sugar but the most vitamins and minerals and the most distinctively molasses taste.

The dark "swamp" desserts of Louisiana, like Buster Holmes' Louisiana Mud Cake, generally take their taste and color from powerful blackstrap molasses for pies, cakes, gingerbreads, and puddings. Mulatto-colored desserts use cane syrup, which is halfway between molasses and brown sugar. Cane syrup, molasses, and brown sugar crystals were once staples of southern kitchens because these sweeteners were cheaper than white crystals purified of molasses. By the twentieth century, however, commercial corn syrup had replaced cane, and commercially processed white and brown sugars had replaced both molasses and the sweeter stickier crystal of the past. To taste a locally produced cane syrup like Steens on a pecan waffle or in a sweet potato pone is to recapture the sumptuous flavor of the past the way a good maple syrup does.

Cajuns, according to Prudhomme, were never dessert folks. The women were too busy helping their men skin alligators to whip up cakes in order to show off newfangled ovens. Also gumbos and jambalayas were so filling that they precluded desserts. Creole cooking, however, expanded the perimeters of the dessert course with candies like New Orleans' famed pralines, pulled molasses taffies, and the molasses-coated popcorn called "tac-tac" (which eventually became Cracker Jacks when some Chicago Yanks packaged and renamed it in 1896).

Celestine Eustis, in *Cooking in Old Creole Days* (1904), gives us an idea of how the dessert course completed a typical festive dinner of the last century, when the New Orleans Press Club staged "A Small Creole Dinner" at the Atheneum on February 19, 1898:

> Absinthe & Anisette, Oysters from Mosquito Bayou, Gombo file, Bisque 'crebiches, Small vegetables with salt, Courtbouillon from Bayou Patassa, Chicken Pate, Boiled Crawfish, Hopping John, Pigskin Fricassee, Jambalaya Tschourisses [blood pudding], A runaway pig stuffed & roasted, Sweet salad with chickory, Snipes with laurel leaves en baguette, Watercress from Bayou des Herbes, Popcorn, Sweet potato bread, Pecan Pralines, Thick Molasses Taffy, Ice cream biscuit, Mulatto stomach [gingerbread], Tante Zizine's poundcake, Bananas, Oranges, Sugar cane, Mandarins, Black Creole Coffee, Brulo, Cigarettes perique (in corn paper), Creole cigarettes (in yellow paper).

This is the kind of small dinner that caused the *Picayune* to warn hosts against excess:

> Do not overload your table, and, above all, do not fatigue your guests with long-drawn-out affairs of eighteen and twenty courses. . . . Observe the happy medium, ten and even less, and you and they will be the more satisfied, the more delighted, and the more comfortable for your thoughtful and refined consideration.

PECAN PRALINE TART

The pralines once sold by New Orleans' *pralinières,* roaming Canal Street or Jackson Square "when the little Creole children are taking an airing with their faithful old mammies," says the *Picayune,* were once of two kinds, a white kind and a brown kind: the white made of white sugar and freshly grated coconut, the brown of brown sugar and pecans. Today's praline is a lavender-beige pecan disk made from sugar and milk or cream. The ideal praline is opaque to the eye and it crumbles and melts on the tongue.

The other local sweet-tooth killer is pecan pie, but the layer between the pecans on top and the crust on bottom is too often an excessively sweet glue of cane syrup and eggs. (If you want the classic filling, a local booklet labeled *Louisiana's Fabulous Foods* gives a recipe with promising proportions and real ingredients: 1 cup pecans, ½ cup sugar, ¾ cup molasses, the juice of 1 lemon, ¼ cup butter, and 3 eggs.) I prefer the creamy crumble of a good praline, and so I fill my crust with a praline mixture and top the pie with heavy whipped cream. Not a pie for the timid or restrained.

> 1 cup dark brown sugar
> 1 cup heavy cream
> 6 tablespoons butter
> 2 cups chopped pecans
> 2 tablespoons vanilla extract
> 1 10-inch prebaked tart shell

Topping
> 1 cup heavy cream, whipped
> ¼ cup bourbon
> 12 toasted pecan halves

Melt sugar in a large saucepan with cream and butter, stirring constantly. Once sugar is dissolved, boil the mixture rapidly, continuing to stir until it reaches soft-ball stage (236° on a candy thermometer). Remove from heat, beat in the chopped pecans and vanilla, and continue to beat with a wire whisk until mixture is creamy. Immediately pour it onto a baking sheet to cool.

When mixture is cool, tear off pieces and chop them in a food processor or by hand.

Press the praline mixture into the prebaked tart crust, making an even layer. Before serving, add bourbon to the whipped cream and spread on top of the praline layer. Decorate top with pecan halves lightly toasted 5 to 10 minutes in a hot skillet or oven.

Serves 8.

VARIATION: COCONUT PRALINE TART Use freshly grated coconut meat instead of pecans, and white sugar instead of brown. Sprinkle whipped cream topping with more coconut.

SWEET POTATO PONE

It was Sir John Hawkins who brought the *patates douces,* as the *Picayune* calls them, to England in 1564. By the century following, sweet potato puddings and pies were as common on English tables as lemon creams. *The Country Housewife and Lady's Director* (1727–32) gives a pair of recipes for sweet potato pudding that, except for the orange flower water, might appear in today's collection of prize-winning recipes at a Yambilee. *The Country Housewife* adds candied lemon and orange peel to cut the sweetness of the potato, as does the *Picayune* a couple of centuries later, without candying the peel. One classic way of making this wet rich pudding-bread-cake was to use raw grated sweet potatoes instead of cooked pulp. The result is a bit like our current carrot cakes, with a lovely fresh texture and flavor, baked here on a sheet to cut into flat squares.

½ cup brown sugar
¼ pound (1 stick) butter
¼ cup molasses or cane syrup
½ cup fresh orange juice
1 lemon
rind of 1 orange, grated
4 eggs, beaten
½ teaspoon each nutmeg, cloves, and cinnamon
1 tablespoon brandy or rum
2 cups grated raw, peeled sweet potatoes (1–2 potatoes)

Candied Lemon Slices

2 lemons
¾ cup sugar
¼ cup water

Cream the sugar and butter and gradually beat in the molasses and orange juice.

Grate lemon rind and reserve. Remove and discard white pith from the lemon, seed it, and chop the pulp fine. Add to the sugar-butter mixture, together with the orange rind, eggs, seasonings, and brandy. Add the grated potatoes and mix well.

Smooth mixture into a buttered 9-by-9-by-2-inch baking dish and bake at 325° for 1 hour.

Meanwhile, make the candied lemon slices. Cut lemons crosswise into ⅛-inch slices and remove seeds. Boil sugar with water in a covered pan for 5 minutes, then remove cover and boil rapidly until syrup reaches the soft-ball stage (236°). Remove from heat. Dip lemon slices in the syrup, and put on a baking sheet to dry until ready to use.

As soon as the pone is done, transfer the whole potato square to a rack and let it cool. Cut into squares and top each with a candied lemon slice.

Makes 9 to 12 squares.

CREOLE FRENCH TOAST
PAIN PERDU

"Lost bread," or *pain perdu,* is a Creole pun for "saved bread," since this is a way of redeeming stale bread from the night before. The *Picayune*'s recipe reveals why we call it French toast, since its flavors are sophisticated: orange flower water, lemon zest, brandy. Not quite a children's breakfast dish, even when, as the *Picayune* suggests, you deep fry it in lard and sprinkle it with powdered sugar and grated nutmeg. Mandy, in her *Favorite Louisiana Recipes,* ignores breakfast and suggests that *pain perdu* is a fine accompaniment for meats as well as a rich dessert.

> 1½ cups milk
> 3 eggs, beaten
> ⅓ cup sugar
> 2 tablespoons brandy
> 1 teaspoon vanilla extract
> grated rind of 1 lemon
> 8 (1½-inch-thick) slices day-old French bread, with crusts
> 6 tablespoons butter
> powdered sugar
> freshly grated nutmeg
> cane syrup

Combine milk with eggs, sugar, brandy, vanilla, and rind. Let bread soak about 5 minutes in the mixture.

Melt butter, 2 tablespoons at a time, in a heavy skillet and, when bubbling, fry the bread, 2 or 3 slices at a time, over moderate heat until nicely browned. Sprinkle with powdered sugar and nutmeg and serve with good cane syrup.

Serves 4.

FRENCH MARKET BEIGNETS

You can think of them as a Frenchman's doughnut or as an entremets fritter "from the old mother country," as the *Picayune* says. And if once they were cooked by the dozen by "the fat and cheery old negro cook," today they are eaten by the dozen at Café du Monde, where the French Market joins Jackson Square. You eat them three square pillows at a time, dipping them into an extra bowl of powdered sugar to whiten your clothes along with your face. You wash them down with a cup of French-roast chicory coffee, black or *au lait*, at any time of day or night, before a "small Creole dinner" or brunch.

These beignets are simply a Frenchified version of the *sopaipillas* of the Southwest. They are made with either baking powder or yeast, to produce an airy texture or a chewy one. The recipe here I've adapted from Rima and Richard Collin's *The New Orleans Cookbook* (1975), which attributes the rich taste of the French Market beignets to canned evaporated milk. Since Louisiana heat made canned milk a godsend when first introduced by Gail Borden just before the Civil War, it's an appropriate ingredient for Louisiana fritters.

> 1 package dry yeast
> ¼ cup very warm (110°–115°) water
> ¼ cup granulated sugar
> ½ teaspoon each salt and nutmeg
> 1 egg, beaten
> ¾ cup canned evaporated milk
> 2 tablespoons vegetable oil or shortening
> 3½ cups all-purpose flour
> oil for frying
> powdered sugar

Dissolve yeast in the water, add sugar, seasonings, egg, evaporated milk, oil, and flour. Beat well until smooth. Cover with plastic wrap and let rise in a warm (75° to 80°) place until doubled.

Punch down, knead 4 or 5 times, and roll into a long, 18-by-12-inch rectangle ⅛-inch thick. Cut into rectangles 3 by 2 inches, cover lightly with plastic, and let rise again about 20 minutes.

Heat oil in a wok or heavy skillet to 365° and fry 2 or 3 at a time until the beignets puff and turn golden brown on both sides. Drain on paper towels.

Drop them in a paper bag filled with powdered sugar and shake until coated. Serve hot.

Makes about 36.

FIG CAKE

While figs in most parts of the United States are an expensive luxury, a backyard fig tree is still common in Louisiana, and recipes for fresh figs or fig preserves sweeten old and new cook books. Many add raisins and nuts to make a figgy fruitcake, as moist as the swamps, dark with brown sugar, and elevated to tea-table status baked in a tube or Bundt pan.

"Use the broom wisp test," the *Picayune* advises us to test doneness. "If not done, bake longer, till the straw comes out clean and dry." This is a very wet cake to come out dry, but a broom wisp or toothpick will tell you when the batter is cooked.

> 1 cup brown sugar
> ½ pound (2 sticks) butter
> 2 eggs, beaten
> 3 cups all-purpose flour
> 2 teaspoons baking powder
> 1 teaspoon cinnamon
> ½ teaspoon each ginger and nutmeg
> ¼ teaspoon salt
> 1 cup milk
> 2 cups fig preserves (or canned figs), chopped fine
> 1 cup sultana raisins
> 1 cup chopped pecans

Cream sugar and butter together and beat in the eggs. Mix the flour with the baking powder and seasonings, and add it alternately with the milk to the sugar-egg mixture. Stir in the figs, raisins, and nuts.

Spoon batter into a well-buttered and floured 12-inch tube or Bundt pan. Bake at 325° until cake tester comes out clean, about 1½ hours. Cool in the pan before turning cake out.

Makes 12 servings.

NEW ORLEANS BREAD PUDDING
WITH PRALINE CREAM

Bread pudding is one of those traditional thrift dishes that appear on high tables as well as low, although most folk remember it as either loved or hated nursery food. Nora Ephron loves the bread pudding at Chez Helene in New Orleans because "It tastes like caramelized mush." Commander's Palace up-scales it into a Bread Pudding Soufflé, while Prudhomme thickens it with raisins and pecans and smothers it in Lemon Sauce and Chantilly Cream. I've taken the middle road here, with a rich pudding for kids, glazed with a praline-bourbon-cream sauce for grownups.

    4 tablespoons butter
    1 cup brown sugar
    4 eggs, beaten
    1 tablespoon vanilla extract
    1 teaspoon each nutmeg and cinnamon
    1 cup each milk and heavy cream
    ½ cup sultana raisins
    ½ cup pecans, toasted and chopped
    4 cups stale French or Italian bread, with crusts, cubed

Praline Cream
    1 cup pulverized pecan praline (see page 152)
    2 cups heavy cream
    ¼ cup bourbon, or more to taste

Cream butter and sugar and gradually beat in the eggs. Add the seasonings and beat again. Beat in the milk and cream; add raisins and pecans.

Put bread into a buttered baking dish. Pour egg-milk mixture over it and let soak 15 minutes. Set baking pan in a larger pan of hot water (to keep the custard from overcooking) and bake at 350° for 40 minutes, raising heat to 425° for an additional 10 minutes to brown and puff the top.

Make the cream sauce by beating the praline into the cream. Add bourbon to taste and beat until cream is thick but not stiff.

Serve the pudding warm with the praline cream.

Serves 8.

MULATTO GINGER CAKE

The *Picayune* explains that Estomac Mulatre, which appears on the menu of the New Orleans Press Club banquet of 1898, was a folk food sold "by the old darkies around New Orleans" and sometimes called "stage planks," which it resembled. Their virtue was economy and the historically curious can taste them by combining one cup molasses, one cup sour milk, half cup lard, three cups flour, one teaspoon baking soda, and one tablespoon powdered ginger.

Although there were dozens of recipes for ginger cakes, most Louisiana ones favored swamp-black batters. "Molasses must be the unrefined black New Orleans molasses and the sugar must be the coarse, dark, unrefined brown sugar," Celestine Eustis specifies in *Cooking in Old Creole Days*. I've made a kind of compendium of ginger cakes in the one here, which is black with molasses but lightened with eggs and smoothed with sour cream.

½ pound (2 sticks) butter
1 cup brown sugar
½ cup blackstrap molasses
2 eggs, separated
½ cup sour cream
2 cups all-purpose flour
2 teaspoons baking powder
½ teaspoon baking soda
1 tablespoon powdered ginger, or 2 tablespoons grated fresh
    ginger
1 teaspoon each salt and cinnamon
½ cup chopped pecans
powdered sugar

Cream together the butter and brown sugar. Beat in the molasses and egg yolks. Add sour cream and beat until light. Mix the flour, baking powder, baking soda, and seasonings. Stir gradually into the molasses-butter mix.

Beat egg whites until stiff but not dry, fold them into the mixture, fold in the nuts, and pour into a buttered 9-by-9-by-2-inch baking pan. Bake at 350° for 25 to 30 minutes. When cake is cool, sieve a little powdered sugar over the top for contrast.

Makes 9 to 12 squares.

PART III

Planters and Slaves

SOUTHEAST DIXIE

RECIPES IN PART III

"I used to stan' and see how Mama clean her greens and I thanks the Lord that what learned me how to clean mine."

—Shirley Ritter, of Allendale, South Carolina

"**I** just saw a recipe in a new Southern cookbook for 'Fried Grits Balls' and my family hooted," says Carolina Gribble in the kitchen of her modern colonial house in Columbia, South Carolina. Carolina Gribble is one of those southern ladies she calls, laughingly, "iron butterflies," as she shows me how to work her grandmother's tin syllabub churn. Put the churn in the middle of your bowl of cream and pump it like a bicycle pump until the liquid froths and flies all over the place. "I hope you're not going to talk just about grits and greens and chittlins but also about all the fine elegant dishes, like syllabub, we've always served at our tables," Carolina says. "That's the South nobody up North knows."

I'd just driven four hours northwest to Columbia from Charleston, where I'd talked to Charlestonians like Beth Sparre. Beth's great-grandmother had been born on a plantation in Estherville, and when the Union troops got close she walked her children fifty miles to Charleston. Beth lives on Bedon's Alley, south of Broad Street ("South of Broad or dead," as the gentry of Charleston say), in the midst of eighteenth- and nineteenth-century houses painted apricot, bisque, peach, and yellow—Barbados colors, dating back to the seventeenth century, when Charles Town was an outpost of Barbados, "a colony's colony." "Charleston is still an eighteenth-century colony," Beth says, "a close-knit family of kin—English, French Huguenots, Barbadoans."

In Beth's walled brick garden, smelling of jasmine and crepe myrtle, her friends can't talk food without talking family because in the South food *is* family. Betty Verner Hamilton talks about her Huguenot ancestors who fled to this colony of Good King Charles' Lord Proprietors after the Edict of Nantes. "We were the original boat people," she says. Charleston cooking is plantation cooking, and that means rice cooking, since Charleston sits on top of a marsh. "Scratch dirt and you get water," Betty says. Recipes were saved in plantation kitchens "time out of mind," she explains in her foreword to the 1976 edition of *Two Hundred Years of Charleston Cooking* (1930), a collection indebted to the notebook of Miss Elizabeth Harleston of the Bossis Plantation, handed down to her niece, Mary Leize Simons, who bequeathed it to her daughter Elizabeth Harleston Fraser. In the South, recipes are handed down like family jewels.

Following my week in Charleston and Columbia, trying to put names to recipes, I got as far north as Greensboro, North Carolina, halfway between Raleigh and the Blue Ridge Mountains. In Greensboro they were talking rice and gravy but I didn't know it because in the Carolinas nobody calls rice "rice." Down in Charleston they call it "perlew" and up in Greensboro they call it "pie-low" and cook books spell it "pilau," to mean "rice pilaf." The South hangs on to its regional dialects the way it hangs on to its recipes and the War between the States.

In Greensboro, I talked to Mary Louise "Squeezer" Ravenel, a trim little blonde who works a couple of acres of vegetables every day and who inherited from the mother of her husband, Tom, the family recipes of their rice plantation at Green Pond, near Charleston. Squeezer grows, cooks, and cans the produce of the land just as her mother did and Tom's mother did. "We have rice three hundred sixty-five nights a year," says Squeezer, "with dish gravy, pot liquor, and red pepper I grow and grind and keep in a big bottle on the table."

Squeezer also cooks what Tom hunts and fishes, and the freezer is full of bream (pronounced "brim") and dove. Tom's mother makes pressed dove by splitting the birds down the back and weighting them with a brick to fry them blood rare, Squeezer explains. But after looking in the Junior League cook book the other night, Squeezer told her husband, "Listen, Tom, to the way Anna Transome cooks her doves. She puts them in the oven and cooks them for hours." To which Tom said, "Thank God I didn't marry Anna Transome."

A rare photograph of a family dinner in Charleston, South Carolina, in the 1890s. Even today, Charlestonians seldom allow their privacy to be invaded by a camera, preferring to show their table settings as works of art unencumbered by people caught in the act of eating.

If you think Cajuns and Creoles talk food down in Louisiana, stop off sometime in the Carolinas. This is the South nobody up North knows because it is at once the most vocal and the most "silent," the least public, of all of America's cooking. You find it not in restaurants (except for barbecue shacks on back roads) but in private houses, the legacy of plantation hospitality. Recipes are both traditional and intensely personal. A recipe can chronicle a family history of some two hundred years and, to a Southerner, can indicate place of birth, family relations, and social position as neatly as the Columbia Assembly or Cotillion.

If you ask about southern cooking, a Southerner will ask, "Which South?" There's white South and black South, rich South and poor South and coast South and the South that moved north when slaves were freed. To draw the line somewhere, I picked the two Carolinas, North and South, in that large quilt called "Dixie," where folks number the accents not just region by region or state by state but town by town. Three cities—Charleston, Columbia, and Greensboro—had to stand for three major ecologies: the lowlands and tidewaters of the coastal plains that stretch from Florida to Chesapeake Bay; the central plain of the Piedmont; and the long chain of the Appalachian mountains from Georgia to Maryland. In the South, where you come from means not just what family but what land, and nowhere are the products of the table more rooted in the land.

Southern cooking, I discovered, was earth cooking the way the Southwest was sun cooking and Louisiana was swamp cooking. A respect for the earth and what came out of it bound the owners of the land to the workers of the land. "Land, land to use, to waste, to divide among one's children," Daniel Boorstin writes in *The Americans*, "was the foundation of all the governing families and the fortunes of Virginia." Land was the foundation of those eighteenth-century "company towns" called plantations, which brought to America indentured English by choice and black Africans by force after the first settlers landed with Captain John Smith in 1607 at Roanoke Island. Land was a gift as important as freedom to the descendants of those slaves after the Civil War, men like the grandfather of Edna Lewis, who writes, in *The Taste of Country Cooking* (1976), of their fifty acres of land in Freetown, Virginia, and of what it meant to "gather wild honey from the hollow of oak trees to go with the hot biscuits and pick wild strawberries to go with the heavy cream."

How to cultivate the land was the lesson learned by the first settlers of Jamestown after the terrible winter of 1608–9, when "for the most part, they died of mere famine." They died because rats ate the corn they had got from Chief Powhatan and because they had no nets or hooks and found frying pans useless to catch fish with. They were reduced to roots and berries, dogs and cats, snakes and rats, and finally people. "So great was our famine," Captain John Smith wrote, "one amongst the rest did kill his wife, powdered [salted] her and had eaten part of her before it was known." But even then Captain Smith foreshadowed the manner in which southern life would center on food and traditional recipes: "now whether shee was better roasted, boyled, or carbonado'd [grilled], I know not: but of such a dish as powdered wife I never heard of."

How to dig pits in the land to roast fish and fowl is the lesson settlers learned from the native Algonkians. Thomas Harriot, in *A Briefe and True Report of the New Found Land of Virginia* (1590), provided the first recipes for southern barbecue and Brunswick stew in his descriptions of "the browyllinge of their fishe over the flame" and "their seetheynge of their meate in earthen pottes," where they put in "fruite, flesh, and fish, and lett all boyle together like a galliemaufrye, which the Spaniarde call, olla podrida." Spaniards called the broiling of fish over flames on a framework of sticks *barbacao*, after a Haitian word and custom. When the English enclosed the fire pits and wooden frameworks, they called them "smokehouses."

The plantation ideal was founded on the fertility of southern land in weather softer and warmer than the hard North. Land produced the cash crops of indigo, tobacco, cotton, and rice, but it also produced the food for each self-supporting fiefdom. The kitchen garden was the heart of the plantation, linking the manor house up front to the kitchen out back and to the other one-room dependencies of dairy, icehouse, smokehouse, grist mill, pigsty, chicken coop, and slave quarters. Jefferson wanted to turn the entire estate of Monticello into an ornamented garden, integrating farmlands, orchards, herbs, vegetables, and greenhouses, "the pleasure garden being merely a highly ornamented walk through and round the divisions of the farm and kitchen garden."

The fabled hospitality of the southern plantation was rooted in farms and gardens so civilized they put the North to shame. With the help of a gardener imported from Italy, Jefferson produced for his White House chef imported from France such delicacies as Pisa carrots, salmon radishes, Lattuga lettuce, Windsor beans, Tuscany wheat, angelica apricots, *boccon de re* plums and *poppe di venere* peaches. Southern climes were hospitable to the Frenchification of food and drink, which may have offended Patrick Henry (Jefferson returned from France, he said, "so Frenchified that he abjured his native victuals") but delighted visitors like Henry Barnard from Yale, in 1833, who couldn't get over the sumptuous breakfasts and dinners. At 3 p.m. dinner, there was turtle soup, turkey with oysters, ham, venison, saddle of mutton,

The slaves of the Stirrup Branch Plantation in Bishopville, South Carolina, arranged by rank on the occasion of Captain James Rembert's seventy-fifth birthday, June 8, 1857. Nearly invisible are four uniformed house servants on the porch. The foreman, Nero, stands at the left of the group of field hands. In the middle stands the second yard boy; in front of him and at the left stands the first yard boy. The cook stands at the right, in front of all.

wild ducks, vegetables, custards, plum puddings, ice cream, bananas, oranges and almonds, champagne, and "the richest madeira, the best port and softest malmsey wine I ever tasted."

The same kind of hospitality was shown at low tables and high ones, loaded with the produce of backyard gardens and of the woods surrounding the slave quarters. While families without kitchen gardens fared badly before the Civil War on a standard issue of three pounds of pork and a peck of corn-meal per slave per week (plus "toting privileges" from the manor house), after the war freed slaves with gardens often ate better than their former masters without gardens. The hospitality of black families, no less than white, expressed itself through food shared at the hearth or cabin table or iron pot in the yard. And the tradition of that hospitality was passed down from generation to generation, like the manuscript recipe collections of the plantation manor. Even today a black woman from Georgia remembers family dinners where "everybody come to eat and to see each other. And there's plenty of food for everybody's likes—fried chicken and ham, cream potatoes and sweet potatoes, string beans and corn and peas, sliced tomatoes and cucumbers and home canned pickles and onions, hot biscuits and corn bread and iced tea and apple pie for dessert, or cake if anybody don't like the pie. Yes, sir, nobody ever left my Aunt Zoe's table without being filled up."

I remember hearing from a Virginian who moved north, a woman who cooks now for a farm in Rosemont, New Jersey, of her stepfather's big garden in Lily-of-the-Valley, near Roanoke, and of the food they ate. "You didn't set down to one meat, you had two or three meats every day," she said. "I didn't know we was poor 'til I got grown and come north and learned, 'Hey, we grew up poor.' We're still poor, of course, but my stepdaddy still got a *big* garden."

"Gardeners know, better than most people, that everything man has came out of the earth," wrote the late Stringfellow Barr, a Virginia gardener, gentleman, and scholar. I learned the truth of his words from a black woman and her family who were sharecroppers in Allendale, South Carolina, until the Second World War brought them north to Trenton, New Jersey. Virginia loved to cook the way her mama, Shirley Ritter, cooked and Virginia loved to talk about "those olden days, those days in time," on a Sunday "when the preacher come and we'd bake sweet potatoes and cracklins in the ashes and make chicken and dumplins and put a big pot of dried peas on the woodstove that had four 'eyes' in it and another big pot of okras with lots of green 'scunions' [scallions] from the garden, where we growed everythin."

In her backyard in Trenton, Virginia still grows everything and eats everything they had down south. She gets home-raised chickens in Hightstown and homemade butter in Lancaster and 'coon and 'possum and "all that old-timey food" from a fish store on North Broad Street and grits loose in a barrel at Sam's Superstore by Creech Temple. Virginia and her mother think

---

A Fourth of July picnic at St. Helena, South Carolina, 1939. A painting of their church has been hung from a tree at the left to bless the congregation and their food.

A family picking peas in their garden at Flint River Farms, a Farm Security Administration Project near Montezuma, Georgia, 1939.

nothing of forty for Christmas dinner, with country ham and turkey, forty pounds of chittlins, rice in chittlin gravy, green beans and collards and yellow turnips from the garden, potato and macaroni salads, and fruit salad "we calls Waldorf" with oranges, grapefruits, tangerines, nuts, raisins, shredded coconut, and milk to thin the mayonnaise. And there'll be apple jelly cakes, coconut cakes, pound cakes, sweet-potato pies and sweet-potato breads and a mixed drink of Hawaiian Punch and 7-Up with three kinds of fruit sherbet to thicken it up.

From Virginia I learned about her hunger for eating the earth itself, a tradition slaves brought with them from Africa. "When it's good and dug from the right place, dirt has a fine sour taste," Fannie Glass of Mississippi told a *New York Times* reporter in 1984. Dirt bred connoisseurship like any other food, and Fannie Glass held that the best dirt was good hill clay, rather than gritty delta "gumbo dirt," hill clay which she baked and seasoned with vinegar and salt and kept in a bag on her person for convenient snacking.

In the Southwest food is symbolic of man's place in the universe. In the Southeast food is symbolic of man's place on the earth and on his specific patch of land. That's why voices rise when the talk is of barbecue: the dry vinegar and pepper barbecue of Stamey's in Greensboro or Uncle Don's in Raleigh or the mustard barbecue of Greenville, South Carolina, or the ketchup barbecue of Orangeburg, or the wet smoky barbecue south of Pawley's Island at George C. "Yum" Young's or up at Foo K. Farina's Pig Pick in Holden Beach. That's why I could spend a whole evening at Carolina Gribble's listening to fifty family and friends dispute the best way to make grits, with which kind of water from what place or how much milk or how finely ground, and agreeing on only one thing, that the North doesn't know beans about grits.

That's why food is the tie that binds every social event, whether a church supper, a debutante ball, or a family funeral. Only in the South would a guest book for a funeral be called "The Food Record," in which the bereaved records the name of each donor, the name of the dish brought, a description of the food and of the container the food was brought in. "The first thing when mother died I called my best friend and said, 'For goodness sake come help me clean,' " Carolina recalled, "because people would be pouring in with food right after church, cooked by both men and women and some bring whole meals and we must have had forty-five for smorgasbord lunch and everybody said, 'I never had such a good time.' " And that's why game is still so much a part of the cooking of the South, ever since William Byrd in the seventeenth century noted "the edibility of the bear, the sweet flavor of polecat meat." And why a living descendant of Sarah Rutledge, a "Lady of Charleston" who wrote *The Carolina Housewife* (1847), still remembers the cooter pens all over Mount Pleasant when the decapitation of a sea turtle for turtle soup was a major social event. And why a game warden–cook in Charleston, Ben Moise, knows how to barbecue whole hogs in a giant wild gum-tree bowl or alligator snapping turtles weighing twenty-six pounds.

That's why the streets of Charleston once echoed with the cries of fish

A stereopticon slide labeled "Roasting Pigs at the Great Barbecue," Grand Army of the Republic Encampment, Louisville, Kentucky, 1895. The Southern barbecue is still a male ritual.

men from the "mosquito fleet" calling "Swimps" and why the arches of the eighteenth-century marketplace still echo with the voices of black women whose mothers sold the same foods from the same baskets woven of sweet marsh grass. "Don pass me by, you gonna buy from me today, so don put your purse away." And in the baskets, heaps of green and brown crowder beans, little field peas, civy peas, green and white butter beans, tiny lady beans, scuppernong grapes the size of purple marbles, baby okras, cukes, and peanuts—boiled, roasted, and green—the same as two hundred years ago.

When a Southerner leaves the South, he loses neither his accent nor his sense of place because he takes his cooking with him. Whether it's earth foods like grits and greens, rice and gravy, or country foods like ham biscuits and crackling breads, or fancy foods like syllabubs and brandied peaches, hospitality betrays his origins. For an eighteenth-century traveler from France, hospitality distinguished North from South. In the North inns were frequent but the people inhospitable, he complained, whereas in the South inns were few but the "hospitality of the people abundant and generous."

It takes more than the industrialized ghettoes of Trenton to kill the traditions of hospitality passed down from mother to daughter even when country South moves north. "My mother cook and that what learn me how to cook and I glad to the Lord I can cook," Virginia's mother tells me in Trenton. "When I cooks greens I cuts em up so fine and puts in jus a tiny little bit of spring water less all the sumption be cooked outta em and when I gives people a plate I love for it to be a satisfaction to em."

OPPOSITE: In an abandoned plantation house in Green County, Georgia, 1937, a Negro woman stirs her cast-iron fry pan next to the aluminum coffeepot. Behind her, a cast-iron muffin pan is a ghostly reminder of hot baked breads three times a day.
FOLLOWING PAGE: Three women planting corn on a plantation in Moncks Corner, South Carolina, 1941.

11
Earth Foods

"These people live so much upon swine's flesh," William Byrd complained during his eighteenth-century travels through Virginia and North Carolina, "that it . . . makes them likewise extremely hoggish in their temper, and many of them seem to grunt rather than speak in their ordinary conversation." The earth foods of the South are variations on the theme of hog and hominy and how to preserve them in damp southern heat. Barbecue, country ham, and grits all spring from Indian methods of preserving meat and corn by fire without the aid of salt. "For preservation, a barbecue is erected," a European traveler to the South wrote in the early nineteenth century, "and the fish are smoked over a fire." Since the discovery of salt, Europeans had preserved foods by pickling them in brine, but here were men who "barbecuted" their game and fish by dehydrating them with mere smoke.

Smoke did for the southeastern tribes like the Catawbas and Cherokees and Creeks what the sun did for the tribes of the Southwest. A gathering of men around a raised platform of saplings above a fire pit to smoke the day's catch was a social occasion celebrating the gift of fire by which man tamed the wilderness and turned raw food to cooked before it rotted. Vestiges of this primal meaning hung on in the communal barbecues of plantations, of Fourth of July picnics, of political rallies in nineteenth-century America and down to our own day, so much so that the barbecue has come to mean the quintessential method of American cooking and the abundant hospitality that goes with it.

Typically, American barbecue crossed West Indian smoked meats with

East Indian *kejap,* which English tea traders had Anglicized into "ketchup" and "catsup." Until tomatoes became plentiful in the mid-nineteenth century, ketchup was made of oysters or walnuts, anchovies or mushrooms. Mrs. Mary Randolph, who wrote one of America's earliest cook books, *The Virginia Housewife* (1824), calls for a mushroom ketchup "To Barbecue Shote" (also spelled shoat), the name Southerners give "to a fat young hog." She directs the housewife to cut the shote in quarters, season it with garlic, pepper, salt, red wine, and mushroom ketchup, and bake it in broth until well browned.

Most barbecues today are based on the four elements of salt, sweet, sour, and hot in the seasoning, varied according to the cut of meat, the kind of wood, and the length and intensity of the smoking. Smoking is usually no more than eight to ten hours, largely for flavoring and tenderizing rather than preserving. The meat is sloshed with brine or vinegared water during the smoking to help tenderize it before it is shredded, sauced, and slapped between thumb-thick slices of bread. "I love the barbecue I sho do," Virginia's mother says, "and when anyone on the street smell my barbecue, they wants it too."

The famous country hams of the South take barbecue a step further by salting and smoking pork for much longer periods of time. "I'll tell you how I kills a hog," Virginia's mother tells me. "I hang him up by his back feet, cut his throat, and starve the blood out of him so the meat will be clear and then I butcher em up and salt em down and after he sets in the salt so long, I wash em and smoke em over an oakwood fire and that's your country ham."

The salting of country ham comes from the "sea pickle" of English sailors and the land pickle of European peasants identified especially with Westphalia, in Germany. To make Westphalian ham, sixteenth-century English cook books instructed the housewife to brine it in water, salt, and "peeter-salt" and "so hang it up asmoking" in the chimney above the hearth. Early in the nineteenth century, English cooks began to add a sweetening like sugar, honey, or molasses to the pickle, following the advice of cooks like Louis Eustache Ude. Ude's *The French Cook* was one of the first books on French cooking to be published in the States (1828), and Monsieur Ude carried weight with the English because he had cooked for the Duke of York. His "Receipt to make a Ham better than those of Westphalia" was praised by Eliza Acton in her *Modern Cookery* (1861), copied by Mrs. Beeton, and made famous through York hams. Ude added to the brine both sugar and vinegar before smoking the ham for a month, "as high as possible from the fire, that the fat may not be melted."

By building a separate enclosed smokehouse, a cook could control flame and smoke better than in the chimney hearth, but a house was not required. A hogshead would do, inverted over a pile of sawdust with hams hung from tenterhooks inside. In the South the smokehouse became a standard fixture among plantation outbuildings and because the South clung to its country ways, we still look to the South for our best country hams.

"Their bacon cured here is not to be equalled in any part of the world, their hams in particular," an enthusiastic English visitor to Virginia wrote in 1775. When Mary Randolph tells the Virginia housewife how "To Cure Bacon," she begins by telling her how to fatten a hog, no older than four years and no heavier than 160 pounds, with corn for at least six weeks before slaughtering. Her method of dry salting is the one used by the town of Smithfield today, which mixes salt and saltpeter with black pepper and sugar to cure a ham for three to six weeks before it is dried and smoked for a couple of months over hardwood chips of red oak, apple, pecan, and hickory and finally aged six to eighteen months. The heavy salting and smoking for long preservation requires the cook to soak and boil a Smithfield or similar country ham. Milder cured hams such as those of Parma, Westphalia, and Bayonne require no soaking or "cooking," any more than a smoked salmon does, but are sliced paper thin to be eaten "raw."

Squeezer Ravenel in Greensboro remembered the country hams of her Uncle Royal Hewitt, who cured them in brine and molasses and wrapped them tight in brown paper so the varmints couldn't get in. "At slaughtering time," she recalled, "you'd see hogs hanging in the yard from all the trees and Uncle Royal trained his men to slice his country ham so thin you could read a newspaper through the slice."

As the South clung to its smokehouses, so it clung to its grist mills, and none is more beautifully sited than Mabry Mills in the Meadows of Dan, just across the Virginia border from North Carolina in the Blue Ridge Mountains. This is foxfire country, where farmers like Ed Mabry are still blacksmiths, tanners, and millers, living in a pocket of time as remote from my New York kitchen as Mary Randolph's kitchen is, and yet linked by recipes for hushpuppies and spoon breads and just plain grits. At Mabry Mills a massive waterwheel turns the massive granite stones that grind the meal into grits and that make clear the meaning of "water-ground" or "stone-ground" meal.

Mountain people here still make their own hominy. As Laura George of Robbinsville, North Carolina, says, "To make hominy you have to have a black iron washpot." Laura George's washpot came from her husband, Grady's father, who bought it in 1911 and who was "plumb foolish about hominy." In Laura's day every family had an ash hopper in the backyard to turn wood ashes into lye by dripping water through a hopper filled with ashes into a tub below. To make hominy, Laura says, you build a fire under your washpot and fill it with lye water and shelled corn and let the kernels soak until the hulls float free, but "you pay particular to it and see that the corn kernels don't overcook and lose the hearts of the kernels along with the hulls."

Laura in the Blue Ridge today was doing what Pueblo Indians in New Mexico and Creoles in New Orleans had been doing for centuries, turning corn into big hominy and little hominy. Any foreigner in the South has trouble with the vocabulary of hominy and grits. "Nobody *ever* ate big hominy," said a friend in Columbia. "I ate it once and thought I'd choke, just couldn't squeeze it down it was so awful." "And nobody *ever* says 'hominy grits,' " she went on. "It's just grits." Down in Charleston, however, nobody says "grits," they say "hominy." "One buys grits, cooks it, and the result," Betty Hamilton says, "is *hominy*." It's enough to drive a poor Yank back where he came from, which is maybe the point, for the South still speaks a kind of self-preserving pig-Latin that William Byrd mistook for hoggish grunts.

VIRGINIA'S BARBECUED PORK

"We used to call our place Buzzard's Roost," Virginia Ritter remembers of the farm in Allendale, "cause everythin would come collectin round—pigs and chickens and folks." Also goats. "When Mama used to barbecue goats," Virginia says, "she'd cut em up in slabs and cook em in big Aga pans and make the best barbecue goat you ever had. Up North I buys spareribs. You buy em packaged you get a lot of fat stuck under the bottom, so you get the man at the market to pick up your slab and you looks and see what you want."

Up North I buy spareribs, but down South the favored meat for barbecue is pork shoulder. For early-twentieth-century cooks like Marion Harland, "barbecue" meant "roasting any animal whole . . . usually in the open air." The animal most commonly barbecued was shote, a pig too old to be a suckling but too young to be a hog—a pubescent pig. Mrs. Henrietta Dull's recipe in her *Southern Cooking* (1928) is typical of early barbecue recipes when she directs her man to "make pit four feet wide, 16 or 18 inches deep and as long as necessary." She further directs him to baste the whole pig with a mop of cheesecloth, on the end of a long stick, dipped in a strong salt solution. Down in Atlanta, Georgia, where Mrs. Dull comes from, barbecuing was man's work.

Because it was relegated to men, few recipes for barbecue appear in ladies' cook books until after the Second World War. Women made up for it, however, with recipes for soys and ketchups that evolved into today's spicy tomato-based chili or barbecue sauce. Tomatoes were a late addition to the bottled sauces such as HP and Worcestershire, which English traders developed early in the nineteenth century from the spiced brines they found in India and Malay. Sugar was an even later addition, and a sweet-sour-hot combo became the state of the art for American bottled ketchup only after Francis Heinz of Philadelphia began his pickle factory in 1876.

A sauce called "barbecue sauce" is relatively recent. A *Collection of Choice Recipes* (1903), assembled by The Ladies of Des Moines, Iowa, includes a pair of "chili sauces" based on tomatoes, sugar, salt, vinegar, red peppers, cloves, cinnamon, and allspice. But the earliest sauce named "Barbecue Sauce" I've found is in Louis De Gouy's *Chef's Cook Book* (1939), which uses a French brown sauce, spiked with ketchup, onions, mustard, and Worcestershire sauce.

You can't talk barbecue without talking sauce, because the point is to balance the sweet unguent richness of pork with the cutting edge of a sharp sauce, spiked with mustard, hot peppers, and/or vinegar. You also can't talk barbecue without talking smoke. Deprived of an outdoor pit or a home smoker, you can still get good flavor by baking a salted pork roast and then smoking it quickly on a charcoal grill, using hardwood chips of hickory, oak, cherry, mesquite—whatever—for flavor. Once cooked, the meat is cut from the bone, chopped, and slopped with sauce to eat on a toasted bun. Most public barbecue shacks, up and down the South, put their exactingly smoked and sauced meat on bread no goat or pig would choke down. I like to stuff the meat into pita bread because it makes a good container, but any honest loaf will do.

> 2 tablespoons salt
> 1 tablespoon black pepper
> 1 10-pound pork shoulder (for 5 pounds meat)

Rub seasoning into meat on all sides. Place pork on a rack in a roasting pan and sear in the oven for 10 minutes at 500°. Lower heat to 275°, cover the pan with a lid, and bake until interior temperature of the meat is 170°, about 5 hours.

Toward the end of the baking, heat charcoal on an outdoor grill and place a few hardwood chips on the hot coals. Remove meat from the roasting pan and place it to one end of the grill, away from the direct heat of the coals. Cover the grill with a hood (or improvise one with heavy aluminum foil) and smoke the meat about 20 minutes to flavor it.

When meat is cool enough to handle, remove it from the bone and chop it fine with a cleaver.

Put 1½ cups meat and ½ cup barbecue sauce of your choice on each serving of bread or bun.

Serves 10 to 12.

TOMATO-SOY BARBECUE SAUCE

Virginia says of her barbecue sauce, "The older it is the better it gits. I does my sauce at least two days ahead and I likes the sweety-sour taste the sugar gives, but you can leave it out." I don't like the sweety-sour taste, so I do leave it out. To get a really nonsweet ketchup, I've started here with a version of Mary Randolph's Tomato Soy from *The Virginia Housewife* (1824) and then intensified the sours and the hots to make a nonsweet barbecue sauce.

Mary Randolph calls for a bushel of ripe tomatoes, to be salted for three days, after which "they must boil from early in the morning till night." If boiled sufficiently, she says, "It will keep for many years." Now that we know about the acidity of tomatoes and their keeping qualities, we need boil the tomatoes no longer than it takes to release their juices and evaporate the water to make a thick purée.

4 pounds ripe tomatoes
2 large onions, chopped
⅔ cup red wine vinegar
2 tablespoons salt
2 teaspoons black pepper
1 teaspoon each cayenne pepper and mace
½ teaspoon each allspice and cloves

¼ cup peanut oil
½ cup each red wine vinegar and prepared mustard
¼ cup Worcestershire sauce
3 tablespoons Hungarian paprika
several dashes of Tabasco sauce
juice of 2 lemons

For a tomato-soy sauce, remove core of tomatoes but leave skins on. Stew tomatoes with the onions, vinegar, salt, peppers, mace, allspice, and cloves, covered, for half an hour. Pour into a blender and liquefy. Return to pot and boil the mixture until thick, stirring to prevent burning. Sauce should be very thick and peppery.

For the barbecue sauce, beat remaining ingredients into the thickened tomato purée, bring to a simmer, and adjust seasonings to your taste. If you have any homemade pure ground chili sauce left over from cooking New Mexican, add that too for body and flavor.

Makes 4 to 5 cups.

COUNTRY HAM WITH
BEER AND MOLASSES

If you like dishes made out of a piece of lettuce and ground-up peanuts and
    a maraschino cherry and marshmallow whip and a banana
You will not get them in Savannah,
But if you seek something headier than nectar and tastier than ambrosia
    and more palatable than manna,
Set your teeth, I beg you, in one of these specialties de Savannah.

—Ogden Nash, in *The Savannah Cook Book* (1933),
by Harriet Ross Colquitt

One of the specialties de Savannah is a country ham soaked in blackstrap molasses, tea, and beer, then braised and glazed with mustard, ketchup, and brown sugar. "Good? Well, you'd be surprised," writes Harriet Colquitt, who assembled these recipes for the Colonial Dames House, formerly home of the founder of the American Girl Scouts, Juliette Low. As a former Girl Scout, I was willing to try Harriet's ham, since the packer's directions on most commercial country hams leave the thing too salty, stringy, and tough.

I've learned to soak a Smithfield type of ham two to three days, not just overnight, and here the tea helps counteract the salt. I've also learned not to time ham cooking mechanically by the pound, because the longer you cook it, the less time per pound the ham needs. Old cook books say cook until the bones of the small end are loose. More accurate is a meat thermometer. You should cook until the interior temperature (away from the bone) is 160°. (Remember that the ham is already "cooked" by curing, and 140° is enough to bring out the flavor.) For a ten- to twelve-pound ham, I find three hours' braising is usually enough, particularly since it will cool in the cooking liquid. Braising with molasses and beer tenderizes the meat and again moderates the salt.

Carving is not a problem if you cut a wedge on top near the hock end (in contrast to the big ham end) and slice on the diagonal from the small end to the big one, slicing as paper thin as possible. The cooked ham will keep several days refrigerated, but I freeze the bones for soups and stews. I also like to keep a bag of frozen slices on hand for use in pastas and omelets and vegetable stir-frys.

The main problem with a country ham is finding a pan big enough for soaking and braising. Get a butcher, if you can, to cut off the hock end and you'll have a more manageable beast. Remember that the process is to soak, braise, and glaze, so you do need to start two or three days ahead of serving time.

    1 10- to 12-pound Smithfield or similarly cured country ham
    4 quarts weak tea, cooled
    1 15-ounce bottle blackstrap molasses
    2 quarts beer (any brand)
    1 cup brown sugar
    ½ cup Dijon or similar mustard

Scrub the outside of the ham to remove mold. Cover with the cold tea and add enough cold water to cover the ham in its pan. Soak in a cool place 2 to 3 days.

Drain off the tea and return the ham to the pan. Add molasses and beer, cover pan tightly with foil and a lid. (If you are using a roaster, close the vents to aid steaming.) Bake ham 30 minutes at 500° to bring liquid to the simmer. Lower heat to 290° and bake 1½ hours more. Remove lid and foil, turn ham in its liquid, re-cover tightly with foil and lid, and continue baking until thermometer reads 160°, another 1½ to 2 hours. Remove from oven and let ham cool in its liquid.

Remove rind and all but a thin layer of white fat. Mix together the sugar and mustard and spread over the top, thinning if necessary with the molasses-beer mixture. Return to oven and bake at 400° for about 15 minutes to brown the top. Let ham cool thoroughly before slicing.

Serves 20 to 30.

HUNTER BEEF

Until this century, beef in the American South was, like mutton, a luxury. Where salt pork was a staple of the poor, salt beef, sanctified by its English-ness, was a centerpiece for the rich. The method for preserving a thirty-pound beef haunch, called "hunting beef" or "spiced beef" in seventeenth-century England, was the same as that for a pork haunch: by salt, saltpeter, and spices from the medieval trade routes—cloves, nutmeg, allspice. By the eighteenth century, raw or Barbados sugar was added to preserve and tenderize. Most Americans today are familiar with this salt- and sugar-cured beef through Jewish pastrami, which takes its name from a Rumanian verb meaning "to preserve."

Mary Randolph gave Americans a classic hunter beef recipe in her *Virginia Housewife,* beginning, "Select a fine fat round weighing about twenty-five pounds." Marion Cabell Tyree, in *Housekeeping in Old Virginia* (1879), lists no less than four recipes for this beef, with minor variations in the spicing. The basic method was to hang the beef in a cool place or put it in a tub and rub in the spice mixture every day for three or four weeks. The Virginia housewife then covered it with suet and braised it in a Dutch oven sealed with a flour and water paste, or *en daube*.

Instead of a twenty-five-pound haunch, I use a five- to ten-pound beef roast that I can put in a plastic bag and keep in the refrigerator. Both the salt and sugar draw the meat's juices from within to create brine, and you need to turn the bag once a day for a week to ten days until the beef is thoroughly pickled. (The meat will shrink by a third.) You then braise it in a little liquid, cool it, and weight it so that you can slice it thin.

> 1 5-pound rump or round roast
> ½ cup kosher or sea salt
>   optional: ½ teaspoon saltpeter (for color)
> ¼ cup brown sugar, packed
> 3 tablespoons black pepper
> 2 tablespoons each ground cloves and nutmeg
> 1 tablespoon allspice
> ½ cup beef stock

Remove all fat and skin from the outside of the roast. Mix salt with saltpeter, sugar, and seasonings and press the mixture into the meat on all sides. Put meat into a plastic bag and refrigerate, turning the bag every day, for 7 to 10 days.

When ready to cook the meat, remove it from the marinade, place in a tightly fitting casserole with the beef stock (or place the meat in foil within a casserole, pour the stock over the meat, and seal the foil), cover closely with a lid, and bake at 290° for about 2 hours.

Turn the meat over and let it cool in its own juice. Drain, wrap it in plastic, weight it down with a board and heavy can, and chill in the refrigerator until ready to use. It will keep for weeks. "It is a delicious relish at twelve o'clock, or for supper," Mary Randolph says, "eaten with vinegar, mustard, oil or salad." Or with the spicy hot peanut sauce that follows.

Serves 10.

SPICY PEANUT SAUCE

"A remarkable peculiarity of this plant is that the flowers insert their ovaries into the ground, where they complete their growth, and where the seeds or nuts ripen." So Vilmorin-Andrieux's *The Vegetable Garden* (1885) explained the peanut to Europeans. Although native to Brazil, the goober or ground-nut, as it was called, became part of southern earth-food by way of the Portuguese slave trade. Because the nut was as nutritious as it was transportable, slavers cultivated the plant in West Africa in order to fatten slaves on the long Atlantic crossing.

When George Washington Carver boosted the peanut to replace cotton as the staple crop of the South, the names of peanut varieties boosted the South: Georgia, Tennessee red, early bunch Virginia, Virginia running. By the time the peanut arrived, settlers had already learned from the Indians how to turn indigenous nuts into butters and "milks," so peanut uses were more varied in the South than elsewhere. While nothing is more delicious than green peanuts boiled and salted in the shell, as sold in the market at Charleston, peanut sauce is also fine with the salt meats of the South. If we've discovered spiced salt beef through pastrami, we've also discovered spiced peanut sauces through the cooking of southern China and Malaysia. In such sauces peanuts provide a bland oil to bind the salt of soy and the heat of chili to the sweetness of fruit.

> 1 cup dry roasted peanuts, or more as needed
> 1 cup beef broth, or more as needed
> 2 tablespoons pure ground chili
> 1 tablespoon soy sauce, or to taste
> ¼ cup plum, cherry, or raspberry jam

Put ingredients in order in a blender and liquefy. Taste and adjust seasoning. To thin, add more broth; to thicken, more peanuts. Serve in a sauce bowl with beef or pork.

Makes about 2 cups.

COLLARD GREENS

I got yellow yams
From Birmingham
I got greens from New Orleans.
I got the greenest greens I ever seen.
And I sure seen
A whole lot of greens.

Anyone born in the South has seen a lot of greens, especially collard greens. "Mosly I remember everybody in the South plantin collards on Good Friday cuz that was good luck," Virginia remembered. "They be ready by August up North but I never eat my collards until the frost falls cuz they seems to be more tender. In summer they be more bitter and on the chewy side and in summer they takes maybe thirty minutes to cook. Winter greens don take no more than half that time. I don like em on the cooked up side. I likes to know what I'm eatin."

Everybody in the South has his own way of fixing greens and is as proud of them as Virginia's mother was. A lively friend of Carolina Gribble's in Columbia told me that collards were the high point of her annual Christmas dinner of okra, rice, tomatoes with bacon and green pepper, field peas, pork loin roast, cornbread, and *greens*. "I make the *best* collards," she says, "because I remove the stems, roll the leaves, cut across them, parboil them, throw the water out and start all over. Parboiling takes the bitterness out." You don't have to cook greens with a hog jowl or fatback or pig's foot, but "it do taste more better that way," Virginia says.

> 1 smoked ham hock, or ½ pound fatback
> 3 pounds collard greens
> 1 small hot pepper
> black pepper to taste

Split ham hock and cover with cold water. Bring to a simmer and let cook, covered, until tender, 2 hours.

Meanwhile, wash the greens well and strip the large leaves from their stalks. Fold or roll several leaves together lengthwise and cut them crosswise into ¼-inch-wide strips.

Add them to the cooked ham hock with the seasonings, cover tightly, bring to a boil, lower heat, and simmer about 15 minutes for winter greens, 30 to 45 minutes for summer greens.

Serves 6 to 8.

YELLOW AND WHITE TURNIP ROOTS

In the South the turnip hill and sweet potato hill were both root cellars to protect the garden harvest through the winter. The manuscript collection called *Martha Washington's Booke of Cookery* (1749) tells us how to dig a turnip trench in the root cellar in the basement of the house or in the yard outside: "though it be out of dores, it matters not" after Michaelmas. A winter turnip hill was necessary to Mary Randolph's many recipes for turnips mashed, puréed, ragouted, and in the spring there were turnip tops—"the shoots which grow out, (in the spring,) from the old turnip roots"—to be simmered with bacon and salt and served as a hot salad.

Mixing together white turnips and the yellow turnips sometimes called Swedes or rutabagas remains a custom of the South, although the yellow turnip is little appreciated elsewhere in the States. Virginia likes to slice up a large yellow turnip on top of her collard greens to steam. "I likes the look of it," she says, "because it's all green and yeller on the plate."

> 2 large yellow turnips (rutabagas)
> ½ pound salt pork, diced
> 1 teaspoon sugar
>   black pepper to taste
> 4 large white turnips

Peel yellow turnips and cut each in half. Lay cut side down and slice vertically into ½-inch slices. Cut the slices in half.

Sauté the salt pork in a heavy casserole about 5 minutes to render fat. Lay the yellow turnips on top, sprinkle with half the seasonings, cover tightly, and simmer 20 to 30 minutes.

Peel white turnips, cut them the same way, and place them on top of the yellow turnips. Season, cover, and steam until both turnips are tender, 10 to 15 minutes more. Pour into a serving dish and mix the two.

Serves 6 to 8.

CORNFIELD PEAS AND COCONUT RICE

In *Housekeeping in Old Virginia* (1879), Marion Cabell Tyree quotes verbatim Mozis Addums' "Resipee for Cukin Kon-Feel Pees": "Gather your pees 'bout sun-down. The folrin day, 'bout leven o'clock, gowge out your pees with your thum nale, like gowgin out a man's eye-ball at a kote house. . . . It fattens you up, makes you sassy, goes throo and throo your very soul." "Some says cornfield and some says black-eye peas," Virginia explains, and like the hoppin' John of Louisiana, these beans are a staple of soul food because they are cheap and nourishing.

Mozis Addums cooked his peas with fried saltback, raw tomatoes, and brown sugar. Virginia favors hog jowl and coconut juice. Coconuts were plentiful in the South because of the West Indies, which accounts for the region's plentiful coconut cakes and pies. Here the whiteness of coconut milk shows off the black-eyed look of the peas, besides adding a creamy sweetness to the rice.

2 cups dried black-eyed peas
1 hog jowl, ham hock, or split pig's foot
1 onion, chopped
2 cloves garlic, mashed
1–2 small red hot peppers
salt and black pepper to taste
1½ cups long-grain rice
1 cup coconut juice and milk (from 1 coconut)*

Put the peas and hog jowl in a pot with the onion, garlic, and seasonings and cover with cold water. Bring to a boil, remove scum, cover pot, lower heat, and simmer gently for 1 hour. Add rice and liquid to cover, return to the simmer, cover tightly, and cook until both rice and beans are tender, 20 to 30 minutes.

Remove jowl and cut meat from the bone. Chop meat and put back with the peas and rice. Stir in the coconut liquid and warm it over low heat without letting it simmer.

Serves 6 to 8.

VARIATION: To make a delicious cold salad, drain the peas and rice, mix with chopped red and green peppers, green onions, and celery tops, and dress with a little warm bacon dripping or oil and vinegar.

---

* With an ice pick punch 2 holes through 2 of the black spots in the shell known as "eyes." Shake out the juice inside and save it. Bake shell at 350° for 20 minutes. Put it on a chopping board and cover it with a towel. Split the shell by hitting the shell through the towel with a hammer. Peel off the shell and inner brown skin and put pieces of white coconut flesh in a blender. Add 1 cup boiling water and liquefy. Press the coconut milk from the shredded coconut through a strainer and add the milk, plus the reserved juice, to the rice.

CHITTERLINGS WITH RICE

In the South I didn't encounter a single white person who had ever eaten chitterlings, or pig intestines. "Chittlins? You gotta draw a line somewhere." I did meet a few blacks who admitted their mamas used to make them, but I didn't find any enthusiasm for them until I talked to Virginia's mama. "You got to wash them chittlins good," she said. "You pour warm water through them, then cold water, then turn them inside out and wash some more. We used to soak em in salt for a day to soften em up, then wash em again and put em in a pot with salt and pepper and two or three pods of red pepper and they gets tender in about an hour. Then we cut em in pieces three or four inches long or tie em in knots and cut where the knot is at. Then we roll em in a little bitty flour and deep-fry em or leave as they is and pour vinegar over em. Then we cook the rice in that chittlin gravy and it get so dry it just fall apart cause I don't cook no gummy rice."

If you slaughter your own hogs, there's no shortage of chittlins. Up North, however, I found that the only way to buy them was in ten-pound frozen blocks, fortunately cleaned. But they still need to be washed thoroughly and turned inside out to remove all particles of fat. The only container big enough in my apartment to hold them was the bathtub, where they defrosted overnight in cold water, then lay in salt water six hours before they were ready for washing and defatting. They looked like a tub of dirty laundry and I cannot deny that my bathtub retained their distinctive odor long after they left tub for pot. Their taste is distinctive as well, chewy and filling, and unlikely to replace potato chips as a national finger food. But for innard lovers like myself, who savor the peculiar textures of tripe or of sausages like *andouille* made with pig guts, there is a satisfaction to this earthy food as primal as the imitative magic by which you eat guts to get guts.

Ten pounds, however, is a heap of chittlins. Once you have thawed, cleaned, and stewed them, freeze half of them for later use. Five pounds at a time will go a long way.

10 pounds chitterlings, cleaned and frozen
1½ pounds kosher salt
   optional: 1 hog maw
1 large onion, chopped
2 stalks celery, chopped
3 carrots, chopped
2 cloves garlic, mashed
1 bay leaf
2 red pepper pods
¼ cup vinegar
1 tablespoon black pepper
2 cups each corn flour and all-purpose flour
   oil for deep frying
4 cups long-grain rice
   garnish: 2 large onions, chopped

In a large container, cover chitterlings with cold water and defrost overnight. Clean them under running water and remove all fat particles. Return them to the container and pour in the salt. Cover again with cold water and let sit for 6 hours to soften them. Wash well to remove the brine.

Put chitterlings in a pot for cooking with ½ cup water. Add the optional hog maw, chopped vegetables, and seasonings. Cover tightly and steam until they are fork tender, adding more water if needed—about 1 hour. Cut them in 3-inch lengths and shake them in a paper bag full of flour to coat them. Heat oil in a wok or heavy skillet and deep fry the chitterlings a few at a time. Keep them warm in a low oven while cooking the rice.

Pour 6 cups of the pot liquid into a smaller container for the rice, add the rice, bring to a simmer, stir once, cover pot tightly, and steam 15 minutes. Serve on a platter surrounded by half the chitterlings and pass a bowl of chopped onions along with it.

Serves 15 to 20.

HOG'S HEAD CHEESE

Among southern blacks and whites, hog's head cheese and hominy are still a good-luck meal for Christmas and New Year's, just as *posole* is in the Southwest. In nineteenth-century cook books, the head of a hog was one of the most important of its many parts. In *Housekeeping in Old Virginia,* we find Jowl and Turnip Salad and four or five recipes for Pig's Head Stew, including an interesting one in which you remove all meat and bones from inside the head, chop the meat with liver and hard-cooked egg yolks, sew up the head with the mincemeat inside, stew it, and serve it in brown gravy with walnut ketchup.

The head was also a valued part of soused pig, "soused" being a word we get from the English to mean "pickled" in salt and vinegar. From the French we get the notion of "head cheese" (*fromage de tête de porc*), to mean meat from a pig's head, stewed and chopped, preserved in a vinegared aspic made from its own gelatinous bones. It's the bones that make a good head cheese, but getting the head can be troublesome.

In Mary Randolph's day the Virginia housewife could easily follow her directions to first "take out the brains." Today a hog's head, which must be sought in a specialty butcher shop, comes split in half, clean as a pig's whistle, all bristles gone, teeth sweetly bared, the eyes conveniently removed along with the brains. Half a head is as good as a whole one unless you're serving an entire plantation, but an additional pig bone from tail or foot will help produce the stiff gelatin that makes head cheese good.

> half a hog's head, cleaned
> 2 pigs' tails, or 1 split pig's foot
> 1 large onion, chopped
> 4 carrots, chopped
> 2 stalks celery, chopped
> ⅓ cup white vinegar
> 1 tablespoon salt
> 1 teaspoon black pepper
> ¼ teaspoon each cayenne pepper, powdered ginger, nutmeg or
>   mace, and allspice
> 2 bay leaves, crushed

Put hog parts in a deep kettle and cover with cold water. Bring gently to a boil and remove scum. Add remaining ingredients and simmer until the meat falls from the bones, 2 to 3 hours.

Remove pork pieces from the liquid and chill the liquid so that the fat solidifies and you can skim it from the top. Cut meat from the bones and chop it. Reduce liquid by boiling until the taste is strong and spicy.

Pack meat in a large mold (or 2 or 3 small ones such as bread pans), pour the liquid over, and refrigerate. The flavor improves if you make this 2 or 3 days ahead.

Serves 10 to 15.

GREEN CORN AND CRACKLING BREAD

Books like *Housekeeping in Old Virginia* are invaluable in showing how long the corn-pone and ash-cake tradition lasted in the rural South. Here is a recipe contributed by "Mrs. S.T." for the 1879 collection, which tells the cook to knead her cornmeal with water, make it into cakes, "sweep a clean place on the hottest part of the hearth," put the cakes on it, cover them with hot ashes, then wash and wipe dry before eating. If you put the cake on a cabbage leaf and cover it with another, you can dispense with the washing.

The same collection tells a modern reader how "To Cure Lard" and get cracklings from it. As soon as the fat is taken from the hog, it is washed, chopped, and boiled briskly with a little water "until the cracklins begin to brown." They should be light brown and crisp and sink to the bottom when done. In the South you can buy cracklings in a bag at the supermarket. Up North, you'll have to beg fresh pork fat from the butcher and render your own cracklings or else substitute fried and crumbled bacon. I've tried using crisply fried pork rind but the bits don't dissolve in the cornmeal the way cracklings or bacon does. Nuggets of fresh sweet corn (called "green corn" in the old days) give an added texture and sweetness to this most southern of all corn pones.

1 ear corn (to give 1 cup kernels)
2 eggs, beaten
2 cups yellow or white stone-ground cornmeal
2 teaspoons baking powder
½ teaspoon salt
1 cup buttermilk
1 cup pork cracklings
2 tablespoons pork fat

Hold corn cob vertically and cut the kernels down in rows. With the dull side of the knife, scrape the "milk" from the cob. Mix corn and this milk with the beaten eggs. Mix the meal thoroughly with the other dry ingredients and add. Beat in the buttermilk and cracklings.

Heat pork fat on top of the stove in a heavy cast-iron skillet or baking pan. When fat is bubbling, pour in the batter and smooth the top. Put in oven and bake at 400° for 25 to 30 minutes. Cut into wedges or squares.

Makes 9 to 12 pieces.

CREAMY GRITS

Never call it "Hominy Grits"
Or you will give Charlestonians fits!

So warns the Junior League of Charleston in their *Charleston Receipts* (1950). Columbians also give Charlestonians fits by calling cooked grist "grits." Columbians are very particular about their grits. Fred Gantt of Columbia explained to me how he would grind corn kernels in a home grinder to get the exact texture he wanted in the cornmeal. Creaminess would come in the cooking. Fred achieves creaminess in his grits by an initial fast boil, followed by long and slow cooking partly in milk to "meller them down." Some add salt, some a pinch of soda, some use only soft spring water in quest of ultimate creaminess. Some go so far as to add peanut butter to their grits, but classicists deplore such innovative lengths.

Everyone agrees that creamy grits requires lengthy cooking. You first add water to the meal and boil it hard five minutes, stirring constantly to avoid lumps. Then you cover and simmer on the lowest possible heat for at least one or two hours. "The longer you cook it, the better it gets," says Fred. Some, of course, resort to a pressure cooker, which does the job in thirty to forty-five minutes. And some cheat altogether and buy quick or instant grits. But if you don't make grits 365 days a year for breakfast, lunch, and dinner, it's worth tasting the real thing by buying stone-ground meal and by cooking it lovingly and slowly until it's as creamy as the large hunks of butter you will add at the end.

    1 cup stone-ground grits
    3½ cups water
    1 cup milk
    1 teaspoon salt
    ¼ pound (1 stick) butter

Cover grits in a saucepan with the water, bring to a boil while stirring, and boil hard uncovered, stirring constantly, for 5 minutes. Add milk and salt, return to the simmer, cover tightly, and steam over lowest possible heat. Remove lid after an hour, stir, and add more water if meal seems too stiff and in danger of scorching. When meal is smooth and creamy, beat in the butter and serve.

Serves 4.

OWENDAW HOMINY BREAD

Leftover grits are as important to southern cooking as grits freshly made. Many people simply pour their hot grits into a tall glass tumbler, which serves as a mold. When the grits are cold, they stick together the way any cornmeal mush does, so it's easy to slide them out, slice them, and fry the slices in butter or bacon fat until they are crisp and brown.

One of the oldest recipes for leftover grits is a breakfast bread called variously "old-time hominy bread," "grits bread," and "Owendaw or Awendaw bread." The final name suggests an Indian origin, but it is really a kind of spoon bread using raw grist and cooked grist, leavened with eggs and enriched with milk and butter to make a batter like a "rich boiled custard," says *Housekeeping in Old Virginia.* Proportions vary widely, from a custardy to a grainy cornbread, depending on the amount of uncooked grist used. "Like all of the spoon breads," Blanche Rhett writes in *Two Hundred Years of Charleston Cooking* (1930), "it should be eaten very hot with much butter." Because this is a flat batter bread leavened only with eggs, it will puff slightly and fall back as it cools. I like a little black and red pepper in it, but that's not orthodox Owendaw.

> 1½ cups cooked grits (½ cup uncooked)
> ¾ cup uncooked grits
> 1 cup sour milk
> 3 eggs
> 4 tablespoons butter
> 1 teaspoon salt
> ½ teaspoon black pepper
> ⅛ teaspoon cayenne pepper

Put all ingredients but 2 tablespoons of the butter into a blender and process until smooth. Heat the reserved butter in a 10-inch cast-iron skillet until bubbling, pour in the batter, and then bake at 375° until the top is nicely browned, 30 to 45 minutes.

Serves 6 to 8.

12
Country Foods

The difference between cooking up North and down South is the ruralism of
the South. It's tempting to put a high nostalgic gloss on the pleasures of country cooking, but there are voices past and present to remind us of the costs of
rural life. One voice, from 1856, is Sally Baxter Hampton's, a New Yorker
who married the owner of Woodlands Plantation near Columbia, South Carolina, and despaired of Christmas dinner. "In luxurious and well-trained New
York households, Christmas preparations consist of little more than an order
to the butcher, the confectioner, and telling the cook how many are coming to
dinner," she wrote, but here her duties were "daily and exhausting." She had
to measure and distribute all the ingredients needed for the day by the cook,
to preside over the hops and yeast kettle for the Christmas loaves, to select the
poultry and game, to direct the cutting of a saddle of mutton, and to supervise
all the cakes, pies, and confections. "These are all necessary chores of the
Southern housekeeper," she said, "and I am afraid that as a Northern woman,
I am woefully untrained for my job."

Another voice is Virginia Ritter's, in 1984, recalling life as a sharecropper a century after Sally's complaints as the mistress of Woodlands. "We wuz
always workin when we were sharecroppers to pay off our debts at the end of
the year but it seem like the end never come," Virginia told me. "The owner
say you owe so much for fertilizer, so much for seeds, and we jes keep on
workin. My mama come through because she was always doing extra.
Mama'd make fish sandwiches and chicken sandwiches for the big dance on
Saturday nights or we'd go out and collect straw for brooms and sell em and

we'd go round and work for white folks houses on the weekends and I said when I was a kid that onc't I got away I wuzn't ever goin to work for no farm man agin."

But even when Virginia shed the farm, she couldn't shed her country roots. I asked her for a recipe for raccoon when she told me that her sister had six 'coon in her freezer from the fish man who sells 'coons, 'possums, mushrats, rabbits, squirrels, and turtles, whenever they come around. "What you doin given her a 'coon recipe?" her sister asked. "White people don eat 'coon." I never did coax a 'coon from Virginia but I did coax a recipe. "You have to muss it, take the fat off around the neck and shoulders and thighs— that's what we call the 'muss,' the oil glands that smell strong—cuz otherwise you taste all that wildness in it. Be sure you buys it with the head on so's you know what you're buyin and then cut it up like a rabbit and let it soak over- night in a little vinegar and salt and pepper. Then you wash it off, put it in a pot with fatback and red pepper, and simmer 'til it gets real tender. Then I brushes it with barbecue sauce and puts it in the oven so's the sauce gets all through. You pick it up one bone at a time and the meat jus slides right off the bone."

Game cooking is still part of daily cooking in the South because the tra- dition of game privileges never ended. Anna Wells Rutledge, in her 1979 in- troduction to *The Carolina Housewife* (1847), quotes a traveler named Lawson who stopped with the French in 1701 along the Santee River and wrote that there were so few laws about game privileges in Carolina that "A poor Labourer, that is Master of his Gun, hath as good a Claim to have con- tinued courses of Delicacies crowded upon his Table, as he that is Master of a greater Purse." Native Indians, on the other hand, may have had laws of their own, for Lawson was later burned at the stake by Indians in North Carolina.

Squeezer Ravenel told me that the hunting was so good on her father- in-law's plantation at Hickory Hill in South Carolina that he sold it to E. F. Hutton up North, who wanted land to hunt on. After the deal was made, Mr. Hutton is reported to have said, "Mr. Ravenel, it's been nice knowing you but you're about the poorest business man I know. I would have paid you twice the price for it." And Mr. Ravenel smiled and said, "I would have sold it for half as much."

Game didn't get into the cook books much because game cooking was taken for granted, but recently the South Carolina Wildlife and Marine Resources Department republished their fine *South Carolina Wildlife Cookbook* (1981–82), with recipes ranging from how to skin a rattlesnake to how to pluck a marsh hen. "You don't pluck a marsh hen, you peel it," Betty Hamilton notes. "The skin, feathers and all, comes off like a glove." "Nothing comes into my house unless it comes cleaned," Carolina Gribble says forcefully, suggesting an endless succession of marsh hens and wood ducks and grouse that some of us up North would give an eye tooth for the opportunity to clean.

That game birds were not wholly unappreciated in early cook books, however, is clear in a recipe for "rice birds," or bobolinks, quoted by Anna Rutledge from *The Carolina Rice Cook Book* (1901):

> Select the fattest birds, remove the entrails, bake them whole or split them up the back and broil. Permit no sacrilegious hand to remove the head, for the base of the brain of the rice bird is the most succulent portion. . . . Use no fork in eating. Take the neck of the bird in the left hand and his little right leg in the right hand. Tear away the right leg and eat all but the extreme end of the bone. Hold the bill of the bird in one hand and crush your teeth through the back of the head, and thank Providence that you are permitted to live.

Low-country cooking meant, as we have seen, rice cooking, whether it was the rice birds that haunted the marshes, rice breads (for which *The Carolina Housewife* gives thirty-six separate recipes), or rice main dishes with tomatoes, shrimp, or beans. "Charlestonians take rice very seriously," Betty Hamilton warns, and cites a local joke about the difference between a Charlestonian and a Chinaman: "A Chinaman lives on rice and worships his ancestors. A Charlestonian lives on his ancestors and worships rice."

"Perlews" are high-table rice dishes and "chicken bogs" are rice dishes so low you don't need a table, just an empty tin can, rice, water, a piece of chicken, and lots of black pepper. A tonier version of chicken bog, Ben Moise tells me, is the ubiquitous Buford (spelled Beaufort) stew, which in Beaufort County is known as "the pot." Here rice is made into a kind of nonthickened gumbo, full of sausage, shrimp, corn, and celery. A rice-loving insurance executive, Bill Shealy, was happy to spell out details. "Put on a pot of water and salt, add your smoked sausage, your corn, your shrimp, and turn the fire off for the shrimp. Scoop it all out onto a big platter and let them at it. They gotta peel the shrimp themselves. It's a drinking man's meal. In fact, it tastes better after you've had a whole lot to drink."

A lot of one-pot cooking in the South springs not only from the improvised campfires of drinkers and hunters, but from the communal cooking pots of the blacks. In the 1930s a former sharecropper who became a maid for white folks in Memphis liked to "recollect how us Prentices had the grab habit at the table, most everything we had to eat all in one pot on the hearth or kitchen table, and now me steppin' round like a bird on sore claws, passin' eats one at a time."

Many traditional dishes of the South are still one-pot dishes, although the contents may have changed. Until the turn of the century, Brunswick stew, named probably for a hunters' stew cooked for a political rally in 1828 in Brunswick County, Virginia, contained squirrels and not namby-pamby chickens. Southerners were always big on squirrels. Marion Harland's *Common Sense in the Kitchen* (1884) has an entire section labeled Squirrels—Ragouted, Broiled, Stewed, noting that "the large gray squirrel is seldom eaten in the North, but is in great request in Virginia and other Southern States."

Besides one-pot cooking, there should be a category for down-home southern cooking, halfway between the earth cooking of collards and the fancy cooking of syllabubs, that covers the fry pan and pickle jar. All those good fritters of fresh garden corn and okra, not to mention chicken crisp as only hog's lard can make it. And all those vegetables and fruits preserved in brine or sugar or both, the sweety-hots like "chow-chows" and the clove-spiked watermelon rinds, tiny crab apples, pickled peaches and chutneys, and that southern serendipity, Jerusalem artichoke pickles. No wonder it made Twain cry to think of what he'd left behind: "The North seldom tries to fry chicken and this is well: the art cannot be learned north of the line of Mason and Dixon, nor anywhere in Europe."

PRESSED DOVE

"I hate to admit it," Squeezer Ravenel says, "but we've got so many doves we've started popping out the breasts and discarding the rest." A mourning dove yields but two good bites per breast, so you need a lot of doves. As with other game birds—quail, woodcock, wild duck—the breast is what you're after, and to get the juicy goodness of it, you should either braise it very slow or fry it very fast. To remove dove breasts, split the bird down the back, peel off the skin covering each breast, insert your thumb under the lower rib end of each breast, and work the flesh loose until you can pull the meat out in one piece.

To speed the frying, Squeezer weights the breasts in a cast-iron skillet or "iron spider," as she calls it, with a cast-iron pot lid. She then makes a little pan gravy for "dove essence."

To freeze uncooked breasts, she puts them in rinsed-out milk cartons and covers them with water, since freezing them in a block of ice prevents airburn.

  ¼ pound (1 stick) butter
  8 dove breasts
    salt and pepper to taste
  ½ cup red wine
    optional: chopped fresh thyme or rosemary

Melt half the butter in a large heavy frying pan, and when it bubbles put in the breasts and weight them evenly with a heavy lid or a smaller skillet. After 3 minutes, turn them over, sprinkle with salt and pepper, and weight them again. They should be done in 2 to 3 minutes. Remove them to a warm platter. Add wine to the pan juices and beat in the remaining butter. Season to taste and, if you like, add some fresh herbs like thyme and rosemary.

Serves 2 to 4.

FRIED CATFISH AND HUSHPUPPIES

The South is particular about its catfish. Whites eat only freshwater catfish from the rivers, while blacks eat seawater catfish at the mouths of the rivers. "Catfish must be cooked quite fresh," Mrs. Porter warns in her *New Southern Cookery Book* (1871), "if possible, directly out of the water." She preferred to fry them whole, scored with gashes and touched with cayenne along the incisions. "They are very nice dipped in a batter of beaten egg and grated bread-crumbs," she finds, "or they may be done plain, though not in so nice a way, with Indian meal instead of bread-crumbs."

The catfish fries memorialized in *Green Pastures* or *Porgy and Bess* were done quite nicely in Indian, meaning corn, meal and buckets of boiling lard to flavor both the fish and the Indian-meal hushpuppies that were fried when the fish was done. But don't believe a word about how hushpuppies got their name, like "Ole Mammy hears the dogs a howlin and throws some pone cakes out the window, hollerin, 'Hush up, puppies.'" The name did not appear in print until 1918, but deep-fried corn batter flavored with minced onions is one of the standbys of nineteenth-century cook books. The virtue of this particular corn pone is the fish-flavored oil in which it cooks, to make it a Yankee version of England's fish and chips.

Of course you can substitute other fish for catfish. Up North, Virginia Ritter favors gray mullet, especially in the winter when the fish have roe. Small fish you can fry whole and nibble from the bone. Otherwise, you need firm-fleshed fish for fillets. "I share my fish when it get done—" Virginia says, "sometimes—if anyone come home before I eats it."

> 2 pounds thick fish fillets (catfish, mullet, halibut)
>   salt and black and cayenne pepper to taste
> 1 egg, beaten
> ¼ cup milk
> 1 cup corn flour (or *masa harina*) or mixed cornmeal and wheat
>   flour
>   fat for deep frying

Hushpuppies
> 2 cups yellow or white cornmeal
> 2 tablespoons all-purpose flour

1 tablespoon baking powder
1 teaspoon salt
½ teaspoon each black and cayenne pepper
¼ teaspoon baking soda
1 large onion, minced
2 eggs, beaten
1 cup buttermilk

Cut fillets crosswise into 2 or 3 large pieces. Sprinkle with seasonings, wrap in plastic, and refrigerate for an hour or more.

Beat egg with milk, dip the fish in the egg and then corn flour. Heat oil in a wok or heavy skillet to 375°—hot but not smoking—and fry fish, a few pieces at a time, until golden brown. Drain on paper towels. Keep fish warm in a low oven while making the hushpuppies.

Mix the dry ingredients together (a processor is useful here). Add onion, eggs, and buttermilk. Drop the batter by small teaspoonfuls into the hot oil you've used for the fish. Don't crowd them and they will brown in a minute or two. Drain on paper towels and serve on a platter with the fish.

Serves 4 to 6.

PINE BARK STEW

In *200 Years of Charleston Cooking* (1930), Blanche Rhett traced this recipe to a Captain John A. Kelley, of Kingstree, South Carolina, who made it for fellow sportsmen of the Otranto Club. It's one of those hearty fisherman stews hoisted on bacon and fatback or butter, spiked with hot sauce, and cooked in a big iron pot over a pine bark fire on the banks of the Pee Dee River. Captain Kelley gave quantities for a party of thirty and suggested sunfish (redbreast), blue bream, bass, or southern sheepshead, but many just stick to catfish. You can use any firm-fleshed fish, preferably one "fresh out de crick." If you're not hoisting fish from the Pee Dee, you'll find it easier to use fish fillets or thick fish steaks covered with a good fish stock. There's the pork-fat school and the butter school of pine barkers, but I like the taste of both, so I use butter and bacon in the version below. As always, you throw into the sauce what pleases your palate, but Captain Kelley liked a sauce as dark brown as the pine bark that cooked it.

> ½ pound slab bacon
> 4 large onions, sliced
> 2 large potatoes, peeled and sliced thin
> 4 cups fish stock
> 2 pounds firm-fleshed 1-inch-thick fish fillets or steaks
> ¼ pound (1 stick) butter
> ¼ cup ketchup
> ¼ cup Worcestershire sauce
> 1 tablespoon each salt and curry powder
> ½ teaspoon each black and cayenne pepper

Cut bacon crosswise into 1-inch pieces and fry until crisp. Remove bacon with slotted spoon and drain on paper towels. Fry the onions in the bacon fat until golden brown.

Bring fish stock to boil and boil potatoes, covered, 10 minutes.

Remove the potatoes, reserving the stock. Put a layer of half the onions in the bottom of a large casserole, cover with a layer of half the potatoes, then the fish fillets, a final layer of onions, and a final layer of potatoes. Pour in the reserved stock barely to cover. Melt the butter and stir in the seasonings. Pour into the casserole. Bring to a simmer and simmer gently until potatoes and fish are fork tender, about 10 minutes. Serve from the pot, sprinkled with the crisped bacon.

Serves 4.

SHRIMP AND GREEN-CORN PIE

If the shrimp man no longer cries his wares in the streets of Charleston and Savannah, there are still a few remnants of the "mosquito fleet" who throw their nets into creeks, inlets, and rivers to reap the tiny sweet shrimp of the low country. These shrimp were once so abundant that they were served three times a day and no breakfast was complete without them. *200 Years of Charleston Cooking* has no less than seven recipes for shrimp "pie" and three recipes for shrimp paste. The shrimp "pie" is really a kind of custard, thickened with bread, rice, crackers, hominy, or the sweet starch of freshly grated corn. If you like a firm custard, don't separate the eggs. If you like a souffléed texture, separate them as I've done here. If your shrimp are not small, cut them up so that they will cook quickly.

        2 pounds shrimp in the shell
        6 ears fresh corn (to make 6 cups grated kernels)
        4 tablespoons butter
        1 small onion, minced
        3 eggs, separated
        1 teaspoon salt
        ½ teaspoon black pepper
        ⅛ teaspoon mace
        1 cup heavy cream

Cook shrimp in their shells in a large skillet with a few tablespoons water, covered, just enough to stiffen the shells so that they will peel easily, 2 to 3 minutes. Peel shrimp and, if large, cut into small pieces.

Melt butter and cook the onion in it until soft. Cut corn kernels straight down from the cob; with the dull side of the knife, scrape the corn milk from the cobs and add to the kernels. Add onion and corn to the shrimp. Beat egg yolks with seasonings into the cream and add to the shrimp. Whip egg whites until stiff but not dry and fold them into the mixture. Bake, covered, in a well-buttered soufflé dish at 300° for 40 to 50 minutes. Uncover and let top brown an additional 10 minutes.

Serves 6 to 8.

CORN OYSTERS

"Mock Oysters of Corn," Mrs. Porter properly calls them in her *New Southern Cookery Book* (1871), because there is nothing oystery about them except their shape. Occasionally you find a recipe using both corn and real oysters, whole or chopped, to make a fritter, but that's a literalism not to be encouraged. Canned or frozen corn is to be actively discouraged, since the beauty of these mock oysters is the sweetness and lightness of "green" corn bathed in its own milk and wrapped in a froth of egg white.

I had them first at the hands of Cleo Johns, transplanted from Spring Hope, North Carolina, to Temple Israel in Maplewood, New Jersey, where she catered her native country cooking as Cleo's La Cuisine Catering. "On the farm, we raised every string bean, butter bean, lima bean, every ear of corn, and picked it fresh," she says, and it's the freshness that makes these fritters fine. They are best hot from the pot, but I have made them perforce hours ahead and they were still, praise God, delicious.

6 ears fresh white corn
4 eggs, separated
1 cup all-purpose flour
1 tablespoon baking powder
1 teaspoon each sugar and salt
¼ teaspoon each black and cayenne pepper

With a sharp knife cut straight down through the middle of each row of kernels to release the "milk" within. Then cut the kernels from the cob.

Beat the egg yolks until light and add the kernels. Mix the flour with the other dry ingredients and beat into the corn mixture. Beat the egg whites until stiff but not dry and fold in (this is easiest to do with your hands).

Heat 2 to 3 inches of lard or oil in a wok or deep skillet and immediately drop the batter by serving-spoonfuls into the fat. Turn fritters over to brown on both sides. Drain well on paper towels.

Makes about 30 "oysters."

MULACALONG CHICKEN

Of this curiously named dish, Blanche Rhett says in *200 Years of Charleston Cooking,* "Its origin is as mysterious as the flavor of the dish itself." Actually it's only the name that is mysterious, but my guess is that mulacalong comes from the same Anglo-Indian drawer as mullagatawny soup, named from the Tamil *molegoo* and referring to the spices of an Indian curry. At any rate, the dish appears in *The Carolina Housewife* (1847) as a chicken dish flavored with lemon and turmeric. The result is a gentle chicken curry, not too assertive, which I like to mix with a few strips of sweet red bell pepper and puréed fresh corn kernels for thickening.

    1 3- or 4-pound chicken
    4 tablespoons lard, butter, or oil
    2 onions, chopped
    2 cups hot veal, chicken, or beef stock
    1 dried red pepper
    2 teaspoons turmeric
    ½ teaspoon coriander
      salt and pepper to taste
    1 lemon
    1 red bell pepper, cored, seeded, and cut into narrow strips
    1 ear fresh white corn, kernels cut off

Cut chicken in 6 to 8 pieces, pat dry with paper towels, and brown in lard until golden on all sides. Remove chicken and reserve. Brown chopped onions lightly in the same lard. Return chicken to the pan with stock and seasonings.

Grate lemon rind and reserve. Squeeze lemon and add juice to the stock. Bring stock to a simmer and add the bell pepper strips. Purée the corn in a blender, add to the stock, cover pan, and simmer gently 8 minutes. Turn the chicken breasts and simmer until breasts are tender but still faintly rosy, another 5 minutes. Remove cooked breasts to a serving platter and keep warm while the other pieces finish cooking, 15 to 20 minutes.

Transfer remaining chicken to the serving platter and reduce stock rapidly over high heat. Pour sauce over chicken and sprinkle with the reserved lemon rind.

Serves 4 to 6.

SQUEEZER'S
OKRA FRITTERS

"People think I've gone to so much trouble in my cooking when all I've done is run into the garden and pick some itty-bitty okra or squash," Squeezer says, in explaining what makes a good okra fritter. What makes an okra fritter good is itty-bitty okra fresh from the garden. The rest is easy. Or so she says. When I had trouble making Squeezer's fritters up North, she mailed me a package of them, and not even a four-day journey defeated them. I ate up every one.

Squeezer got her recipe from Tom's mother. She slices the okra thin and puts them in a Bisquick pancake batter, seasoned with red and black pepper. "The okra keeps thickening the batter because of the slime in it," she warns, "so keep adding milk as you go to keep your pancake consistency." She makes them into little pancakes three to four inches round and fries them in an inch of hot cooking oil so that they are more deep fried than sautéed.

If you start with itty-bitty okra, you can simply dip the whole okra into a batter and fry it for finger food. Here you slice the okra, which flavors the batter. If you use Bisquick, you'll need one and a half cups to each four cups of okra, but I've used a beer batter here because I like the richer flavor.

Batter

    2 eggs
    ¾ cup beer
    1 tablespoon peanut oil
    ¾ cup all-purpose flour
    1½ teaspoons salt
    1 teaspoon black pepper
    ½ teaspoon cayenne pepper

    1 tablespoon baking powder
    2 pounds baby okra
    oil for frying

Make batter ahead in a blender by mixing all the ingredients but the baking powder, okra, and oil. Let batter sit at least an hour or two.

Slice the okra quickly into ¼-inch slices. Stir the baking powder into the batter, then the okra. Drop batter from a tablespoon into a heavy skillet containing 1 inch of oil that is hot but not smoking. Turn fritters to brown quickly on each side and drain on paper towels.

Makes about 36 fritters.

RED RICE

"Everybody cooks red rice," Betty Hamilton says, for the simple reason that tomatoes are red and plentiful and their juice is good for rice. While *The Carolina Housewife* has a surprising number of tomato recipes for its relatively early date of 1847, Sarah Rutledge did not put them together with rice. She stewed and baked and fried tomatoes, put them in omelets and salads, put them up for the winter and preserved them as paste in two ways: one as a kind of ketchup and the other as a spiced "Italian" purée dried in the sun or oven and rolled into thin sheets. By the time of *Charleston Receipts* (1950), the tomato paste (or often canned stewed tomatoes) goes into the rice, along with bacon, onion, and sometimes okra, to make what others call "Spanish rice." Squeezer Ravenel tells me that she likes her red rice plain, with tomato paste, butter, and fresh herbs from the garden. If you make red rice in the summer, you can also add fresh chopped tomatoes. The main point is not to overcook or overliquefy, so that the rice grains remain separate. Fortunately today we do not have to begin as Mrs. Rutledge did, with instructions on how to "wash and gravel" rice first to remove the starch and then the gravel by rinsing the rice in "a common piggin" (or wooden pail).

1 small onion, minced

4 tablespoons butter

2 tablespoons mixed fresh herbs (thyme, basil, savory, marjoram, oregano)

1 teaspoon salt

½ teaspoon black pepper

¼ cup Italian tomato paste

1 cup long-grain rice

1½ cups boiling water or chicken stock

Sauté onion in butter until soft, add seasonings, tomato paste, rice, and boiling water. Taste for seasoning and adjust. Bring to a boil, stir once, cover, reduce heat, and simmer 15 to 20 minutes. Fluff with a fork and let sit 5 minutes off heat, covered, to fluff more.

Serves 4.

SCRAMBLED EGG PILAU

"Carolina Gold" began when Captain John Thurber brought rice seeds from Madagascar and gave them to one of Carolina's founders, Henry Woodward, sometime before 1694. By 1698, one of the Lord Proprietors, Lord Ashley, shipped to England 60 tons of rice from Charleston. For the next century England imported some 150,000 barrels a year and nearly wiped out America's rice industry during the British occupation of Charleston in 1780 by sending the entire harvest, including seeds, to London. Jefferson helped to replenish Carolina's stock in 1787 by smuggling some Italian rice out of Italy, and by 1840 Carolina was producing 60 percent of all American rice grown in the United States. After the Civil War, however, the plantations started moving west, first to Louisiana, then to Texas and California.

Carolinians adopted the English and French tradition of naming rice dishes "pilau" or "pilaw," which southern voices pronounced "perloo" or "perlew," from the Turkish method of steaming rice with a little onion and fat. Stuffing the rice into a bacon-wrapped chicken produced what Louis Eustache Ude called in 1828 "Chickens à la Turque." In *200 Years of Charleston Cooking* there are thirteen recipes for pilaus, mostly with chicken, but some with okra, squab, or shrimp, and one with scrambled eggs, "a truly marvelous concoction for Sunday night supper."

    1 large onion, minced
    ¼ pound (1 stick) butter
    2 cups long-grain rice
    1 quart boiling chicken stock
    2 teaspoons salt
      black pepper to taste
    6 eggs

Sauté onion in the butter until soft. Add rice and let kernels puff slightly and turn white (3 to 5 minutes). Add boiling stock, salt, and pepper, stir once with a fork, cover pot tightly, and simmer over low heat for 17 to 20 minutes. Beat eggs well with a fork and stir them quickly into the rice. Taste for seasoning.
    Serves 4 to 6.

SWEET-POTATO CORNBREAD

When Virginia cooks up sweet potatoes fancy, she puts half of them into pies and the other half into "poon," or sweet potato bread. Sweet potatoes are as rampant as the kudzu vine all over the South, for the sweet-starchy yellow-orange flesh was a natural staple for breads, cakes, puddings, and pies, not to mention waffles, biscuits, and buns. An early recipe for bread appears in *The Carolina Housewife* under an Indian name, Espetanga Corn Bread, using equal parts of sweet potato pulp and cornmeal, along with milk, eggs, and butter, to make a good pudding, says Rutledge, when served with sugar, wine, and butter as a sauce. She also turns sweet potatoes and cornmeal into a tea cake, made plentifully rich with half a pound of butter, a pound of sugar, and eight eggs. This is the way Virginia likes to enrich her sweet-potato poon, with about a pound of homemade butter, a can of Carnation evaporated milk, and cinnamon "to your taste cuz that's what make sweet potato poon taste good." I've made a much less sweet version, using yogurt instead of milk and cutting down the sugar.

> 1 large sweet potato (to make 2 cups pulp)
> ¼ pound (1 stick) butter
> 4 eggs, beaten
> ½ cup brown sugar
> ½ teaspoon baking soda
> 1 teaspoon each salt and cinnamon
> 1 cup yogurt
> 2 cups finely ground white cornmeal
>   optional: ½ cup each sultana raisins and pecans

Bake or boil the sweet potato in its skin; when cool enough to handle, peel it and purée the pulp. Mix together butter and puréed pulp. Beat eggs with sugar, soda, cinnamon, and salt, and add to the purée. Beat in yogurt, cornmeal, and optional raisins and nuts. Pour into a buttered 9-by-9-by-2-inch baking pan and bake at 350° until browned, 45 to 60 minutes.

Makes 9 to 16 squares.

SALTED BENNE WAFERS

For years the only benne wafers I knew were sweet crisp square cookies that came in a green and white tin box with an old-time kerchiefed mammy on the lid. Sometime during the 1960s the black mammy changed to white, still ker-chiefed, still grinning, in a revisionist denial of the African slaves who intro-duced sesame seeds into this country as "bennes." Oddly enough, more Americans know the unctuous taste of sesame through Near Eastern foods like tahini or sesame pita breads than through the many soups, candies, cakes, and cookies of our own Deep South. Once upon a time, Charlestonians could buy their benne candy from "Maum" Sue, along with groundnut cakes and monkey meat, when she sold her wares in Bedon's Alley. The 1963 edition of *The Carolina Housewife* has a photo of her doing just that. Since recipes for sweet benne cookies are so common, I've opted for a nonsweet salted wafer that makes an excellent drink food and a welcome alternative to pretzels and peanuts.

       1 cup sesame seeds
       2 cups all-purpose flour
       2 teaspoons salt
       ¼ teaspoon cayenne pepper
       ¼ cup lard or shortening
       ¼ pound (1 stick) butter, chilled, cut into 8 pieces
       1 egg, beaten
    2–3 tablespoons ice water
       1 tablespoon sea salt

Toast sesame seeds until golden brown in a skillet or low oven, 4 to 8 minutes. Mix flour with the seasonings. Work in lard and butter with your fingertips as if making pie crust. Beat egg with 2 tablespoons ice water. Mix flour and liquid lightly with a fork. Add sesame seeds and more water, if needed, to make dough barely stick together.

Put dough in a plastic bag and shape it into a long roll about an inch wide. (The easiest shape is a squared roll.) Refrigerate for 3 to 4 hours.

Cut roll into ¼-inch slices and place them on a baking sheet. (They won't spread, so you can place them close together.) Bake at 325° on top rack of oven for 15 to 20 minutes. Sprinkle them with sea salt while still warm.

Makes about 30 wafers.

SESAME SEED SOUP

Among *The Carolina Housewife*'s many intriguing soups is one Sarah Rutledge calls "Soup with (So Called) Green Frogs," which is a broth poured over spinach leaves wrapped around a dumpling of butter, bread crumbs, peas, and egg—the so-called green frogs. Another is Seminole, which asks for one boiled squirrel and broth thickened with hickory nuts, sassafras leaves, or "the tender top of a pine tree." A third one, Bennie Soup, is also based on the Indian method of thickening broth with ground nuts, only this time with sesame seeds. This is a delicious variation on the slightly more usual peanut and oyster soup.

> 1 cup sesame seeds
> 1 pint shucked oysters with their liquid
> 4 cups good fish stock
> 1 dried red pepper, or cayenne pepper to taste
>   salt and black pepper to taste

Toast seeds in a heavy skillet until lightly browned, 4 to 5 minutes. Grind them in a blender with liquid drained from the oysters and with half the fish stock.

Put mixture in a saucepan, add seasonings and remaining stock, and bring liquid to a simmer. Taste for seasoning. Add oysters and simmer until oysters just begin to curl, 2 to 3 minutes.

Serves 4.

CAROLINA SOY SAUCE

Two centuries before Americans identified soy sauce exclusively with China and Japan, Sarah Rutledge and other Carolina housewives were bottling mixtures of highly flavored pickled sauce to enliven broths and sauces and gravies just as we do today. I've included a recipe here for such a soy sauce to indicate how sophisticated these sauces might be in the hands of a good cook accustomed to making everything from scratch. Since the soy sauce calls for mushroom ketchup and walnut pickle, the recipe is in three stages. "Gather your mushrooms early in the morning," Sarah advises the makers of mushroom ketchup. "Take one hundred walnuts, and run a needle through them," she advises the makers of walnut pickle. To get green walnuts so tender they are prickable, one recipe contributor specifies walnuts gathered between the tenth and twentieth of June. Walnut pickle was often turned into walnut ketchup by grinding the walnuts in a mortar, boiling them with spices, adding vinegar, and then straining the liquid into bottles with an addition of grated fresh horseradish.

Walnut Pickle (1 cup)

> 1 cup green walnut meats (or substitute regular walnuts)
> salt for brine
> ½ cup wine vinegar
> 1 slice fresh ginger
> 1 small piece dried red hot pepper
> ¼ clove garlic, mashed
> mace, nutmeg, and cloves to taste

Mushroom Ketchup (1 cup)

> 2 cups chopped fresh mushrooms
> ½ tablespoon kosher or sea salt
> ½ clove garlic, mashed
> cloves, allspice, and mace to taste

Soy Sauce

> 1 can anchovies
> 1 cup Walnut Pickle (see above)
> 1 cup Mushroom Ketchup (see above)
> 2 cups Madeira
> ¼ cup black mustard seeds

To make walnut pickle, boil 2 cups water with 2 tablespoons salt and steep walnuts in this brine for one week. Drain and then soak them in fresh water for 1 to 2 hours. Drain again. Mix vinegar with the seasonings and bring mixture to a boil. Pour over the walnuts.

To make mushroom ketchup, purée mushrooms with salt in a blender or processor, put in a bowl, cover with plastic wrap, and let sit 24 hours. Mix mushrooms, garlic, and spices and boil, covered, for 10 minutes. Strain, bottle, and chill.

To make the soy sauce, put all the ingredients in a pan and boil, covered, 15 minutes. Then liquefy the sauce in a blender, bottle it, and seal in mason jars. "In ten days the soy will be fit for use."

Makes about 4 cups.

JERUSALEM ARTICHOKE PICKLES

When a Southerner says "artichoke," he means that strange root, Jerusalem artichoke. (When he means the globe artichoke that is a thistle and not a root, he says "bun artichoke.") The South is the one place in the country that still loves the tuber Samuel Champlain found the Indians growing on Cape Cod and that the Italians named *girasole* because it was indeed a type of sunflower. The English found it by way of Italy and in typical English fashion transformed *girasole* to "Jerusalem" and *articiocco* to "artichock," but why they put the two words together remains a mystery unless it was a means of damning all things Italian. Gerard in his *Herbal* (1597) provides a clue when he says of the Artichocks of Jerusalem, "which way soever they be dressed and eaten, they stir and cause a filthy loathsome stinking wind within the body."

The South did not pickle artichokes to reduce wind but to preserve their garden produce from southern heat. Southerners must have grown Jerusalem artichokes in untold quantities because old recipes for them are usually by the bushel and not the peck. To make a light (or yellow) pickle—in contrast to a dark (or green) pickle—*The Carolina Housewife* suggests bleaching the tubers in a brine bath before their vinegar soak to keep them from darkening. *Charleston Receipts* has several recipes for artichoke pickle, with small variations in the seasonings, but this one I've adapted from Squeezer's recipe, handed down from Tom's mother, Millie Archer Ravenel, and cut down from three bushels of artichokes to one quart.

4 cups Jerusalem artichokes
2 tablespoons salt
2 cups sliced onions
2 cups cider vinegar
2 tablespoons dry mustard
2 tablespoons sugar
1 teaspoon celery seeds
¼ teaspoon turmeric
pinch of cayenne pepper
1 teaspoon mustard seeds

Wash and scrape artichokes. Dissolve salt in 2 quarts of cold water and soak them overnight. Drain and slice artichokes ⅛- to ¼-inch thick. Layer the slices with the sliced onions in six scalded half-pint jars.

Moisten the mustard with vinegar until it is smooth. Add remaining vinegar and seasonings except for the mustard seeds. Bring vinegar to a boil in a pan and pour over the artichokes and onions. Add several mustard seeds to each jar. Let stand 4 to 6 weeks before using.

Makes 3 pints.

13
Fancy Foods

One of my favorite southern recipes is a recipe for tea rolls handed down in a black family: "1 quart flour; 1 yeast cake; 1 tablespoon lard; 1 tablespoon sugar; big pinch of salt; 1 heavy stone jar; 1 warm place in winter; 1 cold place in summer." Weather conditioned the whole world of southern cookery because the plantation kitchen was kept separate from the house. The cold weather of New England demanded that additional rooms be attached to the main house. The hot weather of the South demanded a separate fire room so the main house could keep cool.

The separation of dining room from kitchen enforced, in turn, the division between white mistress and black cook and produced the kind of specialization of labor that turned slaves into America's first group of professional chefs. When Thomas Jefferson hired a French cook for the White House by offering twenty-eight dollars a month when the going rate was twenty dollars, his chief aim was to guarantee a succession of good cooks at Monticello. "Having been at great expense in having James Hemings taught the art of cookery," Jefferson wrote in 1793, he promised the slave his freedom if he would but promise to train a successor. In the Carolinas slaves were often sent to the eating houses of Charleston for training in the Anglo-French arts of cookery, arts they were expected to pass on to the next generation.

Even if what the planters sat down to eat was "a decanted version," as a southern friend says, of what their slaves ate, the sumptuous hospitality of the South sprung from an abundance of servants. The variety of hot breads in the South and their appearance thrice daily were impossible without a Dinah or two in the kitchen. An English visitor to Virginia in the eighteenth century found its colonists "eating too much hot and new bread, which cannot be wholsom." These were quick breads largely based on corn, which had to be baked fresh since they did not keep the way yeast-leavened wheat loaves did. When wheat became more available, the South clung to soft rather than hard wheat, as it does even today, because soft wheat makes for tenderer shortcakes and biscuits.

With servants, southern colonial housewives could maintain English traditions of manor house cooking, and it is no accident that the first cook book to be produced in America was published in Williamsburg, Virginia, in 1742: *The Compleat Housewife: or, Accomplished Gentlewoman's Companion,* by an Englishwoman, Eliza Smith. The cook book was in its tenth edition in England by the time William Parks, printer, decided to pirate the work for the benefit of his pocket and of colonial housewives aiming for English fashion. The first duty of a gentlewoman, with servants, was to oversee the sweetmeats, that world of preserves, jellies, distillations, and confections, and only secondly to prepare fancy entrees like "pulpatoon of pidgeons" or a "ragoo of pigs-ears."

If quick breads were the province of the black cook, fancy desserts were the province of the mistress and therefore the main point of many nineteenth-century southern cook books. Cakes were the favored dessert more than pies because pie crust doesn't work in "giffy weather," as Betty Hamilton calls it. Cakes and biscuits stand up better to high humidity. Not surprisingly, then, a book such as Mrs. Porter's *New Southern Cookery Book* (1871) devotes twice as many pages to desserts as to all the rest of the courses put together and includes some two hundred cake recipes with fanciful names like Ancient Maiden's Cake, and the instructions: "if the Ancient Maiden's matrimonial prospects are good, frost or ice with icing of proper flavor, otherwise serve plain." Less sinister is Mrs. Porter's advice to have all the main ingredients— flour, butter, sugar, eggs—at uniform temperature and "*warmer* than their average natural heat." The pride of southern cookery, its angel biscuits and coconut cream cakes, sprang from the heat of southern weather.

SALMAGUNDI SALAD

One of the grand high-table salads that eighteenth-century Southerners imported from England was "salamagundi," later called "sallad-magundy" and even "Solomon Gundy." Mary Randolph printed a recipe for it in her *Virginia Housewife* and indicates its dressiness by instructing the housewife to build a ringed hemisphere of minced meats by inverting a bowl on a dish and covering it in layered rings, beginning at the bottom, with minced anchovies, chicken or turkey, hard-cooked eggs (yolks and whites minced separately), scraped ham, celery, and parsley. Around the bowl should go a ring of capers and on top a pyramid of butter. With it should go a small glass of egg dressing "as for sallad." Mary Randolph's probable source was Hannah Glasse, in *The Art of Cookery Made Plain and Easy* (1796), who suggests, in addition, using shredded lemon pulp and greens like sorrel, spinach, lettuce, and shallots with a garnish of horseradish and sliced lemon. She also suggests that this makes a good second course or middle dish for supper, but in these servantless days it makes a good supper dish in itself, composed easily in layers within a glass bowl, as one might compose a California Cobb Salad.

   1 small bunch fresh spinach (or other greens), washed and
      shredded
   1 can anchovies, minced
   4 cups diced cooked chicken
   1 cup diced Smithfield or other smoked ham
   4 stalks celery, chopped
   6 hard-cooked eggs, whites and yolks chopped separately
   3 lemons
   1 cup chopped parsley
   2 tablespoons grated fresh horseradish

Dressing
   2 tablespoons Dijon mustard
   ½–¾ cup olive oil
   3 tablespoons lemon juice
   1 egg, beaten
      salt and pepper to taste

Place spinach in bottom of the bowl for a green "bed." Add in layers the anchovies, chicken, ham, celery, egg whites and yolks, and pulp and chopped peel from 2 of the lemons. Thinly slice remaining lemon. Top bowl with parsley, put the horseradish in a mound in the center, and surround it with overlapping lemon slices.

Make the dressing by beating together the remaining ingredients. Pour into a bowl and serve with the salad.

Makes 4 to 8 servings.

CHARLESTON SHE-CRAB SOUP

As late as the 1930s Blanche Rhett could remember the soft Negro voices of the Charleston crab men waking ladies in their high-ceilinged bedrooms along the Battery with the cry, "She-Crab! She-Crab!" And she could remember the she-crab soup prepared by her able butler, William Deas, "one of the great cooks of the world." In an ideal world, we would all have fresh crabs from the crab man and a butler-cook to clean them and pick out the white meat and roe from the she-crab's shell.

Deprived of these luxuries, anyone can nonetheless make this fine cream soup, flavored English style with sherry, if he can get hold of the orange roe that she-crabs carry in their bellies in spawning season and that gives a quintessential richness to a cream. Since he-crabs, among "the pugnacious Blue Crab," as Euell Gibbons calls them, outnumber she-crabs by 5 to 1, she-crabs are more expensive and more precious. You can of course use good fresh packaged crab meat and even crumbled hard-cooked egg yolks, as *Charleston Receipts* advises desperate housewives, but I would rather substitute some other kind of fresh roe, from cod, salmon, whitefish, or scallop.

Many nineteenth-century recipes call for a flour-thickened soup, English style. I prefer to use egg yolks for thickening and, instead of Worcestershire sauce, grated lemon rind.

1 small onion, minced
4 tablespoons butter
1 pound crab meat (about 12 crabs)
1 quart milk
2 cups light cream
¼ teaspoon each mace and white pepper
½ teaspoon salt, or to taste
¼ cup dry sherry
2 egg yolks
¼ cup orange crab roe
  rind of 1 lemon, grated

Sauté onion gently in the butter, add crab meat, and set aside. Heat milk and cream in the top of a double boiler, add crab meat and onion, seasonings, and sherry, cover, and let steep over very low heat for 30 to 45 minutes.

Beat the egg yolks, pour a little of the hot liquid into them, and then stir the yolk mixture slowly into the soup. Put a spoonful of roe in each soup bowl, ladle in the soup, and sprinkle the top with grated lemon rind.

Serves 4 to 6.

BEEF AND OYSTER SAUSAGES

Another English-derived eighteenth-century recipe calls for minced beef mixed with minced oysters to make round "sausage" cakes of delicious flavor. This is the kind of "made" dish the lady of the plantation would teach her black cook to do or would prepare herself, along with Caveached Mackerel or Ragout of Veal with Sweetbreads. Sarah Rutledge's recipe of 1847 in *The Carolina Housewife* is probably from the same source as that of the "Boston Housekeeper" (Mrs. N. K. M. Lee) who included in *The Cook's Own Book* (1832) an identical recipe. Since our Bostonian got most of her recipes from either Hannah Glasse or Dr. Kitchiner's extremely popular *The Cook's Oracle* (the first American edition published in Boston in 1822), the line from the homeland to the northern and southern colonies is fairly direct.

½ pint shucked oysters, plus their liquid
1 pound beef chuck, ground fine
2 tablespoons butter, softened
4 egg yolks
2 teaspoons salt
½ teaspoon black pepper
¼ teaspoon cloves
⅛ teaspoon mace
1 cup fresh bread crumbs
4 tablespoons melted beef suet or butter for frying

Bring oysters to a simmer in their own liquor. Immediately drain and mince by hand or in a processor. Put in a bowl with the ground meat and 2 tablespoons butter. Beat in 3 of the egg yolks, together with the seasonings.

Form the mixture into patties of about 3 tablespoons each. Beat the remaining egg yolk with 2 to 3 tablespoons oyster liquor. First dip each patty into this mixture, then roll in bread crumbs. Heat the beef suet in a skillet and sauté patties until browned.

Serves 4.

EASY BEATEN BISCUITS

Beaten biscuits were once as indispensable to the old South as slavery. Eliza Leslie reflected Union sentiment when she wrote in her *Directions for Cookery* (1837) that this Maryland biscuit was "the most laborious of cakes, and also the most unwholesome," albeit "there is no accounting for tastes." Confederate sentiment, on the other hand, was reflected postbellum by Mary Stuart Smith, in her *Virginia Cookery-book* (1885). "Let one spend the night at some gentleman-farmer's home and the first sound heard in the morning, after the crowing of the cock, was the heavy, regular fall of the cook's axe, as she beat and beat her biscuit dough."

As cooks left for the North, housewives began to rely on beaten-biscuit machines, which "beat" the dough until it was glossy and "blistered" with air bubbles by cranking the dough between rollers, much like an old-fashioned clothes wringer or modern home pasta machine. Today, however, the food processor or mixer easily substitutes for the hand-cranked biscuit machine or the outdoor "biscuit block" on which the cook would beat her dough with an ax handle.

Beaten biscuits probably date back to the days when biscuits were best preserved by mixing flour with water or egg and without fat. Karen Hess points to a sixteenth-century Bisket Bread of this kind that appears in the *Booke of Sweetmeats* given to Martha Washington. Mary Randolph in *The Virginia Housewife* calls a version of this biscuit "Apoquiniminc Cakes," after a town in New Castle County, Delaware. She adds butter to her flour, egg, and milk, and beats the dough half an hour with a pestle before cutting it into round cakes and baking the cakes on a gridiron.

> 2 cups unbleached white flour
> 1 teaspoon salt
> 4 tablespoons lard or vegetable shortening, chilled
> 4 tablespoons butter, chilled
> ¼ cup each milk and ice water, mixed

Mix flour with salt. Cut lard and butter into small pieces and work into flour, as if making pastry. Pour in milk and water and beat until mixture forms a ball. Continue to "beat" the dough 2 minutes in a processor, 5 minutes in a mixer.

Roll out dough ⅛-inch thick on a lightly floured surface and cut out circles with a 1½-inch biscuit cutter or the lip of a small glass. Or make rounds by hand and flatten them with a rolling pin. Place the rounds on ungreased baking sheets, prick on top with fork tines, and bake at 350° until they just begin to brown on the edges, 15 to 20 minutes.

Makes 36 biscuits.

ANGEL BISCUITS

My major discovery about biscuit making in the South is that, first, the flour is different and, second, practice may not make perfect, but without practice, forget it. In Greensboro, I met up with Ella Barham, who's been catering since the age of fourteen and who learned to cook from her mother and her grandmother, who had eleven children to cook for. Ella gave me a rundown on that cocktail staple of the South, ham biscuits. Ham biscuits are short biscuits, small as a quarter, thin as a dime, split in two, buttered, layered with a thin slice of country ham, put back together, and eaten by the bushel and the peck. "Everybody's weight conscious," Ella says, "so they like them small and then they can ignore how much they're eating."

Ella, like most of the Carolina cooks I met, favors Red Brand flour, made by General Mills "for Carolina families" who insist on soft-wheat flour for tender biscuits. Columbia, South Carolina, produces Adluh flour named for the founder's wife, Hulda (spelled backward). And over in Knoxville, Tennessee, there's White Lily flour. All of these flours are more like pastry flours than bread flours because they are low in gluten, which allows them the crumbly texture of pie crust or "shortenin' bread." All are sold with baking powder and salt already mixed in to make "self-rising" flours.

For regular short biscuits, Ella mixes in two tablespoons Crisco for each cup of Red Brand flour and adds just enough cold milk to hold the dough together, less than a quarter cup. She lets the dough sit a minute or two after mixing, then rolls it out, cuts it into rounds, starts them on the bottom shelf of a 450° oven, and finishes them on the top shelf: total seven to ten minutes maximum. "Most people overcook them," she warns, "and if the tops aren't browned, I just run them under the broiler." To freeze them, she splits them open, puts a slice of butter inside, and freezes them in foil.

When I asked her about angel biscuits, she said, "They're not what I do. I love em but I don't do em because you do what you know how to do." Angel biscuits are a double-light biscuit because they use both yeast and baking powder to leaven the flour. Essentially they are made of very moist buttermilk dough more easily shaped into biscuit blobs than rolled. I'm fond of a Savannah cook book that tells the cook to "de-gunk fingers" after mixing the biscuit dough, then to "scoop" up a blob and "plop" it on a baking sheet.

1 package dry yeast
2 tablespoons very warm (110°–115°) water
5 cups soft-wheat flour
1 tablespoon each sugar and baking powder
1 teaspoon baking soda
1 cup lard or shortening, cut into small pieces
1½–2 cups buttermilk

Dissolve yeast in water. Sift together the flour, sugar, baking powder, and soda. Cut the chilled lard into the flour mixture with your fingertips or pulse a few times in a processor until mixture is crumbly. Turn mixture into a bowl, make a well in the center, and gradually work in yeast and 1½ cups buttermilk, flipping the flour from the outside into the middle. Add more buttermilk as needed to make a dough soft enough to knead. Knead lightly 20 to 30 times, place in a lightly greased bowl, sprinkle with flour, cover with plastic wrap, and refrigerate 6 hours or more.

When ready to bake, shape dough quickly into blobs about 1 inch high and 2 inches wide and place on an ungreased cookie sheet. Let rise in a warm place until doubled. Bake at 400° until lightly browned, 12 to 15 minutes.

Makes 36 to 48 biscuits.

FRESH CORN AND PECAN SPOON BREAD

Spoon bread is to the South what johnnycake is to the North, a matter of endless controversy but most often made with white cornmeal, eggs, butter, and milk and baked either on a griddle or in a greased pan, as *The Carolina Housewife* suggests in its Corn Spoon Bread. You will find dozens of recipes for spoon breads, all "authentic" and widely varied in proportions and results. Spoon bread nowadays has come to mean a form of grits soufflé, with the eggs separated and the whites used for extra leavening. I've taken spoon bread evolution one step further by adding freshly grated corn and some ground pecans, not at all "authentic" but hopelessly good to eat as a dish in itself or as a companion to ham, chicken, and shrimp.

1 cup stone-ground white cornmeal
1 cup boiling water
1 cup buttermilk
3 eggs, separated
3 tablespoons butter, softened
1 ear fresh corn, kernels scraped off or grated
1 teaspoon salt
2 teaspoons baking powder
½ teaspoon baking soda
½ cup pecans, ground fine

In a large bowl, soften cornmeal in boiling water. Mix buttermilk with the egg yolks and add to the cornmeal. Beat in the butter and the grated corn with its corn milk.

Beat egg whites until stiff but not dry. Mix together the salt, baking powder, and soda, and add to the corn mixture. Then mix in the nuts, and finally fold in the egg whites.

Scoop batter into a well-buttered 1½- or 2-quart baking dish and bake at 375° until the top is well browned and a cake tester comes out clean, 50 to 60 minutes.

Serves 8.

NUNS PUFFS

Two names that have disappeared from common usage suggest the airy fancies of southern housewives and their cooks. One was a biscuit or cracker dough of flour and butter rolled no thicker "if possible, than a sheet of paper" and called "zephyrinas." The other was a batter of egg, yeast, and milk meant to rise quickly like a popover and called "nuns puffs." Early recipes call for yeast but later ones for a leavening of beaten egg whites, baked in cups or tins and sprinkled with white sugar, "Very nice for tea." Without the sugar, this makes an eggy, buttery popover that is very nice for dinner.

> ¼ pound (1 stick) butter
> 1 cup milk
> 2 cups all-purpose flour
> 1 teaspoon each baking powder and salt
> 4 eggs, separated

Melt butter with the milk in a saucepan and remove from heat. Mix the flour with the baking powder and salt and beat into the milk. Beat in the egg yolks, one at a time.

Beat the egg whites until stiff but not dry and fold into the batter. Spoon mixture quickly into buttered muffin tins and bake at 350° for 40 to 50 minutes.

Makes 12 puffs.

LEMON CURD IN A CRUST

Lemon chess pie of the South is really a lemon meringue pie without the meringue, but the name "chess" comes from a specifically English use of the word "cheese." The English and the French of the seventeenth and eighteenth centuries were extremely fond of custards, puddings, and creams, which they often thickened by heating milk until it curdled or made clabber, the first step in domestic cheese making. Eggs were added to the clabber, along with a flavoring like "orringes" or lemons, vanilla, brandy, or rosewater, and the custard was then strained "in a clean cloth that ye whey may run from it."

Even when the mixture was made without milk, the words "cheese" and "curd" meant thickening eggs with heat. Thus Mrs. Tyree in *Housekeeping in Old Virginia* (1879) can instruct a cook to make Lemon Cheese Cake without any milk or cheese but with eggs, butter, sugar, and lemon and to "Stir all well together till it curds." Significantly, Mrs. Tyree includes recipes for three such lemon "cheese" cakes, for four lemon puddings and two lemon meringues, not to mention six or seven lemon pies. By 1879 many recipes for such pies call for egg whites to be "frothed and sweetened" and set in the oven to brown, but such meringues are a late refinement. More typical is the Lemon Pudding of the *Carolina Housewife*, which incorporates separately beaten egg whites into the yolk mixture to bake "in a puff paste." Sarah Rutledge flavored her lemon curd with nutmeg and rosewater, but I've substituted brandy or bourbon for roses.

> 6 lemons
> ¾ cup sugar
> 6 ounces (1½ sticks) butter
> 8 eggs, separated
> 1 tablespoon brandy or bourbon
> ¼ teaspoon nutmeg
> 1 partially baked 9-inch pie shell
> garnish: powdered sugar or sugared lemon slices

Grate the rind of 3 lemons and reserve. Cut the 3 lemons into quarters, remove seeds, and scrape out pulp with a sharp knife. Squeeze juice from remaining 3 lemons to make a total of ¾ cup pulp and juice.

Dissolve the sugar in the lemon mixture over low heat and beat in the butter. Beat the egg yolks well and mix in a little of the hot liquid. Then add the yolks to the rest of the butter mixture, stirring constantly over low heat until it thickens enough to coat a spoon. Let cool to room temperature.

Beat 4 of the egg whites (freeze the rest for another use) until stiff but not dry, add brandy and nutmeg, and fold into the lemon curd.

Pile into the partially baked pie shell and bake at 350° about 30 minutes. Sprinkle the top of this tart with powdered sugar or decorate with a lemon, sliced paper thin and dipped in sugar syrup (see page 154).

Serves 6 to 8.

PEANUT BUTTER CHEESE CAKE

Another version of the "cheeseless" cheese cake is offered by *The Carolina Housewife* in Sarah Rutledge's recipe for a Groundnut Cheesecake, which thickens the custard of sugar and eggs with peanuts. The nuts, she says, are to

be ground very fine in a marble mortar, "adding a little brandy while pounding, to prevent oiling." She suggests putting the mixture into puff paste in tins
like patty pans. But you don't have to put your filling in a pie crust: You can
make a crunchy nut "crust" in a ring mold, as I've done here. I prefer to use
another kind of nut than peanut for the "crust," to avoid peanut overkill.

    ½ pound roasted peanuts
   1½ cups brown sugar
    ½ pound (2 sticks) butter
    5 eggs
    2 tablespoons bourbon
    2 tablespoons each flour and sugar
    ¼ cup walnuts or hazelnuts, chopped fine

Grind peanuts in a processor or blender but keep them somewhat
crunchy. In a bowl, cream sugar and butter until light, beat in the eggs and
bourbon, and fold in the peanut butter.

Butter a ring mold. Mix together the flour, sugar, and chopped nuts and
use to sprinkle interior of ring mold. Press peanut-butter mixture into the
mold. Bake at 300° until mixture is solid, 1½ to 2 hours.

Let cool in the pan and refrigerate. Unmold and serve cold.

Serves 8 to 12.

SALLY WHITE CAKE

The delectable coconut cream cakes of the South evolved from the dark fruitcakes of the English, which were originally sweetened yeast breads made from
ale barm, studded with currants or raisins, and spiced with cloves, mace, nutmeg, and rosewater or liquorous spirits. These medieval yeast breads flavored
with fruit evolved into richer pound cakes of butter, sugar, and flour, eventually substituting eggs for yeast. Such cakes were called "great cakes" because they were celebration cakes for special occasions like weddings and were
made in great quantities, like the one printed in *The Savannah Cookbook* and
attributed to "an old manuscript dated Mt. Vernon, 1781," "made by Martha
Custis for her grandmama." This Martha Washington Great Cake called for

forty eggs to four pounds of butter, four pounds of sugar, and five pounds each of fruit and flour. Actually, those quantities were fairly small in comparison to a Plum Cake for Weddings given by *The Carolina Housewife,* which calls for twenty pounds each of butter, sugar, and flour to bind twenty pounds of raisins, forty pounds of currants, and twenty glasses each of wine and brandy.

A spin-off from these dark fruitcakes were white fruitcakes often called "lady cakes," made white with almonds and egg whites. When only egg whites were used, the cake was often called "bride cake" or "angel cake" (as in our later angel's food cake). In the South, where coconut was added to a basic white fruitcake, it came to be called "Sally White Cake," allegedly after a famous cook of Greensboro, North Carolina. The ladies I met in Greensboro were unanimous in praise of the Sally White Cake recipes found in *Favorite Recipes of the Lower Cape Fear,* collected by The Ministering Circle of Wilmington, North Carolina, in 1964. "The original recipe" for a Sally White Cake, according to this book, was brought from Petersburg in 1830 by Mrs. Kate Walker Whiting, whose name was appropriate for her mission.

> 1 pound butter
> 2½ cups sugar
> 4 cups all-purpose flour
> 1 whole nutmeg, grated
> 1 tablespoon each cinnamon and mace
> 1 pound freshly grated coconut meat
> 2 pounds citron, chopped
> 1 pound almonds, chopped fine
> 12 eggs, separated
> 1 cup each sherry and brandy

Cream butter with sugar until light. Sift flour with the seasonings. Take 1 cup of the spiced flour and mix with the coconut, citron, and almonds. Beat the egg yolks into the sugar-butter mixture, then fold in the remaining spiced flour alternately with the liquor. Add the floured fruits and nuts.

Beat the egg whites until stiff but not dry and fold into the batter. Pour it into 2 tube or angel-food cake pans, well buttered. Bake at 275° until a cake tester comes out clean, 1½ to 2 hours.

Makes 2 5-pound cakes, which will improve with age.

SOUTHERN SYLLABUB

When Captain and Mrs. Basil Hall journeyed from Canada to New Orleans in 1827, they stopped in Columbia, South Carolina, to dine with Mr. and Mrs. Taylor, who "belonged to the old stock families of South Carolina, families who pique themselves on their ancient standing, quite old aristocracy, in short, and possessing immense wealth." After a first course of hams, turkeys, chickens, ducks, beef, fish, and several kinds of potatoes and vegetables, the second course was "eight pies down the side of the table, six dishes or glasses of syllabub and as many of jelly, beside one or two 'floating islands' . . . and odd corners filled up by ginger and other preserves."

Syllabub in the seventeenth century was the Englishman's cream soda, which he got by milking his cow straight into a bucket of cider, beer, or ale until it frothed. Eighteenth-century ladies turned this into a more refined dessert by whipping the milk and ale with willow twigs or a flat whisk or rod that became known as a syllabub "ventilator." "The Whisk ought to be made of fine small twigs of Birch, or such like wood," Eliza Smith specified in her *Compleat Housewife,* "neatly peeled, and tied up in a quantity a little bigger than your Thumb, and the small ends must be cut off a little, for fear of breaking in your Cream, and so you come to be made ashamed."

Before the invention of the rotary egg beater, the syllabub maker was instructed to skim off the whipped froth onto a hair sieve set over a bowl, to pour the remaining liquid into the bottom of tulip-shaped syllabub glasses, and to spoon the froth onto the top, the whole to be eaten with a special syllabub spoon. It didn't take the syllabub maker long to discover that, by increasing the amount of cream, she could whip a froth that would hold its shape overnight to be served at dinner on a pyramid of silver salvers, surrounded by glasses of colored jellies and plates of preserves.

The English cook Eliza Smith suggests using a quart of cream to a pint of sherry sack and the juice of two lemons, proportions followed by our *Carolina Housewife,* who adds a little Madeira, sugar, and spice. If you think of a syllabub as an eggless eggnog or zabaglione, with the slight sour taste of a yogurt, you'll be heading in the right direction and can alter the liquor to your taste.

4 cups heavy cream
½ cup superfine sugar
½–1 cup sherry, Madeira, or Marsala
grated rind and juice of 2–3 lemons
1 teaspoon freshly grated nutmeg

Whip cream with the sugar until stiff. Mix the sherry with the lemon rind and juice and fold the cream into this mixture. Pile into parfait glasses, topped with the grated nutmeg.

Makes about 5 cups, serving 6 to 8.

A GRAND TRIFLE

"Trifle" originally meant a cozening or a cheat, but not so when it became an ironic name for an eighteenth-century extravaganza that combined four desserts in one and caused Oliver Wendell Holmes to rhapsodize, "That most wonderful object of domestic art called trifle . . . with its charming confusion of cream and cake and almonds and jam and jelly and wine and cinnamon and froth." The froth was from a syllabub, the cream was often an almond cream custard, and the cake was sometimes Italian macaroons. Sarah Rutledge called for macaroons and ratafia, a cordial that Sarah made by steeping 1200 peach kernels in a gallon of brandy to extract their bitter almond flavor.

Since southern hostesses prided themselves on the quality of their syllabub glasses, no high table was complete without a cut-glass trifle bowl, which would reveal the charming confusion of its ingredients layer by layer. The bowl thus gave the lie to the name of the dish in a far wittier way than the late-nineteenth-century vulgarization of it called "tipsy pudding" or "tipsy squire."

Until this century, almond creams had been made for centuries with bitter almonds, but since America's excessively zealous food laws prevent the selling of bitter almonds in this country, you have to get the flavor of bitter almonds from peach kernels. I keep a few dried ones on hand to crack open and extract their kernels. The flavor is quite different from that of chemically made almond extract, but if you have no peach kernels, use the extract.

   1 cup ground almonds
   2 cups half-and-half
   2 whole eggs plus 2 egg yolks, beaten
   ½ cup sugar
   1 teaspoon vanilla extract
   4 crushed and ground peach kernels, or ¼ teaspoon almond
      extract
   ½ pound Italian macaroons (Amaretti), crumbled
   ¼ cup brandy
   1 cup raspberry jam
   2 cups Southern Syllabub (see page 236)

For the custard, heat the ground almonds in the half-and-half. Beat a bit of this cream into the combined eggs and egg yolks, and beat in the sugar, vanilla, and the kernels or almond extract. Combine with remaining cream and stir constantly over low heat until the custard thickens enough to coat a spoon. Remove from heat and chill.

Line the bottom of a deep glass bowl with a thick layer of macaroons. Sprinkle brandy over them. Spoon a layer of jam on top. Cover with the almond custard and top with the cold syllabub.

Serves 8 to 10.

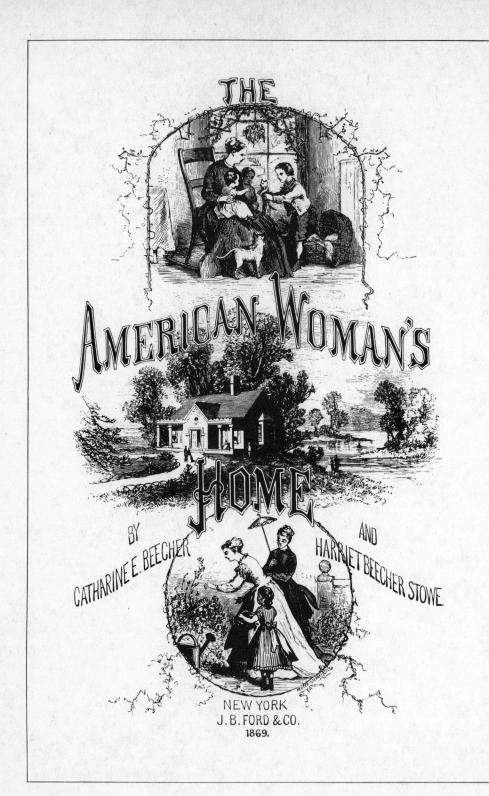

THE

AMERICAN WOMAN'S

HOME

BY
CATHARINE E. BEECHER

AND
HARRIET BEECHER STOWE.

NEW YORK
J. B. FORD & CO.
1869.

PART IV

Seafarers and Settlers

THE NEW ENGLAND COAST

ILLUSTRATION FACING PART TITLE PAGE:
The title page of the first edition
of *The American Woman's Home*, 1869.

RECIPES IN PART IV

The luxuriously rich are not simply kept comfortably warm, but un-naturally hot; as I implied before, they are cooked, of course à la mode.

—Henry David Thoreau, "Economy,"
Walden, or, Life in the Woods (1854)

I am sitting in the kitchen of an eighteenth-century farmhouse in Bedford, Massachusetts, waiting by the cast-iron Glendale stove, covered with wine bottles, for Teapot to move so that I can make some tea. Teapot is twelve and arthritic and favors a spot between the stove, where the ovens serve as wine bins, and a counter where pots are full of books and books full of knitting and embroidery. In the kitchen also are Judy Lindau McConnell, who was born in this house, her husband, Isham, from Kentucky, and several more arthritic dogs and cats, who occupy their favorite spots on floors, chairs, tables. "We never throw anything away," Isham laughs. "We recycle through the house the dogs, the cats, the chickens, the fish; everything comes back."

The kitchen is the heart of this house, as it was once of every New England house and barnyard. Everything collected there. In 1750 on a "drisely wet" night, Justice Joshua Hempsted, a Boston man, found his young mare almost dead from the cold and so took it home to the kitchen, "gave it warm milk & Dryed it by the fire." Judy's kitchen began in 1746 when Deacon Israel Putnam gave twenty-seven and a half acres to his son, "For Love," and son Israel built a one-room house with a chimney and a lean-to kitchen attached. The house evolved around the kitchen chimney as Israel sold his house to Mashach Penniman, who sold it to James Lane, who sold it to Joel Mansfield, who sold it to Fairfield R. Davis, whose widow sold it to Nathaniel Cutler, who sold it to Francis Rodman, who sold it to the Poors (of the Stickney & Poor Spice Company), who sold it to the Ameses of Boston who raised Airedales, who sold it to the McPeakes of New York, who sold it to the Lindaus of Baltimore.

The house, like its genealogy, rambles through time. "At the end of a long driveway stands a rambling house," as Judy describes it, "with seven doors and no front door, four chimneys built at different times, and a room that looks into a greenhouse with an old acacia tree." Next to the decaying greenhouse, the green light of a gurgling aquarium flickers on the silver tea paper of the living-room ceiling, which shows patches of damp. Outside, the screen porch has collapsed and the wisteria tree withered and died. Even as the house rambles, it huddles around its kitchen as another New England winter takes its toll.

It's the cold that determines those "necessaries of life" which Thoreau sought and found at Walden Pond in the winter of 1845. And in his one-room hut with a chimney, he discovered that all the necessaries boiled down to one—fuel. In his chapter on Economy, in which he explores the nature of unaccommodated New England man, he concludes: "The grand necessity, then, for our bodies, is to keep warm, to keep the vital heat in us." Food, Shelter, and Clothing are necessary only as fuel: "Man's body is a stove, and food the fuel which keeps up the internal combustion of the lungs."

If in the South food was family, in the North food was fuel and was measured as carefully as lumps of coal. In the North the keeping power of food was crucial: to keep in the heat of the body, to keep in the heat of the soul. Only in New England was food calibrated on those religious and moral scales that the Pilgrims preserved intact across the cold Atlantic. Preserving food to keep body and soul together was a first culinary principle for an island of seamen accustomed to salt fish, salt pork, and ship's biscuits. When Englanders from the Old World sailed to the New they applied the same methods of salting and drying to preserve the purity and heat of their religious principles. To keep warm was in the service of keeping pure. To family the North added church. "They were a family and a church," Thoreau wrote in *Cape Cod* (1864) of the Pilgrims who first landed on the Cape, "and were more anxious to keep together, though it were on the sand than to explore and colo-

---

Thanksgiving dinner in Ledyard, Connecticut, 1940, at the home of Timothy Levy Crouch, a Rogerene Quaker farmer and stonemason. Pumpkin pies, mince pies, and a fruit cake are ready for dessert, to supplement the fresh fruit on the table.

nize a New World." To keep body and soul and church together was the first duty of a colony that equated godliness with thrift.

Where the South extended its plantation families by the hospitality of its tables, the North withdrew, like Thoreau, into the woods to find economy holy. Itemized cost of food for eight months, $8.74, Thoreau notes, "but I should not thus unblushingly publish my guilt, if I did not know that most of my readers were equally guilty with myself." The voices of the North spoke of sin, guilt, and the evils of luxury. When Mrs. Lydia Maria Child published *The Frugal Housewife* in Boston in 1829, she dedicated her cook book "to those who are not ashamed of economy," and quoted Ben Franklin's "A fat kitchen maketh a lean will." Lydia Child was the daughter of a Medford baker who made Medford crackers famous, and Lydia knew about economy first-hand because she was the sole support of an indigent and incompetent husband. "Books of this kind have usually been written for the wealthy," she writes. "I have written for the poor. I have said nothing about *rich* cooking; those who can afford to be epicures will find the best of information in the 'Seventy-five Receipts.' I have attempted to teach how money can be *saved*, not how it can be *enjoyed*."

Heaven forfend! Let the wicked of Philadelphia follow Miss Eliza Leslie's *Seventy-five Receipts* (published in Boston in 1828) down the primrose path of "pastry, cakes and sweetmeats." Boston was made of sterner stuff. When John Adams visited Philadelphia, he wrote home of a "most sinful feast" of "curds and creams, jellies, sweet meats, tarts, fools, trifles, floating islands, sillabubs, etc." At home in Boston, John regularly sat down to a first course of Indian meal pudding with molasses and butter (an indulgence) and a second course of veal with bacon and neck of mutton with boiled vegetables. Thoreau fled such luxurious waste and took satisfaction in a dinner of wild purslane, boiled and salted, and then got rid of the salt. "As for salt, that grossest of groceries," he writes, "I do not learn that the Indians ever troubled themselves to go after it."

Only in New England were cook books primarily conduct books of morals and manners. The author of our first American cook book, Amelia Simmons, "an American Orphan," who published *American Cookery* in Hartford, Connecticut, in 1796 on the presses of Hudson & Goodwin, was of course a New Englander. "The orphan must depend solely upon *character*," she writes. "How immensely important, therefore, that every action, every word, every thought, be regulated by the strictest purity." Purity a century and a half later was the concern of Judy McConnell's Aunt Clem, who visited Bedford every spring in her blue serge suit and high button boots for a meal of broilers and asparagus. Occasionally, Judy says, they took Aunt Clem to Longfellow's Wayside Inn and Farm, where she once suffered a considerable shock. Perceiving a boiled onion in the center of her plate, she cried, "Great heavens, an onion!" and left the table forthwith.

In New England's cook books, the purity of American food was a function of its politics. Although most of Amelia's recipes were devoted to "Pastes, Puffs, Pies, Tarts, Puddings, Custards & Preserves and All Kinds of Cakes from the Imperial Plumb to Plain Cake," she was careful to state on her title page that they were "adapted to This Country & All Grades of Life." In *The Cook Not Mad, or Rational Cookery* (1830), much indebted to both Child and Simmons, the author speaks of "Good *Republican dishes*," purified of the vitiated tastes of English, French, and Italians, and devoted to health, temperance, and "the science of domestick economy." Those remarkable sisters, Catherine and Harriet Beecher (Stowe), who were as typical of America as the Brontë sisters of England, founded their principles of domestic science on the sanctity and purity of "The American Woman's Home." In their 1869 book of that title, they propose that the aim of a Christian house, which is necessarily centered in the stove and stove room and kitchen, is to enable "every member of a family to labor with the hands for the common good" and thus "to secure health, thrift, and domestic happiness to persons of limited means."

Limited means was a problem from the outset for Pilgrims and later Republicans, who had preserved the class structure of England while denying its political structure. For the abolitionist North, how to keep a house without servants posed a problem as severe as how to keep warm. The Beecher sisters expressed the paradox precisely: "America is the only country where there is a class of women who may be described as *ladies* who do their own work."

In New England purity was confused with propriety as morals were confused with manners. If food in the South is still symbolic of a man's patch of earth, in the North it's still symbolic of his morals and manners. Judy's same Aunt Clem, who like all the Lindau ladies kept a journal from cradle to grave, was appalled at the manners of an American family staying at her hotel in 1913 while she was traveling in Italy. "When she had gravy on her plate," she remarked of the woman at the next table, "she took a piece of bread in her fingers, not only dipped the bread in the gravy, but drew it around the plate, all in her fingers." Aunt Clem concluded that "she certainly must come of very plain people, as she looks very plain, not only plain of face as regards looks, but she comes of the plain people."

In the colonies manners originally centered not on fingers but on the proper use of knives. Forks were not even in question, since table forks had come into general use in England only late in the seventeenth century and were considered until then an affectation of the Italians. The first table fork to reach America was sent in a leather case with knife and bodkin to Boston's governor John Winthrop in 1633. Children were instructed in knife etiquette, as in *A Pretty Little Pocket Book* of 1776: "Hold not thy knife upright, but sloping; lay it down at right hand of the plate, with end of blade on the plate." When eventually the two-pronged carving fork was replaced by the three-pronged table fork, diners were instructed not to eat directly from the knife as before, but to change the fork from left hand to right to convey food to mouth. New Englanders thus distinguished themselves from Old Englanders, who took the shortest route from fork to mouth and economized labor by not changing hands.

In all other respects, however, colonial rebels transported English table manners whole as symbols of civility in a savage world. Medieval England, for example, had developed the art of carving to such a degree that any wealthy household hired a carver as well as a cook. Carving developed its own lexicon of proper terms to distinguish degrees of civility. Alice Morse Earle, in *Home Life in Colonial Days* (1898), quotes from an anonymous colonial author: "How must all regret to hear some Persons, even of quality say, 'pray cut up that Chicken, or Hen,' or 'Have that Plover;' not considering how indiscreetly they talk, when the proper Terms are, 'break that Goose,' 'Thrust that Chicken,' 'spoil that Hen,' 'pierce that Plover.'"

In the North, when a household did have servants, servant manners were all the more important in keeping class lines distinct. The first book written by a black American and published commercially was typically, if sadly, Robert Roberts' *The House Servant's Directory*, published in Boston in 1827. His aim was to instruct young servants in the rules of decorum at table and elsewhere.

"I have often heard servants answer their employers in such an impertinent manner as to make my blood run cold," Roberts warns, "to think that any one should be so ignorant as not to know his place better." Roberts' blood would have turned to ice had he heard the complaints of Sarah Kemble Knight about the laxity of Connecticut colonists with their black servants, "permitting ym to sit at Table and eat with them (as they say to save time) and into the dish goes the black hoof as freely as the white hand."

For the lady who did her own work, in the kitchen and elsewhere, the rules of decorum helped establish her claims to ladyhood. Mrs. Louisa C. Tuthill, in *The Young Lady's Home* (published in Boston in 1847), laid down English law. "Although domestic economy must necessarily occupy much of a woman's time and thoughts, it should be made as seldom as possible the subject of conversation," she advised. "The affairs of the kitchen should never be discussed in the parlour, or at table." Or even away from the table, as I discovered visiting friends in Wellfleet on Cape Cod. When I asked a Boston lady about food, her eyebrows shot up. "Food?" she queried. "I know nothing about food, I never cook." She thought a moment. "Who do I know *would* know about food?" she pondered, and came up with nobody. I got the same response from a local lady, Miss Clara Rowells, whose ancestors had helped to found Wellfleet and who had been born in the same seventeenth-century cottage where she had lived for the last seventy-five years. She knew nothing about cooking, she told me. And as for food, "Well, I like anything so long as it comes from the store."

If the cooking of the South was earth cooking, the cooking of the North was subsistence sea cooking, and specifically cooking aboard ship in a big iron pot. On Atlantic sailing vessels a hearth of bricks was constructed on deck and a tripod set above it from which to hang the communal pot. The pot boiled salt fish and meats and softened sea biscuits. The fuel that fed the Pilgrims aboard the *Mayflower* consisted of such pot foods as smoked bacon, dried and salted cod, and smoked herring, plus 15,000 brown biscuits and 5000 white crackers, to be washed down with six-shilling beer in casks. On land, the same pot boiled fresh cod.

Cold waters bred cod in such plentitude that the earliest colonists, nosing their ships past Newfoundland, New Brunswick, New Scotland, New France, and finally New England, complained that their ships were "pestered with cod." And a traveler along the Cape of Cod in the nineteenth century complained of the native cooking, "at breakfast, fish; at dinner, fish—fish fried, broiled, boiled, baked, and chowdered!" So synonymous was food with fish chowder that Herman Melville wrote in *Moby Dick:* "Fishiest of all fishy places was the Try Pots, which well deserved its name, for all pots there were always boiling chowders. Chowder for breakfast, and chowder for dinner, and chowder for supper, till you began to look for fish-bones coming through your clothes."

Provincetown cod fishers, their drag nets hoisted to dry, sail home from the banks off Cape Cod, 1942.

Cod fishers dish up a chowder aboard the *Francis and Marion,* a Portuguese drag trawler from Provincetown, fishing off Cape Cod, 1942. The New England iron pot, here enameled, has been the center of seafarers' and settlers' tables from the time of the Pilgrims.

What English seafarers brought to the land of cod was the pot to cook it in. Francis Higginson, in his *New England Plantation* (1630), advised prospective colonists to carry with them "1 iron pot, 1 Kettel, 1 Frying Pan, 1 Gridiron, 2 Skellets, 1 spit," and an array of wooden platters and trenchers. The Narragansets and other Indian tribes who had been boiling fish in containers of bark were quick to see the utility of iron. Mrs. Mary Rowlandson, who was captured by the Indians in 1675 and carried in twenty "removes" through the wilds of Vermont and New Hampshire, discovered during her captivity new uses for the colonial pot and kettle. "I went to the same Squaw, who had a Kettle of Ground nuts boyling," Mary wrote. "I asked her to let me boyle my piece of Bear in her Kettle, which she did, and gave me some Ground-nuts to eat with it; and I cannot but think how pleasant it was to me." She confessed that she'd been timid about bear, but soon learned to eat, from the Indian kettle, broths made of maggoty bones and horses' hooves and rattlesnakes and tree bark.

Mary Rowlandson had been captured during the Indian Wars waged by the grandson of the very chief whom Squanto had brought to Pilgrim tables to feast on wild duck, geese, venison, cod, bass, eels, clams, leeks, watercress, cornmeal bread and white bread, wild plums, dried berries, and wild grape wine, "very sweete & strong." Fifty years after that first Thanksgiving, the wine had soured and "King Philip," as the grandson of Chief Massasoit called himself, was massacred along with a thousand of his tribe while they sat down to dinner at Narragansett Bay. Here the English discovered new uses for the colonial skillet for, a colonist reported, the Indians "fryed together":

> Had we been *Canibals* here might we feast
> On brave Westphalian gammons ready drest.

The pot that boiled chowder soon began to boil cane and turn molasses into sugar and rum. I discovered that the fortunes of New England, founded on cod, slaves, and rum, hung by a single pot in which the colonists added sugar to salt. In England, sugar refinement had also been a matter of class refinement. Not until the seventeenth century was brown crystallized cane sugar of the coarsest kind, the kind they called "Muscovada," available to tables lower than royal. Not until the eighteenth century were cook books addressed to "The English Hus-Wife" principally to instruct her in the new art of sugar cooking or the making of sweetmeats. Martha Washington, on the occasion of her marriage to Daniel Custis in 1749, was given a manuscript collection of recipes divided in two parts, *A Booke of Cookery* and *A Booke of Sweetmeats*. And when such a collection was first published by Eliza Smith in America in 1742 as *The Compleat Housewife: or, Accomplish'd Gentlewoman's Companion*, sugar exploded in her receipts for "pastry, confectionery, preserving, pickles, cakes, creams, jellies, made wines, cordials."

The accomplished gentlewoman transported to Plymouth Rock found a forest of native sugar trees. "The Sugar-Tree yields a kind of Sap or Juice, which by boiling is made into Sugar," Robert Beverley wrote. "This Juice is drawn out, by wounding the Trunk of the Tree, and placing a Receiver under the Wound. The Indians make One Pound of Sugar, out of Eight Pounds of the Liquor . . . bright and moist, with a large full Grain, the Sweetness of it being like that of good Muscovada."

The gentlewoman also found the compleat Indian housewife seasoning her meats with this native sugar as her counterpart would have with Muscovada. A colonist captured in 1755 described how Indians mixed their sugar with water to drink and how they put sugar "in bear's fat until the fat was almost as sweet as the sugar itself, and in this we dipped our roasted venison." Another colonist noted that sugar was to the Indian what salt was to the European. "That great cookery symbol, the salt-box, which is regarded among salt-consuming nations with a species of superstitious reverence, is hence hardly ever found in an Indian lodge," wrote Johann Georg Kohle in 1859. The great cookery symbol of the wigwam was the sugar-*makak*, or *mokuk*, a box of white birch bark, stiffened and stitched with thongs of elm. "When the children are impatient," Kohle observed, "the mother gives them some of the contents, and they will sit at the door and eat sugar by handfuls."

Early settlers called this sugar "Indian melasses" and consumed it only as a last resort. "It is brown to be sure, and somewhat dirty and viscous," a German traveler wrote in 1788, "but by repeated refinings can be made good and agreeable." Settlers refined the "sugaring-off" methods of the Indians by replacing bark buckets and log troughs with the old iron pot. Since maple sap is 35 percent water, refining was simply a matter of boiling. Boil thirty gallons of sap and you get a gallon of syrup. Boil a gallon of syrup and, when reduced by three eighths, you get the grain sugar Vermonters call "Indian sugar." If you pour the syrup on a snowbank, you get through rapid cooling a soft, chewy sugar called "wax" or "gum sugar."

From the Indians, settlers learned to collect tree sugar during "maple moon," when at the end of February sap began to rise during the day and descend at night. "In the daytime the sap surges up from the roots and at night it rushes back so that it doesn't freeze," recounted an old New Hampshire syrup maker, H. D. Merrill, now removed to New Jersey, where he still plugs a nearby "sugar bush." "Every time the sap goes by your plug, you take your share." In the old days, Merrill recalled, he'd be out on snowshoes collecting sap from milk pails to pour in the huge iron vat his team of oxen pulled on a sled to take to the sugarhouse. In the shanty, a series of four successively smaller iron pots would turn sap to sugar and in the process cover ceiling and sugarers with sticky sweet grains. Nowadays, sugar-making economy dictates plastic tubes and stainless-steel evaporators, but now that Indian melasses has become more costly than Muscovada or even a lily-white grain, maple cooking may take on a new status.

I began in a kitchen in Bedford, Massachusetts, culling recipes from a woman whose family of Keltons had sailed from Ware to land in Boston in the 1660s. I ended in a kitchen in Arcadia, Rhode Island, culling recipes from a woman whose family had been there for centuries before that. When I talked to Pretty Flower, whose non-Indian name is Eleanor Dove, she had just sold her restaurant, Dovecrest, because her husband had died. Roaring Bull had been war chief of the Narragansets, as well as town moderator, tax assessor, and postmaster for the town of Exeter, and he was much missed in the Tomaquag Indian Museum and Trading Post adjoining Dovecrest. He was missed also in the kitchen of Pretty Flower, who was making johnnycakes, quahog pie, venison, Indian pudding, and sassafras tea. "People ask me where all the Indian foods have gone," Pretty Flower says in a voice as soft as her dove-brown eyes. "You had the woods in the winter and the sea in the summer and food was bountiful—fish, game, berries, greens, mushrooms, there for the picking," she recalls of her childhood. "The life we led then is the life of the rich now."

I wondered if Thoreau would have approved such bounty even if it were free. Or if he would not have found nature's abundance luxurious for bodies to be kept warm but not unnaturally hot. Pretty Flower made her life in the woods so easy, so natural, so unlike Thoreau's. Perhaps she was innocent of the Christian dimensions of economy or perhaps she simply enjoyed food that would keep the body not just warm but cooked, of course à la mode.

Frank H. Shurtleff and his son running maple sap to the sugar house on their farm in North Bridgewater, Vermont, 1940. The farm of four hundred acres, purchased by Mr. Shurtleff's grandfather in 1840, one century later produced five hundred gallons of syrup from a stand of two thousand sugar maples.

14
Bread and Breakfast

"Bread I at first made of pure Indian meal and salt, genuine hoecakes, which I baked before my fire out of door on a shingle or the end of a stick of timber sawed off in building my house; but it was wont to get smoked and to have a piny flavor." Thoreau at Walden describes precisely the "genuine hoecakes" or "Johny cakes" (as Amelia Simmons spells them in *American Cookery*) that were the staple breads of the colonists from the moment they discovered Indians wrapping cakes of corn in corn husks or grapeleaves to bake in the ashes of their fires. Such a wrapping would have prevented the piny flavor Thoreau complains of from his shingle, or stick of timber (called earlier a "spoon," hence "spoon bread" and "pone").

Thoreau's method of baking a cake on a shingle is a later refinement on the ashcake, which English colonists would have baked in the ashes of their native hearths, using barley, oats, or rye. The shingle stood in for the gridiron or griddle, which colonists were advised to pack in their trunks along with the skillets, kettles, and iron pot. "In America there is seldom a house without a griddle," Eliza Leslie writes in her *New Receipts for Cooking*. "Still, where griddles are not, these cakes may be baked on a board standing nearly upright before the fire, and supported by a smoothing-iron or a stone placed against the back." This method worked well for a coal fire, but Miss Leslie suggests for a wood fire that the cook wrap the cakes in paper and cover them with red-hot ashes.

The hoecake takes its name, Eliza declares, from the practice "in some parts of America" of using instead of griddle or shingle "the iron of a hoe, stood up before the fire." Dough for the hoecake should be made the night before, she advises, so that early next morning, as soon as the fire burns well, you can put the griddle on and shape your cakes "the size of a common saucer, and half an inch thick." Hoecakes were individual rounds like the maize cakes Spaniards called "tortillas." The "common griddle cake," on the other hand, covered the whole surface of a greased griddle, to be browned on one side and then the other and when served, "cut into three-cornered pieces."

Johnnycake uses the same dough of Indian meal, salt, and water but is made lighter by beating it with a spoon "for a quarter of an hour or more, till it becomes light and spongy." You then spread the dough to cover a "johnny-cake board" (a piece from the head of a flour barrel will do, she says), which is propped before the fire with a flatiron or stone and "placed so as *slightly* to slant backwards; otherwise the upper part of the cake, being opposite to the hottest part of the fire, may bake too fast for the lower part."

The details of Eliza's instruction may shed light on the johnnycake wars which continue to be fought in Rhode Island the way chili wars are fought in Texas. Until the cook books of the nineteenth century, johnnycake was synonymous with hoecake because the names had a common source in the Englishing of Indian terms, which varied according to tribe. "No-kake," "joniken," and "nokehick" were all English phonetic renderings of Indian words for corn parched in hot ash and beaten into powder to make it transportable over long distances for long periods of time. "Nokehick" had shelf life, as Roger Williams described it: "Parch'd meal, which is a readie very wholesome food which they eat with a little water, hot or cold, every man carrying a little basket of this at his back, and sometimes in a little Hollow Leather girdle about his middle." An Indian could snack from his backpack or, with a campfire, bake a corncake in the ashes.

Linguists have tipped *slightly* backward in deriving the word johnnycake from "journey" cake. More likely, I think, is that "john" and its diminutives, "jonakin" and "johnny," were nicknames once as familiar for the common man as today's "mac" or "joe" or "man." Hoecakes and johnnycakes were the commonest of common cornmeal cakes, a kind of people's cake, and it would be easy to confuse Indian sounds with the familiar sounds of "john" and "cake." Imagine linguists a few centuries from now trying to etymologize "Big Mac."

In New England, which thriftily recycles the past the way Judy recycles dogs and cats, these linguistic quibbles are matters of state. In the 1940s the Rhode Island legislature, after a century of dispute over the proper spelling, the proper ingredients, and the proper method of making "the johnnycake," passed laws making "jonnycake" the official spelling and whitecap flint corn the official grain for this regional specialty. A century ago it even hauled stoves into the capitol building in Providence to settle the matter hot off the griddle, but hot words led to blows and hurled johnnycakes, and the war went on.

For the rest of the country, whitecap flint corn scarcely exists. Flint, one of the six native American corn kinds, by the twentieth century had been hybridized almost out of existence and replaced, commercially, by the more malleable dent corn. "The original flint died out entirely. It's extinct," says Paul Drumm, Jr., shouting above the whirr of the mills at Usquepaugh, where his family keep their noses to the grindstone at Kenyon Grist Mill, built in 1886. These are fighting words to the agronomist Robert Wakefield, the Johnny Cornseed of his time, and to members of The Society for the Propagation of the Jonnycake Tradition in Rhode Island, whose mission is to preserve, propagate, and develop new varieties of flint. The *Jonnycake Journal* notes that a Massachusetts flint grower has produced a variety he calls "Old Glory," because each kernel displays red stripes in the pericarp and blue dots in the aleurone against a white endosperm.

The grinding of corn matters more than the kind of corn, young Paul believes. They use the softer dent corn but grind it between nineteenth-century hard granite stones. Softer stones crush the grain rather than shave it into paper-thin flakes. The grooves, which are cut into the face of each stone according to the tradition and whim of the carver, also affect the grind. When the grooves wear down, the face must be recut, but genuine millstone carvers are nearly as extinct as genuine flint, and it is no easy matter to remove stones weighing two and a half tons each.

Paul shows me how the grain is fed through a hopper into a rectangular opening called a "shoe." The shoe is then agitated by a rod called the "damsel" because it clatters. The damsel controls the flow of grain down through the "boot," so called because it was once made of leather, and into the hollowed center of the "giant" or "runner stone." From here the grain spreads out evenly over the "bedstone," where it is ground or flaked and then swept by "sweeper rods" into a chute which fills barrels or bags. (Those curious about the language and lore of stone milling should read Thomas Robinson Hazard's *The Jonny-Cake Papers of "Shepherd Tom,"* published in Boston in 1915.)

New England made a meal of breakfast cakes—breads, griddlecakes, and flapjacks—for the same reason Old England did. Carbo loading on a cold morning stoked the body's furnace. As soon as wheat and rye were grown, they were mixed with cornmeal to make a lighter loaf. "I have tried flour also; but have at last found a mixture of rye and Indian meal most convenient and agreeable," Thoreau wrote of his experiments with hoecakes. "In cold weather it was no little amusement to bake several small loaves of this in succession, tending and turning them as carefully as an Egyptian his hatching eggs."

"Ryaninjun" was the staple mixture everywhere for those for whom wheat either cost too much or was not to be had. While rye had less gluten than wheat and would respond less to the leavening of yeast, still, rye had more gluten than corn, which had none. One reason corn was in such low repute as a grain for bread was not just its Indian origin but the resemblance of the baked product to the "black" loaves of peasant bread at home. While city bakers made loaves of refined "white" flour in brick ovens, country folk had perforce to bake their bannocks or ash cakes with flour that still contained the "black" husks of unsieved grain. In the colonies, to mix wheat with rye and Indian flour was a step up the social, as well as the culinary, ladder.

In the 1830s, however, two New Englanders in typical Pilgrim fashion reversed this pecking order and declared "black" good and "white" decadent, luxurious, sinful, and blasphemous. Grain with the husk on made the only proper flour for a white man who called himself Christian. Such was the faith both of the Reverend Sylvester Graham of Connecticut and Boston and the Reverend Amos Bronson Alcott of Boston and Concord, father of Fruitlands and Louisa May. Both reverends had been converted to the Bible Christian Church by the preachments of a homeopathic clergyman from Manchester who had migrated to Philadelphia, the Reverend William Metcalfe. Metcalfe preached a vegetarian fundamentalism based on total abstinence from meat, alcohol, sex, and baker's bread. In the 1830s dyspepsia was the monster evoked the way calories and cholesterol are today, whenever a mythic devil is required. Dyspepsia, the moral reformers proclaimed, was the result of a diet too intense, too concentrated, too stimulating for the sensitive and pure. Unhusked grain would dilute the concentration and bulk out the meal. "Every farmer knows that if his horse has straw cut with his grain, or hay in abundance, he does well enough," Dr. Graham wrote. "Just so it is with the human species." In the 1830s in Boston and Philadelphia, the only way to get a loaf of bread baked with unhusked grain was to bake it at home. The conclusion was inevitable. The first duty of the American female was to stay in the kitchen of her Christian home and bake bread for the salvation of the soul.

In the name of exorcising "dat ole debil" dyspepsia, Graham let in a new devil, which New Englanders thought angelic. Since unhusked grain, or "Graham" flour, did not leaven nearly as well as "refined" flour, home bakers had to intensify the strength of their yeast. As long as yeast was brewed at home, the cook added sweetening to the barm to speed the fermentation and prevent souring. With graham flour they increased sweetening from a spoonful of sugar to a half cup of brown sugar or molasses. "Use molasses instead of sugar if the bread is eaten for constipation," Maria Parloa advises bakers of graham bread in *The Appledore Cook Book* (1872). Use molasses instead of sugar to act with saleratus, or baking soda, in a quick bread. The acid of molasses combined with the alkali of soda to produce the carbon dioxide we now get from baking powder. Unfortunately, Graham's "health" flour intensified the taste for unhealthy amounts of sweetening in a populace already conditioned by a British sweet-tooth tradition, evident even today in the sweetened breads, muffins, and crackers of health-food stores and factory graham crackers.

In Thoreau's day, breakfast was much like supper, as we can tell from Thoreau's account, in his *Cape Cod* journals (1864), of breakfasting with a Wellfleet oysterman and his wife. While his wife prepared food at the hearth, the oysterman stood with his back to the fire and ejected tobacco juice right and left without regard to griddle or pot. "At breakfast we had eels, buttermilk cake, cold bread, green beans, doughnuts, and tea," Thoreau reported. "I ate of the applesauce and the doughnuts, which I thought had sustained the least detriment from the old man's shots, but my companion refused the applesauce, and ate of the hot cake and green beans, which had appeared to him to occupy the safest part of the hearth." Either way, each ate a substantial breakfast by today's standards and, for once, Thoreau did not tally in the cost of the tobacco juice as an added and entirely unnecessary expense.

JOHNNYCAKES

The Rhode Island legislature will not approve of this spelling, but neither will they approve any cornmeal other than white flint. Other parts of New England are rigorous in their own way. Judy McConnell remembers her grandfather's breakfast, which was always corned beef hash and johnnycake made of yellow corn. Ruth Rose Barrett, in *The Block Island Cookbook* (1962), compiled by the First Baptist Church, remembers her father's directions for No Cake, "handed down by the Indians on Block Island." "No Cake must be made on a clear day when the wind was from the Northwest," Ambrose said. On such a day he would shuck year-old field corn, parch it in a heavy iron skillet with sand to keep the kernels from scorching, stirring the while with a corn cob until the kernels turned cocoa brown. He would then sift out the sand, cool the kernels in the northwest wind, and grind them in a coffee grinder.

Pretty Flower at Dovecrest remembers when they had "johnnycakes in the morning, johnnycakes for lunch, and if there were any leftover johnny-cakes, johnnycakes for supper." Jamestown grows some flint corn, she tells me, but flint was so expensive they used white dent. "Some swear they can tell the difference, but I can't," she says, "as long as it's stone ground." She gets her grain from a grist mill in Maryland and sifts out the finest meal in a hopper her husband designed. Her cakes are white, light, crisp, and browned at the edges, three inches in diameter and an inch thick, and served with venison steak as one might serve potato pancakes.

In the recipe below, I've compromised between the "Thin East-of-Nar-ragansett Johnnycakes," as June Platt calls them in her *New England Cook-book* (1971), and the "Thick West-of-Narragansett Johnnycakes." East means a rather elegant and Frenchified thin cake with a lacy edge, almost like a crepe, which uses milk in addition to water. Eliza Leslie calls this a "Nice Johnny Cake," in contrast to a "Plain Johnny." In her nice cake, she adds to the meal and water "A small teacup of molasses (West India is best)" with two tablespoons of butter and a teaspoon of ginger. Her plain johnny, like the cake of the West, is simply meal, water, and salt, although she concedes, "You may eat molasses with it." A plain johnny best reveals the taste and texture of the grain, but I believe with June Platt that a little milk with the water does no harm. A useful tip from Pretty Flower is to put your cakes as you finish them on a cookie sheet in a 400° oven to puff slightly as the grains expand.

> 1 cup stone-ground cornmeal (preferably of white flint corn)
> ¾ teaspoon salt
> 1 cup boiling water
> ¾–1 cup cold milk

The cake will be lighter if you warm the meal, mixed with the salt, in the oven before you begin. Gradually stir in the boiling water and then the milk until you have the dilution desired (these cakes will be medium thin to very thin).

Heat a griddle or cast-iron skillet, grease it lightly, and pour on a large spoonful of batter to make a 3-inch cake. Repeat until the pan is full but leave room to turn the cakes. Brown about 6 minutes, then turn carefully and brown 4 to 5 minutes on the other side. Serve with lots of butter.

Makes 8 cakes.

GRAHAM GEMS

Dr. Sylvester Graham's name was so strongly associated with the flour we now call "all-bran" that his name became attached to breads, crackers, muffins, or gems. The evolution of the gem pan from muffin hoops is as curiously Anglo-American as the evolution of Graham's flour from English "whole-meal" flour. Originally, the batter for muffins was leavened with yeast, as Hannah Glasse makes clear in her 1796 recipe "To make Muffins and Oat-Cakes." Hannah leavens a bushel of Hertfordshire white flour with ale yeast, shapes the dough into little balls, rolls them flat, then lets them rise, and finally toasts them on both sides on an iron griddle laid flat over the coals. When you pull them open, she says, "they will be like a honeycomb." Americans would recognize these as English muffins, but Englishers now call them "crumpets."

In nineteenth-century America, however, yeast was replaced more and more by the leavening action of saleratus or pearl ash, before these alkalines were packaged with a powdered acid as baking powders. A batter made with baking powder was thinner than a yeast dough and therefore tin hoops were devised in which to pour the batter for baking on the griddle. Americans soon welded these hoops together or cast them in a single piece of iron with seven to twelve shallow cups and called them "gem pans," each cup guaranteed to produce a "gem." Often the cups were shaped to form decorative molds like scallop shells, Turk's heads, pears or apples, and of course ears of corn.

The transition between the English and the American muffin, or gem, is apparent in Eliza Leslie's recipes for English muffins in 1837, baked in rings on a griddle, and in Maria Parloa's recipes for American muffins in 1872, which she bakes in "muffin-cups" in a quick oven. Miss Parloa mixes graham with white flour and uses saleratus, cream of tartar, and eggs for her leavening. By the time of Fannie Farmer's 1896 *Boston Cooking-School Cook Book,* we find Graham Muffins I and II: number I is a rather heavy cake leavened by the action of molasses and sour milk with soda; number II is a lighter cake with sugar, sweet milk, egg, and much baking powder.

In this recipe I've mixed equal parts of graham flour with white flour, added molasses and blueberries for flavor, a little soda to counteract the sour milk, and baking powder for leavening. If you want a richer muffin, add eggs. There's almost nothing you can't add to this kind of batter, as twentieth-century American muffinry will attest.

> 1 cup each whole wheat and unbleached white flour
> 1 tablespoon baking powder
> ½ teaspoon each salt and baking soda
> 1 cup sour milk
> ¼ cup molasses
> 4 tablespoons butter, melted
> 1 cup blueberries

Stir or sift the dry ingredients together until well mixed. To sour the milk, add 1 teaspoon vinegar and let stand 10 minutes. Beat the molasses into the soured milk and add to the flour. Stir in melted butter and berries and turn quickly into well-buttered muffin pans. Bake at 425° until a cake tester comes out clean, 20 to 25 minutes.

Makes 12 to 15 muffins.

THIRDED BREAD

In order to persuade the French of the virtues of American maize, Benjamin Franklin wrote his friend Cadet ae Vaux in 1785, "The Flour of Mayz, mix'd with that of Wheat, makes excellent Bread, sweeter, and more agreeable than that of Wheat alone." Franklin's missive to France was really aimed at the English who, like Mrs. Frances Trollope, found every kind of cornbread or corncake "all bad." A mixed meal, on the other hand, pleased even fastidious Frances, who declared that cornmeal "mixed in the proportion of one-third, with fine wheat, makes by far the best bread I ever tasted."

Her one-third proportion is based not, as one might think, on one third corn to two thirds wheat but on the early colonial formula for "thirded bread," meaning one third each corn, wheat, and rye. Any bread with wheat in it was a luxury for New England, where wheat was subject to a form of smut called "blast," making wheat crops harder to maintain here than elsewhere. Lydia Child in *The Frugal Housewife* explains that many think this thirded bread "the nicest of all," and as late as 1896 Fannie Farmer still gives a recipe for Third Bread in her *Boston Cooking-School Cook Book*.

I've followed Fannie's proportions here because they produce a lighter loaf, more in accord with today's tastes, than one that uses equal parts of corn, rye, and wheat. As always with Fannie, I've cut down the sweetening, but a small bit of molasses brings out the flavor of both corn and rye. You can omit sweetening altogether, and you can mix your flours to taste. The corn gives sweetness and crunch, the rye a nutty flavor and body, the wheat elevation. If you want a finer crumb for this coarse-textured loaf, add butter, or substitute milk or buttermilk for some of the water.

Miss Eliza Leslie in *New Receipts for Cooking* provides her usual precise directions to determine when the brick oven is hot enough from the wood fire built within. "If you can hold your hand within the mouth of the oven as long as you can distinctly count twenty, the heat is about right," Miss Leslie advises, although "distinctly" gives one pause, as if the baker may feel faint from a blistered and shriveled hand. When Miss Leslie advises caution, it is well to pay heed, as in "The vapour of charcoal in a close room is so deleterious as to cause death."

1 package dry yeast
2 cups very warm (110°–115°) water
¼ cup molasses
1 cup stone-ground cornmeal
1 cup rye flour
3 cups unbleached white flour, plus more if needed
½ tablespoon salt

Dissolve yeast in the water and add the molasses. Mix the 3 flours and the salt and stir in the yeast mixture. Since the dough will be very sticky, add more white flour if needed to make the dough workable. Knead about 10 minutes by hand or 5 by machine with a dough hook.

Put dough in a buttered bowl and let it rise until nearly doubled, 2 to 3 hours, since the dough will not rise as fast or as high as an all-wheat loaf. Punch down and shape into a single round loaf or 2 standard-size greased bread pans to rise again for 1 to 1½ hours.

Slash the top with a razor blade (a cross for a round loaf, 3 parallel slashes for a rectangular loaf) and bake at 375° until loaf sounds hollow when rapped on the bottom, 25 to 40 minutes.

Makes 1 large loaf or 2 small loaves.

INDIAN SLAPJACKS

"We had a splendid breakfast," Hawthorne wrote in his *American Notebooks*, "of flapjacks, or slapjacks, and whortleberries." A batter thin enough to be poured on a griddle, rather than shaped into hoecakes or johnnycakes, was called indiscriminately "flap", "slap," or "flatjacks," sometimes "flips" or "slappers," and eventually "pancakes," "flannel cakes," "flatcars," and "sweatpads." There is no end of names, any more than an end to the stack of cakes on a plate.

Americans, however, distinguished slapjacks from pancakes by ingredients as well as name. In Anglo-Saxon usage "jack" like "john" meant a common fellow (as in "jack-of-all-trades"); the "jack" suffix in America implied a common man's cake in "slapjack," or a common man's drink in "applejack." Although H. L. Mencken takes "flapjack" back to the fourteenth-century poem *Piers Plowman,* in England the word became obsolete when "pancake" replaced it. In the colonies, however, flap- or slapjack meant a pancake with cornmeal in it, as in Amelia Simmons' Indian Slapjacks.

Another influential New England cook-book author, Sarah Josepha Hale, clarifies the slapjack-pancake division in her *New Book of Cookery* (1852) when she calls cornmeal batters "Indian Slappers" and flour batters "Pancakes." "Although egg forms the chief foundation of all pancakes," she says, "they are yet made in various ways according to different tastes and countries." The most *"common sort"* of pancake, made simply of egg, flour, and milk, is still more elegant than a slapper. And the better sort of pancake will be flavored with brandy or orange flower water, or perhaps a little lemon peel or Seville orange. Significantly Mrs. Hale puts Indian slappers in her chapter "Bread, Breakfast Cakes, Etc.," but devotes a separate chapter to "Pancakes and Fritters," which she models on the recipes of Hannah Glasse. The terms remained confused, however, for Lydia Child states that "Either flour, Indian, or rye, is good" for "Flat-jacks." As for "Pancakes," she likes to flavor them with New England rum or "Flip," where "nothing is done but to sweeten your mug of beer with molasses; put in one glass of New England rum; heat it till it foams, by putting in a hot poker; and stir it up with flour as thick as other pancakes."

The most unusual pancake recipe I've come across is Mary Lincoln's in her "First Lesson in Batters" in her *Boston School Kitchen Text Book* (1896). These are Snow Pancakes appropriate to New England, since they call for flour, salt, milk, and a heaping tablespoon of "freshly fallen" snow. You are instructed to mix the salt with the flour, beat in the milk, and "fold in the snow," before pouring the batter onto the griddle with, one would trust, all deliberate speed.

Below I've eschewed snow for a dash of New England rum to enliven a batter of cornmeal and white flour, flavored with spices and leavened with baking powder and egg.

1 cup cornmeal
½ cup boiling water
½ cup unbleached white flour
½ teaspoon each baking powder and salt
¼ teaspoon cinnamon
⅛ teaspoon nutmeg
1 egg
2 teaspoons each molasses and dark rum
½–1 cup milk
3 tablespoons butter, melted

Moisten the cornmeal with the boiling water. Mix the white flour with the other dry ingredients. Beat the egg with the molasses and rum and then beat into ½ cup milk. Add to the cornmeal. Stir in the white flour mixture and 2 tablespoons melted butter. (Use the remaining tablespoon to grease griddle or frying pan.) If the batter seems thicker than you like, add more milk. Cornmeal takes longer to cook than wheat flour.

Brown cakes until golden brown, 2 to 3 minutes on each side.

Makes about 24 small (2-inch) cakes.

YANKEE NUT CAKES

One breakfast bread that took off in the colonies was indebted not to the English but to the Dutch. When the Pilgrims made a fuel stop in Holland in 1607 on their way to Plymouth, they fed on the oil cakes, *olykoeks,* of the Dutch, which were the same as the fat cakes, *fettkuchen,* of the Germans. These were balls of bread dough, left over from making bread, which were boiled in oil instead of in water, as the English did to make dumplings. To make yeast dumplings English style, Hannah Glasse advises the lazy house-wife to "send to the Baker's for half a Quartern of Dough (which will make a great many) and then you have only the Trouble of boiling it." Elizabeth Raffald in her *Experienced English Housekeeper* (1769), a very popular book in the colonies, called these dumplings "Barm Pudding," made by forming the barm dough into little balls, tying them in little nets, and boiling them in water. But do not cover them, she warns, or "it will make them sad."

Americans began to call these boiled dough cakes or balls "dough nuts." Eliza Leslie acknowledges their Dutch origin when she explains that the "New York Oley Koeks" are doughnuts with currants and raisins. Eliza adds cinnamon and nutmeg to her dough and cuts it in "thick diamond shaped cakes with a jagging iron." Only late in the eighteenth century were these nuts or diamonds of dough cut in circles with a hole in the middle to speed their cooking. The first doughnut cutters were made of wood, then later of tin (an idea patented on October 15, 1889), with scalloped edges to reproduce the mark made by a jagger or pastry crimper for trimming pie crust.

The circular doughnut evolved, in part, from the Dutch *krullen,* or kruller. Crullers were essentially a sweetened noodle dough, made with eggs and not yeast, shaped into braids or love knots or twisted, as one writer says, "so as to form small cakes united in a circle." By Sarah Josepha Hale's time, in the mid-nineteenth century, we find crullers and doughnuts side by side. Her crullers are either plaited or cut into strips with the ends joined to make a ring. Her doughnuts add yeast to a noodle dough and are either cut in small pieces or dropped from the end of a spoon into the fat. With Fannie Farmer at the end of the century, doughnuts and crullers are distinguishable only by shape. The dough is now leavened by baking powder, with or without the help of eggs, and doughnuts made with yeast are now called "Raised Doughnuts."

I've returned to a yeast-leavened dough shaped into the little "balls of sweetened dough, fried in hog's fat, and called doughnuts" that Washington Irving observed on the tables of "genuine Dutch families" in New York. New Englanders, Irving added, usually ate them for breakfast.

> 1 package dry yeast
> ¼ cup very warm (110°–115°) water
> 1 cup milk, room temperature
> 2 cups all-purpose flour
> 1 cup sugar
> 1 teaspoon cinnamon
> ½ teaspoon nutmeg
> ¼ teaspoon each mace and salt

2 eggs
4 tablespoons butter, melted
oil for deep-fat frying
powdered sugar

Dissolve yeast in water, add milk, and stir in 1 cup flour to make a sponge. Cover with plastic wrap and let the sponge rise overnight.

Mix remaining flour with the sugar and spices. Beat the eggs and add to the sponge. Stir in the flour mixture. Add the butter, and mix well. Cover dough and let rise.

"When of a spongelike lightness," tear off pieces of dough and shape them into 2-inch balls. Let them rise again, about 20 minutes, and drop them a few at a time into a wok or skillet of oil 2 inches deep and heated to around 375°. Turn them with a slotted spoon to brown on all sides. Drain them well on paper towels and sprinkle with powdered sugar or cinnamon mixed with granulated sugar.

Makes about 48 balls.

EELS IN GREEN SAUCE

On June 17, 1857, Thoreau wrote in his *Cape Cod* journal, "This morning had for breakfast fresh eels from Herring River, caught in an eel-pot baited with horseshoe clams cut up." Eel recipes, for breakfast and other meals, were common in New England cook books until this century, when apparently fishermen tired of unhooking these slippery beasts and housewives tired of skinning them. Euell Gibbons, however, is probably more to the point when he says that "wherever Eels are scarce and hard to catch they are eagerly sought and considered a delicacy, but where they are abundant and easily caught they are disliked." Only Rhode Island seems to have escaped this snobbery and retained its ancient reputation as a colony of eel eaters who asked nothing of life but "a jug of rum and a string of eels."

Louis Eustache Ude, in *The French Cook* (1828), thought the easiest method of skinning eels was to throw a couple of live ones into the fire: "As they are twisting about on all sides, lay hold of them with a towel in your hand, and skin them from head to tail." I find dead eels easier to manage but not by much. If you have a live one, throw him in the freezer to knock him out, then put him in a pan and cover him with kosher salt. The salt will remove his slime and allow you to get a purchase on his head while you skin him. Cut the skin below the head, all the way around, with poultry shears or a single-edge razor blade (the skin is too tough for most knives). Grab the head with one hand and with the other take a pair of pliers and pull hard. The skin will start to peel off in one piece. Gut along the belly with the same poultry shears and cut eel into chunks.

New Englanders derived their taste for eel from the homeland, where the English, like the French, were wont to stew eel in vinegar and wine, sweet herbs and aromats, as in Martha Washington's *Booke of Cookery,* "To Souce an Eele." Since eel is a fatty fish, the vinegar and wine cut the fat and flavor the delicious stock enriched by eel bones.

If eel is no longer a breakfast dish, it makes a fine and satisfying lunch or supper. The only way to eat soused or sauced eel is with the fingers, picking the eel pieces from the parsleyed broth and nibbling the meat from the bones.

2 pounds skinned and gutted eel, cut into 2-inch lengths
1 onion, chopped fine
1 carrot, chopped fine
1 celery stalk, chopped fine
1 clove garlic, minced
1½ cups white wine
2 tablespoons white wine vinegar
1 herb bouquet of thyme, bay leaf, and parsley
1 teaspoon salt
½ teaspoon black pepper
4 tablespoons butter, melted
2 egg yolks
½ cup minced parsley
  lemon juice to taste

In a saucepan put the eel with the vegetables, wine, vinegar, and seasonings, bring to a simmer, cover the pan, and simmer gently for 15 to 25 minutes.

Beat the butter slowly into the egg yolks. Add a little hot broth to the egg mixture, then stir it into the eel pot. Add the minced parsley and lemon juice and serve in soup bowls with wide plates beneath on which to put the bones.

Serves 4.

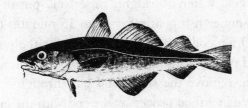

SALT-COD FISH CAKES

"There is no way of preparing salt fish for breakfast so nice," writes Lydia Child, "as to roll it up in little balls, after it is mixed with mashed potatoes, dip it into an egg, and fry it brown." Fish balls, like dough balls, stoked the furnace and got a body going. Fish balls also used up leftovers, and recipes for salt or fresh fish cooked with potatoes were a staple of the frugal housewife throughout the nineteenth century.

Unfortunately, memories of the Depression have put codfish cakes in bad odor in this country, but call it *brandade de morue* and fine eaters snap to attention. The French blended their salt cod and potato with oil, cream, and garlic. Americans added butter, egg, and pepper, and sometimes pork scraps. Much of the good flavor of codfish cakes came from the pork fat in which they were fried, but I've fried these in butter and added garlic because I love the taste of it with cod, even for breakfast, and because I want attentive rather than depressed eaters at any meal.

1 cup salt cod
2 large potatoes
½ cup heavy cream
1 egg
4–6 tablespoons butter
2 cloves garlic, mashed
¼ teaspoon black pepper
    cayenne pepper to taste
1 cup fresh bread crumbs

Soak cod in cold water overnight, rinse well, put in a pan, cover with fresh water, and simmer fish gently for 10 to 15 minutes (do not boil or you will toughen it). Drain cod, reserving the water for the potatoes.

Cut unpeeled potatoes into quarters and boil in the fish water for 10 to 20 minutes. Drain, remove the skins, and put through a ricer or food mill.

Blend or purée in a food processor the cod with the cream, egg, half the butter, garlic, and pepper. Mix together the cod and the potato lightly with a fork. Shape into 2-inch balls or thin round cakes. Roll in bread crumbs and fry in the remaining butter until golden brown.

Makes about 16 balls.

15
Potboilers

When the first seafarers came upon American Indians boiling their meats in vessels of bark or wood, into which they had dropped hot stones, they would have been less astonished than we because they would have recognized the ancient British potboiler. The same hot-stone method that originated in neolithic Britain continued there in remote areas into the eighteenth century. "Otherwise being destitute of vessels of metal or earth, they put water into a block of wood, made hollow with the help of the dirk and burning," a Captain Edward Butt observed of some remote island Scotsmen in the 1720s, "and then with pretty large stones heated red-hot, and successively quenched in that vessel, they keep the water boiling, till they have dressed their food."

Ancient Britons used these potboilers until migrating tribes from the Continent brought with them caldrons of earth, then of bronze, and finally of iron. Evidently the Britons were stewing fish with cereals and herbs in earthern pots as early as 4000 B.C. and adding salt to the pots by 600 B.C. when they discovered how to evaporate seawater. During the Celtic Iron Age they forged huge caldrons and suspended them on hooks over the central hearth for stewing whole carcasses of mutton, beef, and pork. The French called such caldrons *chaudrons* and *chaudières*. American colonists called the contents of such caldrons "chowders," mingling New France with New England in a common linguistic pot, or *caldaria*, from the Latin *calda*, meaning "heat."

For a nation of seafarers, the contents of such caldrons were chiefly fresh or salt fish and salt pork. Hannah Glasse identifies the word "chowder" with a seagoing caldron in her recipe "To make Chouder, a Sea Dish," in her chapter of receipts "For Captains of Ships." Her Sea Chowder is no mean dish, however, for she adds to the layers of pickled pork, salt cod, onions, and biscuits a glass of hot Madeira, "a very little India pepper," rather a lot of butter and oysters, and any truffles or morels lying about the ship's galley, the whole to be covered with a nice brown crust.

On this side of the Atlantic, seafarers-turned-settlers were forced to substitute cheaper ingredients for Hannah's classic chowder, made on land in the same iron pot. In 1751 the *Boston Evening Post* printed one of colonial America's first recipes, for a chowder as above, substituting red wine for Madeira and omitting truffles and morels. Lydia Child, befitting the frugal housewife, substituted for wine a cup of tomato ketchup or beer, and for truffles, "a few clams." The hazards of cheap substitutes are apparent in the warning of Amelia Simmons to housewives against the "deceits" of fishmongers who would substitute for fresh fish an illusory freshness, created by peppering the gills, wetting the fins and tails, or painting the gills with animal blood.

As for method, Hannah Glasse had directed the housewife or ship's cook to cover the stew kettle tightly, supply it with live wood embers, and keep it over a slow fire about four hours. Stewing had turned into steaming or poaching. Rebecca Price's recipe in *The Compleat Cook* is typical of fish boiling a century earlier. "Hang your fish kettle over the fire with as much water in it as you think will cover your fish." Hannah's chowder reversed this process by filling the pot first with fish, then adding liquid and a lid.

Potboilers were to the American North what the barbecue was to the South. One was indoor cooking, and the other outdoor cooking. In their one-pot cooking Northerners economized heat at the same time they economized contents by making tender the toughest meat, the stringiest bird. In this way the North continued earlier English traditions of the pottage, a gallimaufry of minced meats, fowls, or fish mixed with "Violet leaves, Succory, Strawbery leaves, Landebeefe, Spinage, Marigold flowers, Scallions & a little Parsley," as Gervase Markham advises the 1623 *English Hus-wife*. The pottage was a soup, a stew, a pudding, a pie. When French methods began to sophisticate British pottage later in the seventeenth century, the stew pot became the basis for a new range of "made dishes," now fricasseed, hashed, stuffed, collared and ragouted. Thus Hannah Glasse labels a recipe "To stew Beef-Steaks," where we would say "to braise" them, because she simmers them in red wine and seasonings in a pot.

In the North, slow cooking in a pot was the best way to keep vital heat within, so into the pot went not only fish and salt pork for chowders, but also briskets of beef for corning, rumps for pot roasting, oysters and clams for scalloping, lobsters for saucing, beans for tenderizing, hasty puddings and brown breads for steaming, along with numerous pudding-cake-pies put in a Dutch oven for "baking." Even when summer weather permitted the Northerners to cook out of doors, still they improvised a pot—the earth pot of a clambake that steams a gallimaufry of seafoods and vegetables. Where the enclosed heat of a clambake typifies the North, the open flame of a barbecue typifies the South: the one introverted, the other extroverted. Not hospitality but conservation is the watchword of the North, noted by Robert Frost in "Provide, provide."

SPICY FISH CHOWDER

"A *chowder*," Mary Lincoln says in her pedagogic way in *The Boston School Kitchen Text Book*, "is a stew of fish." New England chowders began not with clams but with fish like cod or haddock or bass. Clams and blackfish were "tolerably good" substitutes, Mrs. A. L. Webster advises in *The Improved Housewife* (1842), but only if the hard part of the clam is "cut off and rejected." Clams at first were relegated to soups and only later in the nineteenth century did chowders of clam become interchangeable with chowders of cod.

What made chowder *chowder* was the mixture of seafood with salt pork and ship's biscuit. In *Moby Dick* (1851), Melville describes the Try Pots chowder of Nantucket, "made of small juicy clams, scarcely bigger than hazel nuts, mixed with pounded ship biscuits, and salted pork cut up into little flakes! the whole enriched with butter, and plentifully seasoned with pepper and salt." In her cook books of 1872 and 1887, Maria Parloa furnishes a number of fish chowders and clam chowders unified by pork, onions, potatoes, and split crackers, sometimes identified as "white browns." These were the round, white, lightly puffed and browned ship's biscuits that came to be called Boston common crackers. If you cannot get "white browns," Maria Parloa says, "pilot bread will answer." Pilot bread was the standard sea biscuit or hard tack that became a staple of New England bakers.

Maria Parloa is very specific about her clams. First put them in a tub of clean water and add cornmeal to fatten them. To open them, cover with boiling water and let them stand for ten minutes. Cut off "the black heads" and use only the soft parts, to be added to the chowder at the last minute: "In cooking clams in any manner, remember that they are toughened by long cooking."

Fanatic regionalists who think the addition of tomatoes to chowder began in Manhattan should note Parloa's use of tomatoes in her Danbury Clam Chowder and in Fannie Farmer's 1896 recipes for Connecticut Chowder and Rhode Island Chowder. Louis de Gouy in his *Chef's Cook Book* (1939) had the right idea when he called Manhattan clam chowder a misnomer, since the same tomato-based stew was eaten in "Gloucester, Swampscot, Nehant, Cohasset, Scituate, all around the Cape, and up and down Narragansett Bay from the Point to Providence."

My guess is that tomatoes snuck into fish chowder by way of tomato ketchup, a frequent colonial substitute for the costly and often unavailable "hot Madeira wine" recommended by Hannah Glasse. Today's standard milk-based flour-thickened New England Clam Chowder is another example of the degradations wrought by the Prohibitionists in turning the lively into the bland.

Here I've concocted a mildly spicy cream broth, flecked with a bit of fresh tomato, layered with salt pork, onions, and potatoes and fishified with cod and clams. If I had a fresh lobster, I would throw it in, along with oysters and mussels. The secret, and the only secret, of a good chowder lies in the quality of the fish stock that binds the whole. It's worth buying an extra fish with bones to make a stock before you begin. It's also worth making the chowder a day before you eat it to let the flavors mingle and to intensify that stock. If you make chowder ahead, add the fish at the last moment off heat because it will finish cooking when you reheat it, and no chowder worth its salt has mushy fish.

2 pounds cod or haddock fillets
½ teaspoon each black pepper and thyme
   cayenne pepper to taste
24–36 hard-shelled clams
4 cups boiling fish stock
¼ pound salt pork, diced
2 large onions, chopped
3 potatoes, diced
1 cup each milk and heavy cream
⅛ teaspoon each mace and cloves
   dash each Tabasco and Worcestershire sauces
2 fresh tomatoes, peeled, seeded, and chopped
¼ pound (1 stick) butter
   common crackers or oyster crackers

Cut the fish into 1½-inch pieces, sprinkle with the peppers and thyme (salt will come from the clams and salt pork), and put aside.

Scrub the clams well under cold water to rid them of sand and put them in a pot with a little water on the bottom. Cover pan tightly and steam the clams until the shells open, about 15 minutes. Remove clams from their shells, saving the broth for the stock. Slip the black skin from the foot. If the clams are large, chop the meat of the foot, and leave the soft part in one piece. If clams are small, use whole. Strain clam broth through cheesecloth into the stock. Add water, if needed, to make 6 cups.

Fry salt pork until crisp in a ceramic-lined or nonmetallic kettle and add onions to soften gently without browning. Add potatoes and then cover with the fish stock. Simmer about 5 minutes. Add milk and cream, the seasonings, and the chopped tomatoes. (If you have chopped clam meat, add it now.) Simmer another 5 minutes and taste for seasoning.

Remove pan from heat. Add fish and clams (whole or the soft bellies) and refrigerate overnight. Reheat in a 200° or 225° oven just below the simmering point. Put a tablespoon of butter in each soup bowl, add soup, and crumble crackers on top or serve them separately.

Serves 8 to 10.

TOMATO-CINNAMON CHURCH SOUP

The Meeting House Cookbook of Concord, Massachusetts, provides a soup that Judy McConnell (in nearby Bedford) remembers drinking from a mug in a Concord church parlor on a more than usually icy morning. If cinnamon seems odd for tomato soup, think of a bloody mary without booze but with the spices and peppers of tomato ketchup. Because the tomato is botanically related to deadly nightshade and because it reached England from the New World by way of Spanish ships, England and other cold countries of the north regarded the plant with distrust. Gerard, in his sixteenth-century *Herball*, warned his countrymen that these "Apples of Love" might engender heat of a dubious kind, since they were known to be eaten by the people of "Spaine and those hot Regions." As a result England did not grow tomatoes for food until the middle of the eighteenth century.

Distrust, however, remained. Eliza Leslie warns that baked tomatoes will "not lose their raw taste in less than three hours' cooking." Lydia Child found them "a delicious vegetable" when stewed, but the best and safest way to use them was as a ketchup, where they were better than oysters or mushrooms. For a ketchup, tomato pulp might be boiled for hours to evaporate its water while the Eastern spices of clove, mace, allspice, and cinnamon did their work.

In the kitchens of Concord, the association of cinnamon and other aromats with tomatoes was natural. For a Concord church soup, you can turn this tomato-bouillon into a thin drinkable temperance brew or into a thick purée to be eaten with a spoon. The blender or food processor will purée the vegetables in a trice and you can add beef bouillon to your taste.

3 cups stewed tomatoes
1 onion, chopped fine
1 large stalk celery with leaves, chopped
2 cups beef bouillon
2 teaspoons each red-wine or balsamic vinegar, and sugar
½ teaspoon each black pepper and cinnamon
¼ teaspoon allspice
⅛ teaspoon mace
salt and cayenne pepper to taste

Stew all ingredients together, covered, in a saucepan until the vegetables are soft, about 20 minutes. Purée in a processor or blender. Reduce to thicken or add bouillon to thin.

Serves 4 to 6.

LOBSCOUSE

"Lobscouse" is one of those suggestive British dialect words, like "loblolly," that came from the sea and were retained by seagoing New Englanders. On board ship, lobscouse was a treat. Elsewhere, it was a dish for country bumpkins. "Lob" meant a heavy lump and therefore a yokel; "loblolly" meant a bumpkin's heavy broth or porridge; and "lobscouse" meant a navvy's heavy stew. A sea chowder made of salt meats instead of salt fish, it was not always appreciated by its eaters. "He has sent the Fellow to the Devil," an eighteenth-century Englishman opined, "who first invented Lobscouse." But as seafarers became settlers and then pioneers, the dish survived as a Dutch-oven meal for land travelers. As James Fenimore Cooper noted in *Pioneers:* "He acquired the art of making lobskouse."

Today, it appeals still to thrifty New Englanders anxious to use up leftover meats. I found a recipe for it in Marjorie Mosser's *Foods of Old New England* (1957), originally published in 1939 as *Good Maine Food.* Because I seldom have leftover beef these days, I've started with fresh beef to mix with corned. The cut of beef and the size of the cubes will determine how long to cook the beef. The saltiness of the corned beef will determine whether to add any additional salt, as in the anchovies suggested here. Your own taste for thick or thin chowders and stews will determine whether to flour your beef cubes or leave them without.

¼ pound salt pork, cubed
1 cup all-purpose flour
1 teaspoon black pepper
  pinch of cayenne pepper
4 cups cubed bottom-round beef
4 large onions, sliced
1 quart or more boiling beef stock
4 cups cubed potatoes
4 cups cooked and cubed corned beef
  optional: 2 or 3 anchovy fillets and/or Worcestershire sauce to
    taste

Fry the salt pork until crisp in a Dutch oven or heavy iron pot. Remove with a slotted spoon and set aside.

Mix the flour with the pepper in a paper bag. Add the fresh beef cubes and shake to coat them before quickly browning in the pork fat, adding more fat or oil if needed. Remove beef as it's browned and add to the reserved salt pork cubes. Lightly brown the onions in the same fat.

Return beef cubes and pork to the pot, cover with broth, and simmer until beef is barely tender, about 30 minutes. Add potatoes and corned beef and simmer 30 to 45 minutes more. Halfway through, taste for seasoning and, if salt is needed, add anchovies. For a heftier taste, add Worcestershire sauce.

Serves 4 to 6.

ALAMODE BEEF

To chart the course of cooking in New England is to see how the mighty fell between the beginning of the nineteenth century and the end of it, when the domestic arts converted to utilitarianism and justified that faith by science. The climate of Boston fostered not only Mary Baker Eddy's science and health but Fannie Farmer's as well. Science's gain was art's loss, as we can see in the decline of eighteenth-century "alamode beef" into twentieth-century "Yankee pot roast."

Hannah Glasse had codified the eighteenth-century classic beef roast the English named after the French, "alamode." Hannah specifies a "leg-of-mutton-piece of beef, or a clod, or a piece of buttock of beef," to be braised in red wine, porter, or ale and spiced heavily with cloves, mace, cayenne pepper, "all sorts of sweet herbs," bacon and mushrooms and bread raspings for thickening the gravy. Amelia Simmons follows Hannah in citing two ways to "Alamode a Round of Beef." In one, Amelia pokes holes in a round of beef and stuffs them with herbs and spices as one might lard a roast. In the other, she marinates the round for a week or two, then pokes and fills the holes with a bread and ground-meat stuffing.

The stuffed roast proved very popular in the colonies because it was both filling and fancy. Even the frugal Lydia Child "alamodes" her beef with a stuffing of grated bread, sweet herbs and spices, suet and egg yolks, and shapes the rest into balls, like quenelles, to be poached in claret gravy. Philadelphia, as usual, far exceeded Boston in the fancy, as we see in Eliza Leslie's Alamode Beef, which is boned and stuffed, then stewed with vegetables and calves' feet and pickled mushrooms and bathed in port. Served cold, however, her beef is fancier yet, glazed with egg white and covered with grated potatoes for a field of white, in which Eliza plants flowers and stars cut from turnips and carrots and beets fixed on skewers. From a distance, she says, her alamode beef will "look like a large iced cake decorated with sugar flowers."

Compare Maria Parloa's 1887 recipe for Pot Roast, flavored with salt, pepper, and cloves in a gravy of flour and water. She does give a Savory Beef, which recalls some of the exotic spices of the alamode, but Maria adds sugar to the marinade and omits all mention of claret or port. With Fannie Farmer, we find Beef à la Mode stuck with lardoons of pork fat seasoned only with salt, pepper, parsley, and bay leaf and cooked with vegetables in water. When beef is cooked without the lardoons and vegetables in a smaller amount of water, "it is called Smothered Beef, or Pot Roast," Fannie advises, and suggests that the best pot for the roast is a Boston bean pot.

In this alamode I've put the spiced beef in a marinade for a couple of days, then braised it with flavoring vegetables to thicken a gravy made with wine for color and beer for body. This beef, even cold, will never look like "a large iced cake," but it tastes as good cold as hot because the flavorings have slowly had their way with obdurate flesh.

> 1 4-pound beef round
> ¼ pound salt pork, minced,
> ½ cup minced parsley
> optional: 2–3 beef marrows removed from marrow bones
> 1 teaspoon each black pepper and cloves
> ½ teaspoon each allspice and mace
> cayenne pepper to taste

Marinade
> 2 large onions, chopped
> 2 cloves garlic, mashed
> 3 bay leaves, crushed
> ½ cup dried mushrooms, soaked in 1 cup water
> 1 tablespoon red wine vinegar
> 1 cup red wine
> 1½ cups beer or ale

> 3 tablespoons beef or pork fat or oil for frying

Poke about a dozen holes, top to bottom, in the round of beef. Mix together the salt pork, parsley, marrow, and spices and stuff the holes with the mixture.

Make a marinade of the remaining ingredients (except for the frying fat) and put in a plastic bag with the beef. Refrigerate 1 to 3 days, turning the bag occasionally.

Drain the meat well, dry it with paper towels, and brown it on all sides in hot fat in a heavy kettle like a Dutch oven. Set the meat on a trivet, pour the marinade over it, cover the pot tightly, and bake at 295°, or cook on top of the stove at a bare simmer, until the meat is fork tender, about 3 hours.

Remove the meat to a hot platter, degrease the sauce, and purée the liquid with the cooked vegetables in a blender. If the sauce is too thick, thin with beef stock, beer, or wine and simmer long enough to mingle flavors.

Serves 6 to 8.

SCARLET BEEF
WITH VEGETABLES

Say "corned beef and cabbage" to anyone other than a Boston Irisher and the spirits sink. The New England boiled dinner of salt beef and vegetables in a pot can be a thing of beauty, like a French *pot au feu,* but for many the very name reeks of poverty. Say "scarlet beef," on the other hand, as Mrs. Chadwick calls it in her *Home Cookery* (1852), and spirits perk with suggestions of Hawthorne's *Scarlet Letter.* Since we consume images when we consume our food, names matter.

The name "corned" beef comes from the grains or "corns" of salt used to preserve it. Instead of buying the often overly salted brisket, commercially corned and immured in plastic for supermarket permanence, try making scarlet beef on your own. Brisket, or breast, is the traditional cut for corning, not only because it's cheap, but because it's layered with fat to flavor the meat as it simmers.

"When you merely want to corn meat," Lydia Child advises, "you have nothing to do but to rub in salt plentifully, and let it set in the cellar a day or two," protecting it in summer from the "cellar-flies." Lydia adds a little saltpeter to tenderize and keep the meat red, as Mrs. Chadwick does to keep hers scarlet. Mrs. Chadwick also follows the English mode of adding sugar and spice to the salt. Three to five days is long enough to give the beef good flavor, and if you keep the meat refrigerated, you can salt it so lightly that you won't have to soak it before simmering.

Vegetables depend on the purse and the season. Maria Parloa suggests beet greens, dandelions, chicory, and brussels sprouts, along with the usual turnips, carrots, onions, and parsnips. In the early part of the nineteenth century, cabbage was possible but not necessary, and Eliza Leslie warns against boiling cabbage in the same pot: "it is a much nicer way to do the greens in a separate vessel, lest they become saturated with the liquid fat." Beets did not enter the pot until late in the century, when beets became so popular that ways of cooking them were called "Harvard" and "Yale." If you add beets, heed Mary Lincoln's advice to cook them separately lest you turn the whole pot scarlet.

1 5-pound beef brisket
½ cup kosher or sea salt
⅓ cup brown sugar
   optional: 1 teaspoon saltpeter
2 tablespoons black pepper
1 tablespoon allspice
⅛ teaspoon mace
2 bay leaves, crumbled

6 of each: beets, small carrots, turnips, parsnips, and onions
4 medium potatoes
1 small Savoy cabbage
¼ pound (1 stick) butter, melted
½ cup minced parsley

Mustard

¼ cup each dry mustard and olive oil
½ cup wine vinegar
1 clove garlic, mashed
½ teaspoon each salt and dried tarragon or thyme
¼ teaspoon black pepper
   cayenne pepper to taste

To corn the beef, mix the salt, sugar, and seasonings together and rub into the beef on all sides. Put beef in a plastic bag and refrigerate 3 to 10 days, turning the bag once each day. When ready to cook, rinse off the seasonings, cover beef with water, and simmer gently until meat is almost fork tender, 2 to 3 hours. Skim fat from the broth.

Bake or boil the beets, unpeeled, until tender (bake at 300° for an hour or boil about 30 minutes). When the beets are cool, peel and quarter.

Scrape or peel the carrots, parsnips, turnips, and onions; cut them into halves or quarters. Quarter the cabbage and cook it with the other raw vegetables and the beef in its broth until the vegetables are tender but still crisp, 7 to 15 minutes. Drain well.

Cut beef into thick slices and surround them on a platter with the vegetables. Pour melted butter over the vegetables, sprinkle with parsley, and serve with homemade mustard. To make the mustard, blend all the ingredients together. "Very nice with corned beef," says Eliza Leslie.

Serves 8 to 10.

BEAN TOWN BEANS

Kenneth Roberts, the New Englander who wrote *Northwest Passage,* recalled with nostalgia the one-horse bean carts of his youth, carts that ameliorated "the lot of the New England housewife who was so unfortunate as to have no professional help." The driver perched under a roof with a box in front, a box behind, and a bell "like a broken front-door bell." In the box in front were beans and salt pork; in the box behind were brown bread, white bread, cakes, and pies. The Saturday night bean pot gave Boston its nickname of "Bean Town" and consummated its need to combine thrift with morality.

Roberts, an unregenerate fictioneer, attributed the origin of the bean pot to the Sephardic Jews of North Africa and to a Boston Irish sea captain, shipwrecked off Morocco in 1815, who learned to eat a dish of dried peas and beef marrow bones wetted with "Jew's brandy, distilled from figs and aniseed, and bittered with wormwood." The boring truth, however, was that the bean habit began with the Puritan commandment to keep the Sabbath holy from Saturday sunset to Sunday sunset, with no cooking in between.

While the colonists found Indians cultivating several types of beans among their cornstalks, the English had brought seeds with them to plant the crops of home, "wheat and rye, barley, oats, beans and pease," as William Bradford wrote. And while colonists found Indians baking beans in their hot-stone pits, which the English soon labeled "bean-holes," the English had for centuries "baked" beans and pease in a hearth pot to make their daily "pottage." Pease pottage was still the national dish as late as the seventeenth century, when the middle and upper classes began to wrap the pottage in a pudding cloth and boil it in broth flavored with bacon.

Colonists maintained the more primitive form of the one-pot meal in their bacon and beans, to which they added "a Littell suger." Until the first shipment of West Indian molasses arrived in Boston harbor late in the seventeenth century, settlers had to use "Indian sweetening." As soon as they could, however, they replaced maple sweetening with molasses and added mustard to render the beans "less unhealthy," in Lydia Child's euphemism. The secret to good baked beans, says Lydia, lies in the pork, which should alternate fat and lean and supply a substantial part of the dish, a pound of pork to a quart of beans.

Fannie Farmer, as usual, ups the sweetening and adds sugar to molasses. She also indicates why the dish became identified with Boston even after beans had to be imported from the Midwest. "The fine reputation which Boston Baked Beans have gained has been attributed to the earthen bean-pot with small top and bulging sides in which they are supposed to be cooked," she writes, and adds that a five-pound lard pail will cook them as well. The only advantage of a bean pot is that it retains heat long after the beans are cooked and in that way helps to keep the Sabbath holy.

> 2 cups dried beans (pea, navy, or soldier)
> ½ pound smoked slab bacon, with rind on
> 1 large onion, chopped
> ¼ cup blackstrap molasses
> 1 tablespoon dry mustard
> 2 bay leaves, crushed
> ½ teaspoon each salt and black pepper
>   pinch of cayenne pepper, or dash Tabasco

Pick over beans to remove grit or stones. Cover beans with cold water, bring to a boil, and boil 1 minute. Remove from heat, cover pot, and let the beans sit 1 hour. Drain.

Score the bacon in squares without cutting through the rind. Put half the beans in the pot in which you will bake them and add onion, molasses, and seasonings. Add remaining beans and bury the bacon, rind up, in the top layer. Add just enough boiling water to cover. Cover the pot tightly and bake at 300° for 4 to 6 hours or more to melt the pork fat and meld the flavors. Add boiling water from time to time if needed. Remove lid for the last 30 minutes to make a brown crust.

Serves 6 to 8.

SCALLOPED OYSTERS

Judy McConnell makes scalloped oysters the way Mrs. Champney did. Cora Ambrose Champney was born in 1885 in Rowley, Massachusetts, and she died at age ninety-seven in Bedford. Cora made oysters "the way I used to see my grandmother make them," she said, "starting with a layer of crumbs rolled with a rolling pin and moistened with oyster liquid and butter and put in the oven." Her grandmother might have added, as Mrs. Chadwick did in her 1852 recipe for Scalloped Muscles and Oysters, "a *very little* nutmeg" and a glass of Madeira.

The tradition of seasoning oysters thus exotically, as well as the custom of baking oysters in scallop shells with crumbs to soak up the juice, dates back to the Lenten meals of the Middle Ages. Hannah Glasse used real scallop shells and set them in a tin reflector oven to brown before the fire. Eliza Leslie suggests clam shells or "the tin scollop shells made for the purpose," which she puts on a gridiron over the coals and then browns on top "with a red-hot shovel." Eventually even a simple buttered baking dish allowed the recipe to retain the name "scalloped oysters," provided the oysters were baked with crumbs.

In New England those dry ship's biscuits, now manufactured as Boston common crackers, made the best crumbs because they absorbed juice best. Judy remembers being able to buy the round mushroom-shaped white-and-brown crackers from a barrel in any Massachusetts general store. Originally Artemus Kennedy in the early 1800s baked them thrice weekly in his Dutch oven at Menotomy, Massachusetts, packed them into his saddlebags, and sold them on horseback. Soon a Captain Joseph Bent made a similar cracker known as Bent's common crackers, made still in Milton and rightly labeled "Famous for Years."

Saltines are not a good substitute for the saltless common cracker. If you can't get common crackers, use bread crumbs instead. The point of scalloped oysters is to keep the oysters in a single layer in whatever dish you bake them in, so that the crumbs on top will crisp and the ones on the bottom will soak up juice and oyster flavor. I like both crumbs and oysters flavored with sweet herbs and spices, but Sarah Josepha Hale did not approve. "These although they may please an epicurean palate," she warns, "will destroy the natural flavor of the oyster." So go the Puritans, but I go with the epicures.

> 2 cups common cracker crumbs (or bread crumbs)
> 1 quart shucked oysters
> ¼ pound (1 stick) butter
> ¼ cup each minced green onions and parsley
> 1 tablespoon fresh thyme, or ½ teaspoon dried thyme
> ¼ teaspoon mace
> salt and black and cayenne pepper to taste

Spread half the crumbs in a large shallow baking dish where the oysters will form a single layer. Drain the oysters (saving their liquor for another use) and place them on the crumbs. Melt the butter and soften the onions a minute or two by sautéing gently. Add the parsley and remaining seasonings.

Pour half the butter mixture over the oysters, cover them with the remaining crumbs, and pour over them the remaining butter mixture. Bake on the top rack of an oven at 450° for 7 to 10 minutes. If the top layer is not brown, run the pan under a broiler for a minute.

Serves 4.

CLAM FORCEMEAT PIE

Although the entire eastern seaboard abounded in clams with thick hard shells and clams with thin "soft" shells, English colonists did not hold them in high repute. The word "clam," in fact, related to "clamp" and "cramp," was an Anglo-Saxon generic term for all kinds of bivalves, and bivalves even in neolithic Britain were a main source of food only for "very poor and backward groups of people," Anne Wilson tells us in *Food and Drink in Britain* (1973). When John Josselyn tried to describe the most common of bivalves in his *New England Rarities* (1672), he named the "Clam, or Cramp, a kind of Shell Fish, a white Muscle."

Pilgrims picked up the word "quahog," which suggests a hoggish-sized clam, from the Narraganset *poquauhock*. Middle-sized clams eventually were named "cherrystones" after Cherrystone Creek, Virginia. And the smallest-sized clams became "littlenecks" not for their littleness but their location in Littleneck Bay, one in Long Island and another in Ipswich, Massachusetts.

Recipes for clams seldom appeared in English cook books because of their low status, but Hannah Glasse did furnish a recipe for Muscle Pie, which became the standard for New England bivalve pies to come. New England favored oysters for its pies and left clams to chowders and broths, pancakes, and fritters. Lydia Child, for example, tells us how to make a clam soup by steaming clams in their own juice. Mrs. A. L. Webster tells us how to roast clams in a skillet over the coals. Indian methods of roasting shells in their campfires or steaming them in earth pits would have seemed to the new settlers a reversion to the barbarisms of their own Celtic tribes. As soon as they could, they substituted pots and pies.

One of the most delectable bivalve pies I've come across is an egg and oyster pie in an eighteenth-century manuscript receipt book in Salem, Massachusetts (quoted by Kathleen Smallzried in *The Everlasting Pleasure* [1956]). This Salem pie, misleadingly called "a fine Potatoe Pye," is a countrified version of Hannah Glasse's Lobster Pie, in which she pounds lobster meat and roe to make a forcemeat thickened by egg yolks and bread crumbs. Fannie Farmer continues this forcemeat tradition by chopping oysters or clams to be shaped and cooked as quenelles. For a clam pie, I have found that a layer of clam forcemeat inside a pie crust does wonders in preventing the crust from turning soggy with a clam filling. If you are dealing with large clams, or qua-hogs, a forcemeat is a good way to tenderize those tough clam "feet." Don't take alarm at the large quantity of egg yolks—fourteen! The eggs are as important here as the clams.

pie dough for a 2-crust 9-inch pie
2 quarts, or 48, hard-shelled clams (to yield 2 cups meat)

Forcemeat
1 small onion, minced
6 hard-cooked egg yolks, chopped
1 tablespoon minced parsley
½ teaspoon thyme
⅛ teaspoon nutmeg
salt and pepper to taste
6 hard-cooked egg yolks, plus 2 raw yolks, beaten
½ cup grated raw potato
¼ cup minced onion
¼ teaspoon mace
salt and pepper to taste
½ cup clam broth
1 tablespoon vermouth
6 tablespoons butter, melted

Roll out two-thirds of the pastry to line the pie plate and remaining third to make a top crust. Chill for 30 minutes. Steam open the clams in a covered pan with a little water and strain the broth carefully to remove any sand. If the clams are large, remove and discard the black skins, then cut off and mince the hard feet (for the forcemeat). Reserve the whole soft bodies. If the clams are small, mince half of them for the forcemeat and leave the rest whole.

Add the minced clams to the onion, chopped egg yolks, and seasonings and line the bottom and sides of the pie crust with this forcemeat.

Layer the remaining clams and 6 hard-cooked yolks on top of the force-meat, then add potato, onion, and seasonings. Mix the broth, vermouth, and butter, beat in the 2 raw yolks, and pour the mixture over the clams and potatoes. Quickly cover with the top pie crust, sealing the edges and cutting a vent in the top. Bake at 325° for about 1 hour.

Serves 6 to 8.

MARIA PARLOA'S LOBSTER NEWBURG

As with clams, so with lobsters. Steaming lobsters in hot stones and seaweed was okay for Indians, but not for civilized colonists. Lobster was not a class dish until it was parboiled and stewed with butter, wine, and spices and poured into the emptied shell to make what Hannah Glasse calls "a fine side-dish at a second course."

There were two major concerns for our cook-book ladies with lobsters: the freshness of them and the killing of them. With a fresh lobster, Hannah explains, "the tail will, when opened, fall smart, like a spring; but when stale, it has a rank scent, and the tail limber and flagging." Lydia Child elaborates on the spring action of a fresh tail. "The end of a lobster is surrounded with what children call 'purses,' edged with a little fringe," she writes. "If you put your hand under these to raise it, and find it springs back hard and firm, it is a sign the lobster is fresh; if they move flabbily, it is not a good omen." Omens extended to lobster killing. Hannah finds that boiling lobsters in a pot is not half the trouble of roasting them alive in the coals, "not to mention the cruelty." Sarah Josepha Hale defends the lobster cook from cruelty even in the boiling of lobsters. "Many people are shocked at the apparent cruelty of thus killing, but death takes place immediately," she says, "and life cannot be taken without pain."

After the painful parboil, the lobster meat should be cut into pieces and stewed with wine, butter, elderberry vinegar, and maybe an orange or lemon slice, according to the seventeenth-century *Compleat Cook*'s recipe "To Butter Lobsters: my second Cousen Clerkes Receipt." When Maria Parloa in her *Kitchen Companion* (1887) adds brandy and sherry to her buttered lobster and calls it "Lobster Newburg," she follows a venerated English tradition. The Newburg name got attached to this lobster dish sometime during the nineteenth century for reasons obscured by time and publicists. The fabled origin of the name in a sea captain named Wenberg is clearly the invention of a Delmonico Restaurant publicist. The Delmonico brothers had made French names so fashionable in the 1880s and 1890s that "à la" dishes began to litter not only menus but cook books. The "à la Newburg" is probably a misspelling of Newburgh, either the one in Scotland or the one up the Hudson River, where the New York Central Railroad of Commodore Cornelius Vanderbilt had established an important station. An intriguing clue is provided by Madame Saint-Ange, whose formidably important *La Cuisine* (1927) supplies a lobster recipe named "à la Newburg or Van Der Bilt."

2 large lobsters (2 pounds each)
¼ pound (1 stick) butter
2 teaspoons salt
¼ teaspoon each white pepper and nutmeg
pinch of cayenne pepper
4 egg yolks
1 cup heavy cream
¼ cup brandy or Madeira

Boil lobsters in salted water for 10 to 15 minutes (they will finish cooking in the sauce). Split shells in half and remove the tail meat and all the coral and tomalley (the orange roe and green liver). Discard the stomach sac from the shell, rinse the shells, and save. Split the claws and remove their meat. Cut meat into chunks.

Melt butter with seasonings in a saucepan, add all the lobster, and simmer very gently for 1 to 2 minutes. Mix egg yolks with the cream and brandy. Pour mixture slowly into the simmering lobster and stir until sauce barely begins to thicken (remember that high heat will curdle egg yolks). Spoon mixture into the emptied shells and serve.

Serves 4.

16
Garden Stuff

Early Americans have been much maligned for their presumed lack of fresh vegetables, particularly salads, as if our colonists had had to wait for the arrival of the Swiss Delmonico brothers to "discover," as too many historians have said, not only salads but "endive, watercress, artichokes, sorrel, and eggplant." The claim is nonsense, as we have seen in the gardening South. In the wintry North, the kitchen garden was harder dug and therefore all the more treasured. When Thoreau was not out gathering wild purslane for his salad, he was digging his bean field and moralizing on the virtues of husbandry. "Those summer days which some of my contemporaries devoted to the fine arts in Boston or Rome, and others to contemplation in India, and others to trade in London or New York," he writes in *Walden*, "I thus, with the other farmers of New England, devoted to husbandry."

Where winters were long, the husbanded root cellar was as important as the garden plot, and Thoreau was not alone in turning defects to virtues when he asserted, "The house is still but a sort of porch at the entrance of a burrow." If husbandry was harder work in the North than in the South, husbandmen were also harder workers. John Josselyn noted in his *New England Rarities,* among wild edible plants, the numerous cultivated plants of kitchen gardens, the same "English Herbs we have growing in our Gardens that prosper there as well as in their proper Soil." His list was exceeding long and included such salad greens as "lettice, sorrel, parsley, marygold, French mallowes; chervel, burnet, wintery savory, summer savory, time, sage, carrats, parsneps of a prodigious size, red beetes, radishes, turnips, purslain, spearmint, smalledge [parsley], sparagus, tansie, cucumbers, Gillyflowers."

Our orphan authoress Amelia Simmons was far more a gardener than she was a cook, as one can tell from the particulars of her gardening instructions. She tells how to keep parsley through the winter by transplanting the roots to a cask drilled with holes for the leafy branches to poke through, so that "I clip with my scissors the fresh parsley, which my neighbors or myself have occasion for; and in the spring transplant the roots in the bed in the garden, or in any unused corner—or let stand upon the wharf, or the sash shed."

Herbs, greens, flowers—all were eaten raw in salads and all were treasured for specific medicinal properties, as they had been since the Middle Ages, based on the four elements and the four humors. The New World added a new salad flower, the nasturtium, called "Indian cress" from its origin in the West Indies, and much valued for its blossoms, leaves, and peppery seeds. Because of their newness, nasturtiums were more highly prized than the more common salad flowers like gillyflowers, marigolds, violets, and primroses.

Wherever salads are mentioned, not just freshness but early-morning freshness is required. Americans did not have to wait for Alice Waters to "discover" that fresh is best. Mrs. A. L. Webster in *The Improved Housewife* begins her instructions for garden salads, "To have this delicate dish in perfection, pick your lettuce, pepper-grass, chervil, cress, etc., early in the morning." If ice is available, use it, she says, to keep the greens fresh. *The Cook's Own Book* (1832) has a long section on Salad Mixtures, all "morning gathered" and washed and trimmed of "all the worm-eaten, slimy, cankered, dry leaves," before they are drained and spun dry in a clean napkin.

Sarah Josepha Hale in 1852 enumerates so many salads and salad dressings that she resorts to subcategories of winter, summer, vegetable, French, Italian, Spanish, vinaigrette, chicken, tomato, "coldslaw," radish, and cucumber salads. She also explains the niceties of greens. The English cut lettuces extremely fine, she says, while the French break their leaves in pieces because they object "to the *flavor of the knife*." For summer salads she asks that the dressing be left in the bottom of the bowl, "to be stirred up when wanted," and even recommends garlic if "sparingly and judiciously used." Again, Americans did not have to wait for James Beard or Craig Claiborne to "discover" the classic French vinaigrette. These nineteenth-century cook books almost always specify dressings of two kinds: the French vinaigrette of oil, vinegar, salt, and pepper; and the English dressing, which adds to the vinaigrette a mashed hard-cooked egg yolk and some dry mustard. Soy is also sometimes added, or essence of anchovies. Dressings were ordinarily not sweetened until Fannie Farmer began to make sweetened dressings the rule and unsweetened "French" or "Club French" the aberration. By the time of the 1924 edition of Fannie Farmer, salads have run amok and we begin our modern baroque salad era with names like Nile Salad, Hindoo Salad, Oyster & Grape Fruit Salad, Fruit and Ginger Ale Salad, Mexican Jelly Salad, Porcupine Salad, Heliofolis Salad, Wiersbick's Salad—why go on? Americans have always liked salads, and today's salad bar is as natural to the American style as the Western saloon bar.

HOT SLAW

When Amelia Simmons describes cabbage, her description "requires a page," she says, "they are so multifarious." She lists the Low Dutch, Early Yorkshire, Yellow Savoy, and the fine and tender Green Savoy, which is the best of our supermarket varieties today. "All Cabbages should be grown on '*new unmatured grounds,*'" she warns, for "if grown in an old town and on old gardens, they have a rankness, which at times, may be perceived by a fresh air traveller." Since cabbages were a staple of the colonial kitchen garden, fresh air travelers in summertime may not have delighted in cabbages as much as Amelia Simmons did.

Garden cabbages had been brought to Britain by the Romans, and for centuries the cabbage or cole family (sprouts, kale, headed and unheaded cabbage types) supplied those "buttered worts" or green pottages which foreshadowed, Anne Wilson explains, "the more general boiling and buttering of vegetables in years to come." Hannah Glasse reflects eighteenth-century uses of cabbage, which combined food with medicine: "dressed after the Dutch

Way, good for a Cold in the Breast." The Dutch way was to simmer shredded cabbage in butter and oil, water and vinegar, seasoned with onion, pepper, and salt, to make a sort of hot slaw.

Americans following the Dutch way confused "cold" with "cole" (the Dutch word *koolsla* means cabbage salad hot or cold), and Fannie Farmer's 1896 cook book exhibits the confusion in listing both a Cole Slaw and a Hot Slaw. The Cole Slaw calls for cold crisp shredded cabbage in Cream Salad Dressing. The Hot Slaw calls for simmering shredded cabbage in vinegar and butter, thickened with egg. Even if not eaten for a cold in the breast, such Hot Slaws remained popular, possibly because New England weather encouraged hot salads more than cold.

⅓ cup white wine vinegar
½ teaspoon salt
¼ teaspoon black pepper
4 tablespoons butter
1 Savoy cabbage, shredded
2–3 stalks celery, sliced thin
1 small cucumber, peeled, seeded, and sliced thin

1 tablespoon Dijon mustard
2 egg yolks
½ cup olive oil

Mix vinegar with salt, pepper, and butter in a skillet or wok. Add the vegetables and toss them in the mixture until slightly wilted, then set aside.

Beat mustard and egg yolks together and gradually add the oil, while beating, to make a mayonnaise.

Add mayonnaise to the vegetables; toss to mix thoroughly.

Serves 6 to 8.

INDIAN CRESS SALAD

Wild and cultivated cress salads were eaten in England wherever the wild cress grew, which was almost everywhere. But because the English were fond of hard-cooked egg yolks in their dressings, and of hard-cooked eggs in their salads, there evolved a classic English combination of egg and watercress. In the colonies, wild cress was also abundant, but so was Indian cress, the bright orange-yellow blossom and the round tender leaf of the nasturtium. The New American cookery's discovery of flowers as food is really a rediscovery of the Old World's flower-covered salads served up to Shakespeare's Elizabeth and, on this side of the Atlantic, to John Alden's Priscilla.

2 bunches fresh watercress
6 hard-cooked eggs
2 green onions, with tops
a handful of young nasturtium leaves

Dressing

1 teaspoon dry mustard
½ teaspoon each salt and anchovy paste
¼ teaspoon nasturtium seeds or ground black pepper
2 tablespoons white wine vinegar
½ cup olive oil

4 nasturtium or marigold blossoms

Rinse watercress, spin dry, and remove thick stems. Slice 4 whole eggs, or chop them coarsely. Chop the onions fine and mix eggs and onions with the cress and nasturtium leaves.

Prepare dressing by blending remaining 2 yolks (discard the whites) with all remaining ingredients except blossoms until the mixture is smooth. Pour dressing over greens, mix well, and top with the flower blossoms.

Serves 4.

PARSNIP FRITTERS

One vegetable that thrived in the cold was the parsnip, as ancient Britain learned very early: the parsnip and its cousin the water parsnip, or skirret, figured in the earliest English recipe for a vegetable, a pottage of broccoli rabe (or "rapes") seethed in a broth with minced onions, saffron, salt, and "powder douce" (powdered sugar). Do likewise, the recipe maker instructed, for parsnips and skirrets. Since parsnips are sweet in themselves and sweetest after the first frost, they were frequently put into tarts and pies, as *Martha Washington's Booke of Cookery* shows, flavoring the roots with rosewater and wine, sugar and lemon juice, and thickening the liquid with eggs, grated crumbs, and butter.

New England toned down these rich mixtures and frequently stewed parsnips in milk, thickening them with butter and cream in the newly fashionable white sauce. Boiled parsnips with carrots was a favorite combination, and Miss Beecher advises in her *Domestic Receipt Book* (1846) that the cook make sufficient quantity to fry next day for breakfast. Parsnip fritters were another favored way of using leftover mashed parsnips, to be shaped into cakes like mashed potato cakes. Toward the end of the century, however, both the Irish and the sweet potatoes began to displace the parsnip and skirret in their triple lives as vegetable, pie filling, and breakfast fritter. Fannie Farmer condemns parsnips altogether, saying, "They are raised mostly for feeding cattle."

We should rescue this sweet root from undeserved obloquy. A parsnip purée is much easier to make than a potato purée, particularly with a food processor. Butter and cream give a beautifully creamy texture; lemon and nutmeg give character. If you don't want to bother shaping the purée into fritters, simply pile it into a buttered baking dish and brown it in the oven.

> 1 pound parsnips
> 2 eggs
> ½ cup heavy cream
> 1 tablespoon lemon juice
>   rind of 1 lemon
> 4 tablespoons butter, melted

> salt and white pepper to taste
> ¼ teaspoon nutmeg
> 1 cup fresh bread crumbs

Cut off the parsnips' root ends and tops. Boil them in their skins in salted water until fork tender, anywhere from 10 to 20 minutes. When they are cool, strip off and discard the skins. Cut them in pieces and purée.

Beat the eggs into the cream and then beat this mixture into the purée with the lemon juice, lemon rind, half the butter, and the seasonings. Taste for seasoning. Shape purée into 3-inch cakes and roll in bread crumbs. Heat remaining butter in a skillet and fry the parsnip cakes, adding more butter if needed.

Serves 4.

THREE-FRUIT ICE CREAM

Bananas were first planted by the Spaniards in the West Indies in 1516, but they did not reach the States in any quantity until three centuries later, when Captain John Chester's *Reynard* brought a shipload of bananas to New York in 1804. Not until 1870, moreover, did banana importing become big business, only after Captain Lorenzo D. Baker of Wellfleet exchanged a cargo of mining equipment for Jamaican bananas and made the banana as common a fruit on New England tables as garden rhubarb.

Nothing could more typify the anomalies of New England than the introduction in 1885 of the hot-climed banana by the Boston Fruit Company (which became the United Fruit Company in 1899 and father of a host of banana republics). Bananas were mostly eaten raw, and recipes for cooking them did not appear until late, when Mary Lincoln in 1887 added a layer of sliced bananas to a Lemon-Jelly Cream and a Fruit Ice Cream, based on three threes—three oranges, three lemons, three bananas.

The ice for freezing ice cream had been a New England industry since early in the century, when Frederic Tudor of Boston became America's "Ice

King" by shipping blocks of winter ice in straw and sawdust south to the hot banana lands and west as far as China. Since ice was cheap and available along the eastern seaboard, so was ice cream, made cheaper and more available still through the ice cream plants of men like Jacob Fussell, of Baltimore, who brought credit to the Fussell name.

In looking for a good banana ice cream recipe, I stumbled on a use for that old-fashioned garden stalwart, the rhubarb. The rhubarb, which came to England from China by way of Russia and the Middle East, was once thought as exotic as the banana. Gerard in his *Herball* recommended the root as a medicine to relieve "pain in the hucklebones," where it "purgeth away naughty and corrupt humours." By the time of *Martha Washington's Booke of Sweet-meats* (1749), the stalk was thought more efficacious than the root, if steeped in a syrup of damask roses. A century later the stalk had worked its way into pies for desserts. Lydia Child calls it "the Persian Apple" and suggests that rhubarb is the earliest pie ingredient "which the spring offers." Later cooks simply call it the "pie-plant," and Lydia warns, "These are dear pies, for they take an enormous quantity of sugar."

While I've always admired the tartness of rhubarb, I've never liked its stringy and juicy texture in a pie. In a cream, on the other hand, strings and juice can be puréed and tartness made as welcome as lemon to a bland banana. Here, then, I've made a three-fruit ice cream using a lot of rhubarb, a little orange, and a frozen banana. Puréed in a processor, the frozen banana makes a texture of iced cream that renders other creams or custards unnecessary. Obviously you can vary such fruits to your taste and sweeten them as desired. Mary Lincoln sweetens her three-fruit ice cream with half a can of apricots and sugar syrup, so anything that goes for you, *goes*.

> 1 pound rhubarb (to make 4 cups, cut up)
> 2–3 slices fresh ginger
> ½ cup sugar
> 2–3 tablespoons honey
> 1 tablespoon fresh orange juice
> rind of 1 orange
> 1 large banana, frozen
> fresh mint

Trim rhubarb of root and top and peel only if the stalks have passed their first youth. Cut into 1-inch lengths and put in a casserole with the ginger, sugar, and honey. Cover tightly and bake at 300° for 45 minutes. Drain the rhubarb in a strainer set over a pan.

Reduce the reserved liquid to just under a cup, add orange juice, and purée with the rhubarb until smooth. Stir in orange rind and pour into a metal pan to freeze quickly.

Peel a banana, squeeze a little lemon juice on it, wrap it in plastic, and freeze.

When ready to serve, put banana and rhubarb mixture together and purée in a processor or blender until smooth. Heap into ice cream glasses and decorate with a sprig of mint.

Serves 4.

CRANBERRY FRAPPÉ

A thrifty fruit for New England, because it grew wild in profusion, was what John Josselyn in his *New England Rarities* (1672) called "Cranberry, or Bearberry . . . a small trayling plant that grows in salt marshes." The name probably came from the Dutch or German *kranbeere* or *kranebere,* for berries that grew where cranes fed, that is, in marshes and bogs. Both Indians and colonists of New England "boyl them with Sugar for a Sauce to eat with their meat, and it is a delicate Sauce, especially for roasted mutton," Josselyn explained. "Some make tarts with them as with Goose Berries."

Fannie Farmer made an ice or sherbet with them. Fifty years after her first Cranberry Frappé recipe in 1896, the 1948 *Fannie Farmer's Cookbook* substitutes cranberry jelly for fresh cranberries and makes a fancier sherbet with egg whites or cream. But our current taste for sharp ices and granités should lead us back to the sharpness of the wild bog berry, intensified by citrus and deepened by currant juice in the form of crème de cassis.

Since boiling cranberries with sugar toughens their skins, it is wise to stew them first in water and add sugar *after* their skins have burst.

>   1 quart fresh or frozen cranberries
>   ½ cup water
>   2 cups sugar
>   2 cups orange juice
>   juice of 1 lemon, or more if needed
>   ¼ cup crème de cassis

Pick over cranberries and put in a pan with the water. Cover and boil until the skins have burst. Purée cranberries in a processor and press the pulp through a sieve.

Dissolve sugar in the orange juice and add lemon juice and crème de cassis to the purée. Taste and add more lemon if needed, remembering that chilling will reduce flavor. Freeze as rapidly as possible. When ready to serve, turn ice into a processor and purée it into a smooth frappé.

Makes a little more than 1 quart.

17
Pudding Pies and Cookie Cakes

When I had my first bite of Indian pudding, from an S. S. Pierce can in 1949, I was gravely disappointed because I expected pudding, not molasses-flavored mush. When I learned that same year the source of Harvard's Hasty Pudding Club in Joel Barlow's famous eighteenth-century mock-epic poem:

> I sing the sweets I know, the charms I feel,
> My morning incense, and my evening meal—
> The sweets of Hasty Pudding

I still expected pudding, however hasty, to be pudding. Pudding was made of Jello-O or junket or tapioca or rice or occasionally bread. I was disillusioned to discover that Hasty Pudding, like Indian pudding, sang "The sweets of Corn-meal Mush."

The problem for a contemporary American looking at the roots of American food is that he must translate doubly: he must first translate Indian dialect into British English and then British English into American English.

To an Englishman, "pudding" meant a cooked dish of grain or pulse and water to make a gruel, porridge, or pottage. A hasty pudding meant a simple gruel, rather than a complex pudding of chopped meats, fowl, or fish added to chopped vegetables, fruits, and spices, all packed into the same bag or sheep's or hog's guts (as in a sausage or *boudin*) and boiled in a pot. A pudding might also be packed in a thick crust for a standing dish that was baked instead of boiled and became known as a "pudding pie." Baked puddings were for the rich, not the poor, because they required some kind of bake-oven in addition to the open hearth fire.

In eighteenth-century England, the "pudding in haste" remained a country dish and a poverty dish. In the north of England, it was usually made of oatmeal boiled with water. In the Midlands and the south, it was often a pottage of bread and milk, enriched like a Christmas pudding with butter and eggs, spices, and dried fruits. The pudding became a national dish for the British, Anne Wilson writes, because it was "rich in fat and carbohydrates to keep out the cold, and in sugar and fruit to build up energy."

In cold New England, a sweetened pudding served the same purpose, and Amelia Simmons has a large section on boiled and baked puddings. In America, a hasty pudding came to mean the simplest form of cornmeal and milk sweetened with molasses, as in the translation of Barlow's Latin motto to his poem, "He makes a good breakfast who mixes pudding with molasses." Indian pudding, on the other hand, came to mean a fancier dish enriched with eggs, sugar, and spices and baked or boiled, in a "strong cloth," Amelia advises, in a metal vessel or earthen pot.

A hasty pudding mixed with rye or wheat flour or both came to be called "Boston brown bread," although it was in fact a boiled pudding wrapped in a cloth or steamed in "a tin pudding boiler five hours," according to an anthology, *New England Cookbook* (1905). Breads were not distinguished from puddings because both were grain dishes and pudding was often made from bread crumbs. Thus Gulielma Penn's recipe for hasty pudding, which called for bread, milk, sugar, eggs, butter, rosewater, and mace to be boiled in a skillet until stiff, then "Stick it with Allmons and so sarve it up." Gulielma Penn, the first wife of William, was spared the ordeal of colonial housewives—substituting corn for wheat in such puddings—since Gulielma never made it across the Atlantic and remained secure among her spigot pots, posnets, and porringers in Worminghurst, Sussex.

Neither were breads distinguished from cakes or cookies. The earliest medieval gingerbreads were an uncooked sweetmeat composed of stale bread crumbs, mixed into a paste with honey, ginger, pepper, and cinnamon and colored red with saffron and sandalwood. In Tudor days gingerbread was still made with stale bread crumbs but was now colored with red wine and black licorice. Only in the eighteenth century did molasses replace both licorice and honey as a coloring agent and sweetener. This molasses bread became known as black gingerbread in contrast to a fashionable white gingerbread made of marzipan, flavored with ginger, and gilded.

In colonial America hard gingerbread was distinguished from soft gingerbread. "Hard gingerbread is good to have in the family," Lydia Child writes, "it keeps so well." Hard gingerbread is what we would now call ginger "cookies." (A very un-English word, since the English use the word "biscuits" to describe both sweetened and unsweetened wafers; the word "cookie" came to America with the Dutch, whose term for "a little cake" is *koekje*.)

Cakes and cookies, breads, puddings, and pies all evolved from the same medieval pottage, which combined grains and sweeteners to be baked or boiled. As kitchen hardware developed, kitchen shelves began to fill with specialized pots and pans and baking tins. An inventory of Gulielma Penn's kitchen in Worminghurst would have included chafing dishes, porringers, posnets (small pots or basins), tin pans for gingerbread, tin sheets for marzipan, patty pans for tarts, pie plates for meringues, galley pots, spigot pots, cheese vats, and preserving kettles. Had she crossed the Atlantic with an elementary pot, skillet, and kettle, she would have had to translate her rich cooking vocabulary into the primal syntax of corn cooking. For her, the language of samp and hominy would have been as strange and unsettling as, for us, the language of a seventeenth-century English kitchen. Imagine if today we were told to move the caldron from the trammel on the lug-pole, to fetch the souse from the gimlin, to put a garth on the slice, stir the posnet with a thible, and heat the goofer iron. We would have to translate each term: move the pot from the hook on the stationary pole across the hearth, fetch the pickled meat from the tub of brine, put a cake hoop on the flat wooden long-handled bread shovel, stir the three-legged pot on the hearth with a spatula, and heat the waffle iron.

A NICE INDIAN PUDDING

Amelia Simmons gives three variations of "A Nice Indian Pudding," two of them baked and one of them boiled. The boiled one is the most primitive—salted and sweetened, put into a strong cloth to "secure from wet," and boiled twelve hours. Her nicest one is sweetened with sugar, then spiced, buttered, egged, and raisined, to be baked for a mere hour and a half because the proportion of meal to milk is so small that the result is more like a thickened custard than a hasty pudding. Lydia Child's Indian Pudding is not nearly so nice, but a frugal one of meal and molasses.

Mrs. A. L. Webster is the one who goes to town on Indian Puddings, in her *Improved Housewife* (1842), listing two boiled and three baked. Here the important distinction is between plain or rich. Her Plain Boiled may be made a little richer, she says, by adding eggs and chopped suet, which, with grated lemon, cinnamon, and nutmeg, make up her Rich Boiled. This one is nice, she says, cut in slices when cold and fried; or when hot, served with a sauce of drawn butter, wine, and nutmeg. Hardly frugal at all. Webster's pudding tips show what the colonial pudding maker was up against. She must first wash the salt from her butter, stone her raisins, avoid stale eggs, and remember to beat them ("When but a single egg, or two, are to be used, cooks often think it useless to beat them: mistake!"), make her pudding bag of German sheeting ("a cloth less thick will admit water, and deteriorate the pudding"), wet the bag in water and then wring it out and flour it inside and remember to leave "room for the pudding to swell." Clearly a baked pudding was easier to make if one had a proper vessel and room in the embers or bake oven. A baked pudding also took less time than a boiled one. "Boil three hours:—if six, the better," Webster advises, "—some cooks boil eight or nine hours." And Amelia boiled hers for twelve. Following her Indian puddings, Mrs. Webster gives a number of lemon and/or orange puddings. All of these are to be baked in "a pudding dish, with a lining and rim of puff paste." It's easy to see here the evolution of the baked pudding into the pie.

Mrs. Webster's cook book was immensely popular at mid-century because she was as practical as Lydia Child but not quite so frugal. Thus her Indian puddings call for grated lemon peel or lemon essence. Often apples were added for variety, as was pumpkin, which I've used here and baked in muffin pans for speed and ease.

1 quart milk

¼ pound (1 stick) butter

1 cup light molasses

2 cups stone-ground cornmeal

6 eggs, beaten

rind of 2 lemons, grated

1 tablespoon each cinnamon and nutmeg

⅛ teaspoon salt

2 cups golden sultana raisins

2 cups pumpkin purée (fresh if possible)

Rum Sauce

¼ pound (1 stick) butter

½ cup rum

2 tablespoons brown sugar, or to taste

2 tablespoons fresh orange juice

Scald milk with the butter and molasses and pour slowly into the cornmeal. Mix well and let sit for an hour, covered, to let the meal absorb the milk.

Add beaten eggs, lemon rind, seasonings, and raisins to the pumpkin purée and mix pumpkin with the cornmeal. Bake in buttered muffin pans at 300° for 45 to 60 minutes.

If you want to be very very nice, serve with a rum sauce made by melting butter and adding remaining ingredients.

Makes 36 muffins and a little over 1 cup sauce.

RAISIN BROWN BREAD

"This is the kind of bread which, outside of New England, is always called 'Boston' brown bread," Maria Parloa explained. By the time of Fannie Farmer's first cook book, it is called "Boston" even inside New England, because it proved to be one of New England's most durable pudding breads. It originated in that old "ryaninjun" yeast-leavened bread dough thinned to a batter "as thick as hasty pudding," as Maria Parloa says. This batter bread was baked or steamed and, if steamed, "I will say here that you cannot steam brown bread too much," Parloa warns. Certainly not less than five hours.

I find a plain soda-leavened brown bread, steamed or baked, so very dark and dense that I want the texture varied with raisins and nuts. That would upset traditionalists, who claim that Boston brown bread must not be cut with a knife but with a taut string. But since I am not from New England, I say to hell with it.

½ cup each white cornmeal and rye flour
1 cup whole wheat flour
½ teaspoon each baking soda and salt
1 tablespoon baking powder
1½ cups sour milk or buttermilk
½ cup molasses
2 tablespoons butter, melted
2 cups raisins
1 cup chopped walnuts

Mix or sift dry ingredients thoroughly. To sour milk, add 1 teaspoon vinegar and let stand 10 minutes. Mix the milk with molasses and butter and stir this gradually into the meal. Add raisins and nuts. Spoon batter into a well-buttered quart mold or 2 one-pound coffee cans (cover the mouths of the cans with buttered foil and tie tightly).

Fill molds only two-thirds full because the dough will expand.

Set mold or cans on a trivet or rack in a steaming kettle and add enough water to come halfway up. Cover closely and steam about 3 hours for a large mold, 2 hours for the smaller cans. When molds have cooled, turn bread out into a baking pan and bake at 400° for 15 minutes to make a thin crust. To reheat, wrap bread in foil and bake or steam. The bread keeps well and freezes well.

Makes 1 large loaf or 2 smaller loaves.

POPCORN PUDDING

Early in the nineteenth century, puddings of green corn were immensely popular. Green corn, Eliza Leslie explained, was "Indian corn when full grown, but before it begins to harden and turn yellow." The corn still had the sweetness of youth, but also the starch of maturity to thicken milk and eggs in a delicate custard. More unusual, however, is the popcorn pudding popular late in the century. Fannie Farmer calls it simply "Corn Pudding," and suggests that one serve it with maple syrup or cream. The advantage of popcorn pudding over green corn pudding is that one was seasonal and the other not. Popcorn one could make any time. Fannie ground her popcorn so that the texture of the custard would be fairly smooth. A recipe in Ella Bowles' and Dorothy Towle's *Secrets of New England Cooking* (1947) leaves the popcorn whole. I've compromised below and have ground most of the popcorn but reserved a handful to float on top and let the eater know what's inside.

> 2 cups popped corn
> 3 cups milk
> 4 tablespoons butter, melted
> 3 eggs, beaten
> ½ cup brown sugar
> 1 teaspoon vanilla extract
> ½ teaspoon salt

Grind all but a small handful of the popped corn in a food processor or grinder. Scald the milk, pour it over the corn, stir in the butter, and let the popcorn sit, covered, for 1 hour to absorb the liquid.

Beat eggs with the sugar until light, add vanilla and salt, beat in the corn mixture, and turn into a buttered baking dish. Sprinkle the reserved popcorn on top. Bake at 300° until custard is set and browned on top, 45 minutes to 1 hour.

Serves 4 to 6.

LEMON RICE PUDDING

What is the matter with Mary Jane?
She's perfectly well and she hasn't a pain,
And it's lovely rice pudding for dinner again!—

By the sound of A. A. Milne's Mary Jane, we can be certain that when Winnie-the-Pooh thought it was time for a little something, the little something was never rice pudding. Rice pudding, however, even in England did not decline into nursery fare until the Victorians. When rice first arrived in England along the Arabian spice trail, it was deemed a luxury for Lenten days and was most often boiled with almond milk, sweetened with sugar, and colored with saffron. Hannah Glasse provides four rich rice puddings (one a S. Carolina Rice Pudding), flavored with lemon peel, rosewater, and chopped apples, along with a number of Cheap Rice Puddings. Even the cheap ones, however, use a good quantity of butter and sugar in the milk.

Like Indian pudding, the plain or cheap could easily be made rich with more eggs and butter and flavorings. Plain ones were apt to be boiled in the pudding bag, but rich ones were baked in a crust. "Butter or puff paste a dish," Amelia Simmons advises for baking rice puddings, for which she gives no fewer than six recipes. Eventually the quantity of rice diminished and the custard increased, until the rice furnished merely a thickening, like tapioca later, for the Quaking Puddings and Cream Puddings so popular in nineteenth-century New England. Eliza Leslie, always elegant, grinds and sieves her rice to make an extremely refined pudding with strips of citron laid across the top. Most American cook-book ladies, following English practice, flavored their rice pudding with a little lemon juice or peel. Even Fannie's very plain 1896 pudding includes a bit of grated rind.

You can vary the texture of the rice to your desire. You can blend or process the cooked rice with the eggs for a texture slightly smoother than whole kernel rice. For a perfectly smooth purée, cook the rice longer (one and a half hours instead of one) and blend or process fully.

2 cups milk
1 cup half-and-half
¼ pound (1 stick) butter

½ cup long-grain rice
pinch of salt
6 eggs, beaten
1 cup sugar
juice and grated rind of 2 lemons
½ teaspoon each nutmeg and cinnamon
½ cup lemon marmalade

Scald milk with half-and-half and butter in the top of double boiler. Add rice and salt, cover, and cook 1 hour. Beat eggs with the sugar until light and fluffy, add lemon juice, grated rind, and spices, and combine this mixture with the rice. (For a somewhat smoother texture, blend or process the rice mixture slightly.) Taste for sweet and sour.

Pour mixture into a buttered 2-quart baking dish and set in a pan of hot water to bake at 300° for about 1 hour. During first 10 minutes, stir custard occasionally to prevent rice from sinking to the bottom. When pudding is done, heat the marmalade and pour it over the top.

Serves 6 to 8.

APPLEDORE BLUEBERRY PUDDING

Maria Parloa made the name "Appledore" synonymous with New England after the publication of her *Appledore Cook Book* in 1872, named for the Appledore House on the Isles of Shoals in Maine, where she served as a cook. Like Amelia Simmons, Maria was an orphan turned cook to support herself, first among private families, then in resort hotels, and finally at her own cooking school in Boston in 1877. Twenty years later she joined the Boston Cooking School, founded in 1879 by Mrs. Sarah E. Hooper and the Woman's Education Association, and made famous locally by Mrs. Mary Lincoln and nationally by Miss Fannie Farmer until it was incorporated into Simmons College in 1902.

In America, the English pudding pies made of custard and fruit, and called "flummeries" or "fools," were named "slumps," "crunches," and "grunts." The self-parodying slang was descriptive of both the dish and the eater of these pudding-batter cakes filled with common fruits like blueberries, apples, peaches, cherries, and grapes. Maria Parloa's Appledore Pudding, in contrast, is quite a fancy dish, based on tipsy pudding and made of stale cake, softened with fruit and liquor, and topped with a baked meringue. If the pudding is any indication, Appledore House was more grand than rustic, and eaters of Appledore Pudding would be expected to recognize its debt to English syllabubs and trifles.

¼ pound (1 stick) butter
1 cup maple sugar, or ¾ cup white sugar plus ¼ cup maple
     syrup
2 eggs, beaten
2 cups all-purpose flour
2 teaspoons baking powder
½ teaspoon salt
½ cup milk

Filling

1 quart blueberries
½ cup maple sugar, or ½ cup maple syrup boiled to reduce by
     half
⅓ cup rum, or to taste

Meringue

3 egg whites
pinch of salt
⅓ cup each granulated white and powdered sugar

To make the cake, cream butter and sugar and beat in eggs until light. Mix flour with baking powder and salt and add the dry ingredients alternately with the milk to the egg-sugar batter. Pour into 1 or 2 buttered cake pans and bake at 350° for 20 to 30 minutes. Turn out and cool on a rack. If you have used only one pan, cut the cake in half horizontally. Either let the cake dry overnight or toast it lightly in a low oven.

To make the filling, mix blueberries with the sugar (or syrup) and half the rum. Put one layer of cake in a baking dish, cover it with the fruit, then top with the remaining layer of cake. Sprinkle with remaining rum.

To make the meringue, beat egg whites with salt until they make soft peaks. Gradually beat in the sugar until the meringue is stiff and creamy. Smooth it over the top.

Serves 6 to 8.

MARLBOROUGH APPLE-CREAM TART

As English as apple pie, colonists must have said before America co-opted the dish for its own. Settlers had brought apple seeds along with wheat seeds to the colonies and it was the Reverend William Blaxton who planted some of America's first apple orchards on what would become Boston's Beacon Hill. When Reverend Blaxton moved to Rhode Island in 1635, he created there the first native American seedling type, the Rhode Island greening. America soon had dozens of varieties that matched the quality of their root stock and dozens of ways of using apples, fresh and dried, rooted in the ancient traditions of the homeland.

When pearmains, costards, pippins, pomewaters, bittersweets, and blanderells—to name but a few of England's traditional apples—came into season, they were eaten in such excess, as was any fresh fruit, that the eaters were stricken with diarrhea. Ill health was thereby associated with raw fruit, and fruit was thought to be "safer" cooked. Cooked apples were usually turned into sauce and, in the "well-loved pottage called 'appulmos,'" decorated with fresh apple blossoms. These sieved apples, boiled in puddings, baked in pies, and whipped into creams, were flavored most often with lemon and orange peel or juice.

Hannah Glasse makes an "excellent" apple pudding of this sort, flavored also with brandy and rosewater and baked in a paste-covered dish. Martha Washington roasts her apples to make "ye pulp or pap" and then turns them into tarts or into little frying cakes, or fritters. Gulielma Penn similarly shreds apples into a pudding batter to make "apell pankecks." Somewhere along the line, Americans began to call an apple pudding thickened with egg and cream, flavored with lemon and brandy, and baked in a crust a "Marlborough pudding." Eliza Leslie calls it by this name in 1837, bakes it in a buttered baking dish with a border of puff paste around the top, and ornaments it with "slips of citron handsomely arranged."

A mere five years later, Mrs. A. L. Webster turns the pudding into a pie or tart in her Sweet Marlborough Pie and Marlborough Tarts. In the former, she grates apples and in the latter she stews and sieves them, before adding wine and lemon. By the end of the century, the Marlborough name has largely disappeared, along with brandy and cream. We now find Fannie Farmer's austere version of raw apple slices flavored with a mere teaspoon of butter and lemon juice and "a few gratings lemon rind." "A very good pie," she says, can be made even plainer, "without butter, lemon juice, and grated rind."

Why New Englanders of the mid-nineteenth century chose to honor the British hero of the war against Napoleon with an apple pudding pie I cannot determine, unless Marlborough was simply a snob name that signified a dish fit for dukes and duchesses and therefore for their Yankee imitators at Chestnut and Beacon hills.

> 6 tart apples, peeled and grated
>   juice and grated rind of 1 lemon
> 4 tablespoons butter
> ⅓ cup sugar
> 6 eggs
> 1 cup heavy cream
> 2 tablespoons brandy
> ½ teaspoon nutmeg
>   pie dough or puff paste for a single-crust 9-inch pie

Mix grated apples with lemon juice and grated rind. Cream butter with sugar and beat in the eggs until mixture is light. Add cream, brandy, and nutmeg. Fold in the apples and put mixture into a buttered baking dish.

Cover with a top crust with slashes to vent the steam and bake at 325° until apples are thoroughly cooked, 1 hour. (If you use puff paste, you will have to bake it separately at 400° for about 20 minutes and then lay it over the cooked apples when they are done.)

Serves 6 to 8.

CONCORD GRAPE PIE

Judy McConnell, like most owners of old rambling New England houses, has a grape arbor of old rambling Concord grapes. The Concord, however, is a relative newcomer. Before the Concord, our wild native grapes, *Vitis labrusca* and *Vitis aestivalis,* rambled undeterred by New England cold, but abundance did not guarantee taste. John Josselyn found that although some wild grapes were "reasonably pleasant, others have a taste of Gunpowder and these grow in swamps and low wet grounds." Even Thoreau, with his penchant for all things wild, confessed the limitations of wild grapes. "In October I went a-graping to the river meadows," he wrote in *Walden,* "and loaded myself with clusters more precious for their beauty and fragrance than for food."

A friend of Thoreau's, Ephraim Wales Bull of Concord, decided to do something about it. He decided to develop "a grape of good flavor with little of the foxy taste of the wild grapes," so he planted wildings in the garden next door to Nathaniel Hawthorne at Wayside. After struggling for a decade, Ephraim presented the Massachusetts Horticultural Society in 1853 with the hybrid he called "Concord." An immediate success, the Concord became America's first commercial grape, enriching both the makers of Manischewitz wine and a teetotaling Methodist dentist in Vineland, New Jersey, who first produced "Dr. Welch's Unfermented Wine," later called Welch's Grape Juice.

After the Concord, civilized grape jellies and marmalades became popular, particularly after the dentist Welch, with what degree of self-interest we do not say, marketed grape jam as Grapelade and sold his entire production in 1914 to the United States Army.

Before the Concord, Eliza Leslie kept wild grapes in brandy or molasses: "They will keep all winter and they make good common pies." Amelia Simmons also made wild grape pie. She put grapes, as she would gooseberries or cranberries, in her No. 9 or Royal Paste, halfway between a short crust and a puff paste.

I find the best way to make a good grape pie is to make grape jam and bake a pie crust separately. Here I've given a recipe for Amelia Simmons' Royal Paste, but of course any short crust will make a good container.

1 pound Concord grapes (4 cups stemmed)
1 navel orange
1 cup sugar
½ teaspoon cinnamon
¼ teaspoon cardamon
1 cup chopped pecans

Royal Paste
¼ pound (1 stick) butter
1½ cups all-purpose flour
1 tablespoon sugar
½ teaspoon salt
1 egg, separated

To make 2½ cups jam, wash grapes and slip their skins, putting skins and pulp in separate bowls. Transfer pulp to a deep saucepan and boil rapidly about 10 minutes, stirring to prevent sticking. Push pulp through a sieve and discard the seeds. Add pulp to the skins. Grate orange rind and save. Remove and discard all the white pith from the orange. Add orange pulp and rind to the grape pulp, along with sugar and spices. Bring to a boil and boil rapidly until thick, 15 to 20 minutes. Stir in the nuts.

To make the pastry, cut one third of the butter into the flour, sugar, and salt. Beat the egg yolk with a fork and add. Beat the white until very light and add. Roll out the dough. Put remaining butter in the center of it and fold the dough over, top and bottom, to enclose the butter, like folding a letter. Roll it into a rectangle and repeat the folds until the butter is incorporated fully. Chill, then roll out a circle to fit your pie plate. Bake paste at 425° until lightly browned, about 12 minutes.

To make the pie, simply fill the crust with the grape jam.

Serves 6 to 8.

CARROT PIE

In eighteenth-century England, many foods that we now think of as vegetables—artichokes, potatoes, carrots—went into cakes, puddings, and
pies. Carrots, in particular, with their natural sweetness, were favored for a

pudding pie that might or might not be baked in puff paste. Hannah Glasse gives two recipes for carrot pudding in puff pastes, both using grated raw carrots in a custard thickened with grated bread and flavored with sherry and orange-flower water. Sugar is almost an afterthought. "Sweeten to your palate," she recommends.

In her *Appledore Cook Book,* Maria Parloa repeats Hannah's recipe for Carrot Pudding in immense quantities—twenty carrots, two cups butter, twelve eggs—and instructs the cook to "Bake like Amherst Pudding." Amherst pudding turns out to be an apple pudding-pie like Marlborough, only with a Yankee name.

Recipes for carrot pudding were as popular in nineteenth-century America as carrot cake recipes today; they used similar spicing but without the overload of sugar and with the helpful addition of alcohol. In the recipe below, I've used orange juice for orange-flower water because of the affinity of carrot and orange, but you can use lemon instead, just as you can omit brandy and overload on sugar as much as you please.

    1 pound carrots, scraped and grated (about 3 cups)
    ⅓ cup fresh orange juice
      rind of 1 orange
    3 tablespoons butter
    ¼ cup sugar, or to taste
    ½ teaspoon cinnamon
    ¼ teaspoon each salt and nutmeg
    ⅛ teaspoon mace
    ½ cup currants
    ¼ cup brandy
    4 egg yolks
    2 tablespoons heavy cream
    1 partially baked crust for a 9-inch pie*

---

* To prepare a partially baked pie crust, roll out pastry and line pie pan with it. Line crust with foil and fill to the top with beans or rice so that the crust will keep its shape. Bake at 425° for 5 minutes, remove foil and beans, poke crust with a fork all over, and bake until shell has stiffened, another 5 minutes.

Mix grated carrots with orange juice and rind, butter, sugar, and seasonings. Simmer very gently, covered until carrots are cooked, 15 to 20 minutes. Plump the currants in the brandy while the carrots are cooking. When done, drain carrots well, reserving the liquid.

Beat the egg yolks into the cream, add the carrot juice gradually, and beat in the brandied currants. Mix this with the carrots and fill the partially baked pie shell with the mixture. Bake at 350° until the mixture has thickened and is no longer runny, about 30 minutes.

Serves 6 to 8.

CHOCOLATE CRUNCH COOKIES

Just as Boston became the unlikely home of the Jamaican banana, so it embraced an equally exotic Jamaican import, chocolate. The first chocolate factory in the country was started in 1780 by John Hanan at Dorchester, Massachusetts, and financed by Dr. James Baker, who began Baker's Chocolate. As a child, I thought those bitter squares of chocolate were called Baker's for Baking in contrast to Hershey's for Eating.

I had no notion that until the late nineteenth century, chocolate was not a food but a drink. When Mary Randolph, in her *Virginia Housewife* (1824), supplies a recipe for Chocolate Cakes, it turns out to be a recipe for brown-sugar griddle cookies served with chocolate drunk in cups. As late as 1852 Sarah Josepha Hale must still explain what chocolate is. "This forms the common breakfast throughout Spain," she reports, "and, is there made by chipping a portion of the cake, and leaving the chips in water for a whole night to soften." Afterwards, the chips were warmed with water or milk and worked constantly with the chocolate mill, inserted through the lid of the chocolate pot, to froth the liquid and prevent it from becoming "clotty."

When chocolate appears in American cook books as an ingredient for something more solid than frothed liquid, it arrives via English puddings, custards, and creams. Only late in the century does chocolate work its way into cookies, and only after Baker's bitter chocolate was supplemented by "German chocolate," which became the generic name for sweetened bars of eating chocolate.

A Dutchman, C. J. Houten, was the first to exploit the Mexican-Indian method of refining cocoa beans with wood ashes to alkalize them and thus separate the fat or cocoa butter from the powdered bean. Recombining the powder and butter with sugar produced the first edible chocolate candy bar. To this mixture, a Swiss chemist added sweetened condensed milk in 1875 and produced the first milk chocolate, which led eventually to Nestlé's sweet and semisweet chocolate bars and morsels.

How significant these discoveries were to the American cookie scene is clear in Fannie Farmer's 1896 *Cook Book,* where she lists four recipes for chocolate cookies, one the precursor of the Oreo and another the precursor of chocolate chip or tollhouse cookies. Fannie's Chocolate Cakes were actually cookies, flavored with Baker's unsweetened chocolate and cut into rounds put together in pairs with a frosting between of White Mountain Cream (egg white, powdered sugar, and vanilla). Behold the Oreo, later named by Nabisco. Her German Chocolate Cookies were a cake-cookie, leavened with eggs and baking powder and flavored with German chocolate and chopped almonds, the batter to be dropped from the tip of a spoon onto baking sheets. Behold the chocolate chip or tollhouse, later attributed to the kitchen of Ruth Wakefield's Toll House Inn in the 1930s. Ruth had converted an eighteenth-century tollhouse at Whitman, on the road from Boston to New Bedford, into an inn, where she experimented one day with "an old recipe" for cookies called "Butter Drop Do." Into the dough she cut a Nestlé's semisweet chocolate bar in hunks so big they didn't melt in the baking, and called the result "Chocolate Crunch Cookies." The old recipe for Butter Drop Do came from Amelia Simmons, who listed it as "No. 3" of her Gingerbread Cakes or Butter and Sugar Gingerbread. Amelia's dough, composed of a quarter pound butter and one pound sugar, one and a half pounds flour, and four eggs, flavored with mace and rosewater, makes a cake-like cookie shaped "to your fancy." One wonders what our American orphan Amelia would think of today's chocolate-chip butter-drop-dough cookies that have made names like David and Amos famous throughout the world. The secret of David's Cookies (and one reason for their cost) is that he uses Lindt chocolate. Go and do thou likewise if you want a quality chocolate cookie.

½ pound (2 sticks) butter
¾ cup each brown and white sugar
2 eggs
1⅓ cups all-purpose flour
1 teaspoon salt
1½ teaspoons vanilla extract
2 cups chopped walnuts or pecans
12 ounces Lindt semisweet chocolate

Cream butter with both sugars until light and beat in the eggs. Mix in flour, salt, vanilla, and nuts. Chop the chocolate into ½-inch hunks and add to the dough. Drop by teaspoonfuls onto baking sheets (leave plenty of room for the dough to spread) and bake at 350° for 7 to 8 minutes.

Makes about 72 small cookies.

MOLASSES GINGERSNAPS

In New England both hard and soft gingerbread were served on Muster or Militia Day, when the local militia paraded arms on the village green and townsfolk celebrated with mugs of foaming cider or ale and ginger cakes bought from the ginger vendors. Such patriotic associations account for Eliza Leslie's names Franklin Gingerbread and Lafayette Gingerbread. Her festive cakes are made with candied orange peel, or orange rind and fresh orange juice, to refresh the gingered dough baked in "little queen cake tins." Other dough she rolls out and cuts into strips to make circles of "straight round sticks (uniting them at both ends,) or coil them into rings one within another, as you see them at the cake shops."

The simplest method of cutting hard gingerbread was to roll the dough very thin—"as thin as the blade of a knife," says Maria Parloa—on the baking sheet and then to cut the dough into strips with a jagging iron, now called a "pastry crimper." The simplest method of baking soft gingerbread was to shape the dough into round balls like nuts. Just as a cook might vary the dough with molasses or brown sugar, eggs or milk, candied peels, blanched almonds, or black pepper in addition to hot ginger, so might she vary the shape. Mrs. A. L. Webster turns her dough into Gingerbread, Gingerbread Cakes, Ginger Nuts, Ginger Cookies, and Ginger Snaps No. 1 and No. 2.

America did not apply "snap" to ginger until 1805, as John Mariani tells us in *The Dictionary of American Food and Drink* (1983). "Snap" came from the Dutch *snappen,* meaning "to seize quickly." Mrs. Webster's Snap No. 2 is almost identical to her Hard Molasses Gingerbread, and her proportions of a teacup of butter to a pint of molasses and a quart of flour produced a snap as black, glossy, and edible as Japanese lacquerware, which also tended to snap the teeth. Here I've modified the ancestral "snap" by adding brown sugar and by using refined instead of blackstrap molasses. I roll the dough directly onto a baking sheet and cut it into diamonds or strips after it is baked but while it is still warm and pliant. "These are very nice," as the cook-book ladies say, "and the longer they are kept the better they will be."

> ½ cup brown sugar
> ½ cup refined molasses
> ¼ pound (1 stick) butter (or half butter and half shortening)
> 2 cups unbleached white flour
> 1 teaspoon baking soda
> 2 teaspoons ginger
> 1 teaspoon each salt and cinnamon
> ½ teaspoon each allspice and coriander

Put sugar, molasses, and butter in a pan and cook over low heat until the butter melts. Mix together the dry ingredients and stir them into the sugar-butter mixture. Scoop mixture into a plastic bag and chill thoroughly.

Roll dough as thin as possible onto a buttered baking sheet and bake at 350° for 10 to 12 minutes on the top rack of the oven (gingerbread burns easily so watch carefully after 8 minutes). While dough is still warm, cut it into strips 1 inch wide and 3 inches long, or into diamond shapes by cutting it diagonally first in one direction, then the other.

Makes 36 strips or diamonds.

ELECTION CAKE WITH
MAPLE CREAM

The American or Hartford election cake is American in name only. The cake itself is a classic English "rich cake," "loaf cake," or "fruitcake," which went by many names and varied many ingredients. Martha Washington supplies the essentials in her many kinds of "great cake," listed in *The Booke of Sweetmeats,* always beginning with barm, the froth produced by fermenting ale. Amelia Simmons calls these "emptins," a contraction of "emptyings," which meant the yeasty dregs in the bottom of a cask of ale. On baking day, a thrifty housewife would use some of this yeast to make a richer dough than bread and she might use some of her raw bread dough as a starter or sponge for cake.

The name "election" did not get attached to the cake until the 1830s, when Eliza Leslie calls a pound cake by this name—in the proportion of sixteen eggs to five pounds flour and two pounds each butter and sugar. Brandy and wine were the usual liquids, as in the Sally White cakes of the South, but Fannie Farmer substitutes sour milk in her Election Cake of 1896. Fannie was going against the grain of this rich cake, named for the Election Day feasts in New England towns like Hartford, Connecticut. According to a number of contemporaries, these week-long January election feasts displaced the Anglican feast of the Epiphany, which smacked too much of popery for Connecticut Yanks. "Families exchange visits, and treat their guests with slices of election-cake," an English traveler wrote in 1807–8, "and thus preserve some portion of the luxuries of the forgotten feast of the Epiphany." Madame Sarah Knight was more openly scornful, "Their Chief Red Letterday is St. Election." The popularity of St. Election is evident in Mrs. Chadwick's *Home Cookery* (1852), where she lists no fewer than four election cakes, plus an Excelsior Election Cake and even a Ratification Cake.

To honor St. Election I've here made the fruitcake in the traditional way with a sponge of yeast and flour, which gives a riper fermented taste and a slightly lighter texture. If you don't want to bother with a sponge, you can simply mix all the ingredients at once and let the dough rise in the pan until doubled. No frosting is needed, but I've found that a frosting of maple cream or maple syrup complements the color, texture, and taste of the cake and ameliorates its dryness.

Sponge

1 package dry yeast
½ cup warm (100°–115°) milk
1 cup unbleached white flour
1 tablespoon molasses

1½ cups golden sultana raisins
½ cup brandy or sherry
½ pound (2 sticks) butter
⅔ cup sugar
4 eggs
2½ cups unbleached white flour
1 teaspoon each cinnamon and nutmeg
½ teaspoon salt
¼ teaspoons mace
1 cup chopped pecans

Maple Cream Frosting

¼ pound (1 stick) butter
⅓ cup maple cream or maple syrup
2–3 cups powdered sugar

To make the sponge, stir yeast into the warmed milk. Mix with flour and molasses to make a stiff paste. Cover with plastic wrap and let sit until sponge becomes bubbly, 2 to 3 hours.

Meanwhile, plump the raisins in the brandy. Cream butter and sugar until fluffy and then beat in the eggs. Mix flour with the seasonings and nuts.

Add the sponge to the egg mixture, then beat in the flour and raisins. Pour batter into a well-buttered large tube pan or 2 loaf pans. Cover lightly with plastic and let dough rise until nearly doubled. Bake at 350° for 50 to 60 minutes. Invert onto a cake rack to cool.

Make the frosting by creaming the butter with the maple cream or syrup and beating in sugar until you have the stiffness desired. Spread on cooled cake and refrigerate.

Makes 1 large cake or 2 standard loaves.

PART V

Trappers and Milkers

THE
GREAT LAKES
OF THE
MIDWEST

RECIPES IN PART V

Stock up now! Today and tomorrow there's beer. Soon there'll be only the lake.

—Sign hung by Charles Mader in The Comfort Saloon,
Milwaukee, Wisconsin, 1919

On Sundays, Mader's Restaurant, which began life in 1902 as The Comfort Saloon serving Cream City Beer at 3 cents a glass, today serves a Viennese Brunch for $9.50. While drinking strawberry champagne, I eat, in order, an apple turnover with vanilla sauce, hot potato salad with bacon dressing, smoked salmon, bratwurst, creamed veal, smoked pork loin, sauerkraut with raisins and almonds, red cabbage and potato dumplings, spaetzle, and hot sausages made by Usinger's Sausage Factory across the street. Mader's is jammed with large German families who look as if they feed here every day and twice on Sundays. The walls and even the ceilings are crammed with Germanica collected by Charles' son Gus: antique Maitlock steins, a sixteenth-century suit of Prussian armor, medieval pikes and halberds, a matched set of German dueling pistols in Damascus silver, a triptych of black oak panels carved at Oberammergau to depict the Mader family roistering in a medieval *Weinstube*, a twenty-foot carved oak table from the castle of Baron von Richthofen. I haven't seen the like since the year I spent in Heidelberg—only here, on Third Street in downtown Milwaukee, it looks and feels like Gothic Disneyland.

After my breakfast snack, I drop in on the annual *Oktoberfest*, held in September in Old Heidelberg Park surrounding the Bavarian Inn. Few members of the five German Societies who gather here to celebrate beer in the fall and May wine in the spring speak fluent German, but you wouldn't know it from the sound of the brass bands in the park, the sight of lace aprons and Bavarian skirts, lederhosen and Tyrolean hats whirling in the polka, the smell of dozens of whole spitted piglets—*spankerfeln*—roasting over coals, the taste of foaming steins of Schlebel and Schoenbach and *weisse bier*. As a tourist I am obliged to sample a bit of everything, and more than a bit of the crisp and succulent pig, while I watch big-bellied men drink beer from a two-liter glass boot, designed to drench the man who drains the last drop from the toe.

But my eating and drinking day is not done. I must have the Sunday night *schlactplatt*, says my friendly Milwaukee tour guide, at John Ernst's Cafe. All German restaurants in Milwaukee are family owned but this is the oldest, known first as Mother Heiser's in 1878 before Joe Deutsch ran it during Prohibition. Prohibition is to Milwaukee what the Civil War is to the South—a watershed. And I was not surprised to learn that the first legal post-Prohibition stein of beer in the country, drawn at the stroke of midnight on April 7, 1933, was served at Mader's. After Prohibition, Deutsch sold Mother Heiser's to an Austrian couple, John and Ida Ernst, and it is their daughter Marianne who now runs the cafe with her husband, Ervin Lindenberg. Beneath antler chandeliers, Bavarian murals, stuffed moose heads, and hunting horns, I dig into my plate of pork shank, sauerkraut, smoked pork loin, and thick sausages with horseradish and mustard, finished off with cherry strudel. I resist a serving of *schaum torte* because I know that on the morrow I must eat at Karl Ratzsch's Restaurant under more antlers and steins to sample the koenigsberger klops and sauerbraten with gingersnap gravy.

"People want things they can count on; they don't want change," Ervin explains when I ask about the uniform German menu from place to place. "If they go to a German restaurant, they expect heavy fare, so our menu and our portions are the same as they were fifty years ago. Our waiters have been here twenty to thirty years. Our strudel lady still comes once a week." "And may she come another hundred years," adds Marianne, toasting the strudel lady with a shot of whiskey. Marianne talks about her Aunt Louisa, her Aunt Julia, her Uncle Charlie, her Aunt Theresa. "They all came over because my great-grandfather said that America was the coming land, so they came to Milwaukee—the Athens of the West, right?" She toasts the Athens of the West.

Others have called Milwaukee "the biggest small town in the world" and it has stayed a small town, a "Little Munich," because of the clannishness of its German tribes. Although it began as a French and English trading post in the late eighteenth century, the building of the Erie Canal in 1825 opened the

A "bus" picnic of the ladies' chorus of a German music club from Milwaukee, 1892. Fresh fruit, cold cuts, celery stalks, and plenty of beer are as essential as the gentlemen's straw hats.

Great Lakes as an avenue to the West and opened Milwaukee to the Germans. The first wave of Germans had come in the seventeenth century from southwestern duchies to settle in Pennsylvania, where they kept their clan together by a hybrid German dialect called "Deitsch." The second wave came largely from Swabia and Bavaria as political refugees after the Revolution of 1848. They came not only from Germany, but from Estonia, Lithuania, Serbia, the Ukraine, Latvia, and Scandinavia. They came from countries familiar with wild game and fish and the ice that made good malted brews.

Milwaukee did not truly begin until the first German brewer arrived to make the city famous with his beer. On a tour of Pabst Brewery, a nineteenth-century Alpine castle except that it is made of brick instead of stone, I learn that Jacob Best arrived in 1844 from Bavaria with four beer-brewing sons. In Milwaukee, a place the Algonquin Indians had named "a gathering of rivers," Jacob found what he was looking for—rivers to make ice. Here not one but three rivers—the Menominee, the Kinnickinnic, and the Milwaukee—joined the lake. The bluffs along the lake would provide caves for storing kegs of beer made the German way, as lager, the very name of which means a storage place. Until the Germans arrived, Americans had brewed ale, made the English way, a top-fermented brew from changeable yeasts. The Germans brought lager or pilsener, a bottom-fermented brew in which the yeast sank to the bottom while the kegs were stored in ice to let the bubbles work. Frederick Miller, who arrived a decade after Jacob Best, called his pilsener the "Champagne of beers" about the time Jacob's son-in-law Fred Pabst began to win so many blue ribbons that he called their beer "Select" and tied a blue silk ribbon around the neck of every bottle.

Joseph Schlitz arrived in 1875 to make Milwaukee "the beer capital of the world," rivaled only by the marketing and manufacturing talents of Eberhard Anheuser and Adolphus Busch, down the Mississippi River at St. Louis, Missouri. Although today Schlitz Brewery has decamped, Milwaukeans remain faithful to the brews that built the grand cream-colored brick mansions along Grand Avenue in the 1890s. While Americans consume an average of six gallons of beer per person a year, the folk of Milwaukee consume forty-two gallons a year. "Wisconsin is slow to change," says Ervin at John Ernst's Cafe. "We've kept our ethnic values."

When I first visited Wisconsin it was not in the fall but in dead winter, in the snow. I wasn't looking for the frozen waters that made German beer but for the fresh waters that made pastures and meadows for cows to turn grass into milk and milk into cheese. Water had made Wisconsin (or *"wees-kon-san"* as the Chippewas called "a gathering of waters") a land of lakes—15,000 of them, bordered by Lake Michigan on the east, Lake Superior on the north, and the Mississippi River on the west. Thirteen thousand years ago aboriginal Indians hunted mammoths here as the glacier of the Ice Age receded to leave behind a moraine pockmarked with lakes. Today German and Swiss descendants milk cows in these same lakelands to make Wisconsin America's number-one dairy state and the last home of the once prevalent cottage industry of cheese.

In the snow Wisconsin is milkland. White and black Holsteins nuzzle barns that look like giant mammaries next to phallic silos of blue. Even the sky is milky. This is a white country of white cookery: a cookery of white cheese, milk, butter, and the white sauces the French call *blanc*; of white meats like milk-fed veal, of white fish literally named "whitefish," of white sausages named *weiss wurst*, of white cabbages for sauerkraut, of white noodles called "spaetzle" and white meringues called *schaum torte*, of white wines like reisling and Rhine, and of white beer called *weisse bier*, made with sour milk.

Milking cows at the Rolla Shufelt farm near Oconto, Wisconsin, around 1900.

Robert and Teddy Sangstad in Vernon County, Wisconsin, 1942, fattening their hogs with whey returned from the creamery. Good Wisconsin milk makes good sausage as well as good cheese.

White was the color of Ralph Widmer's cheese factory, a small frame house tucked into the snow in the village of Theresa, due south of Lake Winnebago. Ralph greets me in a white cheesemaker's cap and apron over his white overalls. The overalls are "Oshkosh, b'gosh," he says with a laugh, referring to the trademark that made Oshkosh as famous for its overalls as Milwaukee for its beer. Ralph shows me lakes of white milk in vats, some ten thousand quarts at a time, that rennet will thicken into curds which are then pressed into blocks of white cheese. "All cheese is white," Ralph explains, "only some like Cheddar and Colby are colored with a natural dye, annatto, from a tropical plant, for cosmetic reasons only." Ralph shows me how they cut the curd with big wires which run at right angles to make cubes. They then steam the cubes to shrink them and expel the whey.

"In the old days the pigs got the whey," Ralph recalls. "A farmer would come with his horse and wagon to exchange his milk cans for whey, and when he was still a mile from his farm the hogs would be hollerin'. My dad drank whey every day and lived to be eighty-three, so that tells you something about whey." Ralph is a lively whey-drinking man in his seventies, the oldest of John Widmer's three sons, who even now are cutting, steaming, and pressing curd to make white brick cheese. "This is an 'original' American cheese," Ralph says, "a version of German-Swiss, in which you press the curds under glazed bricks and cure them for six days."

Ralph takes me into his kitchen next door to sample some brick. Ralph's face is as sharply carved as the figures of the cuckoo clock on his wall. Here he presides over Swiss pillows, flags, calendars, plaques of every canton, photographs of Swiss cows in Swiss meadows, and a framed letter of recommendation for Herr Widmer from the flax-weaving factory at Lausanne in 1906. Ralph translates from the German, " 'He's a good worker and we hate to see him go but we wish him luck in America.' Now isn't that something?" Ralph asks. "He landed with twenty dollars in his pocket from the Swiss government and soon as he could, he sent them back $58 to pay off his loan with interest," Ralph explains. "Forty years ago this land was all woods, and when the Germans came they walked all over Wisconsin looking for the hard maples that grew in the kind of soil and climate they knew how to farm. They pastured their cows when they cleared the woods, and when the Swiss came and saw the cows they started making cheese."

Of course the Germans made cheese too, then the Italians, and now the French. I never saw so much cheese as I did in the next few days. "If you get off the beaten path it seems like every crossroad has a little cheese factory because the farmers had to do something with all that milk," Ralph explains. In Wisconsin "all that milk" means 9.5 billion pounds of milk a year to make 9.5 million pounds of cheese. A fifty-mile circle around Madison embraces most of Wisconsin's 340 small cheese factories. I finally learned to recognize them by the sight of a milk truck at the door and a faint milky smell in the air.

I talked to Elmer Deppler, who makes Limburger and baby Swiss down in Monroe. To Jim Baker, who makes mozzarella and string cheese over in St. Cloud. To "Butch" Suemnicht and his wife, who make Cheddar and Colby near Loganville in a mustard-yellow house as colorful as their cheese. To Ed and Helen Miksellspurger at Penn Hollow, who make Monterey Jack to send to California. To Florian Frank at Bigelow near Avoca, who makes aged Cheddar for love, since there's no profit in it. And to Ferdinand "Ferdi" Nachreiner at Cedar Grove, who couldn't stop talking about curds, the fresh curds they call "squeakies" out here because the little cubes make a squeaky-clean sound when you eat them. "We travel a lot because we have a son in Japan, a daughter in Brazil, and another in Jamaica," says Ferdi, "and what I miss most when I'm gone is cheese, the fresh taste of those curds, I love them, I kinda do."

The largest cheese producer I found was not German at all but Italian-Spanish. In the 1920s José Ramon Tolibia, with his wife, Blondina, found on the shores of Fond du Lac to the north the same kind of "sweet grasses and spring water" he knew in northern Italy. Tolibia Inc. boomed with the pizza boom following the Second World War and is now the center of America's Italian cheese production, processing a million and a half pounds of milk a day into provolone, mozzarella, Gorgonzola, Romano, Roquefort, and their latest experiment, Camemblue. The smallest cheese producer I found was a Frenchman, Jean-Paul Guimont, in Belmont to the west, a crossroads so small that the Do Drop Inn advertises an "After School Special for grades 1 to 12" of hamburger, French fries, Jell-O, and soda for $1.09. Here Jean-Paul is trying to make the Brie and Camembert of his native Normandy with the pasteurized milk of Wisconsin for the pasteurized palates of the midwest.

For the small cheesemaker, life is nothing but cheese. "You gotta keep running with it all the time, twelve to fifteen hours a day, sixteen days a week," Helen Miksellspurger says with a laugh. "Milk is like wine, cheese-making is like breadmaking. Every batch is different and sometimes the cheese just doesn't hold together, it gets pitty and falls apart. You gotta have a feel for it. Some got the knack like my husband and others don't." "How do you like being a cheesemaker's wife?" I ask, because I notice that, like most cheesemakers, they live upstairs above the vats. "Awful," Helen answers. "Even when I was a kid, I never liked cheese."

If Wisconsin smells of yeast from its breweries and of milk from its dairies, Wisconsin kitchens smell of sausages from Germany's many ways with pigs. Not long after the first German, Wilhelm Strothman, landed in Milwaukee Harbor in 1835 aboard the steamer *United States,* the inhabitants of the city complained about the numbers of sows and boars running at large on the sidewalks, attacking small children and crowding ladies into the street. The marshal, however, responded that he'd be damned if he'd "deny the liberty of the streets to any hog." Hog rights were important to Germans. In Germany, farmers had been denied pastures for grazing sheep and cows, for such pasturelands belonged to the nobility. Farmers had been allowed, however, to keep pigs as part of their barnyard stock and they had learned to turn pigs into every edible form.

Across the street from Mader's in Milwaukee, I follow my nose into Usinger's Famous Sausage Factory, a bit of Disneyland Bavaria erected by Frederick Usinger in the 1870s, when he landed here with a handful of sausage recipes from a Frankfort sausage maker. His grandson now runs the factory and the original shop, still sporting murals of gnomes and elves who dream *ein schöner traum* of pigs transformed by magic into sausage links beneath mottoes like *"Doch auch Yankee und Franzosen/ Lieben diese deutschen Chosen."* Proof that even Yanks and French love these German goodies is in the pudding—the blood pudding called "Thueringer blood sausage"—and in the summer sausage of smoked pork and beef flavored with garlic, the liver sausage or *braunschweiger,* the wieners in sheep casings and the frankfurters in hog casings, the knackwursts, beerwursts, *yachtwursts,* and bratwursts that enabled *The Saturday Evening Post* twenty-five years ago to feature on a cover the Usinger *wurstmachers* in their "Quest for the Best of the Wurst."

In Wisconsin I learned the depth of America's German roots, which two world wars have tended to obscure. A quarter of Wisconsin's inhabitants today are descended from Germans on both sides, a half from Germans on at

German gentlemen fishing and wining at a picnic on the shores of Lake Michigan in the 1890s. Rounded vests and good cigars suggest a gathering of *Feinschmeckers.*

least one side. As H. L. Mencken long ago pointed out, America's indebtedness to its second largest ethnic group appears most strongly in the language of food and drink. Think of pumpernickel, wienerwurst, frankfurter, sauerbraten, *blutwurst,* zweiback, delicatessen, hamburger, sauerkraut, torte, lager, rathskeller, beer garden. And think of two of America's most influential cook books of this century, *"The Settlement" Cook Book* of Lizzie Black Kander from Milwaukee and *The Joy of Cooking* of Irma von Starkloff Rombauer from Milwaukee's twin city, St. Louis.

Mrs. Simon Kander, born in 1858 in Milwaukee to an English father and an Austrian mother, became interested in the problems of immigrant Jews after her marriage to a businessman from Baltimore. As president of the Ladies Relief Sewing Society, which evolved into the Milwaukee Jewish Mission and The Settlement, Mrs. Kander printed some of her recipes to save time in the cooking classes she organized for women struggling with new ingredients in a strange land. *"The Settlement" Cook Book,* subtitled *The Way to a Man's Heart* and printed in 1901, brought together recipes for chili con carne and *mandel kloese,* chow mein and matzos chocolate torte. As against mainstream English and French, it was one of the earliest ethnic cook books published in English in this country and one of the first to include the culinary traditions of German Jews.

Pennsylvania Germans had earlier profited from German-American cook books like Friederike Löffler's *Vollständiges Kochbuch für die deutsch-amerikanische Kuche,* published in Philadelphia in 1856. And from a collection assembled by a Harrisburg printer named Gustav Peters, who put out *Die geschickte Hausfrau* in 1848, as if it had been written by a comic dialect-speaking cook, Aunt Pall. (A later writer translates this as *The Handy Housewife* and calls it "one of the first truly ethnic cookbooks to appear in this country.") But these were essentially books for peasant and farmer classes striving to join middle-class America. The more refined classes had to wait until 1931, when Irma von Starkloff, who had met Mark Twain in Europe and had had a youthful romance with Booth Tarkington in Indianapolis, had a little cook book privately printed to assuage the emptiness of her new widowhood at the age of fifty-four. It was a casual collection of recipes "such as any kitchen-minded woman possesses," with plenty of shortcuts and brand names of cans for ladies short of time. But it also had a sprinkling of German recipes from her side of the family and of Hungarian recipes from her husband's side. In 1936 Bobbs-Merrill in Indianapolis took over the publishing and her daughter Marion Rombauer Becker helped with the revisions that, 13 million copies later, have made *The Joy of Cooking* a "record of our American way of life." Certainly it became a record of middle America's way of life in the Midwest, as Mrs. Rombauer corresponded with thousands of housewives until her death in 1962, a task continued by her daughter until her own death a decade later.

Because the Germanic tradition is so pronounced in Wisconsin, not until a second visit did I realize how much of this lakeland is still wild and how much of it belongs in spirit if not in deed to the Indians. At the Oneida Indian Village outside Green Bay, Wisconsin, known best today for the Green Bay Packers, an Indian guide put a tomahawk in my hand. I had just examined a case of moose-hair embroidery, porcupine-quill jewelry, cornhusk dolls, and bread paddles for boiling corn dumplings. And I had just heard Iroquois stories of Creation, how the Iroquois did not come from the Lake of Emergence below, as Pueblo Indians did, but from the Sky-World above. The first Woman fell through the floor of the Sky-World into the waters that became the land of sky-blue waters. This was the land Longfellow claimed for Hiawatha and Minnehaha, Laughing Water, but Longfellow's Christianized Indians are no more anomalous than the Oneidas themselves, who converted to Episcopalianism in the East before migrating West. Nor are they more anomalous than my attempts to throw a tomahawk.

There are 600,000 Indians in the north of Wisconsin, descendants of the Ojibwa, Sauks, Potawatomi, Winnebagos, and Menominee—whose name means "good grain," from the seeds of the grass we now call "wild rice." Long before the Germans came, French explorers and fur traders had crossed Lake Michigan to found a fort at Green Bay in 1634, about the time the English were settling Williamsburg and a good forty years before Jacques Marquette and Louis Joliet passed through the settlement of "Chicagu" on their way north to preach to the Winnebagos. For the next couple of centuries the wilderness was undisturbed except by a few French and English trappers and missionaries, scrapping for furs and souls and the honor of providing Christmas feasts such as that set forth by Captain Thomas Gummersall Anderson in 1806 at the American Fur Company. Anderson had stuffed a rac-

Otto Radke, Andrew Eckstein, and Jake Lange with their bag of squirrels, rabbits, and grouse, shot in the woodlands of Cross Plains, Wisconsin, around 1920–25.

A family in Marinette County, Wisconsin, 1895, displaying their garden produce to help boost the state as a land of agricultural opportunity. The photo appeared in an 1896 volume called *Northern Wisconsin: A Hand-book for the Homeseeker*.

coon of thirty-two pounds, the fattest the Indians could tree. "Toward sunset, I set my cook to chop any quantity of venison for stuffing," he wrote. "In the meantime, I had the pepper and a piece of deerskin, pounding it into a pulverized form, cutting up onions and a little cedar leaves, to give my viand a pleasant taste. No coonskin's body . . . was ever so cram-ful before." Unfortunately, however, to prevent his feast from freezing in the night, he set it by the fire and awoke on Christmas day to find his feast putrid. "Oh misery!" he wrote. "I went without my dinner and was laughed at by my half-famished friends."

The cultures of New England and the South evolved slowly, as settlers either assimilated other inhabitants or else pushed them out. But Wisconsin was a recent arrival, an official territory not until 1836, a state not until 1848. The historical clash of cultures is still raw and bizarre. At the Living History Museum at Heritage Hill State Park in Green Bay, I enter the eighteenth-century house of Mme. Caroline Tank, a Dutch noblewoman who married a Moravian missionary from Denmark. He wished to combine business with religion and failed at both. From these misfortunes, Mme. Tank took comfort in her painting. She had been trained by the best tutors the Baron and Baroness van Boetzelaer could afford, and the walls of her elegantly furnished dining room are covered with oil canvases that brought neo-Rembrandts and Vermeers to the eaters of thirty-two-pound raccoons.

In the woods of the Kohler plumbing empire near Sheboygan, I step into an exact replica of Kohler's ancestral home in the Austrian valley of Bregenzerwald, with wood carvings and ceramic-tiled stoves and a Waelderhaus recipe book of Weinschaumsuppe and Dampfnudeln Mit Pflauman. Inside Milwaukee's Public Museum I walk through the cobblestoned streets of a cloned European village of thirty-three ethnic domestic interiors, heaped with foods and artifacts donated by the immigrants of Wisconsin from the Baltic to the Balkans. How American these contradictions: the arrival of Koenig Gambrinus, the Beer King of Bavaria, on the shores of Gitchee Gummee in the land of sky-blue waters.

18
Lakes and Pastures

White fish, white meat, and white cheese are the triad of Wisconsin's white cookery. At Port Washington, just north of Milwaukee on Lake Mie-sit-gan, I talk to Lloyd Smith in the Smith Brothers' Fish Restaurant, which looks out on the first manmade harbor in the country, built in 1856 to dock the large steam tugs that replaced sails when commercial fishing on the lake was big. Now there's but a single tug left on the lake, and commercial fishing is nearly extinct. The native trout was all but wiped out by lamprey eels in the 1940s, Lloyd tells me, but now the State Department of Fisheries has restocked trout in such numbers that they've endangered the perch.

Lloyd is a large and genial man whose great-great-grandfather came here from the Finger Lakes to start a fishing industry and whose grandmother in 1910 devised a way to process whitefish roe. "Whitefish roe is orange," Lloyd explains, "but we dye it black because folks expect caviar to be black." In Port Washington "caviar" means whitefish roe and most of it goes to Japan, except when an old customer like Jack Lord, one of the stars of *Hawaii Five-O*, calls up and orders a couple of cases flown over to Hawaii for a party. Another local favorite is whitefish liver, but as fishermen grab the livers for themselves they seldom reach the market. "Just dredge them in flour and sauté them in butter with lots of onions and mushrooms," Lloyd explains how to cook them, as I gobble up six small fillets of white perch, sautéed in butter.

As for the trout that gobble perch, the lake teems with German brown trout, rainbow trout, and a deepwater lake trout. They eat yellow perch, the big walleye, and the smaller sauger. But there are fish to spare: bass, pickerel, and pike, and over in Lake Winnebago there are even shovel-nose sturgeon. But now it is September and what I see through the window of Lloyd's restaurant is a line of men and women thick as sardines on the dock outside. The coho salmon are running up Sauk Creek and to cast a line is to reel in flapping silver. "Sometimes the fishers are so crowded they fight each other to get a foot on the dock," says Lloyd.

Fishing is a way of life in these parts: salmon fishing in the fall, pike and sauger fishing in the winter when ice fishing is on, trout and suckers in the spring. Friday nights up and down the state there are fish fries when the whole family eats out, once for Catholic sumptuary laws and now for the sumptuous taste of fresh lake fish with dumplings and kraut or mashed potatoes and raw onions and rye bread, "All you can eat from 4:00 to 10:30," at spots called Phil's Tuxedo Lounge or Paul's Rathskeller.

At the Smith Brothers' Fish Dock, smoking fish is a way of life. A small tug, the green and white *Oliver H. Smith,* unloads the day's catch of chub. Ned runs the smokehouse and Ned explains that they fish chub, a subspecies of whitefish, with gill nets maybe a half mile long stretched tight like tennis nets across the lake bottom to catch fish by their gills. The chubs soak in brine overnight, then are hung by their tails on hooks and rods, row upon row, to smoke five or six hours until they look like leaves of beaten gold, each of which suspends a golden tear of oil. "You can keep smoked fish about as long as a quart of milk," says Ned. "Or you can freeze it or you can eat it right off the hook, like this." Ned pushes his thumb under the fat side of the fish and pushes up a fillet in one piece, then attacks the thin side that covers the ribs. "Just suck it off as if you were playing the harmonica," he says.

If whitefish is a specialty of Wisconsin lakes, white veal is a specialty of the pasturelands. With plenty of cows and plenty of milk, veal for the Germans was not a luxury but the year-round staple of Germanic cookery, which in Austria centered on Wiener schnitzel and in Hungary on paprika veal or goulash. In nineteenth-century Germany, once a Hanover transplanted to Buckingham Palace made all things English fashionable, veal found new uses such as in mock turtle soup, made from a calf's head. In Wisconsin restaurants I avoided the omnipresent Wiener schnitzel because of my year in Heidelberg, where veal was such a staple that it was generally indistinguishable from the bread that covered it in crumbs. But at Milwaukee's Karl Ratzsch

Restaurant, I discovered the pleasures of veal meatballs covered in a lemon-and-caper white sauce.

In the white cooking of German Wisconsin, or of German Pennsylvania for that matter, a white dairy product like sour cream constantly joins the white flesh of chicken or veal. William Woys Weaver, in *A Quaker Woman's Cookbook* (1982), warns the modern reader of old Pennsylvania-German cook books that "cream" meant sour cream and "butter" meant butter made from sour cream. As good dairymen, the Germanic tribes were especially skilled in controlling the cultures that turned milk sour, just as they controlled the cultures that turned milk to cheese and malts to beer. Anyone with a cow made cheese at home, the simplest forms being cottage cheese, or what we now call farmer's cheese, and cream cheese. Farmers made cream cheese by dehydrating sour cream, then letting it thicken for a couple of weeks with its own enzymes until the moisture separated out. Commercial brands of cream cheese today, preserved by gum arabic, bear little resemblance to the exquisite taste and texture of cream cheese freshly made at home.

Along with the taste of homemade cream cheese and cottage cheese, we have lost the taste of homemade buttermilk, except in places like Wisconsin, where the relation of man to cow is still direct. "Mother made butter and father cheese," wrote a Swiss immigrant settling in Sauk County at the turn of the century. When mother made butter, buttermilk was the residue after the butter churn had so agitated the cream that it separated into liquid and solid particles that gathered into clumps. Such buttermilk contains more lactic acid than commercial buttermilk made today from skim milk artificially cultured. Just as you can make yogurt at home, you can make buttermilk at home by adding a starter. Half a cup of commercial buttermilk shaken with a quart of milk and kept warm for twelve hours will make a nice thick food-drink of character for those who regret the Great White Milk Murder in the name of sterilized homogenization, just as they regret the Great White Bread Murder in the name of longer shelf life.

PLANKED WHITEFISH WITH
WHITEFISH LIVER

For those lucky enough to catch their fish and cook it, an oak plank, with pegs or nails to attach the fillets to the board, is all one needs to cook fish by a campfire and a lake. For indoor cooks, however, it is comforting to know that a seasoned hardwood plank was recommended by Mrs. Kander in her 1915 edition of *"The Settlement" Cook Book* for whitefish and trout to be baked in a very hot oven. With today's metal alloys, an ovenproof platter will work as efficiently as wood, but wood does suggest that the fish once lived in a lake by a forest.

The method is simple. Rub the plank with oil on both sides and heat it in a 450° oven for fifteen to twenty minutes, if it has been previously seasoned. If not, repeat the process of oiling and heating. You'll need a little melted butter for basting and that's it. Whitefish is particularly good for planking because it has enough oil in it not to dry out. I've added whitefish liver for the really lucky ones.

> 4 whitefish fillets
> 6 ounces (1½ sticks) butter, melted
> salt and pepper to taste
> 2 medium onions, minced
> 1 pound whitefish livers (if available)

Heat an oiled plank at 450° for 15 to 20 minutes. Salt and pepper fillets on both sides. When the plank is ready, put the fillets skin side down on the plank and pour over them 6 tablespoons melted butter.

Bake at 450° for 5 to 8 minutes, depending on thickness of the fillets.

Stew the onions in a small heavy skillet with the remaining butter for 2 to 3 minutes. Salt and pepper the livers, put them on top of the onions, cover skillet with a lid, and braise over low heat until they firm up, about 5 minutes. Serve the fillets from the plank, placed on a trivet or heat-proof tile, with a serving of the liver and onion mixture on the side.

Serves 4.

DOOR COUNTY FISH BOIL

Door County is a peninsular thumb formed by Green Bay on the left and Lake Michigan on the right. Door County was the landing point for French trappers and traders crossing the lake, but the place was so wild that as each successive wave of immigrants washed up on these shores, it became known as "Death's Door." Today it's a place of cherry orchards and vineyards, small harbors and large fishing boats, and enough avid fishermen to keep the pots boiling year round for a Door County fish boil.

Like a gumbo or pine bark stew in the South, like a fish chowder in New England, a Door County fish boil is one of those communal events in which the major ingredients are fresh air, a freshly made campfire, freshly caught freshwater fish, and a fresh crowd of kibitzers to poke the pot. A proper fish-boil kettle, any Door County fisherman will tell you, requires a wire basket in which to lower the fish steaks into the brine and remove them without the fish falling apart. No simmering here. "The water must boil at all times," say the authors of *Wisconsin Style Cooking* (1980). "We even build up the fire to make the pot boil over at the last minute," says my friend Marlene Dockry up at Green Bay, "to get rid of the oil if you've got particularly oily fish."

Marlene is a pretty blond Catholic mother of eight hunters and fishers. She cooks indoor meals regularly for ten, so outdoor meals for 100 seem natural to her. Most recipes for fish boils begin with fifty pounds of fish, fifteen pounds of salt, and eight pounds of butter, but of course you can scale down the quantities for home consumption. What is peculiar to this method is the heavy brine of two pounds salt to ten quarts water. A. J. McClane explains, in his *Encyclopedia of Fish Cookery* (1977), that the brine raises the boiling point and solidifies the fish without oversalting it. Maybe this works with fifty pounds of fish and one hundred beer drinkers, but it doesn't work in small quantities. I find a ratio of a half cup salt to ten quarts water is salt enough.

    10 quarts water
    ½ cup salt
24–36 small red new potatoes (3–4 pounds), skins on
    24 small white onions (3 pounds)
    8 pounds freshwater fish (lake trout, salmon, whitefish, pike), cut into 1½-inch steaks

1 pound butter, melted
12 lemons, quartered
1 cup chopped parsley

Bring water to a boil with the salt. Add potatoes and onions (cut a cross in the bottom of the onions so they will cook rapidly) and cook until half done (8 to 10 minutes).

Put fish steaks in a wire basket, colander, or steamer top, or wrap them in cheesecloth that you can tie at the top with heavy string to fork out later. Lower fish into the pot, making sure they are entirely covered. Return broth to the boil, cover the pot, and boil until the fish is firm but fork tender, 8 to 10 minutes. Remove fish, then vegetables, and drain both thoroughly. Heap fish on a platter surrounded by the potatoes and onions. Pour butter over the whole, sprinkle with chopped parsley and serve with lemon quarters and a pepper grinder.

Serves 12 to 16.

LIZZIE KANDER'S PICKLED HERRING

At the turn of the century the herring catch in Lake Michigan totaled some 41 million pounds a year. As it proliferated in cans and jars, preserved in harsh wine or brutal vinegar, its very abundance made it scorned. But not among the Germans and other émigrés from the Baltic and north seas of Europe, who brought with them centuries-old traditions of pickling and preserving. Because herring is a relatively fatty fish, it takes well to curing by salt and vinegar to counteract its oil. No country developed better curing methods than the Germany that gave us Bismarck herring, made with *schmaltz* (meaning "fat") herring, split open to make flat fillets and cured in vinegar and spices.

The best schmaltz herring should contain 20 to 24 percent fat and for best flavor should contain sperm, or "milt." In old recipes, you will sometimes see this referred to as "milter" or "milch herring," and so Mrs. Kander calls them in *"The Settlement" Cook Book*. To the usual onions, lemons, and spices, she adds tart apples and chopped almonds, a good way to underline that your pickled herring did not emerge from a commercial jar or can.

        12 whole salt herring, with milts
         4 medium onions, sliced thin
         2 lemons, sliced thin
        12 bay leaves
         2 tablespoons each peppercorns and mustard seeds
         1 teaspoon coriander seeds
         2 tart apples, chopped fine
        ½ cup almond halves, blanched
         1 cup dry white wine
         3 cups sour cream

Soak herring in ice water to cover in the refrigerator 3 to 5 days, changing the water daily and rinsing the fish well each time. (Taste for saltiness to determine length of soaking.) Trim fish by removing head and fins. Slit fish along their bellies and carefully remove the milt sacs. Discard the other innards. Place fish open, flesh side down, on a board, press the backbone with your palm, turn fish over, and remove backbone in one piece. Cut off the tails.

In 1 or 2 wide-mouthed jars, place the fish in layers with the onions, lemons, bay leaves, spices, apples, and almonds. Mash the milt with the white wine, discarding the membrane of the sacs. Beat this mixture into the sour cream. Pour over the fish in the jar. Cover tightly with plastic wrap and refrigerate 48 hours for best flavor.

Serves 12 or more.

SWEET AND SOUR CHRISTMAS FISH

For non-Germans an unusual and intriguing fish dish of ancient Silesian tradition is a Christmas carp, originating in the Middle Ages when carp ponds were part of every monastery garden and when the mixture of sweets and sours, fruits and fish seemed natural. In the Germany of her childhood, Nika Hazelton tells us, a whole carp was served on Christmas Eve, as prelude to the goose or hare on Christmas day. Hazelton describes the sauce as a "rich, dark-brown sweet-and-sour sauce made with crumbled spice cakes, beer, onions, root vegetables, salt, sugar, vinegar and lemon juice."

German-Americans, such as Lizzie Kander, usually substituted ginger cookies for crumbled spice cakes, as Milwaukee restaurants do today in their gingersnap gravies. Mrs. Kander's version of Sweet and Sour Fish is too sweet to my taste, for she adds brown sugar and raisins as well. In *The Flavor of Wisconsin* (1981), the contributor of Christmas Fruited Fish, Mrs. Mae Krueger of Kaukauna, recalls the holiday recipe of her childhood and adds dried fruits and nuts.

Don't be put off by the idea of mixing gingersnaps with garlic, apricots with carp. If you think of the Chinese sweet-sour sauces in which they bathe their carps, this one will seem less idiosyncratic of the Gothic North.

1 cup dried apricots
½ cup golden sultana raisins
¼ cup chopped candied ginger
   juice and rind of 1 lemon
1 3- or 4-pound whole fish (such as carp, pike, trout, pickerel)
2–3 cups fish stock
2 cloves garlic, mashed
4 gingersnaps
¼ cup vinegar
¼ cup dark corn syrup or brown sugar
¼ cup slivered almonds
1 cup thinly sliced celery
1 cup thinly sliced onions

Cut apricots into quarters, add to the raisins, ginger, and lemon juice and rind, and cover with boiling water to soften them. Place fish with the stock and garlic in sealed foil in a baking pan, and bake at 325° until the thickest part of the fish flakes with a fork, 10 to 20 minutes. Drain off liquid by punching a hole in one corner of the foil and draining liquid into a bowl.

Put liquid in a blender with the garlic, gingersnaps, vinegar, and syrup and blend until smooth. Pour into a saucepan, add the soaked fruits, almonds, celery, and onions and simmer until the vegetables are translucent. Remove fish from foil and pour sauce over the fish, cover with plastic wrap, and refrigerate overnight. Before serving, let fish warm to room temperature.

Serves 4.

HERBED VEAL BALLS
KOENIGSBERGER KLOPS

The name Koenigsberger, like hamburger, reminds us of the Germanic fondness for ground beef. Named for a city in northeastern Prussia, these little veal meatballs are enriched with ground pork and sauced in a lemon-caper white sauce, thickened with egg yolk. A change from heavy sauerbratens and *schlachtplattes,* these veal balls are light, white, delicate, and fragrant, poached rather than sautéed, more like quenelles than hamburger patties. I tasted them first under the ministering hand of Karl Ratzsch III, whose grandfather emigrated to Milwaukee to become a busboy in the Minsk Cafe, renamed Old Heidelberg when he married the boss's daughter, renamed again Otto Herman's Cafe and finally Karl Ratzsch. Karl Ratzsch IV is expected to carry on the family restaurant tradition, but he is not yet a busboy since he is only four years old.

> 1 pound ground veal
> ½ pound each ground beef and pork
> 4 anchovy fillets, mashed
> ¼ cup minced parsley
> ½ teaspoon white pepper
> 1 medium onion, minced
> 2 tablespoons pork fat or butter
> 2 eggs, beaten
> ¼ cup sour cream
> 1 cup fresh bread crumbs

Poaching Broth
> ½ onion, sliced
> 1 stalk celery, sliced
> 4 sprigs parsley
> 1 bay leaf
> 3 cloves
> 6 peppercorns
> ½ teaspoon thyme

White Sauce

    3 tablespoons butter
    2 tablespoons flour
    2 egg yolks, beaten
    3 tablespoons lemon juice
    2 tablespoons capers
    ¼ teaspoon pepper

Grind the meats together very fine (if the butcher has not done so, grind them again in the food processor), mix in the anchovy, parsley, and pepper. Soften the onion in the fat or butter until translucent and add to the meat. Mix the eggs with the sour cream and add to the meat, along with the bread crumbs. Fluff the mixture with a fork and taste for seasoning by frying a small bit of the mixture. Add salt if wanted. Shape lightly into 2-inch balls.

Prepare the poaching broth by bringing 6 cups of water to a boil with the seasonings in a large saucepan and simmering 10 minutes. Add the meatballs and simmer uncovered until the meatballs float to the top, about 20 minutes. Remove with a slotted spoon and keep warm while preparing the sauce. Strain broth and reserve.

Make a white sauce by melting butter in a saucepan, adding flour, and cooking 2 minutes while stirring. Add 1½ cups of the reserved poaching broth and beat until smooth. Add another ½ cup broth to the beaten eggs, then add this mixture to the sauce, stirring the while. When the sauce thickens slightly, add lemon juice, capers, and pepper and taste for seasoning.

Pour over the warm meatballs and serve.

Makes about 18 meatballs to serve 4 to 6.

PAPRIKA CREAM VEAL

In the Spice House on Third Street in Milwaukee, down the street from Mader's, I see windows filled with baskets of freshly ground spices and aromats of hundreds of kinds and colors. Here I learn about the Hungarian spice the Spanish called *pimenton* when they first brought this species of *Capsicum annuum* from the New World to the Old. Germans called it "paprika." Northern and Central Europe developed several varieties of this plant, but savored most a powder that was sweet, mild, aromatic, and deeply red. So specialized is paprika in Hungary that it comes in five grades, in descending order: "noble sweet," "semisweet," "rose," "strong," and "commercial." We are lucky in this country if we can choose between two forms of Hungarian paprika: "Hungarian sweet" and "half-sharp."

The traditional Austro-Hungarian dish of paprika veal is really a sweet-sour combination, because the paprika provides the sweet and sour cream the sour. As for other spices, I've added here some caraway, fenugreek, and dill, because they are part of the Hungarian spice palate, but you should vary such spices to suit yourself. The most popular packaged spice at Spice House, I learn, is one they call "Old World Third Street Seasoning," which combines Hungarian sweet paprika with the following: celery and caraway seeds, garlic and onion powders, dill, fenugreek, savory, tarragon, thyme, cloves, cardamon, and cinnamon.

> 2 pounds boneless veal (from leg, breast, or shoulder)
> 1 tablespoon Hungarian sweet paprika
> 1 teaspoon salt
> ½ teaspoon white pepper
> ¼ teaspoon each caraway, fenugreek, and dill seeds, ground fine
>   cayenne pepper to taste
> 2 large onions, sliced thin
> 6 tablespoons butter, pork fat, or olive oil
> ½ cup white wine
> 1 cup veal or chicken stock
> 1 tablespoon flour
> 1 cup sour cream
>   rind and juice of 1 lemon, or to taste

Cut the meat into 1½-inch cubes. Mix the seasonings together and roll the meat cubes in them. Let sit for 3 hours or more.

Sauté the onions in half the butter until softened. Remove with slotted spoon and reserve. Add remaining butter to same pan and brown meat lightly and quickly on all sides. Return onions to the pan, add wine and stock, and cover tightly. Simmer over very low heat for 20 minutes.

Pour off the broth into a saucepan and reduce to 1 cup. Stir the flour into the sour cream and add to the broth, together with the lemon rind and juice to taste. Transfer meat and sauce to an ovenproof dish, cover, and bake in a very low (225°) oven for 1 hour to finish cooking the meat in the sauce. Veal should be fork tender and the onions slightly crunchy.

Serves 4.

HOMEMADE COTTAGE CHEESE

If you've ever tasted and longed for the fresh curds of Wisconsin cheese-makers, those "squeakies" that Ferdi Nachreiner longed for in Tokyo and Brazil, you can simulate that taste in your own kitchen by making clabber or pot cheese, the kind of cheese we now call "cottage" but should call "factory." A description from *The Buckeye Cookbook* (1883) reveals that such cheeses were once as much a part of daily life as making bread or brewing beer:

> Set a gallon or more of clabbered milk on the stove hearth or in the oven after cooking a meal, leaving the door open; turn it around frequently, and cut the curd in squares with a knife, stirring gently now and then till about as warm as the finger will bear, and the whey shows all around the curd; pour all into a coarse bag, and hang to drain in a cool place for three or four hours. . . . When wanted, turn from the bag, chop rather coarse with a knife, and dress with salt, pepper, and sweet cream.

The process of clabbering is as fascinating as the results are delicious, and if you wonder what milk is all about, one way to find out is to turn it into cheese. The main problem for both the home and professional cheesemaker is pasteurized milk. Having killed the natural bacteria, we have to reintroduce bacteria to make the liquid coagulate. Junket rennet tablets, however, are almost as available as packaged yeast and it's the rennet that will clabber or curdle the milk. A little buttermilk also helps to speed the souring.

Since commercial cottage cheese today is made uniformly with skim milk, you'll find the whole-milk product richer in taste and texture. You can make your cheese richer still by adding heavy cream, as in creamed cottage cheese. If you make bread, you can use the whey as the liquid for your dough. Otherwise, it can go into a soup or any place you'd use water or skim milk. Whatever you do, don't throw out all those vitamins and proteins. I have found that a glass of ice-cold whey from the refrigerator is as refreshing as seltzer and far tastier. As Ralph Widmer said, "Good for what ails you and great for slopping the hogs."

1 gallon whole milk
½ cup buttermilk
¼ junket rennet tablet
2 tablespoons warm water
1 teaspoon salt
1 cup heavy cream, or to taste

Warm milk to about 70° in a large pot. Add the buttermilk. Dissolve the ¼ junket rennet table in the warm water and stir into the milk. Cover the pot and let it sit in a warm (70°) place until the curd forms, about 12 hours. The curd is a thick, rather firm layer. Cut it straight down with a long knife, first in one direction, then at right angles to make uniform squares. Then cut through the squares diagonally.

Set the pot of curd in a larger pan of water and heat slowly until the temperature of the curd registers 100° to 110° on an instant thermometer, 30 minutes to an hour. Stir gently every 5 or 10 minutes so that the curd will heat evenly throughout. (While heat firms the curd, excess heat toughens it.) Test doneness of curd by squeezing it between your fingers. It should not leave any liquid residue on your fingers.

Pour the curds gently into a colander lined with a double thickness of cheesecloth and set over a bowl or pan to catch the whey. Cover the top of the curd with plastic wrap to prevent it from drying out. Occasionally stir the curd with your fingers to let the whey drain. When curd is well drained, add the salt and cream and refrigerate. Covered with plastic, the cheese should keep several days, though it tastes best fresh.

Makes about 3½ cups.

COOKED CARAWAY CHEESE

Germans call this *Koch Kaese*, which Lizzie Kander translates as "boiled cheese" and Irma Rombauer as "cooked cheese." It's an easy way for the home cook to "ripen" cottage cheese or pot cheese, domestic or commercial. Because you will add whole milk to the cottage cheese, start with dry cottage cheese. The fermentation with caraway and paprika makes a delicious cheese spread with dark rye bread and beer that should make your supermarket packaged spreads blush for shame.

4 cups dry cottage cheese
2 teaspoons caraway seeds
½ teaspoon salt
¼ teaspoon Hungarian sweet paprika
⅛ teaspoon cayenne pepper
2 tablespoons butter
1 cup whole milk
1 egg yolk, beaten

Mix the cheese with the seasonings, cover with plastic wrap and a lid, and put in a warm (70°) place.

Let it ferment 3 to 4 days, stirring once each day.

Warm the butter in the milk, stir in the cheese, and cook gently about 10 minutes. Put into a blender or food processor and blend until smooth. Add the egg yolk and blend again so that it will be slightly glossy. Scoop mixture into a bowl and cover with plastic. Refrigerate until needed. This will keep up to 2 weeks.

Makes about 4 cups.

BELGIAN CHEESE PIE

One of the largest Belgian populations in the country settled in Door County and they brought with them the tradition of Kermess, the roistering harvest celebration in the fall that evokes Breughel more than the Kirk Messe, or Church Mass, for which it is named. This richly layered Belgian pie associated with Kermess is actually a cheesecake, an early Christian cousin of Lindy's Cheescake and Lizzie Kander's many cheese pies and kuchens.

Mrs. Kander's Kuchen Dough No. 2 in *"The Settlement" Cook Book* provides the rich sweetened brioche dough characteristic of Belgian Cheese Pie. The dough forms a container for dried fruits topped by a light and airy layer of lemon-flavored cheese beaten with eggs. Mrs. Kander frequently incorporates currants and almonds into her cheese cakes, but Belgian pie more typically uses prunes or raisins.

A word of warning. The dough is very sticky and is best kneaded in a food processor or electric mixer with a dough hook. But you should knead it only until barely elastic and smooth; otherwise it won't stay put in the pan.

Pie Dough

> 1 package dry yeast
> ½ cup milk warmed to 110°–115°
> 2 cups flour
> 4 tablespoons butter
> ¼ cup sugar
> 2 eggs
> ¼ teaspoon salt
> rind of 1 lemon, grated

Filling

> 1 cup each cooked pitted prunes and chopped almonds
> ½ cup brown sugar
> juice of 1½ lemons
> ½ teaspoon each cinnamon and nutmeg
> ¼ pound (1 stick) butter
> ½ cup granulated sugar
> 4 eggs, separated
> 2 cups creamed cottage cheese

To make the dough, dissolve the yeast in the milk, add 1 cup of the flour, mix well, cover with plastic, and let the starter ferment 3 to 4 hours in a warm (70°–80°) place.

Cream the 4 tablespoons butter with the sugar, beat in the eggs, salt, and remaining cup of flour. Mix with the yeast starter and knead lightly. Cover with plastic and let rise until doubled. Punch down and chill thoroughly. Shape dough into 12 balls (you may need to keep flouring your fingers) and press them into the sides and bottom of a 9-inch buttered cake pan with a removable bottom.

For the filling, mix together the prunes, almonds, brown sugar, one-third of the lemon juice, and the spices and spread them over the dough. Cream remaining butter with the white sugar and beat in the egg yolks until the mixture is light and fluffy. Beat the remaining lemon juice into the cottage cheese and then beat this into the sugar-butter-egg mixture. Beat egg whites separately until stiff but not dry and fold into the batter. Spread the mixture over the fruit layer. Put a baking sheet under your cake pan to catch any overflow.

Bake at 350° for 20 minutes, then turn heat down to 325° and continue baking until top is browned at the edges and slightly puffed, 30 to 40 minutes.

Serves 8 to 10.

19
Sweet-Sours

Germans in Pennsylvania were called "sauerkraut Yankees" during the Civil War because they remained a clan apart, both by their spoken dialect and the dialect of their cooking. The primary verb of that dialect was "to pickle," and the syntax was that of a peasant culture in which salting or brining large quantities of meat and fish for a winter of ice and snow was every man's work. Slavic tribes passed pickling methods on to Germanic ones, William Woys Weaver tells us in *Sauerkraut Yankees* (1983), and for centuries pickling was salt and sour. Typical flavorings were juniper berries and caraway seeds, added to the vinegar that was always in ready supply from the natural souring of grapes and apples and other fruits. In the vocabulary of Germanic cooking, tart fruit was substantive because its high acid content helped to preserve itself and other foods and its acid taste contrasted well with a diet of fatty meat and bland noodle and dumpling doughs.

Sweets came later. Not until the mass production of refined white sugar at the turn of the century did sweet pickling with sugar typify the pickling not only of the Germans in Pennsylvania but of home canners everywhere in the country. To understand the situation, look at the sugars available to a Philadelphia housewife in 1897: Havana white and brown; Muscovado first quality, second quality, and ordinary; West India clayed white and brown; Calcutta white and Batavia white. Even if the housewife decided to splurge and went for one of the costly "whites," she would still, after she brought her loaf home wrapped in a cone of blue paper, have to wash her sugar to remove any insects and other foreign matter. Next she would have to filter the sugar syrup through egg white and charcoal, then strain it through muslin, and finally boil it in a pot to evaporate the water once again to get sugar crystals.

The seven sweets and seven sours that characterize Pennsylvania-German menus today stem from a very recent tradition of modern sugar processing. A less extreme combination of sweet and sour, however, was typical of Germanic-Slavic cookery that continued the medieval mixing of fruits and spices with meat, fish, and fowl. Germans in the American wilderness found an echo of these mixtures in the way Indians mixed wild fruits and berries with meats to make pemmican. Or they found it in the more sophisticated way Indians fermented maple sap to make a vinegar they called *ciwabo*, in which they marinated venison and other game. Such sweety-sour vinegar was not too remote from the marinade of sweetened vinegar for sauerbraten and other German forms of pickled meat.

What makes Germanic methods of sweet-sour distinctive is that the sweet-sour linkage permeates the entire menu—from fruit soups to pickled meats, pickled vegetables, dressings for salads, sourdough breads, sour cream doughnuts, fruit desserts. Even more than the English colonists who settled New England, German clans preserved their tribal customs wherever they landed.

The Germanic farming families of this lake country and of the lush valleys of Lancaster, Pennsylvania, have preserved a nineteenth-century rural America that is as anomalous in its way as the corn dances of the Pueblo Indians. The corn belt of the Midwest with Wisconsin at the top and Missouri at the bottom is Fat Belt, USA. At John Ernst's Cafe, the portions of the *schlachtplatt*, unchanged since the 1930s, would cause thrombosis in a devotee of the New Cuisine. The foot-high meringue on the lemon meringue pie at Lloyd Smith's restaurant in Port Washington would give an urban Yuppie anorexia. At Siebkin's Inn in Elkhart, the proportions of the meals are as Edwardian as the architecture of this belle époque resort. At Two Rivers, north of Milwaukee, Joe Schmidt, of the Schmidt Brothers Barbershop Quartet, is a double-scooped proof of Two Rivers' claim to fame as the "Home of the Ice Cream Sundae." What I learned eating my way through Wisconsin is that for every sour there's a sweet, for every bland there's a pickle, and there's no status at all in being thin.

PICKLED BEEF
SAUERBRATEN

Sauerbraten and sauerkraut are what most people think of when they think of German food. Beef marinated in wine, vinegar, and spices is a type of French beef à la mode, with the acid hyped to pickle the beef as well as to tenderize tough muscles. Sweetening does not appear in early recipes, such as the one for *Sauerer Rindsbraten* in *Die geschickte Hausfrau* (1848), nor does it appear in any of the marinated beef recipes in *Das Algemeine Kochbuch* (1891), written by Karl Kohler in Chicago "for the general German and German-American Cook." Sugar is a twentieth-century intrusion that increases with the century. While Lizzie Kander calls for a tablespoon of sugar in her sauerbraten gravy, Irma Rombauer calls for a full quarter cup.

As with any marinated meat, the quality of the vinegar is as important as the quality of the beef. If you use a harsh vinegar, the sauce will be harsh. If you use a gentler sour and a full-bodied wine, you'll end with a finely flavored meat that tastes as good cold as hot. Classic seasonings such as peppercorns, juniper berries, cloves, and bay leaves are enlivened in German marinades by ginger. *The Handy Housewife* calls for powdered ginger, but I've used the livelier form of raw ginger. Since gingersnaps provide thickening as well as flavor, I've limited sweetening to a few snaps for the gravy.

1 cup red wine vinegar
½ cup full-bodied red wine
½ cup water
1 onion, sliced thin
4 slices fresh ginger
6 each juniper berries and black peppercorns, crushed
4 each whole cloves and bay leaves
1 4-pound beef roast (top or bottom round and rump are good)
4 tablespoons (½ stick) butter or pork fat
½ cup each chopped onions, carrots, and celery
2 tablespoons flour
4–6 gingersnaps

Bring vinegar, wine, water, sliced onion, and seasonings to a boil and then let cool. Place roast in a plastic bag and pour in the cooled marinade. Refrigerate for 3 to 4 days, turning the meat over at least once a day.

Remove the meat from the marinade, pat it dry, and brown it on all sides in the butter or fat. Transfer meat to a casserole and brown the vegetables in the same fat. Sprinkle with the flour and add the marinade. Bring to a simmer, then pour the sauce over the meat. Cover casserole tightly and keep at a bare simmer on top of the stove or in the oven at 325° for 2 to 2½ hours.

When meat is tender, remove from the sauce, put on a warm platter, and cover with foil to keep warm while finishing the sauce. Add the gingersnaps to the sauce and purée in a blender. If the sauce is too thin, thicken with more snaps; if too thick, thin with red wine. Simmer a few minutes to mingle flavors, and pour over the meat.

Serves 8 to 10.

VARIATION: Some like to add sour cream to the sauce after the sauce has cooked. If the vinegar taste is too strong for you, this is one way to temper it.

TONGUE WITH RASPBERRY VINEGAR

Germans are master butchers, and fresh beef tongue is one of the fruits of good butchering. It is also a delicious and mouth-filling meat that takes well to a sweet-sour sauce. While a raisin sauce spiked with lemon is a common combination with tongue, I was happy to find a sauce based on raspberry vinegar in Friederike Löffler's 1856 German-American cook book. It's easy to make or to buy a fruit vinegar today, but if you don't have any on hand, use a good wine vinegar and add a little fruit juice, such as cranberry or apple or cherry.

Fresh tongues are unfortunately not as easy to find as smoked ones, but the flavor and texture are worth the search.

1 fresh beef tongue
2 onions, sliced
1 carrot, sliced
2 celery stalks with leaves, chopped
8 sprigs parsley
1 tablespoon salt
8 peppercorns, mashed
water to cover, or beef or chicken broth

Sauce

4 tablespoons butter
2 tablespoons flour
2 tablespoons raspberry (or other fruit) vinegar
1½ cups broth
½ cup red wine
1 teaspoon raspberry jam
salt and pepper to taste
1 cup fresh raspberries (or other fruit) for garnish

Put the beef tongue in a large saucepan with the vegetables and seasonings. Cover with boiling water, bring to a simmer, and simmer gently until meat is fork tender, about 3 hours. Remove tongue (reserving broth) and when meat is cool enough to handle, remove skin, fat, and gristle. Slice vertically but not all the way through to keep the tongue's shape.

For the sauce, melt butter in a separate pan, add flour, and cook 2 to 3 minutes, stirring the while. Add vinegar, 1½ cups reserved tongue broth, wine, jam, and seasonings and stir rapidly until smooth. Reduce until sauce is somewhat thickened. Taste, and if the sauce lacks character, add more vinegar. If the sauce is too sour, add more jam.

Put the sliced meat in a baking dish, pour sauce over it, cover dish with foil or a tight lid, and bake at 375° for ½ hour to blend flavors.

Garnish with the cup of fresh fruit.

Serves 4 to 6.

PEPPERED RABBIT
HASENPFEFFER

"Peppered hare" is the literal translation of this marinated game dish, with its sweet-sour cream sauce. At Mader's, *hasenpfeffer* is made with the wild rabbits that can be hunted after the first snowfall in November until the first green of spring. Since these are fairly tough meaty boys with good muscles for long-distance running, a marinade helps tenderize the meat for human eaters. For most of us, wild rabbits are hard to get and even domestic ones aren't easy. Most of them come frozen from Australia or Canada. If you use domestic rabbit, cut down on the vinegar to avoid overpowering the more delicate flesh. If you can get a wild rabbit, or if you shoot your own, save the blood to thicken your sauce.

Marinade

    1 cup full-bodied red wine
    ½ cup red wine vinegar
    2 onions, sliced
    2 bay leaves
    3 whole cloves
    1 teaspoon salt
  12 crushed peppercorns

    6 pounds rabbit (1 large or 2 small), cut into serving pieces
  1½ cups flour
    4 slices smoked bacon, diced
    1 clove garlic, minced
    ¼ teaspoon each rosemary and thyme
    1 tablespoon currant jelly
 ½–1 cup chicken stock, as needed
 ½–1 cup sour cream
    optional: ½ cup rabbit's blood plus 2 tablespoons vinegar

Make the marinade by combining the wine, vinegar, half the sliced onions, the bay leaves, cloves, salt, and pepper. Put meat in a plastic bag and pour in the marinade. Seal the bag and marinate at least 24 hours, refrigerated, turning bag to marinate the pieces evenly.

Remove the meat and pat each piece dry. Roll the pieces in flour and put aside. Fry the bacon until crisp in a large skillet and remove pieces with a slotted spoon. Fry the rabbit in the fat until well browned on all sides and transfer the meat to a casserole. Pour off all but 2 tablespoons fat and sauté the remaining onion with the garlic, rosemary, and thyme. Add 3 tablespoons flour and cook 2 to 3 minutes. Add the marinade and the currant jelly and bring to a boil. Pour the mixture over the rabbit and add stock, if needed, to bring the liquid halfway up the meat. Sprinkle the reserved bacon over the top. Cover tightly and bake at 325° about 1 hour for a large rabbit, 45 minutes for small ones, turning the pieces once in the liquid.

Remove pieces to a serving platter. If liquid is too thin, stir 1 to 2 tablespoons flour into the sour cream before adding cream to liquid. (If you have rabbit's blood, mix it with the vinegar into the cream before adding to the marinade.) Let the sauce warm gently but keep it below a simmer or you will curdle the cream and blood.

Serves 6 to 8.

JELLIED VEAL
SÜLZE

The French call it *tête de veau,* the Germans *kalbs-kopf.* When they take the calf's brains from the brain pan, remove the meat from the bones, and sour the delectable gelatin with a little lemon or vinegar, the Germans call it *sülze.* If you like the taste of head cheese made with pork, you are certain to like the more delicate veal. But in these days, when calves are butchered a thousand miles from the counter where you buy your meat, obtaining a calf's head is an awesome task. I see one occasionally in specialty butcher shops in New York, but the size of it leads one to question what is meant by "calf." The best solution I've found is to use veal knuckle or a calf's or pig's foot, together with meaty veal from less expensive cuts than loin. Mrs. Kander, I note, makes a veal loaf from a four-pound veal knuckle, but those aren't so easy to find either. I've adapted the recipe below from one I found in *The U.S. Regional Cookbook* (1947), edited by Ruth Berolzheimer for the Culinary Arts Institute of Chicago.

1 veal knuckle (or 2 calf's or pig's feet), cracked
4 pounds veal with bone (shoulder, breast, rump, leg)
2 onions, chopped
1 carrot, chopped
2 celery stalks with leaves, chopped
½ cup white wine vinegar
1 tablespoon salt
1 teaspoon peppercorns
3 bay leaves
2 lemons
½ cup minced parsley
3 hard-cooked eggs

Put the meat, vegetables, vinegar, and seasonings in a pot and cover with cold water. Seed and chop one of the lemons and add. Bring to a simmer and lower heat so that liquid barely simmers. Remove scum from time to time. Simmer until meat is tender, 1 to 2 hours. Remove meat from broth and let cool. Strain the liquid, chill, and skim off the fat. Remove meat from the bones and coarsely chop. Mix with the parsley.

Boil the broth rapidly to reduce it by half. Add grated rind from remaining lemon. Taste for seasoning and squeeze in some lemon juice if needed. Chill broth again just until it begins to jell. Spread a thin layer of jelly in the bottom of a loaf pan or mold, add half the meat, then add the whole eggs end to end, so that a slice of egg will appear in each slice of jellied loaf, and cover with remaining meat and jelly. Refrigerate until thoroughly jelled.

Serves 8 to 10.

APPLE SAUERKRAUT
APFELKRAUT

When I lived briefly in Germany, I couldn't get over the bins of freshly sliced crisp cabbage at morning street markets, awaiting the housewife thrifty of time. Cabbage is easy enough to cut up at home, but it's the little niceties that make all the difference between starting from scratch and opening a can. Canning has all but ruined the reputation, let alone the taste, of sauerkraut in this country, since the vinegar is usually far too strong and the cabbage far too tired from mummification in a can.

The only major deterrent to making sauerkraut at home is finding space for a pickle crock, particularly if you deal in the quantities suggested by Mrs. Kander, in her *"Settlement" Cook Book*, for fifteen heads of cabbage and twenty-four apples to fit an eight-gallon crock. In the days of eight-gallon crocks you would also need a wooden tamper, a round board, a square cloth, and a very heavy stone, all to keep the cabbage under the brine during its slow fermentation.

Fermenting apples helped to sweeten the crock, and apples were as plentiful in this country as cabbages. Once the kraut was made, it might be "appled" again with fresh apples, bacon, and potatoes to make a splendid light supper or to accompany a roast. A booklet put out by Mader's Restaurant, *German Cooking and Baking* (1977), includes a good recipe for this kind of *apfelkraut,* as does a valuable regional book, *The Flavor of Wisconsin* (1981), edited by Harva Hachten for the State Historical Society of Wisconsin.

Sauerkraut (2–2½ quarts)

8 pounds cabbage
3 tart apples (such as Granny Smith)
¼ pound kosher or pickling salt
1 teaspoon caraway seeds

Apfelkraut

4 strips bacon
1 onion, chopped
3 apples, peeled, cored, and quartered

½ cup each chicken broth and dry white wine
2 potatoes, grated fine
1 tablespoon white wine vinegar
1–2 tablespoons brown sugar

To prepare the sauerkraut, remove 2 or 3 outer leaves from each cabbage and set aside. Cut cabbages in half and slice very fine by hand or in a food processor. Peel, core, and finely chop the apples. In a large pan, mix the cabbage with the salt, caraway, and apples. Line a gallon crock or a nonmetallic equivalent with the outer cabbage leaves, saving a few to cover the top. Put in a quarter of the cabbage mixture and tamp it down with a heavy clean object like the bottom of a wine bottle. Repeat until all the cabbage is in. From the tamping, sufficient brine should be released to cover the cabbage. Cover the cabbage with the remaining leaves. The cabbage will swell while fermenting, so it should not start out reaching all the way to the top. Lay a plastic bag or a cloth over the leaves. Cover with a plate and then a weight, such as a heavy can or jar of water, to keep the cabbage under the brine and out of the air.

The cabbage will take anywhere from 2 to 6 weeks to ferment: below 75°, 4 to 6 weeks; above 75°, 2 to 3 weeks. Every few days, remove scum from the top of the brine, replace plastic bag or cloth, wash the plate and the rim of the crock, and return plate and weight. When the bubbling stops, fermentation is complete. Cover crock lightly and store in a cool (38°) place, removing scum once a week, or refrigerate and dispense with scumming. Rinse the cabbage before using.

To make the apple sauerkraut, sauté bacon until crisp, remove from pan and drain, and pour off all but 4 tablespoons fat. Add onion and sauté until translucent. Rinse the sauerkraut, drain well, and stir into the onion. Cover pan and simmer 10 minutes. Add apples, broth, wine, potatoes, vinegar, and sugar. Return to the simmer and simmer gently until apples and potatoes are tender but not mushed, 10 to 20 minutes.

Serves 6 to 8.

HOT POTATO SALAD WITH
SOUR DRESSING

This ubiquitous Germanic dish gives potatoes a new lease on low tuberous life. In Old Heidelberg, I remember *kartöffeln,* as potatoes are called, for breakfast, lunch, dinner, and tea. How odd that New World white potatoes were once so suspect that they did not enter the general European diet until the 1770s, when death by potato seemed the only alternative to death by famine. The well-fed Germans in this country, however, did not resort to potatoes until the Hessian fly brought in a wheat disease that caused wheat farmers to go bankrupt. By the mid-nineteenth century, Germans were using potatoes as a wheat substitute in dumplings, noodles, and breads, as a parsnip substitute in puddings, and as the staple of breakfast, lunch, dinner, "Forever and Amen!" Even for those who do not eat potatoes four times a day, hot potatoes sliced and dressed with bacon, vinegar, mustard, and wine is a good way to rediscover what potatoes are about.

> 6–8 potatoes (to make 4 cups sliced)
> salt and pepper to taste
> ¼ cup white wine vinegar, or more to taste
> ¼ pound slab bacon, diced
> 1 large onion, chopped
> 1 teaspoon each flour and Dijon mustard
> ½ cup dry white wine

Boil potatoes in their jackets until just tender, drain, and peel while still warm. Slice, sprinkle with salt, pepper, and vinegar. Cover to keep warm.

Sauté the bacon until crisp, remove with slotted spoon, and set aside. Pour off all but 2 tablespoons fat. Add onion and cook until translucent. Stir in flour, mustard, and wine and let thicken slightly. (If you want a very tart dressing, add more vinegar.) Pour dressing over the potatoes, sprinkle with the bacon bits, and cover again for 5 minutes to let the potatoes absorb the flavors.

Serves 4 to 6.

RHUBARB BREAD

Heritage Hill State Park—where you can look at the paintings of Mme Caroline Tank in her 1776 cottage and sample Belgian pie in the kitchen of the 1824 Beaupré Place—has published a collection of historically minded recipes in the *Heritage Hill Cookbook* (n.d.). Here I found an unexpected use of sour milk and an unexpected use of rhubarb, that stalwart garden stalk, in a bread. The book includes not one but two recipes for this sour-milk soda bread, enriched with eggs and nuts and sweetened with sugars white and brown, so rhubarb bread may be as common in these parts as banana bread elsewhere.

> 1½ cups diced rhubarb stalks
> 1 cup white sugar
> 6 ounces (1½ sticks) butter
> 1 cup brown sugar
> 4 eggs
> 2½ cups all-purpose flour
> 1 teaspoon each baking soda and baking powder
> 1 cup sour milk
> 1 teaspoon vanilla extract
> 1 cup chopped walnuts

Sprinkle the rhubarb with the white sugar. Cream the butter with the brown sugar and beat in the eggs until mixture is light and fluffy. Mix the flour with the baking soda and powder. Add flour and milk (soured by adding 1 teaspoon vinegar and letting milk stand for 10 minutes) alternately to the egg mixture. Stir in the vanilla, nuts, and rhubarb and pour into 2 buttered 9-by-5-by-3-inch loaf pans. Bake at 325° for 45 to 60 minutes. Turn out on a rack to cool.

Makes 2 standard loaves.

20
Barnyards and Woods

In the Old Country, every man who had a farm could keep a pig, but game was the prerogative of the nobility. If dukes celebrated the abundance of their forests with banquets of venison and wild boar, peasants celebrated the abundance of their fields with banquets of pig. The *schlactplatt* so popular today in the restaurants of Milwaukee is named for the medieval *schlachtfest*, a harvest festival when hogs were slaughtered in November to provide meat for the winter. The whole village would turn out to cut up their pigs into chops and loins and hams. Scraps were ground into sausages, or wursts, and parts that could not be processed, such as the shank or foot, were cooked and consumed as the centerpiece of a feast devoted to pig.

The smell of sausage is as strong in Milwaukee as the smell of yeast from Fleischmann's factory or of chocolate from the Ambrosia chocolate factory. But the smell of sausage is strongest in Sheboygan, home of the *brat*. What overalls are to Oshkosh, the bratwurst is to Sheboygan, halfway between Milwaukee and Green Bay. The songwriter who composed a popular song of the 1920s, "Mention My Name in Sheboygan," was no doubt longing for a Sheboygan *brat*.

Elsewhere ask for a frank on a bun. In Wisconsin, ask for a *brat* and a *semmel*. The *semmel* is a hard roll of excellent quality, big enough to hold two large bratwursts, plus onions and pickles and Polish mustard. Every meat market, every restaurant, has its own formula for the richly spiced, juicy pork sausage that originated in Nuremberg and that German Pennsylvanians called *brodwarscht*. In Wisconsin the *brat* fry is a communal wienie roast, where folks collect to grill sausages over the coals and quaff a few steins of pilsener.

In the New Country, Germans could shoot game as well as keep pigs. If fishing is a way of life in this lake land, hunting is a way of life in these woods. The opening of bear season in the northern counties is mentioned as casually as the opening of trout season in most places. Since nearly every crossroads has a butcher shop and a smokehouse, it's easy to get whatever you've shot smoked on the way home or ground into sausages larded with pork fat.

Before beer and sausage and butter and cheese, there was bear and beaver, wild ducks and prairie hens. The Winnebagos were especially fond of beaver tail, and when they feasted the first white man to reach their shores they cooked up a storm. For Baron Louis-Armand de Lom d'Arce, who arrived in the 1680s, the Green Bay chieftains poached whitefish, simmered the tongue and breast of roebucks, roasted woodhens, bear feet, and beaver tails, and served them with a beverage of maple syrup whipped to a froth with water. As late as the 1840s an English traveler described a farmhouse breakfast at Rock River, between Madison and Milwaukee, as a savory stew of "snipes, prairie hens, quails, pigeons and robins, all stewed up together," all of which they had shot the day before. Bear remained so common, even after woods had turned to farms, that a Madison newspaper gave notice on November 23, 1853, that the large bear belonging to Governor Farwell had become troublesome and was therefore now in the market of Messrs Conley & Company: "The animal is very large and fat, and any person desiring a choice bit for *Thanksgiving,* will have to call early this evening, when it will be cut up and distributed."

BRATWURST

One of the best *brat* makers in the Sheboygan area, Bill Hansmann in Glenbeulah, tells me that his butcher shop has been turning out bratwurst for sixty years for firemen's picnics and Sheboygan's annual Bratwurst Day. Every butcher has his own recipe but the meat is usually pork shoulder and pork trimmings, seasoned with salt, much pepper, and a little mace and sugar. The mix is stirred by hand, stuffed into natural casings from the lower intestine, and tied into six-inch links. Since it's not easy for sausage makers to scale down their proportions for the home kitchen, I've picked a bratwurst recipe from *The Handy Housewife* and added a little of Bill Hansmann's mace. If you don't have pig casings, just form the meat into patties or balls, dust with flour, and fry.

                    3 pounds lean pork
            1½ pounds fatty pork
                    3 tablespoons black pepper
                    2 tablespoons salt
            1½ tablespoons sage
                    1 tablespoon cloves
                    1 teaspoon each rosemary and mace

Coarsely grind meats with the seasonings, pack into a crock, and seal the top with a layer of pork fat and aluminum foil to let the flavors ripen overnight in the refrigerator. Form the meat into patties and fry them or stuff the meat into casings and poach in simmering water 45 minutes.

Makes about 16 links or patties.

For a **brat** *fry:*
            16 ounces pilsener beer
                4 large onions, sliced thick
                2 tablespoons Polish mustard with horseradish
                1 tablespoon ketchup
            12 bratwursts in casings
                6 hard rolls

Bring beer to a simmer in a pan with 1 of the onions, the mustard, and ketchup. Add bratwurst and simmer about 20 minutes. Have your grill or broiler hot. Drain the bratwurst. Grill *brats* and remaining onion slices about 5 minutes on each side. Grill the split rolls quickly. Fork a pair of wurst onto each and top with onions. Serve with plenty of extra mustard and ketchup and beer.

Serves 6.

HOMEMADE LIVERWURST
BRAUNSCHWEIGER

Bologna still carries its Italian origin in its name, but liverwurst has forgotten its origin in Braunschweig, in the Brunswick province of Germany. "Liverwurst" is a dishearteningly literal translation from the German of the pork liver of which it is made, a word that German immigrants introduced into American English in 1869. If your liverwurst experience has been limited to supermarket cold meat counters, it's worth making this lovely German pork-liver pâté to eat fresh. As with any pâté, flavor improves with a day or two of aging, and if you have a smoker, a light smoking.

If you are a chronic homemade sausage maker and have a pile of large pork or beef casings, stuff the pâté into the casings, tie them with string in eight- to twelve-inch lengths, and adjust the stuffing in order to leave a good two inches at the end of each length for expansion. Simmer the links about forty-five minutes in a pot of water, then dip them in cold water to keep the fat from settling along the bottom. If you have no casings, bake the pork pâté in a loaf pan, as you would a French pâté. Then you can either serve it in slices or use it as a creamy spread.

2 pounds lean pork
1 pound pork fat
1¼ pounds pork liver
1 medium onion, chopped
2 tablespoons salt
2 teaspoons cloves
1 teaspoon black pepper
½ teaspoon each allspice and nutmeg

If you use a processor for grinding, cut the pork, pork fat, and liver into cubes and freeze for an hour or two, so that they will process without mushing. Sauté the onion in a little pork fat or butter until it is soft. Sprinkle with the spices to warm them, then add the mixture to the pork and process until you have a smooth purée.

Pack the purée into an earthenware baking dish or two 9-by-5-by-3-inch loaf pans and cover tightly with foil. Put the dish in a pan with an inch or two of boiling water and bake at 300° until meat is cooked but not browned (meat thermometer should read 160°–165°), about 2 hours. Remove baking dish from the pan of water and let pâté cool in the dish. Refrigerate 1 to 2 days before using.

Makes 2 standard-sized loaves or 1 large terrine.

PORK POT
HIMMEL UND ERDE

The combination of meat and fruit is another variation on the theme of sweet and sour in Germanic cooking. Some call this combination of pork and apples, potatoes and onions, sweetened with sugar and soured with vinegar, "heaven and earth." A contributor to *The Flavor of Wisconsin* calls it by its humbler name, "Pot Essen," which means roughly "pot-eat." Betty Westra of Waupun, Wisconsin, serves it with a dribble of corn syrup and a little melted butter, which makes it taste even more like the medieval one-dish pottage of its origin.

> ½ cup pearl barley
> 4 cups boiling chicken stock, or as needed
> 2 pounds pork, cut into 1-inch cubes
> 4 boiling potatoes, cut into 1-inch cubes
> 4 tart apples
> 2 onions, sliced
> 4 tablespoons butter
> 1 tablespoon sugar
> 2 teaspoons cider vinegar
> salt and pepper to taste

Put the barley in a deep saucepan, cover with chicken stock, and simmer gently for 30 to 45 minutes. Add pork and cook at a bare simmer for 5 minutes. Add potatoes (and more water or stock if needed), cover pot, and simmer for 10 minutes. Core apples (but do not peel) and cut into chunks, add to pot, and cook 5 minutes more. Meanwhile, sauté the onions in the butter and sugar in a skillet until browned. Add the vinegar, stir the mixture into the pork pot, and season to taste.

Serves 6 to 8.

PRESERVED GOOSE
WITH GOOSEBERRY PRESERVES

Germans have an intimate relationship with geese, so much so that one of the things I remember best from a college art class on Renaissance and baroque art taught by Herr Carl Baumann is not the slides of Michelangelo but the tales of Baumann's pet goose, Hilda. Watertown in Wisconsin was once famous for its force-fed or "noodled" geese, which produced the rich fat livers we call "foie gras." Other German ways with geese might help redeem the commercial geese we raise in this country, which are excessively fatty and often tough and stringy.

One way around a goose "too fat to roast," as Lizzie Kander says, is to strip the fat from the meat, preserve the meat in salt, render the fat to make the most flavorful of all cooking fats, and transform the skin into cracklings the Germans call *greben*. If you like pork or duck cracklings, goose cracklings are for you. The French call a goose preserved in this way *confit d'oie;* the Germans add to their *confit* a garnish of sweet-sour fruit preserves, such as tart gooseberries or sour cherries. You can make a beautiful platter by arranging the pieces of goose meat in the center with the cracklings on one end and gooseberry preserves on the other.

> 1 10- to 12-pound goose
> ¾ cup kosher or sea salt
> 1 tablespoon sugar
> 1 teaspoon juniper berries, crushed
> ½ teaspoon pepper
> ¼ teaspoon allspice

Gooseberry Preserves
> 1 quart gooseberries
> ½ cup water
> 3 cups sugar

Cut up the goose by removing wings and legs at the joints. Cut down the breast from neck to vent and remove breasts in one piece from each side of the breastbone. Remove fat with the skin from the breasts and legs. Remove skin from the back. Mix the salt with the sugar and spices, rub into the goose flesh, and put in a plastic bag to refrigerate overnight.

Meanwhile, cut the skin and fat into 2-inch squares; remove and cube any extra fat from the cavity of the goose. Put skin and fat in a saucepan and cover with cold water. Bring to a boil, cover pan, and simmer 1 hour. Remove lid and increase heat to evaporate the water. Then lower heat and let the skin and scraps turn crisp and brown in the rendered fat. Remove them with a slotted spoon to drain on paper towels. Strain the fat through a couple thicknesses of cheesecloth.

Remove meat from refrigerator, wipe off the spices, and submerge in the rendered fat so that the fat covers the meat by about an inch. Simmer meat until it is fork tender, 1 to 1½ hours. Remove it with a slotted spoon and put in layers into a crock or deep dish. Cook fat for a few minutes to evaporate any water, then cover the meat with it. Refrigerated, this will keep 3 to 4 months.

To make gooseberry preserves, stem berries and put in a pan with the water. Bring to a boil, stir in the sugar, and simmer until berries are almost translucent. Drain the berries and boil down the syrup until thick. When syrup has cooled, fold in the berries.

When ready to serve the goose, let the meat come to room temperature or warm it in a very low oven to melt the fat and warm the meat. Reheat the cracklings in the oven or in the drained fat. Serve with gooseberry preserves.

Serves 8 to 10.

VENISON PEPPER STEAKS
WITH CRANBERRY GLAZE

The first deer meat I ever tasted was in Old Heidelberg, where a pair of venison fillets were served rare in a wine-dark sauce garnished with lingonberries. Lizzie Kander advised her Milwaukee readers that venison should always be served rare, and she suggests serving it in a wine or currant jelly. Creatures of the wood take well to fruits and berries of the wood and, for the venison below, I've made a game sauce of cranberries because they are as native to the marshes of Wisconsin as to those of Massachusetts.

Another wild berry traditional to venison is the smoky gray juniper, as common to German forests as to German-American ones. I came on a particularly flavorful way to use juniper in Nika Hazelton's *The Cooking of Germany* (1969: Time-Life Foods of the World series). She treats venison steaks with a coating of crushed pepper, as if cooking beef steaks, but also adds crushed juniper.

                12 each juniper berries and black peppercorns
                 2 bay leaves, crushed
                 1 teaspoon salt
                 4 1½-inch-thick venison steaks (from the loin or tenderloin)

Cranberry Glaze (1 cup)
                ½ cup raw cranberries
                  juice and rind of 1 orange
                ½ cup game or meat stock
                ⅓ cup port
                ¼ cup red wine
                 1 tablespoon red wine vinegar
                ½ teaspoon black pepper
                ⅛ teaspoon cayenne pepper
                 4 tablespoons butter
                 2 tablespoons olive oil
                ¼ cup port or Madeira

   Grind seasonings together in a blender or mortar and press into the meat
on all sides. Put meat in a covered bowl or plastic bag and let sit at room temperature for 2 to 6 hours, or in the refrigerator overnight.
   Simmer cranberries with orange juice and rind in a covered saucepan
until the skins begin to burst, 4 to 5 minutes. Reserve half the cranberries for
garnish. Purée the other half with the juice, stock, wines, vinegar, and pepper.
Simmer for 4 to 5 minutes to mingle flavors. If sauce is too thick, add more
liquid. Keep warm while sautéing venison.
   Heat 2 tablespoons of the butter with the oil in a heavy skillet and brown
the steaks well on both sides until crusty outside but rare within, 3 to 4 minutes a side.
   Transfer steaks to a warm serving platter.
   Add port or Madeira to the pan and scrape up the pan juices. Add these
to the cranberry-wine sauce along with the remaining 2 tablespoons butter
and stir to melt. Pour sauce over the steaks and garnish with a few preserved
cranberries.
   Serves 4.

WILD RICE WITH
BLUEBERRIES AND MORELS

The first German settlers were delighted to find the lakeland woods sprouting wild mushrooms, among them the familiar ocher-colored fungi we call "morels." The wild grass, which the Indians harvested early in the autumn, Germans would not have known because it is unique to the American-Canadian border, and it gave the name "good grain" to the Menominee Indians who harvested it. While wild rice is now grown and harvested commercially (mostly in Minnesota), it was once simply the affair of a man and a wife and a canoe. The man would paddle his canoe through the family "rice plot" in the marshes, while his wife, armed with a pair of long sticks, would bend the stalks over the canoe and beat out the grains from the stalks. Jacques Marquette was so amazed by the processing of these "crazy oates," as the French called them, that he described it in detail:

> They dry it in the smoke, upon a wooden grating, under which they maintain a slow fire for some days. When the oats are thoroughly dry, they put them in a skin made into a bag, thrust it into a hole dug in the ground for this purpose, and tread it with their feet—so long and so vigorously that the grain separates from the straw. . . . After this, they pound it to reduce it to flour—or even, without pounding it, they boil it in water, and season it with fat. Cooked in this fashion, the wild oats have almost as delicate a taste as rice has when no better seasoning is added.

Now that current taste, long conditioned to the delicate and overrefined, longs for the roughness of the "wild," fresh or dried morels and fresh or dried blueberries provide excellent seasonings for these Indian "oats," although the traditional bear fat is good too when available. Fresh morels, which grow most abundantly in the southwest corner of Wisconsin, begin to appear in May. But they will lend their woodsy flavor as intensely when dried as when fresh. In combination with wild rice, blueberries are actually better dried than fresh.

½ cup dried morels, or 1 cup fresh morels
1 cup wild rice
1 small onion, minced
2 tablespoons butter or chicken fat
½ cup dried blueberries (see page 463), or 1 cup fresh blueberries
3½ cups chicken or beef broth
1 teaspoon salt
½ teaspoon black pepper

Soak the dried mushrooms overnight in salted water. Drain, rinse well, and set aside. Wash the wild rice in a colander under cold water until the water runs clear. Soften the minced onion in butter or fat and add to the rice and mushrooms. Bring broth to a boil, add rice mixture, blueberries, and seasonings. Cover tightly and simmer until rice is dry and fluffy, 40 to 45 minutes.

Serves 4.

21
Soups and Dumplings

From the German peasant one-pot meal comes a full range of soups, soup-stews, and dumplings simmered in broths. Where Rhode Islanders come to blows over the proper way to make johnnycakes and Carolinians over the proper way to make grits, Wisconsinites resort to fisticuffs over a local soup called "chicken booyah." Actually it is neither a soup nor German. It is a Belgian beef-pork-chicken stew, with lots of vegetables and seasonings and a sharp jolt of lemon, as in the *waterzooie* it resembles. Chicken booyah, like Belgian pie, owes its beginnings to the Kermess, centered on a simmering pot big enough to feed hungry dancers, foot racers, and chasers of greased pigs.

The Great Booyah Controversy of 1984 arose when St. Paul, Minnesota, had the temerity to hold a World Booyah Championship. That raised the hackles of men who knew that the Booyah King, Bob Baye, was alive and well in Green Bay, Wisconsin, where he has been cooking booyah batches in fifty-gallon cans for the last forty years. In Green Bay, booyah and beer are as obligatory to Packer fans on a Sunday afternoon as chili to Dallas Cowboy fans. Like the Door County fish boil, a booyah recipe ought to begin with the secret ingredient, "1 clear sunny day."

Soups of other kinds, with other sours than lemon, are a large part of the vocabulary of German cooking. *Das Allgemeine Kochbuch* divides soups into several categories: Meat, Fish, Milk, and Fruit Soups, and the last category embraces Gooseberry, Wild Cherry, Raspberry or Strawberry, Apricot, and Currant Soups. We often think of a fruit soup as a cold summer soup, but when every household dried summer fruits to use in winter, hot winter soups flavored with fruit and thickened with some form of noodle or dumpling were a tasty treat. A pot of broth kept warm in one level of the two-tiered iron stove (which you can see in Kohler's Waelderhaus outside Sheboygan) would allow the the cook to have a hot bowl of soup ready at any time of day, varied with flavors as Germanic as poppyseeds or beer.

WHITE POPPYSEED SOUP

An unusual cold soup comes from Alexa Young, in Madison, who says in *The Flavor of Wisconsin* that her mother called it "mohne-soup," after the white poppyseeds she grew in her garden for Christmas stollen and this poppyseed soup. Essentially it is a milk soup, uncooked, but thickened and flavored with seeds that are first soaked and then ground into a butter the way both Americans and East Indians grind seeds and nuts. I prefer buttermilk or yogurt to regular sweet milk here, in order to spark up the flavor and balance the sweet ening. White poppyseeds are difficult to obtain unless you grow them yourself, but the common dark poppyseeds can be used for this soup provided they are absolutely fresh and not rancid.

> 1 cup white poppyseeds, or regular dark ones
> 2 quarts buttermilk or yogurt
> ¼ cup sugar
> ½ teaspoon salt
> 1 teaspoon cinnamon
>   milk or lemon juice, as needed

Soak seeds overnight in water to cover.

Drain well and purée in a blender with 1 cup of buttermilk and all the seasonings. Mix with the remaining milk, taste for seasoning, and thin if wanted with plain milk or lemon juice. Refrigerate and serve very cold.

Serves 6 to 8.

CHICKEN BOOYAH

The name is a lot less mysterious than it sounds. Since "booyah" is a dialect rendering of bouillon, our soup-stew is really a form of chicken bouillon. There are as many variations as soup makers, but this particular version dates from the 1880s in Fox River Valley. Quantities have been scaled down from the usual one-hundred-gallon cookers favored by Booyah Kings and their Pretenders.

> 1 roasting or stewing chicken, about 4 pounds
> 1 pound each beef and pork stew meat, with bones
> ½ cup minced parsley
> 1 tablespoon salt
> 1 tablespoon each rosemary and thyme
> ½ teaspoon each pepper and sage
> 4 cups quartered potatoes
> 2 cups each chopped onions and celery
> 1 cup each cut-up carrots and green beans
> 1 cup fresh peas
> 1 cup skinned, seeded, and chopped tomatoes
> 2 lemons

Put chicken in a deep kettle with the beef and pork. Cover with boiling water. Bring slowly to a simmer, remove scum from the top, and add herbs and seasonings. Simmer very gently, covered, about 1 hour. Remove chicken and, when cooled, take meat from the bones and cut into pieces. Let beef and pork continue to cook until tender, 45 minutes to an hour more. Remove and let cool enough to remove meat from bones. Add vegetables to the broth and simmer 5 to 10 minutes.

Grate lemon rind and set aside; remove white pith and seeds from the lemons, chop the pulp, and add to the broth. Taste for seasoning. While vegetables are still crisp, return the meat pieces to the broth to heat through. Serve in large soup bowls and sprinkle with the lemon rind.

Serves 12 to 16.

CREAM OF BEER SOUP

Where beer flows like water, there's no reason not to cook with it like water, so that a cream of beer soup sounds perhaps more exotic than it is. Beer flavors at the same time it supplies liquid, which *Das Allgemeine Kochbuch* thickens with sieved bread crumbs and Lizzie Kander thickens with egg yolks and flour in a white sauce. Here I've used heavy cream instead of a flour-based sauce, but I've followed Lizzie in lightening the whole brew with beaten egg white. The combination of a malted brew and creamy milk is as old as English syllabub, which this soup somewhat resembles with its spicing of cinnamon, nutmeg, and sugar. I like to use a mixture of dark and light beers for flavor and I like this soup very cold rather than hot.

> 3 12-ounce bottles of beer (1 dark and 2 light)
> 1 tablespoon sugar
> ½ teaspoon white pepper
> ¼ teaspoon each cinnamon and salt
> ⅛ teaspoon nutmeg
> 3 eggs, separated
> ½ cup heavy cream

Pour beer into a saucepan, stir in the sugar and spices, and bring to a boil. Beat the egg yolks into the cream, add a little hot beer to the mixture, beat well, and pour the mixture back into the rest of the beer, beating constantly with a wire whisk over very low heat to avoid curdling. Refrigerate until cold. When ready to serve, beat the egg whites until stiff but not dry and fold them into the soup.

Serves 4 to 6.

SOUR CHERRY SOUP

This kind of tart fruit soup was common in summertime in Central European countries when the cherry season was on. Sometimes the soup was thickened by boiling the noodle called "spaetzle" in the fruited broth. Since these delicate noodles are delicious cold, they make a fine garnish for cold soups as well as hot ones. Lizzie Kander made a fairly elegant soup of sour cherries, intensifying the sweet-sour of the fruit with sugar and lemon, seasoned with cinnamon and fortified with "claret wine." According to Lizzie, "Strawberry, raspberry, currant, gooseberry, apple, plum or rhubarb soups are prepared the same way, each cooked until tender and sweetened to taste," or as the Germans say, *"nach Geschmack."*

> 2 pints sour cherries, pitted
> 2 cups red wine
> ¼ cup sugar
> 1 stick cinnamon
> 2 whole cloves
> 2 egg yolks
> rind of 1 lemon, grated

Stew the cherries gently in the wine with the sugar and spices until the cherries are soft. Remove cinnamon and cloves. Purée ½ cup of the cherries with 1 cup of the liquid and the egg yolks (beaten with a little of the hot liquid first) and return to the pan. Add the lemon rind and taste for seasoning. Serve cold or hot.

Serves 4.

LIVER DUMPLING SOUP
LEBERKLOESE

Irma Rombauer in her *Joy of Cooking* calls this soup "not exactly a handsome dish, but it has qualities." Handsome is as handsome does, and the delicately seasoned dumplings of calf or chicken liver do very well in the German restaurants of Milwaukee. Mader's Restaurant calls them *Bayerische Leberkloese,* or

Bavarian Liver Dumplings, since the soup is popular in Bavaria. A matzoh-ball version of the soup is a standby of Jewish-American cooking.

> 1 pound calf's or chicken liver
> 2 eggs
> 2 tablespoons minced parsley
> 1 tablespoon each chopped onion and chopped celery leaves
> 2 slices stale bread, moistened in water
> 2 tablespoons each butter and flour
> 1½ teaspoons salt
> ½ teaspoon pepper
> 4 cups beef broth

Remove any skin or connective tissue from the livers. Put into blender or processor and purée the livers with all the remaining ingredients but the beef broth. Chill the mixture in a plastic bag. When it is cold, roll into balls the size of walnuts. Heat broth to a simmer and poach the dumplings in the broth for 5 to 8 minutes.

Makes about 12 dumplings to serve 4.

POTATO DUMPLINGS
KARTOFFELKLOESE

Potato dumplings can be light as quenelles or heavy as Grant's Tomb, depending on the hand of the cook. The hand of Lizzie Kander sprinkled dumplings lightly with cinnamon and nutmeg and fine bread crumbs. Bread crumbs or croutons are often used as a garnish for dumplings and noodles in Central European cooking. Many traditional recipes for potato dumplings call for a few croutons to be hidden in the center of each dumpling, which gives a serendipitous crispness to the soft potato dough. Sometimes a little ground liver or animal fat enriches texture and flavor.

6 medium potatoes
2 eggs
½ cup all-purpose flour
1 tablespoon grated onion
1½ teaspoons salt
¼ teaspoon white pepper
⅛ teaspoon each nutmeg and cinnamon
¼ pound (1 stick) butter, melted
½ cup fresh bread crumbs

Boil potatoes in their skins, drain, peel, and grate or put through a food mill or ricer.

Beat eggs and add flour, onion, and seasonings; beat mixture into the potatoes with a wire whisk to make them as fluffy as possible. Roll this potato dough into balls about 1 inch in diameter. Drop them into boiling salted water and simmer about 10 minutes. Drain well. Pour the butter over the dumplings and sprinkle with bread crumbs.

Serves 4 to 6.

22

Doughs, Batters, and Cakes

When I think of the fine art of baking, I don't think of France but of Austria and the legacy of the Austro-Hungarian empire that spread the arts of *kuchen* and *torten, schnecken* and *stollen,* arts that have given us a range of breads and pastries more imperial and farther-reaching than the baking empires of Britain and France. Perhaps the extreme cold of northern and middle Europe kept cooks close to their tile *kachelofens* and enclosed stoves, where yeast doughs might be turned into fermented rye breads, into sweetened rolls sprinkled with poppyseeds, into tarts and turnovers and fruit-layered pies; where batters of egg dough might be crisped in hot fat for nuts of dough or poured through a funnel to make "funnel cakes," or might be poached to make nutmeg-spiced spaetzle; where flourless egg dough might be leavened with beaten whites, thickened with ground nuts, and flavored with chestnut or chocolate or orange to make tortes.

Torte was a High German word for a baked cake. *Kuche* was a Low German word or folk term for anything baked. "Bache, bache kuchen" was a folk rhyme I learned in Old Heidelberg in order to play "patty-cake" with my baby. The rhyme puzzled me because it was a recipe "To Bake Good Cakes." To bake good cakes, take seven things: butter, eggs, sugar, salt, milk, flour, and saffron. That was the end of the rhyme, but what then? Was this a cookie, a cake, a doughnut, a sweet roll, or what?

As an American in Germany, I had reason to be puzzled, just as Germans in America puzzle over how to translate into Anglo-American their words for cakes and pies. The most common German word for the raised doughs they use for crusts was *kuchen.* Thus Lizzie Kander, in her Pastry section, has a chapter on *kuchen* and a chapter on *torten,* but the terms have become so hybridized that when she explains how to bake a "Blueberry Pie or Kuchen," she calls for a yeast-raised kuchen dough or one of the butter-flour-egg "Cookie Doughs for Pies." (How confusing the language of German-American cook books could be is evident in the recipe for cornmeal muffins in *The Handy Housewife.* The translation reads "Kornmehl Muffins," but for Germans "Korn" meant rye rather than maize.)

Another confusing branch of cookery is what Germans call *mehlspeise,* or "flour foods," as Lizzie Kander translates. This includes *matzos kloese,* or dumplings made with matzos meal; *creplech,* or dumplings filled with meat; *haefen kloese,* or dumplings made with yeast. These overlap with Dumplings and Noodles for Soups, such as *spatzen* and *plaetzchen.* To a non-German, *"The Settlement" Cook Book* reads more like a tale from the Brothers Grimm than a manual from a Milwaukee lady of good works.

Despite the confusing terminology of cakes, cookies, doughs, batters, and pies, what the recipes in the following section have in common is that they are all flour foods, using sometimes potatoes and sometimes eggs as substitutes for wheat flour.

SOURDOUGH RYE BREAD

Perhaps no food for an immigrant recalls more powerfully the home he left behind than bread. Where English settlers tasted "home" in a loaf of white wheat bread, German settlers tasted *die Heimat* in a loaf of crusted rye. Even though white processed flour symbolized for European immigrants undreamt-of affluence, farmer Krohnke of New Holstein, Wisconsin, could write home in 1848, "the old dear black bread still tastes best, and in spite of the fact that we eat white bread, I prefer the rye bread."

Rye and caraway were the paired Germanic flavors that made the "old dear" black bread taste best, and those flavors were intensified by a sour or fermented sponge, started two or three days ahead of baking day. I've become addicted to the earthy aroma that a fermenting sponge gives my kitchen before it is captured in a loaf of bread and, like farmer Krohnke, I miss it when the bread is gone.

Sponge

1 package dry yeast
1½ cups very warm (110°–115°) water
¼ cup blackstrap molasses
2½ cups rye flour
2 tablespoons caraway seeds

Dough

1 package dry yeast
½ cup very warm (110°–115°) water
2 teaspoons instant espresso granules (such as Medaglia d'Oro)
2 tablespoons lard or butter, softened
1 cup whole wheat flour
3½–4½ cups unbleached white flour
1 egg beaten with 1 tablespoon water
1 tablespoon caraway seeds

To make the sponge, dissolve the yeast in the water and beat in the molasses, rye flour, and caraway seeds. Pour into a large bowl so that the sponge can rise to 3 or 4 times its original height. Cover bowl tightly with plastic wrap and put in a warm (70°–80°) place for 2 to 3 days.

When ready to bake, dissolve the second package of yeast in ½ cup water, add the coffee granules, lard, whole wheat flour, and 3½ cups white flour. Mix with the sponge. Knead dough until elastic (by hand, processor, or mixer with a dough hook), adding white flour as necessary if dough is too sticky. Place dough in a greased bowl, cover with plastic, then a towel or a lid (to increase warmth), and let dough rise until doubled, 1½ to 2 hours. Punch dough down with your fist, divide it in two, and shape into high rounds placed well apart (dough will spread as well as rise) on a greased and floured baking sheet. Cut a cross in the top of each loaf to avoid the dough splitting while baking. Glaze the tops lightly with the egg-water liquid and sprinkle with caraway seeds. Let rise again about 45 minutes.

Bake at 375° for 40 to 45 minutes. Bread is done when the bottom crust makes a hollow sound when rapped with the knuckles. Cool loaves on a rack.

Makes 2 loaves about 9 inches in diameter.

ZWEIBACK

An early German settler, Michael Rodenkirch, wrote from "Westkonsin" to his family, who were about to emigrate in 1846, "For your sea voyage, make your own 'Zwieback' and take along sufficient oatmeal and wheat flour." Zweiback means "twice-baked" to make bread dough drier, lighter, more durable, and therefore more portable. The French called their twice-baked dough *biscotte* and the English, "rusks." The word "zweiback" (spelled variously, according to the degree the speller was Americanized) entered the American language late in the nineteenth century, when many German food and drink words were assimilated. In her first edition Fannie Farmer distinguishes between French rusks and "rusks," or zweiback. The French rusk was shaped like a Parker House roll, according to Fannie, whereas the zweiback rusks were made from finger-length rolls, baked once, and then cut into thin slices and browned in the oven.

The rusks of my childhood were called "Holland Rusks," a trade name for a package of uniform slices of crisp toast that had the reputation in my family of being "good for you." It never occurred to me that you could make rusks or zweiback at home until I looked at *"The Settlement" Cook Book* and found two recipes there for an eggy-brioche dough flavored with anise, baked, and then toasted. One of these was labeled "Delicate" because the dough was made even lighter by separating yolks from whites, to make the zweiback doubly digestible and therefore "very nice for invalids."

½ cup milk
4 tablespoons butter
1 package dry yeast
3 cups all-purpose flour
¼ cup sugar
½ teaspoon salt
3 eggs, beaten
½ teaspoon aniseed, ground

Heat milk with the butter. When the liquid has cooled to 110° or 115°, dissolve the yeast in it. Mix the flour, sugar, and salt, beat in the liquid and eggs, add anise, and mix well. Put dough in a buttered bowl and let rise until tripled, 2 to 3 hours. Punch dough down with your fist and divide it into 5 loaves. Shape each loaf by rolling and stretching it with the floured palms of your hands into 16-inch lengths (or the length of your baking sheet) about 1 inch in diameter. Lay the rolls on your buttered baking sheet and let rise again until doubled.

Bake at 350° until lightly browned, about 15 to 20 minutes. Cool the loaves on a rack and when they are cold, slice them vertically ½-inch thick.

Toast the slices at 325° about 5 minutes a side.

Makes about 8 dozen (96) slices.

GERMAN PUFFS

The *fett kuckes* of the Germans, the *oley koekes* of the Dutch, were known to the English as "German puffs." "They will rise and look like a large yellow plumb," Hannah Glasse wrote, "if they are well beat." For busy German housewives, bread dough was the easiest way to make a treat of fried dough balls for hungry children and hardworking husbands. In *The Flavor of Wisconsin* a woman in Illinois remembers the way she would pull bits of dough into thin leaves to make Pigs Ears, before frying the "ears" in lard and sprinkling them with sugar. A woman in Elkhorn remembers the way her mother shaped baking-powder dough into figure-eights before dropping them into bubbling lard.

The number of doughnut recipes in the 1943 *Joy of Cooking* attests to the continued fondness of midwestern housewives for doughnuts of many shapes and ingredients—raised doughnuts and potato doughnuts; orange, chocolate, and pecan doughnuts. To prevent the "fat cakes" from being too oily, Irma Rombauer instructs the doughnut maker to give the doughnuts a dunk in boiling hot water after the oil and to dry them out in the oven. Fortunately, she drops this instruction in the 1964 *Joy*, because dough deep-fried in a quantity of properly hot oil, as Chinese and Japanese know in their wok cooking, will absorb less fat than dough pan-fried or sautéed.

In the recipe below, I've used potatoes instead of flour, and sour cream instead of sour milk or sweet milk, to make a rich, gently spiced soft and tender dough that will taste distinctly different from the doughnuts of your local Dunkin Donuts outlet.

> 2 eggs
> 1 cup sour cream
> ⅔ cup sugar
> 2 cups unbleached white flour
> 2 teaspoons baking powder
> 1 teaspoon baking soda
> ½ teaspoon salt
> ¼ teaspoon each cinnamon and nutmeg
> 1 cup riced or mashed potato (from 1 large boiled potato)
>   fat or oil for deep frying
>   cinnamon and granulated sugar, or powdered sugar

Beat the eggs into the sour cream and stir in the sugar. Mix the flour well with the baking powder, soda, salt, and spices. Mix together lightly the sour cream and flour mixtures with the potato.

Drop the dough by teaspoonfuls into a deep skillet or wok in which the oil is hot but not smoking (about 370°) and fry the balls until crisp. Drain them on paper towels and roll in a mixture of cinnamon and granulated sugar or sprinkle them with powdered sugar.

Makes about 36 doughnuts or balls.

"SPARROW" DUMPLINGS
SPAETZLE

If we get pasta from Italy, from Germany we get *nudeln*, or noodles. From Swabia we get little egg-dough squiggles, poached like dumplings and called "spaetzle," or "little sparrows." The dough is as easy to make as any pasta dough, but the squiggles take a bit of practice and a lot of patience. In Germany there are spaetzle machines, just as there are pasta machines in Italy (and now the world), that work on the principle of a potato ricer. One traditional home method is to rub the dough with a large wooden spoon through the holes of a colander over a pot of simmering water so that the dough will drop directly into the pot. I have no luck with this and use, instead, the method of a German-trained friend, Glenna Putt, who spoons a blob of dough onto a plate, then scrapes off bits of the dough with the tip of a table knife and slips each bit quickly into the pot. The bits should be no longer than an inch and no thicker than an eighth of an inch.

Spaetzle doughs differ widely in how soft or stiff they are, according to the taste of the cook. The point either way is to handle the dough as little as possible to keep from toughening it. My spaetzle friend favors a liquid dough because "the softer the dough the lighter the spaetzle." With a slightly stiffer dough, you can snip off bits with scissors instead of the knife-scrape method. Glenna suggests putting the noodles as they are cooked into a warm bowl with melted butter in order to keep the spaetzle from sticking together.

Some people have a thing for cold pasta and I have a thing for cold, or leftover, spaetzle. But they are also good reheated gently in cream and sprinkled with sugar and cinnamon, or fried in a skillet with a little butter to turn them brown and crisp. Traditionally, they are used hot and fresh from the poaching pot as an accompaniment for roast meat or fowl or sauced stew.

> 3 eggs
> ⅔ cup milk
> 2 cups all-purpose flour
> ¼ teaspoon salt
> ⅛ teaspoon nutmeg
> 3 tablespoons butter, melted

Bring a large pot of salted water to a boil while making the noodle dough. Beat the eggs with the milk. Mix the flour with the salt and nutmeg. Beat egg-milk into the flour to make a very wet dough.

Spoon a large blob of dough onto a small plate. Hold the plate with one hand over the pot of simmering water. Scrape off pieces of the dough by pressing the tip of a table knife against the rim of the plate so that the dough drops into the water. Work as quickly as possible. When the dumplings rise to the surface, skim them with a slotted spoon into a warm bowl of melted butter. Toss the spaetzle lightly with a fork in the butter before serving.

Serves 4.

GERMAN PANCAKE WITH APPLES

Pfannkuchen in German became pancake in English around 1430 and bred an English art of pancakery divided by Hannah Glasse into Pancakes, Fine Pancakes, A Second Sort of Fine Pancakes, A Third Sort, A Fourth Sort called A Quire of Paper, and another sort of colored pancakes made green with tansy and pink with beet-root. The German Pancake, however, of Lizzie Kander and Irma Rombauer varied recipe by recipe but was essentially a single large pancake puffed in a hot skillet in the oven. I first discoverd this pancake from a recipe Craig Claiborne named, for a friend in Hawaii, "David Eyre's Pancake." If Eyre is not a German name, it should be, because his pancake is *the* German pancake, which is sometimes sprinkled with powdered sugar and lemon, sometimes smeared with jam or honey, and sometimes layered with sugared apples fried in butter.

3 eggs
¾ cup all-purpose flour
½ teaspoon salt
⅛ teaspoon nutmeg
1 cup milk
7 tablespoons butter
2 tart apples
2 tablespoons sugar
1 lemon, sliced
½ cup powdered sugar

Preheat oven to 425 °. Make a batter of the eggs, flour, salt, nutmeg, and milk by puréeing them in a blender until smooth. Heat 3 tablespoons of the butter in a heavy 10-inch cast-iron skillet until it is bubbly. Pour batter into the skillet and put the skillet on the top rack of the oven. Bake until edges are browned and crisp, about 20 minutes.

Meantime, quarter, core, and peel the apples and thinly slice them. Heat the remaining butter in another large skillet, add the slices, sprinkle with sugar, and sauté over high heat until apples are browned. Spread them over the pancake, make a row of lemon slices across the top, and sprinkle with the powdered sugar.

Serves 4 to 6.

POTATO-PEAR PANCAKES

In my family, we made potato pancakes from leftover mashed potatoes and fried them in lard or butter to make them crisp. I never heard of pancakes made of raw grated potato and flavored with grated onion until I came East and encountered the world of German-Jewish cuisine and of potato latkes for Hanukah. In exploring German cooking, I have learned how often raw potatoes were combined with raw apples, since both kept well through the winter. But only from Lizzie Kander did I learn the possibilities of combining raw potato with raw unpeeled pears.

Lizzie includes a standard potato pancake in her section "Eggs, Omelets and Pancakes," but in her section "Potatoes" she includes potatoes sweetened with sugar and scented with cinnamon in a recipe for Potatoes and Pears. She cooks the potatoes and pears with onions and gravy as a kind of vegetable-fruit garnish for meats. But the addition of raw grated pears to raw potatoes in the traditional fried pancake turns a potato latke into a dessert pancake, like the German Pancake with Apples on page 399.

        1 firm pear
    2–3 large potatoes, peeled and grated (to make 4 cups)
        ¼ cup minced onions
        3 eggs, beaten
        2 tablespoons flour
        1 teaspoon brown sugar
        ½ teaspoon each baking powder and salt
        ¼ teaspoon each pepper and cinnamon
            butter or chicken fat for frying

Without peeling the pear, cut it into quarters, core, and chop it fine. Mix it with the potatoes and onion. Beat the eggs with the flour, sugar, baking powder, and seasonings, and mix with the potatoes and pears.

Heat butter or fat to make a thin layer in the bottom of a heavy cast-iron skillet. Drop the potato mixture by large spoonfuls into the fat and fry as you would pancakes, turning them to brown on each side.

Makes about 12 pancakes.

HICKORY-NUT COOKIES

A friend from Kewascum, near the Kettle moraine, remembers how he and his many sisters would gather hickory nuts sixty-five years ago in the woods and spend the rest of the week pounding their recalcitrant shells with hammers and stones to get at the tiny nuggets of meat inside. Anyone who has grown up in hickory-nut country will understand why hickory nuts are not part of commercially harvested and processed nut cooking. But more's the pity, for hickory nuts have a dark and smoky taste not unlike the similarly disappearing English walnut.

In the recipe below, I've used hickory nuts instead of almonds in a rich butter cookie often called "Viennese crescents" after their Austrian origin. They are my favorite kind of cookie because they are very crisp and crumbly, held together with a bare minimum of egg yolk and flour and flavored entirely by vanilla and nuts. *If* you have a friend with a hickory tree, arm yourself with a hammer and a bushel of patience. If you find a mail-order source, send for shelled nuts. Someday, when they have entirely disappeared from our forests, you can tell your grandchildren that you once savored the dark smoky taste of the hickory nut.

1 cup hickory (or other) nuts
½ pound (2 sticks) butter
1 cup sugar
2 egg yolks
1 teaspoon vanilla extract
2 cups all-purpose flour
½ teaspoon salt

If using a processor, finely grind the nuts first and set aside. Then cream butter with sugar until light. Add egg yolks and vanilla and process or beat again. Mix the flour with the salt and stir into the butter mixture. Fold in the nuts. Refrigerate dough for ½ hour.

Divide it into thirds and shape into long rolls an inch or so in diameter. Refrigerate again until butter is hard, then slice into ½-inch slices. Place the slices on ungreased baking sheets and bake at 375° for about 8 minutes. Check often because they burn easily.

Makes about 60 cookies.

POPPYSEED TORTE

Because the opium poppy, *Papaver somniferum*, named for its sleep-inducing properties, grew in the cold of northern Europe as sunflowers grew in the hot Mediterranean south, poppyseeds became a dominant flavoring agent in the north. The most common German type is blue-gray in color and its use dates back to the Lake Dwellers of prehistoric Switzerland. Consequently, poppyseeds appear everywhere, from the sweetened doughs of *koclaches* to egg breads like *halvah* and Hungarian tortes like *maktorta*.

Lizzie Kander has a number of sweet noodle puddings flavored with poppyseeds, as well as three recipes for poppyseed tortes. I've combined elements from each of her torte recipes to make a fine, light, and exotic torte, typical of German-American taste at the turn of the century. The spring-form pan is lined either with crushed zweiback or that cookie dough Mrs. Kander refers to as "Murberteig No. 2," which is a mixture of hard-cooked egg yolk, brandy, butter, sugar, and flour. (For a simple zweiback crust, use six large rusks to a half cup sugar and four tablespoons butter, crumbled together.)

Crust

     5 ounces (1¼ sticks) butter
    ½ cup sugar
    2 hard-cooked egg yolks, plus 1 raw egg
1½ cups all-purpose flour
    ½ teaspoon salt
    ⅛ teaspoon mace
    2 tablespoons brandy

Filling

    6 eggs, separated
   ¾ cup sugar
    rind of 1 lemon, grated
    ¼ cup chopped raisins
    2 tablespoons chopped citron
    1 tablespoon brandy
    1 cup poppyseeds, ground fine
    ½ cup almonds, ground fine

For the crust, cream butter with sugar. Mash together (or process) the egg yolks with the flour, salt, and mace. Beat the whole egg with 1 tablespoon of the brandy, mix the egg-brandy lightly into the flour to make the dough, and chill dough 30 minutes. Press dough onto the bottom and sides of a spring-form pan. Refrigerate while you make the filling.

For the filling, beat the 6 egg yolks with the sugar until light and fluffy. Beat in the lemon rind, raisins, citron, remaining brandy, seeds, and nuts. Beat the egg whites until stiff but not dry. Fold the poppyseed mixture into the whites and spoon into the crust in the spring-form pan. Bake at 350° until filling has puffed and browned like a soufflé, 30 to 40 minutes.

Serves 6 to 8.

RASPBERRY "PINCH PIE"
SCHAUM TORTE

"Torten," Lizzie Kander explains, are "cakes that contain no butter, but are made rich with nuts and light with eggs, while bread or cracker crumbs usually take the place of flour." Such tortes were usually baked in spring-form pans of the kind we use for cheese cakes. Lizzie, in fact, gives three recipes for Cheese Torte that we would call "cheese cake." Many of her recipes call for lining a spring-form with the sweetened cookie dough *murberteig,* to make what we would call a fruit or custard pie. Sometimes the egg-nut meringue itself would line the form, filled then with a mixture of fruit or cream. This is the sort of meringue torte Irma Rombauer calls a "Pinch Pie," named I suppose because you pinch up the sides of the meringue to hold the filling. Irma, like Lizzie, reveals an enthusiasm for tortes named Angel, Cream, Schaum. Today, the ubiquitous *schaum torte* of Wisconsin means a baked white meringue, filled with raspberries in a berry sauce and heaped to the rafters with whipped cream, or as they say in the Old Country, *schlagsahne.*

As anyone learns with experience, meringues are easy to make in dry weather but impossible in wet weather. Wait for a clear day, unless your kitchen is completely dehumidified, because a meringue is not so much baked as dried, and moisture in the air makes the whole lovely balloon collapse.

Meringue

> 3 egg whites, room temperature
> ⅛ teaspoon cream of tartar
>   pinch of salt
> ⅔ cup sugar
> 1 teaspoon vanilla extract
> 2 drops almond extract
> ¾ cup pulverized almonds
> 1 tablespoon cornstarch

Sauce

> 2 pints fresh raspberries
> 2 packages frozen raspberries
> ¼ cup crème de cassis
> 2 cups heavy cream, whipped

Beat the egg whites with cream of tartar and salt until stiff but not dry. Fold in the sugar gently, along with the flavorings. Mix the ground almonds with cornstarch and add. Either line a spring-form pan with the meringue, or spread it in a thick 10-inch circle on a buttered and floured baking sheet and pinch up the sides to make an inch-high rim to hold the filling. Bake the meringue at 225° until it is well dried and barely golden in color, 1½ to 2 hours. Leave meringue in the turned-off oven until ready to use.

Keep the fresh raspberries whole, but make a sauce of the frozen raspberries by liquefying them in a blender with the cassis. Mix the fresh raspberries with half the sauce and put them in the meringue. Cover with the whipped cream and a splash of sauce, or serve the torte with the raspberries showing, and the cream and remaining sauce kept separate, as accompaniment.

Serves 6 to 8.

PART VI

Prospectors and
Asiatics

THE
ECOTOPIAN
NORTHWEST

RECIPES IN PART VI

Ocian in view! O! The joy.

—Meriwether Lewis and William Clark,
The History of the Lewis and Clark Expedition,
entry on November 8, 1805,
at Cape Disappointment

As I mount the steep heart-thumping hill from the waterfront of Seattle to Pike Place Market between First Avenue and the Alaskan Way, the ocean is not in view. Elliott Bay is in view and beyond Elliott Bay the glacial peak of Mount Olympus in the heart of the rain forest of the Olympic Peninsula. Beyond Mount Olympus is the imagined Pacific Ocean, "this great Pacific Octian," wrote Clark, "which we have been so long anxious to see."

If I turn to the north, Alaska is straight up the coast. If I turn to the south, the wild woods of the Oregon coast presage the redwoods and sequoias of northern California stretching down to San Francisco. I've never been here before and yet I've come home, because I feel the elongated finger of Baja California pointing me southward. This is my ocean. O! The joy.

Extremes meet in this final coastal frontier as nowhere else in the country. Here mountains sleep under glaciers or erupt with lava. Here cities are shaken by earthquakes and the land may crack and slip into the sea. Here the coastal side of the mountains may expect 140 inches of rain a year and the "rain-shade" side of the mountains as little as 7 or 8. Here silicon valleys lie next to virgin forests. And here the earliest and the latest of America's immigrant races pitch totem poles and television aerials side by side.

Along this Pacific rim, the mammoth scale of the American continent finally goes too far and thumbs its nose at both history and credibility. Its proper scale is myth. Paul Bunyan carelessly drags his ax and leaves us the Grand Canyon. A Fortunate Hunter kills a bear and a moose with a single bullet, falls into a stream, and rises with his pockets full of fish. The peoples of

An Indian dip-net salmon fisher at Celilo
Falls, Oregon, 1956, is silhouetted against
a landscape as timeless as an Albert Bier-
stadt painting and as permanent as the
West that Thoreau imagined when he
wrote: "The West is but another name for
the Wild . . . and in Wildness is the preservation of the world."

Washington, Oregon, and northern California band together in the year 1999 and secede from the Union in order to found Ecotopia. This is the West Thoreau imagined but never saw, when he said that "the West is but another name for the Wild . . . and in Wildness is the preservation of the world."

Here myths of the New World began with the first migrants who crossed land bridges from Siberia to Alaska some 40,000 years ago to settle in the serrated coastal strip from Anchorage to San Francisco. They called themselves Sea People, like the Haidas of British Columbia, born from the sea when Raven, wandering lonely on the beach, heard a sigh from a half-open clam shell and called, "Come out." A row of clam shells softly sighed and opened from within, as little arms pried shells apart and little people clambered out to populate the world.

Seattle is the pivot between the wildness of Arctic wastes to the north and the cultivated European wine valleys to the south. Seattle sees itself, however, as the gateway to Asia and therefore the pivot between Beijing and New York. Seattle began life as a kind of New York, when it was named first "New York-Alki," which meant in Chinook, "New York bye-and-bye." Seattle took its present name from a meeting between an entrepreneurial Indian chief, See-alth, and a dreamer escapist from Ohio, "Doc" Maynard, who in 1852 turned a settlement of seven men, five women, and twelve children into a town with a steam mill and a road for skidding logs from the mill to the sea.

When I reach Pike Place Market and face Elliott Bay, with Skid Road to my left, I am standing literally on buried history. With the gold strikes in the Yukon, Seattle in the late 1880s and 1890s turned from a lumber town to a port city of bars and brothels. The Great Fire of 1889 wiped out most of the shantytown, but a number of streets were later buried intact and exist today as a tourable if ghostly Underground City of Chinese laundries and butcher shops.

It is not so much the past that dazzles, but the present. At Pike Place I stand in the midst of seven acres of produce from land and sea, on the spot where farmers first brought their wagons in 1907 to make this the oldest continuous farmers market in the country. I look at not one variety of salmon but five. Fish stalls are silvered with king or Chinook salmon, silver, sockeye, pink, and chum. They teem with sturgeon, black cod, lingcod, Pacific cod, halibut, Pacific snapper or rockfish, and Pacific perch. They crawl with king

The Palace Fishmarket at Pike Place Market, Seattle, Washington, displaying the day's catch, crowned by serried ranks of Dungeness crab, the monarch of Pacific waters. Prices suggest a date early in this century.

The Oriental influence on the Northwest dates back to the Chinese, who were the first to cultivate vegetable gardens in this part of the world. On the present site of the Multnomah Club, Portland, Oregon, Chinese gardeners at the turn of the century lived in these shacks and peddled vegetables from shoulder baskets to other immigrants.

———————

crabs and Dungeness, octopus and crayfish, cockles, mussels, and gooseneck barnacles, sea urchins, and sea cucumbers, Yaquina Bay and Willapa Bay and Olympia oysters, butter clams and Manila clams and the monster clam called by a name as odd as the duckbill platypus, the geoduck.

To the left and right of me is the bounty of the valleys behind the mountains. Apples with names beyond Delicious: Tydeman, Spartan, Lodi, Gravenstein, Yellow Transparent, Pearmain, King, Cox's Orange Pippin. Pears with names beyond Bartlett: Clapp's Favorite, Forelle, Neli, Comice, Chinese Sand-pear. Here are baskets of apricots, peaches, plums, prunes, cherries, and in summer the wild berries, berries from the forest primeval, berries with names like Himalayan blackberries, dewberries, red huckleberries, black raspberries, salmonberries, thimbleberries, barberries, salal berries, bear berries, buffalo berries, lemon berries, manzanita berries.

Here are green and white baskets of vegetables: sugar snap peas, potatoes with names like Netted Gem, Kennebec, Nooksack, LaSoda; here are onions named Walla Walla, mushrooms called morel, chanterelle, boletus, shiitaki, cèpes; here are whole fields of Oriental greens such as gai lan, bok choy, chrysanthemum leaves, lotus roots, daikon, bitter melon. And here are Tillamook cheese, fresh goat cheese, cream cheese from the Pike Place Market Creamery, and nonpasteurized cream so thick it whips with a shake.

Such extravagant and eclectic bounty is not unique to Pike Place in Washington. What are luxuries in costly specialty markets in the East are bargain staples in the West. Drop in on the Berkeley Bowl Market in Berkeley, California, and you will find, cheek by ethnic jowl, Hawaiian gobo (a kind of root), naga imo (a type of potato), Chinese okra, Japanese cucumbers,

---

McClean, McMillan & Co., Grocers, of Tacoma, Washington, offering Puyallup Valley vegetables and Yakima Valley fruits in the early 1900s. Note the imported pineapples and the decorative use of celery.

Hannah Yallup and Lily Heath barbecue salmon, butterflied on wooden stakes following the method of their ancestors, at a festival in Celilo Village, Oregon, 1967.

Mexican tomatillos, opu (a type of squash), five kinds of persimmons, six or seven kinds of chili peppers, three kinds of avocados, two kinds of kiwi, all kinds of miniature and hydroponic and organically grown vegetables, not to mention prepared foods of equal ethnic diversity—cold sushi, hot tortillas, and warm sourdough breads. Since these products are grown or made locally, prices are not gourmet-high but lower than supermarket low.

Food is the tie that binds classes and races together in this culinary ecotopia. Food is at the center of life because the line to Nature is still direct. Such natural abundance breeds, of course, its own fanatics, as Joel Garreau warns in *Nine Nations* when he says, "It's not hard to find people in the Northwest who get as rigid with distress over the idea of a person eating an additive- and sugar-laden Twinkie as a devout Empty Quarter Mormon does about someone imbibing strong drink."

If New Englanders never start talking food, Northwesterners never stop. "Nothing is just food and nothing more," Ken Hansen tells me. "Everything has its own spirit." Ken, whose size matches the myths of this coast, is tribal chairman of the Samish Indians and he tells me the story of Ko-Kwal-Alwoot, an Indian maiden who was transformed by the greatest of their spirits, The Transformer, into a bride of the sea. At Deception Pass near Anacortes, the headquarters of the Samish that commands the San Juan Islands to the north, the maiden is carved as a "story pole" from a single cedar log which was a sapling when the Pilgrims landed at Plymouth Rock. On one side, as a maiden in cedar-bark dress, she faces Rosario Beach, the site of her ancient Samish village. On the other, she faces Skagit Bay as a fishtailed guardian of the sea. With both hands, she holds aloft a salmon, the symbol of life for these Sea People, as much as corn for the Corn People of the Southwest.

"Salmon are our brothers," Ken explains. "When the salmon return each spring, they give themselves to us and we welcome them with the First Salmon Ceremony by songs and prayers." I had read one of these ceremonial songs, sung by a fisherman's wife who knelt on a mat of cedar bark where the fisherman laid a ring of glistening fish:

> Thank you Swimmer, you Supernatural One,
> that you have come to save our lives,
> mine and my husband's,
> that we may not die of hunger,
> you Long-Life-Maker.

Salmon had saved the lives of Northwest Indians eons before Sir Francis Drake claimed the coast of California for Queen Elizabeth in 1579, or Captain Manuel Quimper claimed the San Juan Islands for Spain in 1787, or Captain George Vancouver and Peter Puget claimed and named Vancouver Island and Puget Sound for the later glory of The Hudson's Bay Company in 1792. By the time these "discoverers" planted their flags, the coastal Indians had developed their technology of catching and preserving fish into a highly skilled industry. Such was the abundance of nature, together with man's art, that they created a culture of prodigality, the feasts of the potlatch in which they had literally food to burn.

Besides salmon, the seas teemed with a fish so rich in oil they called it "candlefish," or "eulachon" in the hybrid jargon of Chinook. From the oil of the eulachon they created a Grease Cuisine. They dipped their dried and smoked fish into eulachon oil as we would dip shrimp into barbecue sauce. They whipped up snow with eulachon oil and flavored it with berries to make Indian ice cream. They put a lump of fat on a stick to make grease popsicles which they called "thumb-chews." In the spring, Indians from as far north as Alaska would journey inland to Grease Harbour on the Nass River in coastal British Columbia to harvest hosts of running eulachon and to render their oil in improvised processing plants.

The greatest of the potlatch feasts was the Grease Feast, in which the host burned such large quantities of eulachon oil in the center of his wooden

Indians in western garb, fishing for salmon with dip nets at Celilo Falls on the Columbia River, Oregon, 1941. Chicken wire and nylon have replaced netting formerly spun from nettle, cedar, or hemp and lashed to a hoop of bent vine maple.

longhouse that the roof would catch fire. Etiquette required that guests keep their cool and continue to dine on large horn spoons filled with grease, lest they lose face by showing concern. The chief guest was forced to give an even larger Grease Feast in return or else lose prestige in this ritual of conspicuous consumption.

Even today the Gitksans of British Columbia celebrate the abundance of the seas in a feast they call *so'o*. From a remarkable collection of Gitksan voices in *Gathering What the Great Nature Provided* (1980), I learn that guests bring large plastic containers, flour sacks, pillowcases, and cardboard cartons to these feasts in an orgy of doggy-bagging. "It took only about three months for a tribe to gather enough food to live for a year," said a young Scotch-Irish fishing friend, Stuart Driver, of the potlatch culture, "so they were heavy into waste." But the Gitksans would disagree. Nothing provided by Great Nature was wasted, one said. "We might reincarnate the eaten creature by carefully burning every bone, but we did not squander any edible part in the flames." The recipes in *Gathering* support his statement, for here the reader will discover recipes for Salted Fish Belly, Boiled Fish Backbone, Fried Rabbit Innards, and Boiled Moose Nose.

Today, when the seas are less abundant than in the past, the crucial issue is not feasting rites but fishing rights. "Ours is a survival economy," Ken Hansen explains of the Samish, "and fishing is *the* territorial issue here." The Samish are a small tribe of only a thousand or so among the umbrella group called "Coastal Salish." By a twist of fate and bureaucratic idiocy, the Samish have been deprived of both land and fishing territories. Although the tools and bones of Ken's ancestors lie beneath the industrial section of Anacortes, the 1855 Treaty of Point Elliott left the Samish without a reservation of their own. Because the tribe had no land, its rights to the sea were not recognized in the 1979 decision by federal judge George Boldt to restore to the Indians of this coast the right to fish its waters without restrictions of any kind.

During the fishing wars that the Boldt decision technically ended, "men were vicious on the waters," Ken recalls. "Fishermen armed themselves, boats were rammed, men were shot." In his early thirties, Ken is young to be a tribal headman, but at three hundred pounds, with flowing hair and a large mustache, he is impressive and he is angry. His name, he explains, is from his great-grandfather, an Englishman who jumped ship and married a Samish woman of the islands. His power, however, is from his grandmother, a medicine woman, blessed by the guardian spirits with the power of healing. Food is never far from medicine in the Samish world, for both restore man to life.

In the kitchen of the Franulovich family in Anacortes, I listen to George and his son Tony explain the plight of commercial fishermen like themselves, who have been deprived of their livelihood by the Boldt decision. The Franulovichs came here in 1949 as Croatian refugees from the Dalmatian coast of Yugoslavia and they have been sea people since the time of Christopher Columbus. "My grandfather came to this coast many times as a ship captain," George's wife, Marija, says, "and one of the captains he knew had a watch fob given him by Abraham Lincoln." Before the Second World War, her grandfather had retired to Alaska and then Anacortes. "After the war, we wait six years to get here," Marija says with tears in her eyes, as she recounts their long journey to the West, the years of exile in Italy, Santo Domingo, and Venezuela, the deaths from typhoid and tuberculosis. "All this time how much we suffered, how much we was scared without country, without nothing, so when we come to the port of New York and see this Statue of Liberty—God bless—I now had a country, that was the most happiest day in my life."

They left behind everything but the cooking traditions of their homeland. I watch Marija and her daughter Maria Petrish shape twenty-five round loaves of Marco Polo bread, called *lumblya* in Croatian, a spicy and wine-sweetened bread traditional to the feast of All Saints Day. The Franuloviches built a brick fireplace in their basement kitchen so that they might spit-roast a leg of pork with rosemary and garlic over alder logs, or barbecue fish in their "all-purpose Croatian marinade" of olive oil, garlic, lemon, parsley, rosemary, and wine. "The Dalmatian coast was a crossroads," Maria explains. "We had anise-flavored creams from Turkey, tortes from Austria and Hungary, olive oils from Italy." For the Croatian community in Anacortes, they now order olive oil by the case from Napa Valley, a thousand dollars' worth at a time. "Here too is a crossroads," her mother says, as she takes a tray of fragrant Marco Polo loaves from her oven and adds, "Marco Polo, you know, was Croatian." A food they did not have at the Dalmatian crossroads Maria discovered when she landed at age twelve on Ellis Island. "All these strange things on our trays," she remembered. "I saw something and it *moved*. I would poke and it moved some more. I was terrified. You shook it and it wiggled. It was Jell-O. I thought it was alive."

At Thibert's Crab Market on Simiok Bay near Deception Pass, Ken Thibert, a large genial white-haired man with blue eyes and a red nose, is getting ready for his annual "North to Alaska" party. Ken is from a French-Canadian logging family who came here from Quebec in the 1880s. Next to his fish store and smokehouse, artificial deer graze his lawn and a trio of cast-iron bear guard the barbecue pit in the patio where he will roast ten salmon at once over the coals. "We barbecue oysters in the back grill, set up some plastic lanterns, a keg of beer, one hundred people come and we have a ball— every year." But Ken, who built his boat, *The Destiny,* himself and numbers eighteen grandchildren in his fishing family, says it's getting harder to take the beating you have to take in the open sea around Alaska. "You talk Alaska, it's an awfully big place," Ken says. "You can travel five hundred miles and catch nothing and now the Japanese are back and they're cleaning out our king salmon. Russians too."

Ken blames the Boldt decision for the fact that the salmon are nearly gone in the local waters of Washington and Oregon. "We're being squeezed out," he says. "Used to have lots of traps here, nine fish canneries in Anacortes and now there are none, 'cause the fish are nearly gone. Upriver you've got dams and loggers and the Indians got gill nets all across the river. Alaska's all that's left."

Ken is the best fish smoker around and he's proud of the hundred-year-old smokehouse out back that his grandfather built. It's a double-decker copied from an Indian tribe, Ken says. He builds a fire of alder and maple and smokes chum or coho salmon or black cod or salmon cheeks—"very special, very sweet." "We rack 'em up, give 'em a two-day air and smoke cure, all natural, and now the Health Department wants us to put in stainless-steel that'll sweat and make the fish soggy."

Later in the week, I drive down to Astoria at the mouth of the Columbia River, a Victorian fishing town once inhabited largely by Scandinavians. In the 1880s there were no fewer than four hundred John Johnsons, named by employers who gave up on unpronounceable foreign names and distinguished their employees by nicknames—Cigar-Store Johnson, Hung-Up Johnson, Just-a-Minute Johnson. The man I was looking for was a squarehead, as they call Swedes in this part, Egil Unander. He was supposed to know all about Columbia River crayfish. Egil was another giant man and he had landed on this coast by as roundabout a route as other exiles and émigrés. He'd run a pulp-and-paper business out of Beirut, had gone into the wine business in California, had smuggled booze from Italy to Corsica, then had developed a crayfish export business in Astoria until the town put in a sewage treatment plant and ruined commercial crayfishing.

It is raining as I sit in Egil's kitchen—it rains a lot in Astoria—and snap and suck my way through a large platter of crayfish as red as the geraniums in his window. "The Swedes buy four million pounds of crayfish a year for their August Crayfish Festival," Egil says. "It's the last blast before winter—outdoor tables, candles, lanterns, mountains of crayfish with vodka and a beer chaser. We've got a great tradition of feasting, for the last four thousand years. Everyone gets totally drunk and do two things they never do normally. They fall in the water and screw other men's wives."

The crayfish of Columbia are very different from Louisiana crawfish, Egil maintains. Down there, crawfish grow in the rice paddies to full size in a year. Here they take three or four years to mature in the cold clear waters and there's no mud taste. Louisianans, he says, use all those hot spices to kill the mud taste, but here he cooks them the Swedish way with branches of crown dill. When he is not boiling crayfish, Egil is smoking sturgeon in his smokehouse or making caviar. "I learned how to do it from the Russians when I lived in Cannes." Or he is collecting wild mushrooms or hunting wild ducks, "going out at five in the morning, with new ice crunching under your boots, watching the sun rise over Mount Wahkiakum."

In this ecotopian wild, Egil speaks for all those for whom eating is feasting and for whom love of food is love of life. When I hear Egil talking, I hear also Alice Waters telling me at Chez Panisse in Berkeley, "I went to France and fell hopelessly in love with eating." Egil speaks the same language. "Like France," he says, "here you eat with the season, you wait for it, you savor it, it puts an order in your life. With me, eating is a sensual experience. Women too, but food you can count on." Here the source of food is direct, immediate, and therefore an organic part of daily life. "When I was last in Sweden, someone asked me, 'Don't you miss the security of Sweden with its social system?'" Egil says, "And I said, 'Look. I've got a river full of crayfish and sturgeon and salmon and caviar. There's oysters in the bay, mussels on the rocks, crab in the sea. *That* is security. God knows how long your social system is going to last.'"

This Northwest corner is still wild because it was the last corner in the country to be settled. And when it *was* settled, in the 1880s, it was settled by wild men—traders and prospectors and adventurers from all over the world. Explorers from Europe fought it out here with migrants from Asia, and the culture clash still booms. Here Russian, Chinese, Japanese, Vietnamese, Thailanders, Koreans, each with their own cooking traditions, meet Spaniards, Mexicans, Frenchmen, Canadians, Englishmen, Croatians, and Scandinavians.

Chinese butchers gutting and filleting salmon at a canning factory in Astoria, Oregon, at the mouth of the Columbia River, around 1900. Their expertise enabled them to butcher a thirty-pound Chinook salmon in forty-five seconds, and each was expected to butcher one ton of salmon per hour.

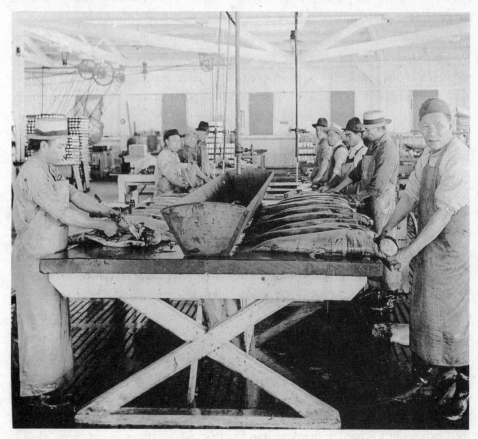

Here more than elsewhere *cuisine improvisée* is a necessity. I think of Lewis and Clark trading their blue beads for food they had never imagined eating. "As a great mark of respect, they were then presented with a fat dog, already cooked," Captain Clark wrote of a gift from the Sioux to their expedition, "of which they partook heartily and found it well flavored." By the time Lewis and Clark reached the coast and were presented by the Clatsop tribe with roots, berries, three dogs, and fresh blubber, they had become as discriminatory as Frenchmen confronting gastronomic novelties. On the matter of whale blubber, Clark wrote, "It was white and not unlike the fat of pork, though of a coarser and more spongy texture, and on being cooked was found to be tender and palatable, a flavor resembling the beaver."

I think too of a teenage Wisconsin girl named Hannah Brain Campbell, born of Norwegian parents in Haugen, Wisconsin, in 1880, who landed a job as a cook for gold miners in Specimen Gulch, Alaska. With the help of an Eskimo nicknamed "Toadstool," she learned how to make wild blueberry jam, how to bank the cookhouse with horse manure to keep it warm in winter, how to turn a snowbank into a deep freeze for the reindeer Eskimos would drive to the camp and kill so that the meat could be put instantly "in our snowbank refrigerator." "The Northern Lights was our Opera," she wrote home, and on Christmas Day, they spread out sheets for tablecloths, toasted the folks back home with blueberry wine, and feasted on roast reindeer with dried huckleberry pies.

In the Northwest, the improvisations, innovations, and hybrids that make American cookery are usually radical and sometimes bizarre, but so is the landscape they come from. This is the quintessence of sun-and-sea cookery, produced by the hybrid crossing of wilderness with high tech. The Transformer Spirit of the Salish is reinforced by the horticultural transformations of Luther Burbank in Santa Rosa, California, in the second half of the nineteenth century. That was the period that brought a whole new world of transplanted

————————

Seedlings of the red Delicious apple were transplanted from Iowa to the Yakima and Wenatchee valleys of Washington in the 1890s. Here crews pick an abundant harvest at the Birchmount Orchard of the American Fruit Growers, Inc., of Wenatchee.

and hybridized fruits and vegetables to the West: the navel orange to Riverside, date palms to Coachella Valley, avocados to Santa Barbara, Calimyrna figs to Fresno, persimmons to the American River Valley, prunes to Santa Clara, sultana grapes to Madera, olives to Corning, garlic to Gilroy, walnuts and almonds to the San Joaquin Valley, apples to Yakima Valley, Washington, and pears to Medford, Oregon.

One of the Picking Crews on Birchmount Orchard of the American Fruit Growers, Inc. Chelan, Wash. Frank A. Ayres, Manager

Spanish missionaries to California had earlier planted in their mission gardens the olive and the grape, but pioneering agriculturists of the late nineteenth century transformed nature's fruits into today's wine and olive industries. After the first boom-and-bust efforts of the Hungarian Colonel Ágoston Haraszthy to found a wine industry in California in the 1860s, Eugene Hilgard in the 1880s started a winery and an unprecedented program of viticulture at the University of California at Davis. Soon after, Hilgard helped an olive grower named Freda Ehmann devise a mild-cure for the black mission olive that put California olives and the town of Lindsay on the map: "A nice town, a great olive."

Many people think of California wine as a post–World War II invention, when French, Germans, and Swiss invested heavily in the vineyards of the Sonoma and Napa valleys. But a Frenchman named Georges de Latour had come to San Francisco to mine gold before the turn of the century and ended mining grapes in the Beaulieu (B.V.) Vineyards. As long ago as 1889, a California booster wrote of the burgeoning wine industry, "It is to California that the American people are to look for wines that will in time make them forget Bordeaux, Rhine, Epernay, Oporto, Madeira, and Tokay." Now that California wines provoke memories of their own, America's wine revolution of the 1960s and 1970s has spread north to Oregon and Washington in the 1980s. Perhaps the wines of the future are the pinot noirs, rieslings, and chardonnays in the Willamette Valley of Oregon and the Columbia Basin of Washington.

In the Northwest, America's home cooking has come into its own in a holistic blend of health and hedonism peculiar to the latest migrants to this coast. For the first time America has bred a generation of homegrown chefs, who pride themselves on being professional amateurs. Alice Waters, whose offspring are Jeremiah Tower, Debra Welch, Mark Peel, Jonathan Waxman, Mark Miller, Joyce Goldstein, Judy Rogers, and Susan Nelson, is the earth mother of this California commune of cooks and Alice is all of forty years old. "I was looking for a restaurant that would be like my house," Alice says of the beginnings of Chez Panisse, "so I could feed my friends every night and get paid for it." Loving and sharing are words that come easily to this family of cooking friends, as well as to their suppliers in the food chain, most of whom began life as students of law, literature, medicine, architecture, almost anything but food. "As important as location and quality," says John Challik of

Berkeley's mini-specialty markets called Curds and Whey, "is that we all feel that we really share this thing together, that we're helping each other." "We're like an extended family," says Alice. "People come and go and everyone contributes to *The Idea* of using always only the freshest and the best."

Like other good ideas in the culinary regions of America, Alice's credo, transported from the Mediterranean of Marseilles to the Bay of San Francisco, is not transportable to other climates and cultures in states less favored by nature or more hampered by the detritus of man's art. Not everyone can run into the back garden at any time of year to pick a handful of tiny young greens—rocket and lamb's lettuce and red oak-leaf lettuce and fresh thyme and a few nasturtium blossoms—to surround the fresh chèvre supplied by Laura Chenel's goats up the road. The New American cookery produced by California and the Northwest is the result of a unique ecology and three decades of affluence after the Depression, Prohibition, and the Second Great War. I can wonder at and admire this brave new world and yet feel a foreigner here.

Ecotopia means "home-place" in Greek and in returning to that "Great Western Ocian" which Captain Clark said was misnamed Pacific "as I have not seen one pacific day since my arrival in its vicinity," I had in a sense returned to my home place. But time had so transformed the place where I grew up that I was forever a stranger to my Riverside home. "Strange people, strange people these Americans," I had heard the Zunis say through their translator a century ago, when they visited the Ocean of Sunrise in the East. Here I was visiting the Ocean of Sunset at the other end of the continent to feel again the strangeness of this land of strangers, wanderers, and exiles, banding into communes, looking for roots, hungering for home.

23
Rivers and Seas

"Puget Sound," a friend from the Northwest who had spent time as a beach-comber in Sitka told me, "is as good as Alaska for eating off the beach." When Lewis and Clark first arrived on these Pacific shores, they were puzzled by large numbers of Indians who seemed to be inspecting the sand, until they realized they were looking for fish freshly stranded by the tide. Eating off the beach was as simple as picking up a fish and roasting it on a spit over a fire. But these coastal Indians had developed a sophisticated spit for their salmon barbecues. "The spit for fish is split at the top into two parts, between which the fish is placed, cut open, with its sides extended by means of small splinters," Clark wrote in 1805.

The same method is used today, as you can see and eat for yourself if you visit the Kah-Nee-Ta resorts on the Warm Springs Indian Reservation one hundred miles southeast of Portland or take a ferry from Seattle to Tillicum Village on Blake Island in Puget Sound. What the Indians learned centuries ago was to butterfly a whole salmon so that it would cook quickly and evenly over the fire of alder wood that flavored it. The only trick was to find a green branch large enough to split partway to hold the fish, as in this contemporary recipe from Earl N. Ohmer in *The PTA Cookbook* of Petersburg, Alaska (printed in *Cooking Alaskan,* 1983): "Cut two straight boughs or willows of medium size and split each down one end. Place a side of salmon between each split willow. Whittle some small sticks and place them crossways on both sides of the salmon, between the split willow to hold the salmon flat. Draw the split end of the willow tight and fasten it." Earl Ohmer suggests basting the salmon with butter, vinegar, pepper, and salt, but as Ken Thibert says, "With barbecue you can do anything—brown sugar, garlic, butter, whale oil."

For the Northwest Indians, roasting and baking are both forms of "barbecue": one in a shallow open pit and the other in a deep sealed pit. To slow-bake fish in a sealed "earth oven" was a good way in a cold wet climate to cook large quantities of fish, say for a potlatch of 2400 guests. An earth oven works simply: heat stones in a pit by building a fire above or beneath the stones; line the hot stones with greens, such as moss, skunk cabbage, or hemlock, or wrap the food in cedar bark to protect and flavor it; seal the top with earth to bake the food from twelve to twenty-four hours.

A refinement on the earth oven was the steam pit, in which a layer of kelp, seaweed, thimbleberry, or wet fern is added to enclose the fish or roots. A long pole is inserted from top to bottom and the pit sealed with earth. The pole is removed and water poured into the hole, which is then sealed to create a kind of steam cooker, as in a New England clambake.

Another refinement was "The Cooking Box" for rendering oil from the eulachon. A three-man canoe filled with eulachon might produce five to six gallons of oil, which was rendered by letting the fish ripen in a pit until oil oozed from the flesh. The oil was heated with hot rocks in a large cooking box made of watertight cedar bark, then strained through strainers made from the curved rib bones of seals, and finally poured into bottles fashioned from kelp bulbs for storing.

Fishing for the Indians was a seasonal affair, so that for most of the year the staple was not fresh fish but fish that had been dried and smoked by the particular methods of these coastal tribes. The very name of the Kwakiutl tribe of British Columbia means "smoke of the world." The tribal smokehouse built entirely of cedar from floor to shingled roof was the special domain of the chieftain's wife. The simplest form of drying was to air-dry the fish on wooden racks built on rock ledges above a windy river valley such as the Fraser River that flows into Vancouver Bay. Smoking helped to speed the drying process and keep insects away. Rotted alder, poplar, or cottonwood was smashed into chips for the fire.

Hilary Stewart in *Indian Fishing: Early Methods on the Northwest Coast* (1977), records in her drawings ancient methods still in use by coastal tribes. She shows whole salmon butterflied and spread with their backbones and dorsal fins removed, so that they look like a row of ponchos hung on racks. She shows salmon backbones hung in pairs, side flanks hung on cedar-bark strands, dozens of eulachon strung through the mouth on a looped cedar bough, thin fillets of salmon sliced on an A-shaped cutting board with a knife honed from slate. After a couple of days in the smokehouse the fish is "half-smoked" and ready for eating. But fully preserved fish is "twice-smoked" and remains in the smokehouse until completely hard and dry. This is the fish you boil to freshen, says Ken Hansen of the Samish tribe, then dip in seal oil or butter. "Give me boiled potatoes and dried fish in the winter," says Ken, "and I'm happy." Twice-smoked fish is so very dry, he adds, that you just stack the fish up and put them in your cupboard.

So identified were Indians with smoked salmon on this coastal rim that white folk used to say you could detect an Indian a mile away by the smell of salmon on his breath, just as the Scotch-Irish said you could detect an Italian by the smell of garlic. The identification of Chinook salmons with Chinook Indians took strange forms in the imagination of the white man, as we see in the editor's comment in the 1893 edition of the *Lewis and Clark Expedition* on the visit of Chief Comcommoly to the expeditionary camp in Astoria:

> "This one-eyed potentate, Comcomly," as Washington Irving calls him, still lived and reigned over the amphibious Chinooks of fishy odor and renown, in 1812, when McDougal of the Astorians indulged the romance of marrying the chieftain's daughter. How the sagacious savage played the father-in-law, and how the unctuous nuptials slid on into the piscivorous honeymoon, forms an irresistibly humorous chapter in Astoria.

One of the reasons the salmon industry became so powerful when traders turned to fish as well as furs is that the amphibious Chinooks had already developed a fishing industry that lacked only iron to make it "modern." What the white man brought was salt for brine, and the Hudson's Bay Company shipped the first salmon pickled in barrels of brine not only east to Europe and London, but west to Hawaii and south to Argentina. By the 1830s Hawaiians were eating their first *lomi-lomi*, which Europeans called "lox." When American packers broke the Hudson's monopoly in 1860, they experimented with milder cures and shipped their fish in refrigerated holds to London and

Hamburg, where the fish would then be cold smoked like Atlantic salmon and returned to United States markets.

One of the early canneries along the Columbia River was Seufert's, which built its first fishwheels at The Dalles in 1884 and its first cannery in the same year at Seuferts, Oregon. In *Wheels of Fortune* (1980), the founder's grandson, Francis Seufert, describes the history of this typical salmon cannery with family photographs dating back to the turn of the century. Sockeye was the favorite salmon of the canners because it was the reddest, but for Francis the spring Chinook surpassed them all. "As they passed The Dalles in their prime," he writes, "they were unsurpassed by any other salmon in the world." By the time they reached The Dalles, fresh water had purged their bodies of sea lice, emptied their stomachs of food, and firmed their flesh, still rich in the oil they would need to leap many further miles upstream to their spawning grounds.

The Coulee Dam changed all that. "The Grand Coulee wiped out six hundred miles of spawning grounds," says my young fisherman friend, Stuart Driver. "Man screwed up their habitat, they built the dams without fish ladders, loggers stripped the land, fishers used gill nets, and now they use trawlers with radar to catch the fish by computer before they can even make it into the river." If the young are angry, old-timers like Francis—who remembers Indians catching salmon in dip nets, the China boss blowing the steam whistle for his crew, the madams of the first-class whore houses at the Crescent and Washington hotels—are elegiac. "When man changed the Columbia River from a free-flowing stream to a series of quiet water pools, the Columbia River salmon were doomed," Francis says. "No amount of propaganda or money will ever bring them back."

"Alaska today is the way it was here twenty years ago," Stuart said, as others say who, in the last ten years, have seen the red tide destroy the razor clam, El Niño wipe out cold-water fish such as herring and squid, the Japanese drill decimate the Pacific oyster, and overfishing threaten the Dungeness crab and almost anything that swims. "They say shark fishing is virtually unlimited now, which is next door to saying it's extinct," Stuart said. "As soon as you tell people anything is unlimited they go fish the hell out of it."

But abundance is relative and for me the Washington-Oregon coast today is the way the California coast was twenty or maybe thirty years ago, although Helen Brown wrote even then that abalone had gone the way of the great auk and sand dabs were bound to follow. Now the tiny briny Olympia oysters, no bigger than a baby's thumb, have "all but vanished into the folklore of Puget Sound and the Northwest Coast," writes Raymond Sokolov in *Fading Feast* (1981). Next to go, according to Ken Thibert, may be the mighty Dungeness crab, which Ken remembers selling a dozen of for a dollar and a quarter—"if you were lucky."

At the same time the Northwest complains it has depleted the harvest of rivers and seas, in comparison to the rest of the country this coast is seafood heaven. Restaurateur Ivar Haglund of Seattle, before his death in 1985, held an annual International Pacific Amateur Free Style Clam Eating Contest and every year crowned a local beauty, "Miss Halibut Cheeks." At Ray's Boathouse overlooking Shilshole Bay and the locks to Lake Union, I can today sit down to a dozen iced Olympias, sparkling like diamonds in their lavender shells. At Jake's 1892 Fish House in Portland, I can sample grilled sturgeon, lingcod, Oregon scallops, yellowfin tuna, or Pacific snapper. And at Dan and Louis' Oyster Bar by the waterfront at Portland, unchanged since 1907, when every inch of its beached schooner interior was covered with "oysterana," I can feast on Yaquina Bay oysters fetched the moment before from Dan and Louis' beds. If neither Indian nor white man can live off the beach in quite the way he did ten or a hundred years ago, he can still die happy of a surfeit from river and sea.

Smoking and Curing

There are two kinds of smoking, cold and hot. Cold smoking, a process that results in food halfway between raw and cooked, tenderizes the flesh, flavors it, and helps to preserve it for short periods. Cold smoking is the method traditional to Scotland, Nova Scotia, and Scandinavian countries for Atlantic salmon. The source of heat is indirect and removed from the smoke box in order to keep the temperature at 70° to 90°. Anyone can make a smoke box from a cardboard box, barrel, metal trunk, oil drum, et cetera, provided he vents the smoke into it from a separate container of smoldering chips.

In hot smoking, the method traditional to the Pacific Northwest for Pacific salmon, the source of heat is direct and the temperature is over 110°, and may be as high as 170°, so that the flesh is fully cooked. But if the flesh is to be preserved for long periods, it must be smoked so thoroughly that all moisture evaporates: thus the "twice-smoked" method of the Indians. Anyone can improvise a smoker in a heatproof container with a rack set above wood chips or sawdust sprinkled over coals. Or he can construct a sealed dome of heavy-duty foil over an outdoor charcoal grill.

The length of smoking time is as variable as the cure. If preservation is the aim, a good rule for cold smoking is to smoke the fish at 90° for eight hours, then lower the temperature to 70° by dampening the coals to build a denser smoke for forty-eight hours; if flavor is the aim, two to three hours will impart good flavor to one-inch-thick fillets. With hot smoking at 110°, you can test for doneness with a fork as you would in baking fish in an oven. When the flesh flakes, it's done. A one-inch-thick fillet may take one to two hours, a five- to six-pound fish eight to twelve hours.

A bulletin from the Washington Department of Fisheries, *Smokehouses and the Smoke Curing of Fish,* warns the home smoker that "smoking is not a sufficient preservative in itself" because the fish may sour before it becomes fully smoked. Therefore a salt cure, either dry or wet, is also necessary. In a dry cure, salt is mixed with sugar, which also tenderizes and preserves, and with herbs and spices for flavoring, such as black pepper, bay leaves, oregano, marjoram, cloves, fennel, and chili and cayenne peppers. These are rubbed into the flesh and refrigerated twelve to twenty-four hours for fish fillets or a whole fish of one to two pounds; forty-eight hours for a larger fish of three to four pounds. Proportions vary widely but a good rule of thumb for a medium salt-strength cure is one cup pure salt (noniodized, as kosher, sea, or pickling salt) to a half cup white or brown sugar, to one tablespoon mixed spices for every ten pounds of fish. (Many, however, prefer equal amounts of salt and sugar.)

In a wet cure, water is added to the salt-sugar-spice to effect the same drawing-out of moisture from the flesh and to help prevent the oxidation of fat. A brine cure works faster, say in two to three hours instead of five to eight hours for a one-inch-thick fish fillet or whole fish. The disadvantage is that you must keep the fish entirely immersed in the brine and therefore weighted down. You can use the same proportions of the dry cure above for a quart or a gallon of water. Since the priority for the home smoker is flavor more than preservation, he can make the brine stronger or weaker according to the length of the soak, the size of the container, the kind of fish.

After either a dry or a wet cure, the fish should be thoroughly rinsed and dried. You can speed air drying by hanging the fish in front of an electric fan. The flesh should form within an hour or two a shiny coat called a "pellicle," meaning a "thin" skin. It is then ready for hot or cold smoking.

Cold-smoked fish freezes well without severe damage to texture; hot-smoked fish freezes poorly. However, the easiest way to slice wedges of hot-smoked fish is to put it in the freezer very briefly (fifteen to twenty minutes) to stiffen the flesh so that you can slice it thin.

Fresh fish that you plan eventually to smoke may be popped into the freezer with impunity because flesh that has been frozen absorbs salt and smoke better than fresh flesh and its flavor and texture may even improve.

BARBECUED SALMON
WITH
ANCHOVY-ORANGE BUTTER

Because it is rich in oil, a salmon takes to barbecue. If you have a flat-hinged "toaster" grill to hold over a bed of coals, you can nail a butterflied salmon to a seasoned plank and prop it against a rock to face the heat of an outdoor campfire. Or, if you have to cook indoors, you can broil a butterflied salmon as close as possible to the heat of your broiler.

To butterfly a whole salmon, slit the fish along the belly and gut it. Insert a sharp knife under the side (pectoral) fins below the gills and cut through to the bone on each side. Then turn the fish on its back and cut the head off just beneath the small (pelvic) fins under the throat. Cut out the back (dorsal) fins and the belly fin. Slit the flesh open from head to tail along the belly and press the fish open, skin side down. Cut flesh on each side of the backbone from head to tail without cutting through the skin. Remove backbone by clipping bone near the tail with sharp scissors, then lifting the bone out. Cut away the rib cage from each side. If you need to, you can cut the butterflied fish into two fillets down the middle. Slash the thickest part of the fillet crosswise halfway to the skin to even the cooking time.

You can use the same method of butterflying thick salmon fillets by slicing a steak horizontally and then spreading it open, after which you can remove the skin from the uncut side. Of course you don't need to butterfly at all; you can barbecue salmon with bone or without, sliced horizontally into fillets or vertically into steaks.

As Ken says, you can do anything with a barbecue, but here I've used a delicious orange juice, garlic, and hot pepper marinade to flavor the fish before cooking. The marinade becomes part of the sauce, not unlike one suggested in a good regional book called *The Portland Woman's Exchange Cook Book,* first printed in 1913 and reprinted in 1973. This book suggests a nice "Sharp Sauce" for fish, with anchovy, vinegar, butter, and cream, thickened with egg yolk. Orange and lemon juice replace the vinegar in my sauce and thickening comes from the puréed garlic and green onion, which supplies a golden green color and texture like mayonnaise.

Marinade

½ cup fresh orange juice
¼ cup olive oil
1 clove garlic, crushed
1 small dried red chili pepper, crushed
½ teaspoon salt
¼ teaspoon each black pepper and dry mustard

2 pounds salmon fillets (from a 3- or 4- pound salmon)

Sauce

rind of 1 orange, grated
1 tablespoon lemon juice
3 green onions, chopped
4 anchovy fillets
¼ pound (1 stick) butter

Make a marinade by puréeing together the orange juice, oil, garlic, chili pepper, salt, pepper, and mustard. Put the salmon fillets in the marinade and refrigerate for at least 4 hours or overnight. Remove ½ hour before you are ready to grill in order to bring the fish to room temperature.

Place the fillets in an oiled toaster grill and sear quickly on both sides—skin side first to release the oil in the skin. Two minutes a side is enough for thin fillets. Put the fish on a platter flesh side up.

For the sauce, pour marinade into a blender, add orange rind, lemon juice, onions, and anchovies. Blend until smooth. Heat the butter until it bubbles and add the hot butter slowly, while the blender is on, as if making hollandaise. If using a whole butterflied fish, to serve, cut the fillets crosswise into 2 or 3 pieces. Pour sauce over all.

Serves 4 to 6.

COLD SPICED SALMON

Helen Brown, in her *West Coast Cook Book* (1952), calls pickled salmon "a pioneer's escabeche." Certainly brined or vinegared salmon was a standard preserving method with prospectors, just as smoking was with Indians. Seufert's cannery put out a brand they called "Spiced Salmon." "The product was delicious, although you either liked the pack or you didn't," Francis Seufert recalls. "I thought it was one of the best products ever put up." In Alaska others agree, for I found in *Cooking Alaskan* a Pickled Salmon recipe contributed from Cordova, Alaska, that echoes Spanish escabeche and the pioneer pickling of Seufert's. While Seufert's brand contained bay leaves, cloves, cinnamon, allspice, and a slice of lemon, Cordova, Alaska, prefers a sweet-sour mixture of white vinegar, brown sugar, and pickling spices, after brining. In the recipe below, I've chosen an escabeche of vinegar and oil, flavored with Seufert's spices.

¾ cup white wine vinegar
⅓ cup olive oil
1 small onion, sliced thin
1 clove garlic, crushed
3 bay leaves, crushed
1 teaspoon each sea salt and whole mustard seeds
½ teaspoon each whole cloves and black peppercorns
¼ teaspoon cinnamon

2 pounds boned and skinned salmon, cut into 1-inch cubes
optional: fresh coriander

Bring all ingredients but the fish to a boil in a saucepan and taste for seasoning. Put the salmon cubes in a glass bowl, pour the marinade over, and refrigerate for 12 to 24 hours.

When ready to serve, drain the salmon and serve on greens as a salad or a first course or in a bowl with toothpicks as an appetizer. If you like, sprinkle the cubes with a chopped herb such as coriander.

Serves 6 to 8.

HOT-SMOKED SALMON
WITH BERRY DIP

Richard Donley, Jr., is a blue-eyed Scotch-Irishman whose dad built his own smoker by the West Village Highway in Meredith, an hour south of Seattle, and called it "The Caveman." "When we opened fifteen years ago," Richard said, "we served smoked chicken and smoked beef and French dip." Since I had never heard of French dip, I asked what it was. "French dip is a beef sandwich you dip in a spiced bouillon sauce or it's a smoked salmon sandwich you dip in a spiced fish stock with lemon peel." Richard thought French dip was worldwide, he said, until a friend visited Europe and told him the French had never heard of it.

The French had never heard of it because it should have been called "Indian dip." It was from the Indians that Washington locals acquired the habit of dipping their smoked meats in a sauce. Acorn dip is a favorite of Indians in northern California, but the Samish preferred seal dip, Ken Hansen says, "until seal oil became so scarce that butter had to take its place."

I remembered a huckleberry sauce I'd had on a smoked salmon somewhere along the Mendocino coast of California and discovered that it makes a fine berry dip. Huckleberries have a good sweet-tart flavor that blends well with the butter and lemon and fish stock of The Caveman's French Dip. But other tart berries are good too. If you begin with Caveman's or your own hot-smoked salmon, dip it in olive oil, grill it quickly on both sides to heat it, and serve it with a dip.

You can hot-smoke a piece of salmon at home even if you don't have an electric smoker by covering your barbecue grill with a hood or with aluminum foil. The recipe below is for dry-cured, hot-smoked salmon with a tart berry dip.

> 1 cup kosher or sea salt
> ½ cup brown sugar
> ½ tablespoon black pepper
> ½ teaspoon each allspice and mace
> 2 pounds salmon fillets (from a 3- to 4-pound salmon)

Dip

    1 cup tart berries (huckleberries, boysenberries, blackberries)
    1 cup strong fish stock
    ¼ pound (1 stick) butter
    rind of 1 lemon, grated, plus lemon juice to taste

Mix the salt, sugar, and spices for the dry cure and rub the mixture into both sides of the salmon fillets. Put them in a plastic bag and refrigerate at least 2 hours. Before you are ready to grill, rinse the salmon well and let it dry for an hour on a rack.

When the coals on your charcoal grill have burned down, add a layer of wet hardwood chips (alder, hickory, apple, cherry, mesquite) or sawdust to create a thick smoke. Place the fish as high as possible above the coals and cover with a hood or a double sheet of aluminum foil, sealed at the edges of the grill to trap the smoke within. Length of smoking time depends on the thickness of the fish and the heat of the coals, but the slower the smoking the better the taste. The fillets are done when they have a golden gloss and the flesh flakes easily with a fork.

To make the dip, liquefy the berries in a blender with the hot fish stock. Strain out the seeds. Melt the butter with the lemon rind and beat into the berry stock. Taste and add lemon juice if wanted. Serve in bowls so that each diner may dip the pieces of salmon as he goes.

Serves 4.

MARINATED TUNA

"You can't believe how good marinated tuna is," says Stuart Driver. "Just get a whole tuna and fillet it—say a ten-pound fish. You can quarter, peel off the spine, and cut in chunks." Out West they call dark tuna "yellowfin" and white, "albacore." You can use either kind for this dish because the teriyaki marinade darkens the meat while flavoring it.

Americans on both coasts are rediscovering fresh tuna—a fish too long known only in a tin as "chicken of the sea," as if that were a recommendation—from the Japanese. I was intrigued to find in Helen Brown's *West Coast Cook Book* a Japanese recipe she calls "Mukozuki" that mixes canned tuna with bean sprouts, onions, and eggs in a kind of egg fu yung. Today, however, we want our tuna straight, either grilled in steaks or raw in geometric slices of sushi or sashimi.

Marinating a tuna, before grilling, flavors its firm meaty flesh all the way through. A strip of bacon around each chunk bastes a meat that tends to dry out.

    1 cup sherry
    ½ cup each soy sauce (mushroom soy is best) and olive oil
    ¼ cup sliced fresh ginger
    2 cloves garlic, mashed
    1 tablespoon each brown sugar and pepper
    5 pounds tuna, cut into 2-inch cubes
    1 pound bacon

Combine all the ingredients except the fish and the bacon and purée until smooth. Combine the cubed tuna meat with the marinade and refrigerate 4 to 8 hours.

Heat an outdoor grill and when the coals are hot, wrap a piece of bacon around each cube, secure it with a wet toothpick or skewer, and broil quickly, turning the pieces to cook the bacon on all sides.

Serves 10 to 12.

SMOKED FISH PÂTÉ WITH
SEAWEED AND CAVIAR

"Bought a sturgeon from the Cowhichans," a prospector wrote at Fort Langley on the Fraser River in 1827, "weight 400 pounds, the guts out." The guts might have included the shiny black sacks of eggs that, processed, we call caviar and that a prospector might well have thrown out because sturgeon roe was once so plentiful on both coasts that America shipped some 100,000 pounds a year of the stuff to Europe.

Coastal Indians would have known what to do with this or any other fish eggs. Roe of all fishes was highly prized for flavor and nutrition. They harvested herring eggs by cutting long blades of spawn-covered kelp or by hanging cedar branches in estuaries to receive the clouds of spawn. They then hung the kelp or cedar branch by pegs on clotheslines to dry in the wind like laundry. Dried roe mixed with fat became roe "pâté" to be stored for the winter in cedar boxes. Salmon eggs, poached in salt water and thickened with seaweed, were beaten to a purée as fluffy as mashed potatoes. Some tribes prized rotted eggs, like Chinese "preserved" eggs, which were wrapped in birch within a cedar box and buried in the ground until they had the texture and taste of cheese. "I remember some wee, tiny little bunches of dried eggs," a contemporary Gitksan says. "A guy could put that little bunch in his cheek and keep it there like snoose [snuff] almost about all day, an' he'd never miss his grub, an' never get hungry."

Should you be temped to try roe "cheese," you can find a recipe for it in John Doerper's good book, *Eating Well: A Guide to Foods of the Pacific Northwest* (1984). In brief, you dig a three- by two-foot pit, line it with maple leaves, puncture holes in the bottom leaf layer to let the oil drain, fill it with skeins of salmon roe, cover the roe with more leaves and a thick layer of earth, leave it for two months, and when the roe is the consistency of cheese eat it raw or boiled.

Dried seaweed was as important to the Indians as dried roe or dried fish. They harvested Pacific sea vegetation like sugar wrack, named for its sweetness; ribbon kelp, which health-food stores sell as Alaria or Wakame; dulsel, sea lettuce, giant kelp, rockweed, porphyra. As with dried fish, the Indians cut dried kelp into pieces, softened them in boiling water, and dipped them in eulachon grease.

Here I've combined these three primary Indian ingredients—smoked fish, fish roe, and dried seaweed—to make a visually spectacular pâté with a triple sea taste. The kind of smoked fish you use will determine the amount of butter: sturgeon is quite dry, salmon or whitefish quite oily. You can experiment with seaweeds according to what's available in your local health-food stores. Here I've used two kinds: hijiki, which looks like black spaghetti, and nori, those black-green sheets the Japanese use for rolling sushi.

4 sheets nori
1 pound smoked fish (such as sturgeon, whitefish, sable, or trout)
1 pound (4 sticks) unsalted butter, room temperature
1 cup sour cream or crème fraîche
juice of ½ lemon
1 teaspoon white pepper
2 cups hijiki
1 ounce black caviar (sturgeon roe)
2 ounces each gold and red caviar (fresh whitefish and salmon roe)

Toast the sheets of nori over a stovetop flame until the brownish black turns green, 30 seconds. Save 1 sheet for garnish. Tear the other sheets into pieces and pulverize in a processor or blender. Cut smoked fish into pieces and remove all bones, add to nori, and process with the seaweed. Add butter, cream, lemon juice, and pepper and taste for seasoning. Process until smooth and pile into a round mold or bowl to ripen a day in the refrigerator. Unmold pâté onto a platter.

Rinse the hijiki in cold water and soak 30 minutes. Drain well and arrange in a circle around the pâté. Cut 4-inch-wide strips of nori and place them vertically over the pâté to make 4 segments. Cover top of the pâté with a disk of black caviar. Fill in the vertical segments alternating gold with red caviar.

Serves 15 to 20 as an appetizer.

Dried Seaweeds

WAKAME *(Undaria pinnatifida)*: grows along the coast of Korea and Japan; multifingered leaves along a side central blade. Dried, it forms gray-black stiff ribbons covered with a white powder, the minerals and sea salt that give the seaweed its flavor. Turns green when soaked and bright olive-green when fried.

ALARIA *(esculenta)*: grows in cold waters of both Atlantic and Pacific coasts; long feather-shaped leaves. Sometimes called "wing kelp" or "ribbon kelp"; in Japanese, *chigaiso*. Same look, dried, as wakame.

HIJIKI *(Hizikia fusiforme)*: grows along coast of China from Japan to Hong Kong. Dried, looks like black spaghetti. Tastes nutty with a trace of chocolate.

NORI *(Porphyra tenera)*: grows along temperate coasts of Japan, where it is called *asakusa-nori*. Tenderest of the long leaflike fronds often called "laver." Dried, forms brownish square sheets. Heated, it turns an iridescent lizard green. Can be cut into ribbons or ground to a powder.

SEAWEED CRISPS

For those who've not yet discovered the romance of seaweeds, an underwater world awaits. Until I got to the Northwest, I knew of seaweeds only in Oriental produce markets, health-food stores, and Japanese sushi bars. Since I was not a member of the miso-tofu club, I knew nothing at all. The Asiatic linkage in the Northwest, however, makes seaweed as natural a flavoring agent in America as salt and pepper and as natural a vegetable as salad greens.

Cooking Alaskan has a section on the harvesting and drying of seaweed taken from *Kaa T'eix's Cookbook* (1977), whose author's non-Tinglit name is Mary Howard Pelayo, of the Alaska Native Brotherhood in Mount Edge-cumbe, near Sitka. She explains that the best black seaweed ripens in February, when they roll the weeds off the rocks by hand between tides. She half-dries the weeds on sheets in her furnace room, sprinkles them with clam juice (or salt or sugar), and when they are fully dried, rolls them up for storage.

I lack the facilities for drying but not for experimenting with these beautiful sea greens. Two of the packaged seaweeds most commonly available are the ribbon kelp called "alaria" (meaning winged) and its Japanese analogue, wakame. Directions on the package usually suggest a thirty-minute soaking to remove the salts, but salt is what you need for deep-fried seaweed to make crisps as addictive as potato chips. The one precaution is to buy a good brand to make certain the weed has been rinsed. If the product is sand-free, you don't have to rinse it at all. Still, it may be somewhat too salty, so a quick rinse in cold water, which also separates the leaves, is advisable. If you find you have washed out too much of the salt, you can always salt your sea crisps after frying them.

> 1–2 ounces dried alaria or wakame
> oil for deep frying
> salt as needed

Rinse the seaweed under cold water and spread on paper towels to dry. Cut the strips into 2-inch lengths and, where needed, into 1-inch-wide strips. To hasten drying, put strips in a low oven for 10 to 15 minutes. It is important they be dry, for if the strips are wet when fried, the oil will splatter.

Into a wok or deep skillet, pour oil 2 inches deep and heat to 375°, hot but not smoking. Put in the strips a few pieces at a time and cook until they float and have turned from gray to bright olive green. Don't let them turn brown. Remove quickly with a slotted spoon and drain on paper towels. Taste for salt. These will keep well a week or two without refrigeration.

Makes 2 to 3 cups.

LINGCOD WITH GREEN OLIVES

Lingcod is a common name for the large Pacific greenling, sometimes weighing fifty to sixty pounds. Indians used to fish for them with a "hee-hee," a tricky lure shaped like a shuttlecock that they pushed into deep water with a long pole so that the lure would rise slowly twirling to the surface, attracting on its way any lingcod curious enough to ignore the Indian waiting above with his spear or dip net.

In tender juveniles, the flesh of the lingcod is a rather startling blue-green, but it turns white in cooking to form a firm flaky flesh somewhat like halibut or cod. I've accented the green with leeks and green olives, bathed in a richly scented green-tinged olive oil and steamed in parchment or foil. The thickness of the fish will determine baking time, which may run from twenty-five to thirty-five minutes for a two- to four-inch-thick center cut. The best test for doneness is an instant thermometer, which should register 140°.

> 1 2-pound center cut of lingcod or other large white-fleshed fish
>   salt and pepper to taste
> ¼ cup olive oil
> 2 leeks, finely shredded
> 24 ripe green olives, pitted and sliced

Season fish lightly on both sides, place in the center of a large piece of aluminum foil or parchment paper, add oil, and bathe the flesh on both sides. Cover fish with the leeks and olives. (If using thin fillets or steaks, stew the leeks gently in olive oil to soften them before adding them to the fish.) Lift foil on all sides and seal tightly along the top edge. Place foil in a baking pan (in case of leakage) and cover with a baking sheet to transmit heat evenly. Bake at 325° until flesh flakes easily or until it registers 140° at its thickest part.
Serves 4.

BUTTERFLIED SMELTS

"I took a canoe from below my window and paddling with a rake had in about an hour 600 smelts in the bottom of the canoe," a British Columbian administrator wrote home to England in the nineteenth century. "You sit right forward and use the rake as a paddle, bringing it behind you into the boat each stroke[.] sometimes I would bring up 9 or 10 at a stroke very large smelts and delicious eating." The herring rake, a long shaft of hardwood set with sharpened teeth or bones of whale or deer, Hilary Stewart explains in *Indian Fishing,* is still used today to rake in small fish like smelts, herring, and grunions.

The oil-rich eulachon is so closely related to smelt that it is often called "Columbia River smelt." James Beard remembers how Portland restaurants during the Columbia River smelt run each spring vied to produce the perfect smelt of delectable crisp skin and buttery flesh. So bountiful were smelts that *The Portland Woman's Exchange Cook Book* stuffed them with anchovies and baked them in milk to dress them up. Because their flesh is so delicate, they do well also in a tempura batter, deep fried as in butterflied shrimp. But a boned and butterflied smelt is a thing of beauty simply sautéed, as here, in butter with a dash of lemon.

24 smelts
1 egg
¼ cup cream
2 cups fresh bread crumbs
1 teaspoon salt
½ teaspoon pepper
¼ pound (1 stick) butter
1 lemon, cut into wedges

If smelts are not already cleaned, remove heads and tails and gut them. Remove their backbones by opening a smelt flat, skin side up, on a cutting board or counter and pressing it with the palm of your hand. Turn the fish over and you can remove backbone and ribs in one strip.

Beat the egg into the cream. Mix the crumbs with the salt and pepper.

Dip each fish into the egg-cream and then into the crumbs and set aside.

When all the fish are crumbed, heat the butter 2 to 3 tablespoons at a time in a skillet and sauté the fish very quickly, less than a minute per side. Arrange them on a platter, pour any remaining butter over them, and garnish with wedges of lemon.

Serves 4.

GRILLED HALIBUT WITH
WALNUTS AND CHÈVRE

Pacific halibut is one of the giant fish that haunt deep waters from central California to the Bering Sea. Because halibuts can reach five hundred pounds, they are nicknamed "halibut whales." Coastal tribes often called a halibut "old woman" or "wrinkled-in-the-mouth" from their special halibut hooks, which they often carved in the shape of an old woman. To outwit the halibut, which sucks in food like a vacuum cleaner and expels what it doesn't want, the Indians constructed these V-shaped hooks of wood, with a bone barb lashed to the bottom. The barb penetrates the cheek of the fish when it tries to expel it. Once a fish was hooked, an Indian would haul it to the surface and club it to forestall an upset canoe.

Any place where halibut is so plentiful that the inhabitants stage an annual contest for Miss Halibut Cheeks will have lots of recipes for halibut. *Cooking Alaskan* suggests cutting the halibut flesh into thin strips, salting it well, drying it, and eating it for snacks like popcorn. Here I've cut it into steaks for grilling and sauced them with a pair of West Coast products, walnuts and chèvre. The chèvre gives a mayonnaise-like glaze and the walnuts give crunch for a contrast of texture and color.

2–4 halibut steaks or fillets (2 pounds total)
    salt and pepper to taste
½ cup dry white wine
1 egg yolk
1 clove garlic, mashed
1 teaspoon Dijon mustard
⅓ cup olive oil
½ cup fresh chèvre
    lemon juice to taste
½ cup walnuts, salted and chopped

Season fish on both sides and marinate in the wine at room temperature about 2 hours.

Make a mayonnaise by first blending the egg yolk, garlic, and mustard, then adding the olive oil gradually and finally the cheese. Add lemon juice to taste.

Remove fish from the marinade and pat the flesh dry. Heat broiler. Place fish on oiled baking sheet or broiler pan and spread top of steaks with mayonnaise. Broil anywhere from 4 to 10 minutes, depending on thickness of the steak (7 to 10 minutes for a 1-inch-thick fillet). Sprinkle with walnuts before serving.

Serves 4.

HELEN BROWN'S CLAM PONE

One of the most surprising pones on my corn-pone trail was what Helen Brown in her *West Coast Cook Book* calls "Clam Pone." Only on a coast that numbers thirty-five kinds of clams would someone think of throwing them into corn pone. But early prospectors on this coast were said to be so clammed up that "the tides rose and fell on their bellies." Indians smoked them, dried them, pounded them, mashed them with eulachon grease, and served them with seaweed on the side. Ships' crews scrambled them with bacon and eggs or served them poached on toast or made raw potato pancakes with them for breakfast. This is the kind of hearty corn-clam pone I imagine Hannah Brain Campbell served to her miners up in Specimen Gulch, Alaska, when the long dark winters bred rebellion and the need for strong blueberry wine.

1 cup minced clams (from about 30 clams)
¼ cup minced onion
3 tablespoons butter
¼ cup clam juice
1 cup each all-purpose flour and stone-ground cornmeal
2 teaspoons baking powder
½ teaspoon salt
¼ teaspoon black pepper
2 eggs, beaten

Grind clams in a food processor or food mill. Wilt onions in the butter and add the clam juice. Mix with the clams. Mix together the dry ingredients of flour, cornmeal, baking powder, salt, and pepper. Stir in the eggs and then the clam mixture. Spoon batter into a well-buttered 9-inch-square baking pan or into a heated and buttered cast-iron skillet. Batter should be ½- to 1-inch thick to make a very flat bread. Bake at 350° for 30 minutes. Cut into squares or wedges and butter lavishly.

Serves 6 to 8.

DUNGENESS CRAB WITH LIME-AVOCADO

To this day I remember my first bite of Dungeness crab thirty years ago. I sat at a table in Berkeley, California, set with candles, newspapers, paper napkins, one hammer, and four brick-red crabs the size of dinner plates. I watched my elegant hostess for clues. She ripped the legs from the body, whacked the claws with the hammer, and dug her thumb into the cavity of the body to get at the "butter." I saw and did likewise and have never looked back.

It is true that James Beard retained a certain bias toward his native coast, but there were no takers when he flung down the gauntlet: "I will match a good Dungeness against the best lobster in America and against the best *langouste* in Europe." The problem is that too many have agreed with him, and while a priest still blesses the crab fleet as it sets forth annually from San Francisco Bay in pursuit of surviving Dungeness, most of the crabs are now flown from Alaska. An Alaskan king crab will run three or four times the size of a Dungeness, which averages two pounds and up, but the king crab has no greater proportion of meat to shell and has less delicate flavor. The Dungeness is an incredible 25 percent meat, as white and sweet as an Irish complexion, although the name comes not from the Ould Sod but from a village on the Olympic Peninsula where the crabs were first harvested commercially.

A crab of this quality needs nothing, not even a splash of lemon, but it is often served with fresh mayonnaise because Nature seems naked unless slightly dressed. I will pick crab for no man or woman, but if you are seriously into seduction, a mound of virgin-white crab meat on a pistachio-green pool of lime and avocado mayonnaise can do no harm.

> 2 Dungeness crabs, about 2 pounds each
> 2 ripe avocados
> juice of 2 limes, or as needed
> ½–¾ cup olive oil
> salt and pepper to taste
> optional: cayenne pepper to taste

Throw the crabs backside down into a pot of boiling salted water, cover, and return to the boil as quickly as possible. Boil about 20 minutes. Lift crabs with a skimmer and plunge them into ice water to stop their cooking. When they are cold, remove the triangular "breastplate" or "tail" on the belly, pull off the top shell, and remove the mouth parts and the feathery gills on either side of the body. Discard the white intestine down the center. Remove and save any of the yellowish white crab "butter." Tear the legs from the body, crack them, and pick out the meat from the legs, claws, and the interstices of the body.

Cut the avocados into quarters, remove the pits, and peel the skin from the meat. Slice 6 of the quarters, saving the remaining 2 for the sauce, and sprinkle them with a little lime juice. In a blender or processor, put the reserved quarters with the crab butter and the juice of 1 lime. Blend until smooth and gradually add ½ cup olive oil. Add seasonings. If sauce is too thick, add more lime juice; if too thin, add more oil or avocado.

Put a pool of the sauce on a cold platter, arrange a sunburst of avocado slices, and top with the mound of white crab meat. Serve extra sauce on the side.

Serves 2.

BARBECUED
WILLAPA BAY OYSTERS

Ninety percent of the Pacific West Coast's oysters are raised in Washington and half of these are raised in Willapa Bay, near the mouth of the Columbia River. Because this is the heart of the canned oyster industry, the giant Pacific oyster has long suffered the contumely of discriminating oyster eaters such as M. F. K. Fisher, who refers unkindly to that "tinned steamed Japanese bastard from the coast." Shucked, washed, tinned, and steamed oysters bear little relation to the fresh reality of any oyster large or small. But it is the blandness of these Pacific leviathans that critics attack, searching for the exquisite brininess of the wild Olympia or the Belon bastard from the coast of Brittany now being raised on the coasts of Maine and Pigeon Point, California.

In the early 1900s, the Pacific oyster, which even in its scientific name suggests something crassly gross, *Crassostrea gigas,* was rightly called the Japanese oyster because oyster seed from Japan had to be imported annually to replace the beds of native oysters depleted by the mouths of greedy gold miners. Oysters were farmed by the "cultch" method of Japan, where the seed is spread on empty oyster shells strung vertically and hung from platforms in tidal waters. Now, however, hybrid species spawn in Pendrell Sound,

Hood Canal, and Quilcene and Willapa bays in Washington, in Yaquina Bay in Oregon, and in Drake's Bay, Point Reyes, in northern California.

Because of its size and relative blandness, the Pacific oyster is ideal for the outdoor grill and barbecue sauce. The Pacific Coast is littered with roadside barbecue oyster stands that you recognize by the heaps of discarded shells outside the door, like kitchen middens on the rise. At the Oyster Creek Inn, near the Rock Point Oyster Company in Washington, I ate an oyster medley—oysters with vermouth and Parmesan cheese, with hollandaise and spinach, with shrimp and capers in a frothy cheese sauce. The cook was, in effect, treating these giants like poached chicken breasts. But I find I prefer stronger stuff like garlic-parsley butter, or Pernod-fennel sauce, or hot chili sauce. A recipe left over from Gold Rush days Helen Brown calls "Carpetbagger's Steak," and the *California Cook Book* (1925), an early regional book by Frances P. Belle, calls it "Spanish Steak with Oysters." This is a good mouthful for Bunyanesque appetites, consisting of a large thick sirloin, smothered in poached Pacific oysters and covered with a hot chili sauce. Here I've omitted the steak and used a fresh red or green chili salsa.

12 Pacific oysters, unopened
2 tomatoes, peeled, seeded, and chopped fine
½ cup green onions, tops included, chopped fine
1 clove garlic, minced
1 jalapeño or *serrano* chili, peeled, seeded, and chopped
¼ cup fresh coriander (cilantro), chopped
¼ pound (1 stick) butter, melted
lemon juice, black pepper, and Tabasco sauce to taste

Crumple a large sheet of foil in a foil baking pan to make a nest for the oysters, placing the shells deep side down. Cover the pan with a sheet of foil large enough to form a sealed lid so that the oysters will steam inside. Place directly on the grill over hot coals or under a hot oven broiler. Medium oysters should open in about 6 minutes, large ones in 8 to 10 minutes.

For the sauce, mix together the prepared vegetables, pour the melted butter over, and taste for seasoning. Remove opened top shells and spoon on the hot sauce.

Serves 4, with about 1½ cups sauce.

Geoducks, Abalone, and Sand Dabs

The word "geoduck" comes from an Indian word, *gwed'uc*, meaning in Nisqualli "dig deep." You have to have an arm as long as an elephant's trunk to dig deep fast enough to get these clams, says Stuart Driver's father, Frank. Frank found himself many a time up to his shoulder, holding on to his clam while friends dug *him* out. Commercially, geoducks are now dug by water power. Once a geoduck hunter has spotted the gray nib of the neck or the dimpled sand from a retracted neck, he rapidly hoses the sand around the clam while he grabs the geoduck by the neck and pulls it gently so that it will come up in one piece. That doesn't sound too bad until you realize these clams weigh at least three pounds and may have burrowed four feet deep into the floor of Puget Sound, where the hunter has to dive with his fireman's hose.

The abalone is another dive-deep shellfish that by 1952 had almost gone, as Helen Brown said, the way of the great auk. Abalone shells with their strange technicolor interiors were so common along the beaches of my southern California childhood that we sailed them like Frisbees back into the sea. Now, I slink to the back doors of seafood restaurants to inquire as discreetly about abalone as if it were Prohibition booze.

Sand dabs, fortunately, are not quite so endangered and much easier to fish. They are miniature flounder, weighing about half a pound when caught, found in waters from southern California to northern Alaska. I link these three Pacific sea creatures because each is sweet and delicate in flavor and should be cooked, if at all, as briefly as possible. Japanese favor geoduck raw in thin slices for sashimi. Abalone must first be tenderized by pounding to make it thin as a veal scallop. Sand dabs are so small they can be sautéed whole and eaten in two bites.

It's unlikely that you will come across a geoduck fresh out of the sand if you don't live near Puget Sound, but if you do, Ken Thibert explains that you skin 'em down and cut around the "shoulder" of that foot-long neck. The bottom part is your steak, the neck the fillet. In a fish store like Ken's, you'll find thin geoduck slices ready for pan frying. A dip into egg beaten with a little cream, a roll in fresh crumbs, and a quick sauté in bubbling butter (about one minute a side) is plenty for any of these sea creatures.

24
Wild Woods

"Camas and cow potatoes, we still use them in our Winter ceremonies," Ken Hansen said. Lewis and Clark learned that the coastal tribes balanced their fish with roots. "Here he treated us with a root, round in shape, and about the size of a small Irish potato, which they call wappatoo," Clark wrote. The other root staple was the camas bulb, which Samish women dug with "digging sticks," from beds they replanted by breaking off the tops of the plants and rooting them in the earth. Camas is a starchy, sweet-tasting bulb and the Samish used "all sorts of sweet bushes to infect it" with further sweetness, plants such as kelp blades, sword ferns, and alder bark to make it red.

Other sweetening came from the manifold varieties of wild berries. For the Gitksans, September is still huckleberry time. All the women of the tribe go into the mountains with their baskets of birch bark to pick berries and take them to the "berry dry house," where they crush the berries, cook them by the hot-stone method, and lay them on skunk cabbage leaves on drying racks made of cedar. When the layer of berries is nearly dried, they roll it up like a blanket, push a rod through the center, and hang it from a roof beam to dry thoroughly. Finally, they take the berry roll down, straighten it out, and cut the dried sheet into squares for storage.

Soapberries are favored for the dessert called "yal," in which the seeds are removed and the berries whipped by hand with a little water until they make a thick creamy foam like beaten egg whites. In winter they beat berries into snow and eulachon grease and pile the mixture into a folded thimbleberry leaf for an ice cream cone. Recipes in *Cooking Alaskan* tell the reader how to whip up soapberries with powdered seaweed, sugar, and bananas, in the manner of the Tsimpshean Indians, or how to make Eskimo ice cream by whipping berries into caribou or moose tallow or seal oil.

Less usual foods of the wild are baked hemlock bark and pine noodles. The Gitksans look for "a sweet tender tasting tree," we learn in *Gathering*. They then strip the outer bark of the hemlock to get at the tender sapwood within, scrape it rapidly, bake it in a sealed pit, crush it fine, and dry it as they do their berries. They use a similar method to get "noodles" from the sweet white inner bark of the jack pine, which they shred with a scraper and eat raw when the sap is milkily sweet.

If the seas are full of fish, so are they too of waterfowl. When Captain George Vancouver first sailed inside the strait of Juan de Fuca to land at what is now Port Townsend, he noted a number of Indian flagpoles along the shore. Actually, they were duck traps of nets woven from nettle and stretched between the poles to entangle whole flocks of ducks as they flew over the marshlands. Similar nets trapped ducks under water as they dove for food.

Another ingenious method for hunting fowl and larger game was the night canoe. While the hunter stood, spear poised, by a fire built in a box of sand in the stern of the canoe, the paddler sat in the prow with a hat large enough to cast a shadow. Waterfowl, startled by the light, would move toward the shadow—and the spear. When hunting deer, Indians in canoes with small fires would paddle along the shore so that the hills were lit with moving shadows. Fearing the shadows, the deer would move toward the water, within range of the waiting hunter.

The most valued game was bear, especially June bear, when the beast had fed on crab apples, salmon, and blackberries. From a Samish account in this century I learned how properly to hunt a bear:

> A bear stays inside his tree four months. He eats his paws, one for each month. To get a bear in the winter, look for a big cedar tree with a little hole; a bear can go in a small little hole. Feel inside, smoke him a little and there may be some scratching inside. To smoke him, make a little fire of dry smashed cedar bark and wrap it in wet moss. Be careful not to set fire to the tree. Blow the smoke inside the tree or fan it with brush. When the bear gets tired of the smoke he will come out.

Once you've got your bear and killed it, *Cooking Alaskan* will tell you how to render its fat and turn the meat into Oven-Barbecued Bear, Roast Bear with Yorkshire Pudding, Garlic Roast Bear, and Sautéed Bear Steaks.

Cooking Alaskan, in fact, is a gold mine of fantasy for the urban armchair cook, strait-jacketed by his local supermarket and numbed by his microwave. In its pages he can learn how to prepare Polar Bear with Onions, Snowshoe Hare with Kraut, Buffalo Cutlets Paupiettes, Lynx Stew, Spiced Walrus, Grilled Caribou Kidneys, Jellied Moose Nose. While today's urbanite fantasizes the wild that once was everywhere, yesterday's pioneer longed for the civilized table he had left behind. Helen Brown points out that early cook books in Gold Rush days would apologetically substitute game for the food that was longed for. Pheasant was a cheap substitute for the real thing in chicken salad, or deer meat for the real thing in hamburger meatloaf, or sage hen for a real rooster in a fricassee.

While Lewis and Clark were dining on roast salmon and cockles, baked roots and wild berries, what Lewis longed for was salt and what Clark longed for was white-flour bread. Through the generosity of their girl guide, Sacajawea, Clark got his bread. "The squar [squaw] gave me a piece of bread made of flour which she had reserved for her child and carefully kept untill this time, which has unfortunately got wet and a little sour," Clark wrote in his journal. "This bread I eate with great satisfaction, it being the only mouthfull I had tasted for several months past."

ALASKAN SOURDOUGH BREAD

Sourdough is the best and most distinctive of "native" American breads, itself a hybrid of the portable dough carried by prospectors to the Yukon in the 1890s, called "sourdoughs," and of the traditional baking methods of French and Italian immigrants to Gold Rush ports like Seattle and San Francisco. Some Alaskans today claim that they possess sourdough "starters" a century old, passed down from generation to generation, and feeling runs high about the precise rules for the care and feeding of a family-inherited starter. By the same token, some San Franciscans today claim that the reason for the superiority of San Francisco sourdough to all other sourdough breads is the peculiar bacterial microclimate of the bay area, which cannot be duplicated any place else in the world.

The truth is that anybody can make a starter. But because the yeast is "wild," in comparison to commercial yeast, its effects are less predictable. The major ingredient of any sourdough bread, however, is time: time for the starter to do its work, then the sponge, and finally the dough. To make a starter from scratch, you need four to five days; for the sponge two days; for the dough a mere four to five hours.

Any grain or starchy vegetable, given time and warmth and moisture, will begin to ferment and produce wild yeast. Adding commercial yeast to the starter helps to control the wildness and therefore the degree and quality of the sourness. A Yukon prospector could have started his bread with no more than a raw potato, but what he probably longed for was a sweet white delicate loaf fresh from the hands of a city baker, who had gone to some trouble and expense to obtain a "refined" yeast from the brewer.

Once the starter develops its own yeast, this yeast needs to be fed with more starch or grain to develop its gassy powers. From the starter, the bread-maker makes a "sponge," which multiplies the power of the yeast to expand each glutinous particle of the flour when it is turned into dough. Any kind of flour can be used—rye, whole wheat, white—and any kind of liquid, such as milk, water, vegetable juice, fish broth. You can mold the dough into any kind of shape, but the long thin loaves we call French or Italian give a good proportion of crusty outside to inside crumb. Sourdough crumb tends to be heavier and more dense than that of sweet-yeasted breads.

Here I've mixed whole wheat with white flour in about equal proportions and added a cup of soaked whole wheat berries because I like their sweetness and crunch. Sometimes I use sprouted wheat berries because their extra sweetness nicely balances the sourness of the dough. But there's almost nothing you can't add in the way of flavorings, from herbs and cheese to cinnamon and raisins and nuts, or if you're all-out Alaskan, a little whale oil.

Starter

1 package dry yeast
2 cups very warm (110°–115°) water
2 cups whole wheat flour

Sponge

        1 cup warm water
        1 cup whole wheat flour
        1 cup whole wheat berries

Dough

        1 package dry yeast
        ¼ cup very warm (110°–115°) water
        1 tablespoon salt
        ½ teaspoon baking soda
        3 tablespoons butter, oil, or lard
        3 cups unbleached white flour

For the starter, dissolve yeast in the water, stir in the flour, and mix until smooth. Put in a deep ceramic or glass bowl, cover with plastic wrap, and put in a warm place until it is very bubbly and smells ripe, 4 to 5 days. It will then keep in the refrigerator in a lidded jar for weeks, or in the freezer for months.

To make the sponge, add 1 cup of the starter to the water and flour and beat until smooth. Add the berries, cover, and let sponge sit 1½ to 2 days in a warm place.

When you are ready to make the dough, dissolve yeast in the water, and add, in order, the salt, soda, butter, sponge mixture, and flour. Knead thoroughly, at least 10 minutes by hand or 5 minutes by electric mixer with dough hook. When the dough is glossy and elastic, put in a well-greased bowl, cover the bowl with plastic wrap, and let rise until doubled.

Punch the dough down with your fist and shape it into 2 balls. Press each ball flat into an oval. Fold ovals in half lengthwise, flatten again, and repeat. Indent each piece lengthwise with the side of your hand and fold it in half, sealing the edges. Lengthen loaves by rolling them back and forth with your palms. Place each loaf in a greased trough in a French bread pan or aluminum foil shaped into troughs. Cover with a kitchen towel and let rise again.

Put a baking pan of hot water on the lower shelf of an oven and heat to 425°. Slash the top of each loaf with a razor blade in three parallel diagonal cuts. Brush the tops of the loaves with water to make a brown glaze. Bake until tops are brown and loaves sound hollow when rapped on the bottom, 20 to 25 minutes. Cool on a rack.

Makes 2 loaves.

HOMEMADE BEEF OR
VENISON JERKY

Captain Clark spelled it "jurk" and sometimes used it as a noun and some-times as a verb. It came from an Indian word for sun-dried meat, *charqui*. I've a number of hunting friends who make venison jerky by cutting the meat into strips, brining them, and then smoking them instead of sun-drying them. *Cooking Alaskan* warns against jerking game like bear, walrus, or wild pig be-cause of the danger of trichinosis, but theoretically any meat or fish can and has been jerked, by sun, brine, or smoke.

Pacific Coast Indians are as fond of salmon jerky as Southwest Indians of venison or beef jerky, but I didn't discover how good jerky was until I made it at home from beef I bought in the supermarket. A cut like flank steak or round steak is good because you want muscle relatively free of fat. You can slice the meat with the grain or against it. If you like crunchy jerky, cut across the grain. I like chewy jerky, so I cut long strips with the grain. Seasoning is entirely up to the jerker, and it's the herbs that turn this portage survival food into a sophisticated finger food.

> 5 pounds very lean beef or venison
> 3 tablespoons kosher or sea salt
> 2 tablespoons black pepper
> 1 tablespoon each thyme and marjoram or oregano

Remove all the fat you can from the meat. Partially freeze the meat so that it is firm enough to cut easily into strips about 1-inch wide and ½-inch thick. Mix together the seasonings, spread strips on baking sheets, and sprin-kle with half the mixture. Turn each strip and sprinkle with remaining sea-soning. Refrigerate strips overnight.

Set oven at lowest heat (175°–200°) and cook meat in it until thoroughly dried, 5 to 8 hours, turning the pieces as needed. Refrigerated, the strips will last for months. If they are totally fat free, the strips can also be stored for months in a lidded jar in sealed plastic bags without refrigeration.

Makes 8 cups.

CRANBERRY PEMMICAN

Once you've done jerky, can pemmican be far behind? Pemmican comes from *pemikan,* an Indian word for grease and one so identified with Indian ways that when the Hudson's Bay Company fought it out with the Northwest Fur Company for trading rights, the battle was called The Pemmican War. Indians everywhere made pemmican because Indians everywhere jerked meat. While meat without fat would keep for long periods, pounding the dried meat with animal tallow and flavoring it with dried berries furnished the traveler with a full portable meal as nutritious as any carried by our astronauts today. Columbia River Indians would pack their cubes in cylindrical baskets that George Catlin called "sally bags" as he watched Indians "sally forth."

Just as you can make jerky from any kind of disease-free meat, so you can flavor pemmican with any kind of dried berry. Huckleberries are a favorite of the Northwest, but since cranberries are more accessible, I've used them to turn my homemade jerky into homemade pemmican. To dry cranberries (or blueberries), I simply spread them in a single layer on a baking sheet and dry them in the oven on the lowest heat, then store them in plastic bags.

Bear grease is a favored fat in the Northwest, but beef suet is easier and butter will do. Where pioneers and Indians had to pulverize their jerky with a stone maul or mallet, we have the processor or food grinder to make quick work of powdering both meat and berries. Next time you want to dazzle friends jaded with the latest ethnic divertissement from Laos or Mozambique, offer a plate of miniature pemmican squares and let them guess.

    2 cups jerky strips (see page 462)
    1½ cups dried cranberries or blueberries
    ¾ cup rendered beef suet, or 6 ounces (1½ sticks) butter

Grind jerky strips in processor or food grinder. Add the dried berries and process until powdered. Melt beef fat and pour onto the mixture. Process until well mixed.

Pour the mixture into a 9-by-9-inch baking pan and press it flat so that it is about an inch thick. Score the top into 24 small squares before the fat hardens. Refrigerate and when the mix is well chilled, cut into squares. Remove them and store in an air-tight container in a refrigerator or cool place.

Makes 24 small squares.

HOT FIDDLEHEAD SALAD

Since ferns are one of our ubiquitous wild foods that have at last reached big-city grocers, it is now worth discovering how to prepare them. Fiddleheads or fiddlenecks refer to young fern fronds, still curled in the fetal position, cut from any number of edible ferns, such as the ostrich, cinnamon, hay-scented, or evergreen. The Samish liked to roast the stems and rhizomes of pasture brake fern or western bracken, after which they would pound them into flour to make ash-baked bread. If the fiddleheads are really fetal, you needn't cook them at all, but simply chop them for a salad or use as a garnish for other foods. I like to serve them whole, however, and to cook them slightly, to avoid bitterness, treating them as if they were a green like spinach, dandelion leaves, or broccoli rabe.

    4 cups fiddlehead ferns, rinsed
    4 thick strips bacon
    2 tablespoons olive oil
    2 tablespoons lemon juice
     salt and pepper to taste

Blanch the ferns in boiling salted water to cover for about 4 minutes. Drain them well. Fry the bacon strips in a wok or large skillet. Remove them when crisp and drain on paper towels. Pour off all but 1 tablespoon of the bacon fat and add olive oil. Add the ferns and stir over high heat until they are coated with oil. Pour into a serving dish, sprinkle with lemon juice and seasonings, and crumble bacon over the top.

Serves 4 to 6.

WILD MUSHROOM RAGOUT

In his San Francisco restaurant Stars, Jeremiah Tower serves a good dish of mixed wild mushrooms, sautéed quickly with a frothed cream and poured over wild rice. "You can say ragout but don't say stew," Jeremiah Tower warns.

"They won't order it." While the word "ragout" came from the French, it has been in English use since the seventeenth century when Samuel Butler in *Hudibras* mocked the new Frenchifications of the English table, "as French Cooks use Their Haut-Gusts, Buolies, or Ragusts." A ragout then meant a highly seasoned stew of meat and vegetables. Since the intense flavor of wild mushrooms is a seasoning in itself, ragout is probably a truer word than stew for these delicious wildings.

Few of America's more than four hundred varieties of edible mushrooms make their way into any market or restaurant. We are more likely to find imports from Italy and France and prices to match, but as we become more aware of the riches of our own woods and meadows, demand should rise and prices may drop.

4 cups mixed wild mushrooms
2 tablespoons each olive oil and butter
1 small garlic clove, minced
2 green onions, with tops, chopped fine
1 tablespoon balsamic vinegar, or lemon juice and red wine
    mixed
  salt and pepper to taste
½ cup heavy cream
  garnish: 1 bunch enoke mushrooms

Avoid washing mushrooms unless the caps contain dirt or sand. Chop off and discard any soiled roots. Slice the mushrooms crosswise to include the stem where possible. Heat oil and butter in a heavy skillet or wok. Add garlic and onions and fry only a minute. Add mushrooms and brown them quickly over high heat, shaking the pan to brown them evenly. Sprinkle with vinegar, salt, and pepper. Heat the cream, whip it to a froth, pour it over the mushrooms, and scrape all onto a platter. Garnish the top with a bunch of tiny white enoke mushrooms for a contrast of white and brown.
    Serves 4.

WILD DUCK WITH PLUMS

Wild ducks tend to be as lean as their cultivated cousins of Long Island are fat. Ducks there are aplenty in the Northwest, both wild on their migratory route between Baja and Alaska and tamed under the careful and exacting scrutiny of Oriental duck fanciers intolerant of fat. As a result you will find better variety and quality in Northwest ducks. John Doerper's duck list includes blue Swedish, Cayuga, Runner, Pekin, Muscovy, Mallard, and Rouen: his list of geese includes African, Chinese, Toulouse, Embden, and Canada—their very names a travelogue.

The Orient has lent a beneficent influence not only to the duck but to its contrasting garnish of fruit. A red-skinned plum like the Santa Clara, with its tart skin and interior sweetness, complements the rich meat of a duck as neatly as a Parisian orange, a Normandy apple, or Peking plum sauce. An Oriental plum sauce is usually spiced with ginger and chili and made both sweet and sour with sugar and vinegar. Here I've used port for sweet and lemon for sour, and you can turn either way to your taste.

> 2 tablespoons each butter and olive oil
> 2 wild ducks, pan ready
>   salt and black and cayenne pepper to taste
> 3 lemons
> 2 onions, quartered
> 1½ cups port
> 16 red tart-skinned plums, halved and stoned

Mix together butter and olive oil and rub ducks inside and out with it. Season inside and out. Quarter 2 of the lemons and put them with the onions in the cavity of each bird. Grate the rind of the remaining lemon and reserve the pulp for juice. Lay each bird in a large square of foil. Pour in ¼ cup port for each bird and seal the top of each foil package tightly.

Bake at 350° for 30 minutes.

Open the foil, pour the remaining port over the ducks, and add the plums. Leave the foil open and roast, basting occasionally, until the meat is tender but not dry, another 20 to 30 minutes. If the skin is not sufficiently browned, put ducks into a broiling pan and give the skin a browning glaze under the broiler. Taste sauce and adjust sweetness or tartness with port and lemon. Add more butter if the ducks are particularly lean. Sprinkle the tops of the birds with the grated lemon peel and surround with the plums.

Serves 4 to 6.

VARIATION: Substitute domestic ducks, but get rid of the fat. First prick the skin all over with a fork, then roast the birds on a trivet in a 450° oven for 30 minutes. Finally, wrap ducks in foil with port and plums and bake 20 to 30 minutes more.

SQUAB WITH FIGS AND OLIVES

For most of us, squab must stand in for a full range of wildfowl that may flock our woods but not our meat markets. Squab, tiny and toothsome, can be partnered with a full range of salts and sweets, among them a California hybrid that began life under the gardening hands of the mission fathers—the Cali-myrna fig. Today's fig industry in the San Joaquin Valley came first by way of the missions and second by way of a minuscule fig wasp, inappropriately named "blastophaga." A nineteenth-century horticulturist, a Mr. Roeding, discovered that the only way to mate a male Capri fig and a female Turkish Smyrna fig was with the aid of this Mediterranean wasp. By 1899 he had arranged enough matings to call the progeny "Cali-myrna," a white plump fig that thrived in the hot valleys of California and rivaled its parents in flavor.

Fresh figs are delicious with a game bird such as squab, but so costly except on the West Coast that we should look to the Calimyrna dried fig, especially when paired with another Mediterranean fruit, the olive. I like the intensity of small black wrinkled oil-cured olives for this dish, but other kinds of olives are worth experimenting with. And so are other kinds of figs.

½ cup dried figs, quartered
1½ cups fruity white wine such as white zinfandel
1 cup black olives, pitted and sliced lengthwise
4 small squabs
  salt and pepper to taste
4 tablespoons butter
2 tablespoons olive oil
¼ cup minced shallots or green onions
2 tablespoons each minced parsley and fresh coriander (cilantro)

Soak figs overnight in the wine to plump them. Mix with the olive slivers. Butterfly the squabs by splitting them down the back with a cleaver or heavy knife and pushing the sides flat. Salt and pepper them on both sides.

Heat the butter and oil in a large cast-iron skillet and quickly brown the squabs (skin side first) on both sides. Lower heat, add shallots, figs, wine, and olives, cover tightly, and simmer until birds are tender but not dry, about 5 minutes. Transfer squabs, figs, and olives to a platter, reduce sauce, pour it over birds, and sprinkle them with parsley and coriander.

Serves 4.

WILD BERRY JAM CAKE

The Indians' dried berry roll is really a form of berry jam made without sugar, since drying concentrates the natural sugar of the fruit while preserving it. To then whip up the jam with eulachon grease is not wholly unlike whipping sugared jam into a batter. In this way the wild berry rolls of the Gitksans have something in common with the Blackberry Jam Cake in *The Portland*

Woman's Exchange Cook Book. The Jam Cake contributed by Mrs. Lincoln Gault of Tacoma is really a nineteenth-century spice cake flavored with home-made berry jam. I find that a jam frosting on such a cake aids flavor and color, since the cake is darkened with spices such as cinnamon and allspice or clove. A butter frosting with a red berry jam makes a splendid deep pink color.

    6 ounces (1½ sticks) butter
    1 cup granulated sugar
    3 eggs
    1 cup berry jam
    ½ cup sour milk
    2 cups all-purpose flour
    2 teaspoons baking powder
    1 teaspoon each baking soda and cinnamon
    ¼ teaspoon each allspice and nutmeg

Frosting
    1 cup berry jam
    ½ pound (2 sticks) butter
    2 cups powdered sugar
    lemon juice, if needed

Cream butter with sugar until light and fluffy. Beat eggs one by one into the mixture. Stir the jam into the milk (soured by adding 1 teaspoon vinegar and letting milk stand 10 minutes). Mix the dry ingredients well and add alternately with the milk mixture to the batter. Smooth the batter into 2 buttered and floured 9-inch cake pans and bake at 375° for 25 to 30 minutes. Cool on a rack.

To make the frosting, cream the jam with the butter and powdered sugar until of a spreading consistency. If too sweet, add a little lemon juice. Spread half the frosting on one cake, place other cake on top, and spread top and sides with remaining frosting.

Makes a 2-layer 9-inch cake to serve 6 to 8.

25
Fruited Valleys

The river valleys that stretch from southern California north to the Alaskan Panhandle, protected on both sides by high mountains, form a giant open-air hothouse where, for the last century, gardening pioneers have produced an extraordinary range and quality of produce. Locals say that there are two Pacific Northwests, a wet one and a dry one, with the Cascade Range of Washington and Oregon forming the rain or watershed. The Cascades link California's coastal ranges on the west and the Sierra Nevada on the east to form the fruit and salad bowl of America in a chain of valleys: Washington's Skagit, Wenatchee, and Yakima valleys; Oregon's Willamette, Rogue River, and Hood River valleys; California's Napa, Sonoma, Sacramento, San Joaquin, and Coachella valleys.

Seedlings from all over the world have migrated here, along with skilled hands to nurse them, to settle and create their own colonies. In Washington, the apple; in Oregon, the pear; and in California a kind of fruit-basket upset that links pomegranates to avocados and apricots to artichokes. Western cooking doesn't distinguish between fruits and vegetables as rigidly as eastern does because in western valleys such plants grow side by side.

While the Franciscan fathers were the first to plant apples in West Coast orchards, Russian immigrants were not far behind, planting apples at Fort Ross as early as 1812. The first commercial plantings began in 1847, when Henderson Luelling and William Meek loaded their covered wagons with seven hundred seedlings in the Midwest and carried them over the Oregon Trail. Apples sold for a hundred dollars a bushel during California's Gold

Rush. When an apple rush hit Oregon and Washington in the 1890s, the red Delicious, transplanted from the orchard of Jesse Hiatt in Iowa, became Washington's and America's prime commercial apple because it was hardy and kept well.

While the mission fathers also planted pears, the completion of the transcontinental railroad in 1869 stimulated a pear rush. Pears thrive in the heavy clay soil, cooled by frosty winters and warmed by gentle summers, found in the valleys of Oregon. While the empress of pears, the Doyenne de Comice, thrives in Harry and David's Bear Creek Orchards in the Rogue River Valley, it is the Bartlett that became America's commercial pear because it stores well.

Perhaps the Shangri-la of west coast valleys is in southern California near Del Mar, the valley of Rancho Santa Fe and the home of the Chino Farm. The litany of names suggests Spanish roots, but typical of coastal hybridization, the Chino Farm is Japanese and its full name is Chino Nojo, meaning the farm of the family of Junzo Chino. For thirty-five years Junzo Chino, now in his nineties, has been experimenting in his fifty-six-acre garden with produce of a quality and variety that probably exceed that grown in any other garden anywhere. Here he grows fifty kinds of melons, thirty kinds of lettuce, twenty varieties of watermelons, fifteen kinds of peppers, five kinds of basil, four kinds of eggplant, not to mention miniature vegetables and edible herbs of every variety. The Chino family has grafted Japanese farming methods onto California's growing climate and the results are spectacular. They have close ties on the one hand with agricultural research at the University of California at Davis and on the other with the freshest-and-best tables of restaurants like Alice Waters' Chez Panisse in Berkeley and Wolfgang Puck's Spago in Los Angeles. Their secret is that everything is done by hand. "Every plant has to count," says Junzo's daughter Kay. Their secret is the secret of the Indians, respect for the gifts of the Great Transformer.

STRAWBERRY AND SPINACH
SALAD

While an Easterner might call a strawberry and spinach salad "weirdo California," a Westerner would find it as natural as berries and fish. The far-out combinations of the West are both natural and traditional to its own ecology. I
first tasted a strawberry and spinach salad at the hands of a pioneer caterer and
chef who was the first woman ever elected to the American Academy of Chefs
and who had been wrastling up salads of this sort for a good fifty years before
anyone heard of either Nouvelle Cuisine or New American Cooking. Lillian
Haines, the Annie Oakley of American cooking, is a native Californian
operating out of Beverly Hills as a lively octogenarian daughter of the True
West. "Nouvelle cuisine may be new to France," she says, "but we've been
doing it for fifty years in California." For Lillian the look of food is primal, so
she puts strawberries with spinach, papaya with shrimp, apricots with beef.
"By the time you put food in your mouth, you've already decided whether you
like it or not," she says. "You've already tasted it with your eyes."

> 1 bunch fresh spinach leaves
> 1 pint strawberries
> ⅓ cup olive oil
> 2 tablespoons raspberry (or other fruit) vinegar
>   salt and pepper to taste

Rinse spinach well, discarding stems, and spin the leaves dry. Hull berries and, if they are large, cut in half. Put the leaves in a salad bowl and sprinkle the strawberries on top. Mix a dressing of oil, fruit vinegar, and seasonings
and pour over the whole.
Serves 4.

WARM KIWI AND PAPAYA SALAD

Because it was as decorative as it was novel, kiwi became the spoiled child of nouvelles cuisines everywhere when kiwi was first exported from New Zealand to Paris, Tokyo, and the bicoastal gastronomic centers of America. Now that California is growing kiwi commercially, it has lost some of its novelty but none of its pleasant flavor or delicate green. The West treats the kiwi as casually as the banana, although kiwi still has the edge on cost. One western use is in a warmed fruit salad that combines papaya gold with kiwi green to good visual effect, particularly if sprinkled with peppery black papaya seeds.

        4 kiwis
        2 ripe papayas
        1 tablespoon lime juice
        2 tablespoons dark rum
        ½ cup green-pepper jelly

Peel the kiwis and slice them crosswise into ¼-inch disks. Quarter the papayas, peel, and remove all seeds, reserving a tablespoon of them; cut lengthwise into ½-inch slices. Barely warm the fruit in a skillet, then arrange the papaya slices in a sunburst on a warm serving platter, with the kiwi in the middle. Heat the lime juice, rum, and jelly in the skillet until the jelly melts. Quickly pour it over the fruit and sprinkle with the reserved papaya seeds.
    Serves 4 to 6.

POMEGRANATE GUACAMOLE

In my California youth, pomegranate trees were as common in backyards as loquats, apricots, and oranges. Spanish conquistadors brought the pomegranate to the Americas and it thrived in climates as hot and dry as its home in the Middle East. But in my childhood pomegranates posed a problem. While the juice of their purply red seeds, popped against the palate, was delicious, to pick each seed from its matting inside the rind was tedious work best relegated to children younger than oneself. If you tried to shorten the process by throwing the seed clusters into a blender, the juice often tasted of tannin. An Englishman, Tom Stobart, familiar with pomegranates in the Middle East, suggests a solution: To counteract excess tannin, dissolve gelatin in water (a teaspoon gelatin to a tablespoon water per pomegranate) and add to the pureed juice, then filter it through filter-paper or cheesecloth.

In the Middle East, where pomegranates are much prized, their juice is often used instead of lime or lemon. With this in mind, spicing a Mexican guacamole of chopped avocado with pomegranate juice will not seem as freakish as it might otherwise. Helen Brown, in fact, mentions that Mexicans are wont to put pomegranate seeds in their Christmas salads and sometimes in their guacamole. A little juice for acid and a sprinkling of seeds for color and crispness are happy variations on familiar Christmas and guacamole themes.

> 2 ripe avocados
> 3 green onions, minced
> 1 clove garlic, minced
> 1 tablespoon hot green chili pepper, such as jalapeño, chopped fine
> 2–3 tablespoons pomegranate juice
> 1–2 tablespoons lime juice
> 1 tablespoon chopped fresh mint or fresh coriander (cilantro)
> salt and black and cayenne pepper to taste
> ½ cup pomegranate seeds

Quarter avocados, remove pits, and peel skin from the flesh. Dice the avocado flesh and mix in the remaining ingredients except for the pomegranate seeds. Sprinkle the seeds over the top.

Serves 4 to 6.

CELERY VICTOR WITH BASIL

Since California is the home of the American salad, we find foods of all kinds there turned into salads. This one is made of celery braised in chicken stock and garnished with tomatoes, anchovies, and eggs in a basil vinaigrette. The name "Victor" comes from a once-famous chef, Victor Hirtzler of the Hotel St. Francis in Union Square, San Francisco. *The Portland Woman's Exchange Cook Book* listed Celery Victor among its recipes in 1913, and in 1952 it was still going strong at the Hotel St. Francis when Helen Brown recorded their recipe.

To the braised celery I've added the roasted red peppers and anchovy familiar to most of us from Italian antipasti. A pesto sauce makes this salad a meal, but for a lighter dish a sprinkling of chopped basil in a vinaigrette displays restraint.

4 celery hearts
3–4 cups boiling chicken stock, or to cover
2 large sweet red bell peppers, roasted, peeled, and seeded (see page 39)
12 flat anchovy fillets
⅓ cup olive oil
2 tablespoons lemon juice or vinegar
½ teaspoon black pepper
½ cup chopped basil leaves

Split the celery hearts in half and trim the root ends, keeping the leaves on. Place the celery in a shallow pan and cover with boiling stock. Cover closely with a lid or aluminum foil and simmer (or bake at 350°) until tender, about 10 minutes. Drain the celery well (save the broth for soup). Cut the roasted peppers into strips and lay over the celery, in an alternating pattern, with the anchovy strips. Beat the oil, lemon juice, and pepper together and pour over the whole. Sprinkle the top with basil. Serve at room temperature.

Serves 4 to 8.

ROASTED ARTICHOKES WITH GARLIC

The artichoke navel of the world is Castroville near Half Moon Bay, just south of San Francisco, and the garlic navel is Gilroy near Monterey Bay, south of Half Moon. Both thistle and bulb were planted in Spanish missions, but few non-Spaniards ate them until Italians arrived in sufficient numbers in the late nineteenth century to cultivate and consume both in quantity. While it was the Palace Hotel in San Francisco that elevated the artichoke to gastronomic chicdom in the 1920s, it was Chez Panisse in Berkeley that finally enthroned the garlic in Alice's annual Garlic Gala, in which garlic stars in every course, including a dessert of garlic sherbet. Here I roast the two vegetables together for a first course or main dish, adding crusty bread and baked goat cheese, in the style of California-Med.

        4 large globe artichokes, or 18 small ones
        2 whole heads garlic
        ½ cup olive oil
           salt and pepper to taste
        3–4 sprigs fresh thyme or rosemary
        6–8 ounces chèvre
        ½ cup fresh bread crumbs or grated Parmesan cheese
        1 loaf French bread

Cut large artichokes into quarters, cut off their tops halfway down, trim their bottoms, and remove the thorny chokes. (Very small ones can be cooked whole.) Drop the cut artichokes into acidulated water to prevent discoloring. Break the garlic heads into single cloves and parboil 2 or 3 minutes, then remove their skins. Put the artichokes and garlic in a shallow baking pan, pour on the oil, season with salt, pepper, and herbs, cover with foil, and bake at 350° for 30 to 40 minutes.

Remove 2 or 3 tablespoons oil to a plate and roll the chèvre in it. Then sprinkle the chèvre on all sides with crumbs (or grated Parmesan), put the chèvre in the baking pan with the vegetables, and bake until the cheese is heated through, 5 to 10 minutes. Serve with toasted or grilled slices of French bread.

Serves 4 to 8.

Hearth-Roasted Apples

As we know, the apple preceded the fire in the sequence of events that led Adam to delve and Eve to spin. And certainly Eve was the first to discover that the taste of an apple raw was seconded only by that of an apple roasted on a stick over a hot coal. So simple and universal is the practice of roasting apples over an open fire that cook books have never bothered to provide instruction. But since I have lost a number of apples in various hearth fires, sticking them on pokers (from which they slid off) or on sticks (which burned), a tip or two may not be amiss for decadent urbanites who have lost the arts of hearth cooking.

The safest roasting method is to put the apples in an aluminum foil nest or a baking pan to one side of the coals and to turn the apples about as needed to toast them evenly on all sides. They should roast slowly enough so that the interior swells with hot juice before the outside skin is entirely charred. Once you have tasted a hearth-roasted apple, the wrinkly-skinned oven-baked product will seem an insipid and regrettable consequence of the fall of man.

CALIFORNIA OMELET

"This is really one of our best original egg dishes," Helen Brown wrote in 1952, "one that is bound to become a world classic." Since nothing in the food world is "original" in a historical sense, the California omelet derives from the American-Chinese egg fu yung, which derives in turn from the classic peasant omelet east and west. Centuries ago, Chinese peasants, like European ones, discovered that eggs could bind. Since China had an abundance of bean sprouts, these could be mixed with chopped leftover meats and fish and folded into beaten eggs to make a thrifty and substantial dish. Since Europe had an abundance of vegetables such as onions, cabbage, and potatoes, these mixed with ham or bacon became staples of the country omelet of Europe.

California has always had an abundance of avocados and, until recently, a superfluity of fresh crab. The California omelet, then, was a wonderful way to use up an avocado about to go over the hill and that small bit of crab left over from last night's feast. Freshened with diced tomato and smoothed with sour cream, what began as a thrift dish ends as a luxurious one, albeit in California's laid-back style.

6 eggs, beaten
    salt and pepper to taste
2 tomatoes, peeled, seeded, and diced
1 ripe avocado, peeled and diced
½ cup fresh crab meat
4 tablespoons butter
½ cup sour cream

Beat eggs with the salt and pepper and set aside. Mix diced tomatoes, avocado, and crab. Heat 2 tablespoons butter in a small sauté pan, add the mixture, and warm through; then, off heat, fold in the sour cream.

Heat remaining butter in an omelet pan until bubbling, add the eggs, and stir them with the back of a fork in a circular motion while shaking the pan back and forth to keep the eggs from sticking. When eggs are nearly set, spoon half the filling in a line across the middle and fold the omelet in thirds over it. Pour remaining filling onto a serving platter and roll the omelet, seam side down, on top of it.

Serves 3 or 4.

VARIATION: For a "classic" peasant omelet, mix the vegetables and crab into the eggs, pour eggs into the heated butter in the sauté pan, brown quickly on one side, place inverted plate over the pan and flip so plate is right side up and omelet is brown side up. Then slide the omelet (uncooked side down) back into the pan to brown on the other side. When ready to serve, cut into thirds or quarters and put a dollop of sour cream on top of each piece.

PERSIMMON-CREAM PEARS

On the east coast, it was the Indians who taught the first settlers of Virginia the difference between ripe and unripe "putchamins," which grew as high as palmetto trees. "The fruit is like a medlar," Captain John Smith wrote, "it is first green, then yellow, then red when it is ripe; if it be not ripe it will draw a man's mouth awry with much torment, but when it is ripe it is as delicious as an apricock."

Our native American persimmon is much smaller, rounder, and darker than the modern commercial persimmon, the bright-orange pointed Hichiya, imported from Japan. Today, the heart of the canned persimmon industry is in Mitchell, Indiana, founded in 1863 by a farmer, Logan Martin, who became known as Persimmon Martin. California, however, is the heart of persimmon growing because the slowly ripening fruit likes those hot sunny valleys, where persimmons were introduced in 1876 in the American River Valley near San Francisco.

A simple but beautiful fruit dessert can be composed of pears poached in a fruity California white wine and sauced with a persimmon-cream purée as delicate as a Japanese watercolor.

    4 ripe pears, such as Anjou, Comice, or Bartlett
    2 tablespoons shredded fresh ginger
    1 large piece lemon peel
    1 cup white fruity wine (white zinfandel, chardonnay, or riesling)
    2 cups water
    1 cup sugar
    2 cups persimmon pulp
    2 tablespoons each lime juice, dark honey, and dark rum
    1 cup heavy cream, whipped

Peel the pears and leave stems on. Mix together the ginger, lemon peel, wine, water, and sugar. Bring to a simmer in a saucepan and add the pears. Cover pan partially and cook as gently as possible for about 25 minutes. Let the pears cool in the liquid. Remove the core from the bottom of each pear with an apple corer.

Prepare persimmon pulp either by peeling the skin down and removing the flesh of the fruit or by cutting them in 2 and scraping out the flesh with a spoon. Purée the pulp in a blender with the lime juice, honey, and rum until smooth. Taste and adjust sweet and sour. Fold the pulp into the whipped cream.

Pour some sauce onto the center of each plate and stand a pear upright in the middle.

Serves 4.

PRUNE YEAST BREAD

In the West, fresh plums are often called prunes because the coast developed its own hybrids of prune-plums for the purpose of drying them. The first prunes reached California's Santa Clara Valley in 1856 from France. "They were cuttings of the famous French prune," Helen Brown writes, "which were stuck into raw potatoes, then in sawdust, and packed in two leather trunks in which they made the long trip around the Horn." A Frenchman named Louis Pellier was in San Jose to receive them and he grafted them to the root stock of the wild native plum, the Klamath—tart but tasty. Other plums were developed by the Luelling brothers in Oregon, but because California had the drying barns, Santa Clara became and remains the center of the prune industry.

Of the many uses of prunes, yeast bread was once one of the commonest. The *California Cook Book* (1925) has a typical recipe for such a bread, although with an excess of sugar characteristic of breads at this date. If you want a distinctively pruny taste in your dough, add some of the liquid in which the prunes have soaked. But you don't have to soak dried prunes at all to soften them. You can steam them for half an hour and avoid any wasted liquid.

1 cup dried prunes
1 package dry yeast
¼ cup prune liquid or water heated to 105°–115°
½ cup whole wheat flour
2–3 cups unbleached white flour
1 teaspoon each salt and pepper

½ teaspoon baking soda
¾ cup sour milk
2 tablespoons butter, softened
optional: ½ cup walnuts, chopped

Soften the prunes either by soaking overnight, by steaming, or by a quick-soak method: bring them to a simmer in ¾ cup water, simmer for 1 minute, then cover pot and let them cool. Pit and chop them. Dissolve the yeast in the warm liquid. Mix the whole wheat flour with 2 cups of the unbleached, and mix in the salt, pepper, and baking soda. Pour the yeast mixture into the flour. Stir in the milk (soured by adding 1 teaspoon vinegar and letting milk stand 10 minutes), butter, and prunes and add more flour until the dough is of good kneading consistency. Stir in the walnuts, if using. Knead 10 minutes by hand or 5 minutes in a mixer with a dough hook.

Let the dough rise in a well-buttered bowl in a warm place until the dough has doubled, about 1 hour. Punch the dough down and divide into two well-buttered 9-by-5-by-3-inch bread pans or a single large round pan. Let rise again about 45 minutes. Bake at 375° until loaves sound hollow when rapped on the bottom, 30 to 35 minutes.

Makes 2 standard-sized loaves or 1 large round one.

BILLY GOAT DATE CAKES

Recipes for Billy Goat Cakes appeared in "old cookbooks" in all three of the Pacific states, according to Helen Brown, but she can explain neither name nor origin. From their ingredients of spices, raisins and nuts, brown sugar and molasses, they appear to be an evolutionary stepchild of the seventeenth-century English spiced cakes called "jumbles." Jumbles, in turn, begat hermits, familiar to many an American child of the late nineteenth century from recipes such as one in *The Berkeley Cookbook* (1884) contributed by a Mrs. Miller, who adds soda and sour cream to her spice cake-cookies. The introduction of the Deglet Noor date from Arabia to Coachella Valley in California in 1890 allowed housewives at the turn of the century to add dates to the usual raisins and nuts and to give a western twist to this ancient cake-cookie, so long a favorite of children that some child may once have thought the cake would also please Billy Goat Gruff.

> 1 pound pitted dates
> 1 cup chopped walnuts
> ¼ pound (1 stick) butter
> 1 cup brown sugar
> 2 eggs, beaten
> ½ cup sour cream
> 1½ cups all-purpose flour
> 1 teaspoon each baking powder and allspice
> ½ teaspoon baking soda
> ¼ teaspoon nutmeg or mace

Cut the pitted dates into pieces with scissors and mix with the chopped nuts. Cream the butter with the sugar and beat in the eggs until light and fluffy. Beat in the sour cream. Mix ½ cup flour into the dates and nuts to coat them. Mix together the remaining dry ingredients, stir into the egg mixture, and add dates and nuts. Drop the batter by spoonfuls on well-greased cookie sheets. Bake at 350° until nicely browned, 10 to 12 minutes.

Makes about 6 dozen (72) cookies.

CHOCOLATE-ALMOND TORTE
WITH APRICOT CREAM

Almonds and apricots are kissing cousins, sharing kernels and habitats. The hot Sacramento and San Joaquin valleys have become the world habitat of the almond, first introduced on a large scale into California in 1853. Apricots are a trickier proposition, but since they are native to northern China they do well in the cooler valleys of Washington and Oregon. One need only hear the voices of Washington apricot eaters to want to live among Wenatchee Moorparks, Tiltons, or the aptly named Perfections.

To combine apricots and almonds with chocolate is to change an alliance into a *ménage à trois*. For an apricot cream to hold the layers of torte together, you can make your own apricot purée from dried apricots, buy ready-made purée in the form of Hungarian *lekvar*, or use apricot jam, puréed and sieved and made less sweet by the addition of a little lemon juice.

> 2 cups almonds
> 6 eggs, separated, plus 3 egg yolks
> ¾ cup sugar
> ¼ teaspoon almond extract
> 3 ounces semisweet chocolate
> ⅓ cup all-purpose flour

Apricot Cream
> 2 cups dried apricots
> ½ cup water
> ¼ cup bourbon
> ¼ pound (1 stick) butter

To make the torte layers, grind almonds fine in a processor or blender. Beat 6 egg yolks until light, add sugar and almond extract, and beat until thick and creamy. Melt chocolate in a double boiler and cool slightly, then beat the chocolate gradually into the yolk mixture. Lightly stir in the flour. Beat the 6 egg whites until stiff but not dry and fold them into the chocolate mixture. Spoon the mixture into two 8-inch buttered and floured cake pans, and bake on the top rack of a 325° oven until an inserted toothpick comes out clean, 45 minutes. Cool cakes in their pans.

For the apricot butter cream, bring the dried apricots, water, and bourbon to a boil in a saucepan, cover the pan, and simmer gently for 15 minutes. Purée the apricots with their liquid; mixture should be very thick. Add the 3 egg yolks, one at a time, beating well after each addition. Cut the butter into small pieces, add, and beat until you have a spreading consistency.

When the cakes are thoroughly cool, spread a third of the butter cream over one cake, place the other cake on top, and spread the remaining cream over the top and sides.

Serves 8 to 10.

26
Stir-Fry Smorgasbord

"I have been to Astoria today," a Swedish girl wrote on August 20, 1903. "I seen the great Chinese dragon. That was nice." The girl was Mary Riddle, who worked on a farm in Svensen, outside Astoria. In Astoria she might have seen in 1903 not only Chinese dragons and gardens but also Italian, Irish, Finnish, Swedish, Norwegian, and Danish fishing boats, German and English beer joints, and Hindu temples. Astoria was a port of entry like Port Townsend, Seattle, Vancouver, Portland, Eureka, and San Francisco, and to these ports refugees from wars and poverty flocked then and flock now. Because this part of America is still the wild and because the peoples who come are so diverse, they remain distinct, unassimilated, not a melting pot but a stir-fry of Koreans and Croatians, Vietnamese and Laplanders, Taiwanese and Iranians, Turks and Thailanders.

The first explorers from Spain and Britain left their names and outposts where Yank and British traders would later dispute boundaries and furs and even pigs (as in the Pig War of the San Juan Islands). Then came in the mid-nineteenth century a wave of Scandinavian fishers and farmers and Chinese laborers. The Chinese were neither colonizers nor immigrants but sojourners. Hidden under sheep hides or in potato sacks, they gambled their lives to work as unacknowledged slaves in gold mines, canneries, and railroads in order to send money home to their starving families. The first official Chinese immigrants were two men and one woman who boarded the *Bard Eagle* in 1848 to work in the gold mines of California. Within three years there were 18,000 Chinese on the coast, largely from what Americans then called Kwangtung province, which included Hong Kong and Canton. America's first Chinese restaurant in San Francisco's burgeoning Chinatown in 1869 was appropriately called "The Canton," and for the next century Chinese food in America was essentially Cantonese.

Unofficially, Chinese were smuggled in by men like Kelly, King of the Smugglers, who hid Chinese laborers in the usual cargo of opium and occasionally among cases of red and white Chinese wine. The Chinese Exclusion Act of 1882 merely enriched the smugglers of coolies and opium and led to the terrible massacres of 1885 in Tacoma and Seattle. Whether they worked for the railroads or the salmon factories, the Chinese lived and ate apart. Seufert's Salmon Company, Francis Seufert remembered, was required to furnish, for each crew of Chinese workers led by a China Boss, a China house, a chef, rice, and pigs. To Westerners, Chinese ways were very strange, particularly their ways with food. Seufert recalls being invited by the China Boss to dinner and managing to eat raw sturgeon in a fresh green salad but being unable to eat baby octopus, which looked like "human baby hands." Citizens less tolerant than Seufert developed Sinophobia as a moralistic cover for economic fears. Typical was the statement of the Port Townsend Immigration Aid Society of 1889: "NO person of American or European birth can begin to compete with these leprous creatures, because they cannot, will not, and OUGHT not live as they do."

The Chinese, in fact, treated food with the same sort of respect that native American Indians did and for much the same reason. The Chinese were considered dirty and leprous because they scavenged muddy streets and garbage dumps for slops to feed their pigs. Whites were oblivious to the fact that the Chinese kept their pigs on floored pens above ground and scrubbed them daily until they were as pink as a baby's hand.

Early cook books attempting to explain the mysteries of East to West were full of apology and defense. *The Chinese Festive Board* (1934) describes a typical Cathay breakfast as a ring of batter fried in fat, "cold, limp, insipid, and shining in its coat of cooked grease." At the same time, Chinese cooks became as common in Caucasian kitchens as Chinese laundries on Caucasian streets. Who can forget James Beard's descriptions of the Chinese kitchen crew—Gin and Poy and Let—battling with recipes and sometimes cleavers in their Thirty Years' War with Beard's mother, who ruled Portland's Victoria

Hotel? Or who would have guessed that the horticulturist Henderson Leulling, of the Oregon apple, named a cherry for his favorite houseboy, Bing?

There are few Chinese cook books in English before Grace Chu's influential *Pleasures of Chinese Cooking* (1962). Most of them are product books put out by such companies as La Choy in 1936 or the Pacific Trading Company in 1928. As late as 1952, Helen Brown could write that "the tremendous interest that we have in Chinese food is a pretty recent one, but at the rate it's developing, we may all end up eating with chopsticks." How right she was. The simple ABC's of Cantonese chop suey, chow mein, and egg roll have now swollen to encyclopedic volumes of Szechuan, Hunan, and Fukien specialties as long as the Great Wall of China. But in our current enthusiasm for "authentic" Chinese dishes and scorn for earlier translations into American-Chinese cookery, we should remember that the empire of Chinese food has undergone constant sea-change wherever it has spread—to Honolulu, London, Tokyo, New York, Seattle, San Francisco, and Los Angeles. It is well to remember that in China cornstarch is unheard of and MSG a staple. It is well to observe that *The Mandarin Chop Suey Cook Book* (1928), put out by the Pacific Trading Company of Chicago, which claims to be "the first and only book of its character published in the English language containing genuine recipes of famous Chinese chefs . . . guaranteed to be authentic and accurately translated," centers entirely on chop suey, chow mein, and egg fu yung. (The earliest Chinese cook book in English I know of was published in Detroit in 1911 and was authored by Jessie Louise Nolton, *Chinese Cookery in the Home Kitchen*.)

If Chinese cooking got a head start on the West Coast, Japanese cooking was not far behind. In the first half of this century, before the Nisei-phobia that created the internment camps of the Second World War, Japanese truck gardens produced ingredients that were unexcelled. After the war, Japanese influence was felt in the health-food and ecology movements and in the semi-religious communes that turned to macrobiotic diets as a path to peace and enlightenment. While sushi bars on the east coast sprouted as fast as mung beans, the West was far more innovative in its expressions of ethnic stir-fry foods. Where but in the West would you find, in the Trumpet Vine Cheese and Coffee Center of Mill Valley, California, a Samurai Hero-Sandwich of brown rice, tofu, bean sprouts, barley miso, and tamai-sesame butter, stuffed into a whole-grain chapati?

If you look at America's new generation of chefs, where but in California would you find Udo Nechutnys of the Miramonte Inn in Napa Valley? Born in Czechoslovakia, Udo became a protégé of Paul Bocuse in France, who sent him to Japan to study under the master Shizuo Tsuji in Osaka and to apprentice in Hong Kong and Paris. Now, with his Chinese wife, Mei, Udo owns a Western-saloon-styled restaurant next to La Belle Helene Hotel in the midst of an Italian community. Where but in Berkeley would you find Narsai David, a half-Turkish, half-Iranian Assyrian? Narsai, a math and pre-med graduate from the University of California, is now a wine and food entrepreneur who creates dishes like Cactus Frittata, Gouda Cheese with Mustard and Nettles, or Chocolate Decadence rich enough to stand up to the port with which it's served. Where but in Cashmere, Oregon, would you find the descendants of a pair of 1920 Armenians turning out Turkish delight from Oregon apples and apricots under the name "Aplets and Cotlets"? Where but in Astoria would you find salmon jerky at Josephson's Smoke House or *frikadeller* and *fiskekaker* at Ellen Madsen's Little Denmark Cafe? And where but in the smorgasbord of Seattle would you find in the same Pioneer Square by Skid Row Eskimos in seal skin coats, Croatian dancers in embroidered vests and black boots, and Zen Buddhists in saffron robes exchanging recipes for whale steaks, plum kolach, and grilled tofu?

CHINESE TSAP SUI

Until the Second World War, Chinese cookery in America was synonymous with *tsap sui*, Cantonese for "miscellaneous things" or, when applied to food, "miscellaneous slops" or "fried miscellaneous." The word comes from Toisan, according to C. Chang's *Food in Chinese Culture* (1977), an area south of

Canton "from which about half of all American Chinese trace their ancestry." While the Americanized term "chop suey" did not appear in print until 1888, "fried miscellaneous" in this country surely began with the first trio of Chinese who landed aboard the *Bard Eagle* in 1848.

So chop-sueyed are we now that it's hard to recall the once weird exoticism of soy sauce, raw ginger, and bean sprouts for the meat-and-potatoes mainstream. One reason chop suey grabbed the Yankee imagination is that its "odd" mixtures, within a single dish, of chopped seafoods, meats, fowl, fruit, and vegetables seemed to symbolize the odd mixtures of a Chinese meal as a whole, served like a miniature smorgasbord of dishes with unpronounceable names and unspeakable contents. It's comic to realize that vegetables cut in geometric shapes and kept crisp and crunchy were once viewed as dubious aberrations.

The Mandarin Chop Suey Cook Book (1928) must explain to readers how to grow bean sprouts or make "Au Jus" Gravy by basting roasts with water and two tablespoons "Chinese sauce." By 1936 La Choy bean sprouts and La Choy soy sauce were required ingredients for dozens of chop sueys, including an intriguing Winkel or Snail Chop Suey, seasoned with ginger-root juice and a tablespoon of "Fun wine." The method, also a novelty, was to chop everything small and fry it fast.

Obviously "fried miscellaneous" was a poor man's way of utilizing every scrap of food, fresh or left over, binding the hodgepodge with "Chinese sauce." While a Mandarin might combine beef with scallops, a coolie would combine bean sprouts with sea cucumber, if he was lucky, and with noodles if he was not. Today downtown labels like Seafood Chop Suey have been replaced by uptown ones like Velvet Shrimp or Uncle Tai's Tri-Color Lobster. Today the "fried miscellaneous" below, which *The Mandarin Cook Book* would have called "Beef Chop Suey," a current cook book would call "Beef and Scallops Mandarin."

Since the secret to cooking Chinese is methodical preparation, I've ordered the ingredients by cooking steps, as I learned to do from a supreme teacher and expositor of Chinese cooking, a Manhattan Jewish mother who fell in love with chopping and changed her name to Karen Lee. The recipe itself updates one provided by her own teacher, Grace Chu, who in 1962 called it "Beef Chop Suey."

½ pound beef (sirloin tip, shell steak, or flank steak)
1½ tablespoons sherry
1 tablespoon soy sauce
1 tablespoon cornstarch
¼ teaspoon black pepper

½ pound ocean scallops
1 tablespoon egg white

½ cup fresh water chestnuts, sunchokes, or jícama
½ cup fresh mushrooms
1 cup fresh snow peas
¼ cup fresh bean sprouts
2 tablespoons peanut oil
2 tablespoons chopped green onions, with tops
1 clove garlic, minced
1 teaspoon minced fresh ginger
½ cup chicken stock

Trim beef of all fat and partially freeze it so that you can slice it in paper-thin strips 1 by 2 inches. Make a marinade of 1 tablespoon sherry, the soy, ½ tablespoon cornstarch, and the pepper and refrigerate the beef in it for an hour.

Partially freeze the scallops and slice crosswise ¼-inch thick. Make a marinade of the egg white and remaining cornstarch and sherry, and refrigerate the scallops in it for an hour.

Slice the water chestnuts and mushrooms very thin. Cut the snow peas in half on the slant. Rinse and drain the bean sprouts.

Heat the peanut oil in a wok or heavy cast-iron skillet. Add the onions, garlic, and ginger and stir-fry 1 minute. Add the beef and its marinade and fry over high heat ½ minute to crisp the meat. Add the mushrooms to brown quickly, then the scallops and their marinade, and stir-fry 1 minute. Add remaining vegetables and chicken stock, stir, and pour onto a platter and serve.

Serves 4.

PHEASANT WITH BEAN SPROUTS

Braising a pheasant with cabbage is a classic French way, with sauerkraut a German way, of keeping this dry game bird moist. Braising pheasant with bean sprouts is a West Coast–Oriental way, which Helen Brown mentions in her *West Coast Cook Book*. I've moved western pheasant west to the Far East by adding Oriental spicing. One bird will serve two, but it's easier to whack the bird in half with a cleaver *before* you cook it than after, and the flavor of the marinade better penetrates the flesh if the bird is split. Oregon does a lot of pheasant farming, but a wild bird, if you can get one, will have better flavor than its tamed chicken-tasting brother.

> 2 young pheasants
> 8 slices fresh ginger, minced
> 3 cloves garlic, minced
> 6 green onions, with tops, slivered into 2-inch lengths
> 2 tablespoons soy sauce
> ¼ cup sherry or vermouth
> 2 tablespoons sesame oil
> ¼ teaspoon each black pepper and Five-Spice Powder (or a
>   mixture of cloves, allspice, and mace)
>
> ¼ cup peanut oil
> 1 pound fresh bean sprouts
> ½ cup chicken stock

Cut each pheasant in half, cutting along one side of the breast bone, spreading the halves apart, and cutting along the backbone on one side. Cut out the backbone from the other side. Make a marinade of the seasonings and pour over the pheasants. Let sit at least 3 hours or refrigerate overnight.

In a wok or heavy skillet, heat the oil. Remove birds from the marinade (reserving it), pat dry, and brown them skin side down until skin is golden. Line a wide casserole with a layer of washed bean sprouts, cover with the pheasants in a single layer, and then with remaining sprouts. Pour in the chicken stock and reserved marinade, cover the dish tightly with a lid or aluminum foil, and bake at 350° until a meat thermometer registers 160°, 20 to 30 minutes, depending on the size of the birds.

Serves 4.

STEAMED ROCKFISH
IN BLACK BEAN SAUCE

Fish markets of the Northwest display fish I've never seen or dreamt of elsewhere. The Pacific rockfish comes in fifty varieties and as many colors— golden, black, canary, vermillion, olive, blotched, turkey red—all of which are names for this multihued fish. The Chinese have taught us how to use such undervalued, because common, coastal fish by cooking it whole so that the flavor of head and bone permeates the delicate flesh of the body. The Chinese score the flesh deeply in parallel cuts so that it will cook quickly and evenly and so that seasonings will better infuse the meat. Often they deep-fry the fish until it is so crispy you can eat the fins like potato chips. But they also like to steam the fish, as I've done here, with seasonings that act as a marinade.

> 1 whole 1½- to 2½-pound rockfish (or red snapper, sea bass, or
>   carp)
> 2 teaspoons shredded fresh ginger
> 2 green onions, with tops, chopped
> 1 clove garlic, minced
> 1½ tablespoons fermented black beans or miso
> 2 tablespoons each dark soy sauce and sherry
> 1 tablespoon sesame oil

Rinse fish inside and out and pat dry. With a cleaver or sharp knife, make 3 deep cuts across the body on each side. Place fish on a plate that you can fit into a steamer or onto a rack you can place in a covered wok or roasting pan. Mix all the other ingredients together and spread on the fish. Bring an inch or two of water to boil in the bottom of the wok or pot, cover tightly, and steam 15 minutes over high heat. Bring fish to the table on the plate on which it cooked and carve the fish into 6 slices, following the cuts on each side.

Serves 2 or 3.

HOMEMADE COCKTAIL SUSHI

On the dubious principle that anything worth doing can be done at home, I've included a recipe for making sushi. Watching the rituals of a seafood samurai behind a Japanese sushi bar is enough to intimidate the most intrepid home cook, but let curiosity overwhelm presumption. Nobody expects you to turn out works of art on a first or even a second try, but to have tried at all is worth comment and meantime you will have learned much about the Japanese.

Since no special equipment is required to make the hand-molded rice balls the Japanese call *nigir-zushi* (to distinguish them from *maki-zushi*, which is rice rolled in a layer with the aid of a bamboo mat called a *sudarè*), we will make the hand-molded sushi. We owe to the popularity of sushi restaurants the fresh fish beautifully trimmed that is now available in big-city fish markets; since raw tuna is easy to find and easy to cut, we will make tuna sushi. The only major ingredient other than rice and fish is the flavoring "glue" of wasabi paste. Wasabi is a type of hot Japanese horseradish seldom found fresh in this country but available in the form of powder or paste in Oriental groceries.

To create the proper texture in the rice for sushi, the Japanese toss the rice in a cedar tub while fanning it to evaporate the steam as quickly as possible. They then season the rice with a special rice vinegar, *sushi su,* also available in Oriental groceries. You can, however, make your own seasoned vinegar by dissolving two tablespoons each sugar and sea salt in three tablespoons rice vinegar, heated just enough to dissolve the crystals.

> 2 cups short-grain rice
> 2¼ cups cold water
> 3 tablespoons "seasoned rice vinegar"
> 2 pounds tuna fillet
> 1 tablespoon wasabi paste
> ½ cup "hand vinegar" (1 tablespoon rice vinegar plus ½ cup cold water)
> garnish: 1 sheet toasted nori seaweed
> soy sauce for dipping
> grated pickled ginger

Wash the rice in a strainer under running water until the water runs clear. Put the rice in a pan with the measured water and let soak 15 minutes. Cover tightly with a lid, turn the heat high until you hear the water boiling (about 5 minutes), but don't uncover. Lower heat to medium and cook 10 minutes. Remove from heat, still covered, and let rice steam, off heat, another 15 minutes.

Spread rice on a large platter or wooden bowl, sprinkle it with the seasoned vinegar, a spoonful at a time, and toss the rice with a wet wooden spoon in one hand while you fan the rice rapidly with a stiff piece of cardboard (or hand fan) held in the other hand. It will take about 10 minutes to cool the rice to room temperature. Cover the platter with plastic or a damp cloth to keep the rice from drying out while shaping it.

Cut the tuna crosswise into slices 1½ inches long, ¾-inch wide, and ¼-inch thick. Dip your fingers into a bowl of "hand vinegar" and use them to lightly press a ball of rice, without mashing it, into a roll the shape of a finger 1½ inches long and ¾-inch wide. Do all the finger rolls at once, covering the molded shapes with a damp cloth to keep them moist. (If the rice is too sticky to work with your fingers, place a spoonful of rice in a dampened napkin and twist the cloth to shape a rice finger.)

Put a small dab of wasabi paste in the center of each tuna slice and stick the slice onto a rice finger. When all the slices have been glued to their rice fingers, wrap a ¼-inch strip of nori around each finger. Arrange on a platter with a small dish of soy sauce in the middle for dipping and a mound of pickled and grated ginger on each end.

Makes 24 sushi.

GRILLED TOFU WITH
MISO SAUCE

While tofu, or soybean curd, has been made commercially in this country by both Chinese and Japanese since the turn of the century, the real impetus for tofu manufacturing began in the Japanese internment camps during the Second World War. At Heart Mountain Camp in Wyoming, some two thousand pounds of tofu were made each day. Tofu is now as common to city supermarkets as fresh bean sprouts, and often several kinds of tofu are available at once. Miso, on the other hand, which is fermented soybean mash, is less understood and therefore still mainly available only in Oriental stores or health-food stores. Typically, the first miso shop in North America was opened in the western state of Utah, in Salt Lake City in 1917. While miso shops began to spring up in Hawaii and California before the Second World War, the war put an end to all that for its duration. After the war, the macrobiotic movement led by George Ohsawa spurred local production of miso and tofu as well as high-quality imports.

The third related soy ingredient, the fermented sauce that Japan calls *shoyu* and we shorten to "soy," began commercially in this country in Columbia City, Indiana, in 1928 with the Show-You Company. America's first modern plant, however, was not built until 1972, by the Kikkoman Company in Walworth, Wisconsin.

Synthesizing health foods, religious foods, and high-tech foods with a country twist, California has made miso and tofu not only mainstream, but upper-middle-class. At the Zen Tassajara vegetarian restaurant in San Francisco, appropriately named Greens, Debra Welch has applied her Chez Panisse training to Oriental tofu. One happy result is a tofu marinated and grilled on skewers with mushrooms and peppers. For this you need tofu firmed by draining the salted water from a square of fresh tofu (as you might find it in the supermarket), covering the tofu with plastic wrap, and refrigerating it for at least two hours or overnight. The sauce below I've made with Tabasco. For a milder sauce, substitute a tablespoon of grated fresh ginger.

> 12 ounces tofu (2 standard-sized squares)
> 2 Japanese eggplants
> 2 green bell peppers, seeded
> 8 large mushroom caps

Marinade
> ½ cup miso (red, barley, or Hatcho)
> 1 cup red wine
> 1 tablespoon each red wine vinegar and honey
> 2 tablespoons sesame oil

½ cup olive oil
2 cloves garlic, mashed
2 tablespoons chopped green onions
1 tablespoon roasted sesame seeds or tahini paste
½ teaspoon black pepper
dash Tabasco sauce or hot chili oil
garnish: 1 toasted nori seaweed sheet, ground

Drain and chill regular tofu to firm it. Cut it into 2-inch cubes and let soak for a couple of minutes in a bowl of hot water. Pierce each cube with a flat bamboo skewer and place on paper towels to drain. Cut eggplants, skin on, into slices ¾-inch thick. Cut seeded green peppers into 2-inch triangles. Alternate the tofu squares with the eggplant, mushrooms, and peppers on 4 long bamboo skewers, soaked in cold water, and place in a shallow pan.

Combine all remaining ingredients except the nori and purée. Pour into a saucepan and bring to a simmer, then pour over tofu-vegetables in the pan and marinate for an hour, turning the skewers from time to time.

On a charcoal grill or under a broiler, grill the tofu skewers about 3 minutes on each side. Sprinkle with ground nori.

Serves 4.

NECTARINE-CHAYOTE STIR-FRY

Is there no end to the mixed breeds of the West? The answer is no. As with strawberries and spinach, the distinction between plants labeled fruits and plants labeled vegetables loses meaning in a culture continuously hybridized botanically and ethnically. Nectarines are another of those crops of which California is the sole commercial producer and chayotes are another of those south-of-the-border crops that have become so acclimated to the North that they will marry whatever pretty companion is ready and willing. Chayotes with their pale pistachio flesh are lovely to look at but faint in flavor. Nectarines with their golden blush can be surprisingly tart. Sliced and heated quickly in a sweet-sour sauce with Sino-Mexican overtones, the pair of fruits complement each other as human couplings are meant and often fail to do.

                4 nectarines
                2 small chayotes
                1 tablespoon white wine vinegar
                ½ teaspoon sugar
                ¼ teaspoon salt
                ⅛ teaspoon each white pepper and cumin
                  pinch of cayenne pepper
              2–3 tablespoons peanut oil
                  garnish: fresh coriander (cilantro)

Cut nectarines in half, leaving skin on, and remove pits. Slice ½-inch thick. Peel the chayotes, cut them in half, and remove flat green seed. Cut flesh into similar ½-inch-thick slices. Mix the vinegar and seasonings together. Heat the oil in a wok or large skillet. Add the sliced fruits, sprinkle with the seasonings, and toss quickly, just long enough to heat the slices through. Transfer to a hot platter and sprinkle with chopped coriander. Excellent as a garnish with grilled fish or meat or as a salad.

Serves 4.

VARIATION: Substitute tender young zucchini for chayote. Cut the zucchini into triangular pieces, Chinese style, leaving the skin on. (Sweet and sour sauces for zucchini are standard in Sicily, so this sort of flavoring is not as wild as you might think.)

SWEDISH-ASTORIA CRAYFISH

"Here," Egil Unander says in his Astoria kitchen, "is my Swedish Bible." He lugs to the table a book as large in proportion to other books as he to other men. "The title means *The Big Cookbook*—twenty-fourth edition, 335,000 copies sold—it has everything, an encyclopedia, only in Swedish of course." Egil, looking for crayfish, is waylaid by Johnson's Temptation, a concoction of onions, matchstick potatoes, and Swedish anchovies layered with cream, to be eaten after a ball to keep "Johnson" away from other temptations. Finally, he finds Dilled Crayfish, Swedish style, beneath a photograph of a Royal Swedish Crayfish Tree, the traditional centerpiece at the August Crayfish Festival. The tree is a multileveled pyramid of plates on a stand, each plate festooned with crayfish, claws forward, tails back, the whole crowned with a spray of dill.

"There's only two things you can do wrong boiling crayfish," Egil says, "not use enough dill and overcook." The crayfish Egil takes from his refrigerator are larger and more deeply red than the Louisiana type. "*Never* boil more than five minutes." Egil glowers and offers me one with the traditional chaser of vodka. In twenty-four minutes we have cleaned the platter of twenty-four crayfish and Egil has laid their little decapitated heads in a ring around the plate. "Swedish style," he explains.

> 4 pounds live crayfish
> 1 cup sea salt
> ¼ cup brown sugar
> 2 bunches fresh crown dill

Soak crayfish in cold water for 10 to 15 minutes to get rid of sand. Bring 8 quarts water to a vigorous boil with the salt, sugar, and a half bunch of dill. Remove dill, add the crayfish and another bunch of fresh dill. Return to the boil as quickly as possible and boil gently no more than 5 minutes.

Remove from heat and discard the dill. Put the crayfish into a crock, pour the stock over the crayfish and add the remaining half bunch of dill. Store in your refrigerator 1 or 2 days to allow the crayfish to absorb the flavors of the liquid. Drain well before serving and decorate with dill crowns. Serves 2 to 4.

DANISH KRINGLE

At Ellen Madsen's Little Denmark Cafe, I make a lunch of her counter of pastries—in the interests of research. While Ellen talks about the fall festival at California's Danish town of Solvang, in the Santa Ynez Valley, founded in 1910 by the Danish Lutheran church, I dream of Christmas and Danish kringles. The reason Danish pastry is so good is that the dough is a butter-layered puff pastry, sweetened and leavened, and filled with nuts, sugar, and spice. The Danes make a Christmas wreath of this dough and call it a "kringle," as in Kris Kringle. The dough is easier to work than straight puff pastry because it contains milk, eggs, and yeast, so it is a good dough for the home cook. As always, proportions vary, but the ones used here I've taken from a booklet by Julie Jensen McDonald, accurately titled *Delectably Danish* (1982).

> 1 package dry yeast
> ¼ cup very warm (110°–115°) water
> 2 cups all-purpose flour
> ¼ cup each cake flour and granulated sugar
> ½ teaspoon salt
> ½ teaspoon vanilla extract
> ¼ cup lukewarm milk
> 1 egg, beaten
> ½ pound (2 sticks) butter

Filling

> 1 cup brown sugar
> ½ teaspoon cinnamon
> ½ cup chopped toasted pecans
> 1 tablespoon egg white, beaten
> powdered sugar

Dissolve yeast in the warm water. Mix the flours with the sugar and salt. Add vanilla, milk, and egg to the yeast, and stir into the flour. Knead the dough until smooth. Wrap in a plastic bag and refrigerate 15 minutes.

Between 2 sheets of wax paper, flatten each stick of butter into a 4-by-6-inch rectangle. Chill. Roll out the dough into an 8-by-12-inch rectangle. Place one of the butter rectangles in the middle of the dough. Fold the bottom third of the dough over the butter and seal the far edge to enclose it. Place the remaining butter on top of the folded dough and fold the top third of the dough over the top layer of butter, sealing the edges. Turn the layers so that the narrow end is toward you and roll the dough into an 8-by-12-inch rectangle. Fold it into thirds and indent one edge with your finger to mark the first turn. Wrap dough in foil and chill 30 minutes (or put in freezer for 10 minutes). Repeat twice for a total of 3 turns, rolling, folding, and chilling between each turn. If butter breaks through the dough, patch it by dusting with flour. After the last turn, chill 6 hours or overnight.

Roll dough into a 6-by-25-by-¼-inch strip. Mix brown sugar, cinnamon, nuts, and beaten egg white together and spread center of dough with this filling. Fold one side of the dough over the center. Fold other side over the center and pinch the edges of the dough together to seal them. Bring the two ends of the strip together to form a ring and pinch the dough together where they join. Invert ring onto a buttered and floured baking sheet with a rim (in case any of the butter leaks from the dough during baking) so that the "seam" is on the bottom. Flatten top of dough gently. Let rise for 30 minutes in a warm place. Bake at 375° until golden brown, 20 to 30 minutes. Slip the wreath onto a cake rack to cool. When ready to serve, sprinkle the wreath with powdered sugar.

Serves 8 to 12.

CROATIAN WALNUT PITA

On the Dalmatian coast, the region of the Maraska has long exported its sour cherries to the rest of the world under the name "maraschino" cherries. Washington state, as it happens, abounds in sweet and sour cherries on both sides of the Cascade Range, including the wild and very tart chokecherry. The Franulovich family feels at home not only among the sea and pines of Anacortes, but also among its cherry trees.

From their Austro-Hungarian side, Croatians have inherited an enormously rich tradition of desserts, as I found in a cook book called *Croatian Cuisine*, published in 1978 by a pair of California university students, Ruzica and Alojije Kapetanovic. One distinctive Croatian pastry is a type of shortbread they call "pita," which for dessert they fill with fruits, nuts, cheese, and chocolate, and for a main dish with meat, cheese, and vegetables. Here I've wedded a dessert walnut pita to a sour cherry pita, blessed by bitter chocolate and rum, following the northwestern rubric "everything in excess."

    3 cups all-purpose flour
    1 teaspoon baking powder
    ½ teaspoon salt
    ½ cup sugar
    ½ pound (2 sticks) butter
    1 egg, beaten
    2 tablespoons lemon juice
    1 tablespoon grated lemon rind
    2 tablespoons sour cream

Filling

    5 eggs, separated
    1 cup sugar, plus some for sprinkling
    2 cups walnuts, ground
    2 ounces bitter chocolate, grated
    2 tablespoons rum
    2 cups tart cherries, pitted
    2 tablespoons butter, melted

Mix flour, baking powder, salt, and sugar. Slice the ½ pound butter into small pieces and cut into dry mixture with fingertips or processor. Combine the egg, lemon juice, lemon rind, and sour cream and mix lightly with the flour mixture until the dough just begins to stick together. Wrap in plastic and chill for 1 hour. Divide the dough in half and roll or pat each half into a rectangle the size of a 9-by-12-by-2-inch baking pan. Butter and flour the baking pan well. Place one rectangle in the pan, wrap the other in plastic, and chill both while preparing the filling.

Beat egg yolks with the sugar until light and fluffy and add the nuts, chocolate, and rum. Beat the egg whites until stiff but not dry and fold into the nut mixture.

Spread this filling over the bottom layer of dough. Spread the cherries on top of the filling and cover with the remaining dough layer. Brush top with melted butter and a sprinkling of sugar. Bake at 350° until top is nicely browned, 45 to 60 minutes. Let cool, then cut into diamonds or squares.

Makes 16 squares.

APLETS AND COTLETS

In 1920, Armen Tertsagian and Mark Balaban were ahead of their time when they tried to sell yogurt to the pioneers of Wenatchee Valley, so the pair of Armenian immigrants turned to apples instead. In Cashmere, they named their orchards "Liberty" and began to experiment with canning and dehydrating the fruit. With an excess of apple juice on their hands, they remembered the sweet of the Middle East known there as *rahat locum* and in the West as Turkish delight. There it was made of mastic, flavored with orange-blossom or rose water and textured with almonds or pistachios. Here they boiled down apple juice for "Aplets" and apricot juice for "Cotlets" to form a thick jelly. Now their descendants turn out nine thousand pounds of "Oregon delight" each day. In the Middle East, Claudia Roden writes, Turkish delight was "largely responsible for the extra weight put on by the ladies of the leisured classes." In the Far West, Aplets and Cotlets are regarded as health-food candy, with good-for-you fruits and nuts.

3 tablespoons gelatin
3 cups apple juice or unsweetened apricot juice
1⅓ cups granulated sugar
2 tablespoons each lemon and lime juice, or more as needed
⅔ cup cornstarch
2 cups walnuts, chopped
1 cup powdered sugar

Soften the gelatin in ½ cup of the apple juice. Boil remaining juice with the sugar for 15 minutes to concentrate it. Mix the lemon and lime juice, and add all but ¼ cup cornstarch to dissolve it in the mixture. Add both gelatin mixture and cornstarch mixture to the boiled juice and boil again rapidly for 10 minutes until very thick, stirring constantly. Taste for sweet and sour and add more lemon juice if wanted.

Mix in the walnuts and pour mixture into a 9-by-9-by-2-inch baking pan that has been dipped in cold water. Let paste harden 12 hours or overnight, then cut with a sharp knife into squares. Mix together the reserved ¼ cup cornstarch and powdered sugar. Remove squares with a spatula and roll each in the powdered sugar mixture (the cornstarch helps keep the sugar dry).

Makes about 64 small cubes.

Index

Abalone, 455
Account of Two Voyages to New England, An (Josselyn), xxxii
Acton, Eliza, 180–81
Alamode beef, 282–84
Alaria, 445
Alaskan sourdough bread, 459–61
Alex's crawfish bisque, 121–23
Almond-chocolate torte with apricot cream, 482–83
American Cookery (Simmons), 248–49
Americans, The (Boorstin), xxix–xxx, 168
Anchovy-orange butter, barbecued salmon with, 437–38
Angel biscuits, 229–30
Aniseed cookies, 83
Apfelkraut, 370–71
Aplets and cotlets, 501–502
Appledore blueberry pudding, 313–15, 319
Appledore Cookbook, The (Parloa), 262, 313, 319
Apples:
  -cream tart, Marlborough, 315–16
  German pancake with, 399–400
  hearth-roasted, 477
  sauerkraut, 370–71
Apricot cream, chocolate-almond torte with, 482–83
Artichokes with garlic, roasted, 476
Art of Cookery Made Plain and Easy, The (Glasse), xxvii, 224
Atole, 14
Avocado-lime, Dungeness crab with, 451–52

Barbecued:
  salmon with anchovy-orange butter, 437–38
  Virginia's pork, 182–84
  Willapa Bay oysters, 453–54
Barbecue sauce, tomato-soy, 184–85
Batter, beer, 55
Beans:
  Bean Town, 287–89
  black, sauce, steamed rockfish with, 491
  Buster's red, and rice, 105–107
  cornfield peas and coconut rice, 192–93
  cowpeas and rice, 107–108
  fried, purée, 54
Bean sprouts, pheasant with, 490–91
Becker, Marion Rombauer, 341–42
Beecher, Catharine, xxxvi, 300
Beef:
  alamode, 282–84
  homemade, or venison jerky, 462
  hunter, 188–89
  and oyster sausages, 226–27
  pickled, 364–65
  scarlet, with vegetables, 285–87
Beer:
  batter, 55
  cream of, soup, 388
  and molasses, country ham with, 186–87
Beignets, French market, 156–57
Belgian cheese pie, 360–61
Belle, Frances P., 454
Benne wafers, salted, 216–17
Berkeley Cookbook, The (Miller), 481
Berolzheimer, Ruth, 369
Berry jam cake, wild, 468–69

Hazelton, Nika, 381
Head cheese, hog's, 196–97
Hearn, Lafcadio, 99
Helen Brown's clam pone, 450–51
Herball (Gerard), xxvi, 220, 280, 302
Herbed veal balls, 354–55
Heritage Hill Cookbook, 373
Herring, Lizzie Kander's pickled, 351–52
Hickory-nut cookies, 401–402
Higginson, Francis, 253
Hijiki, 445
Hiller, Elizabeth, 21, 26
Himmel und erde, 378–79
Hoback, Priscilla and Peter, 47, 53, 58, 77
Hog's head cheese, 196–97
Holmes, Buster, 115–16
Home Cookery (Chadwick), 285, 289, 324
Home Life in Colonial Days (Earle), 250
Hominy, 14
  big, 14
  block, 14
  bread, Owendaw, 199–200
  flour, 14
  grits, creamy, 198–99
  homemade, and *masa,* 23–24
  and pork, 32–33
  posole, 14, 32–33
  small, 14
  and tripe, 33–34
Honey butter, 77–78
Hopi Cookery (Kavena), 23, 28
Hoppin' John, 107–108
Hot slaw, 297–98
Housekeeping in Old Virginia (Tyree), 188, 192–93, 196, 197, 200, 222–23
House Servant's Directory, The (Roberts), 250–51
Hughes, Phyllis, 43
Hunter beef, 188–89
Hushpuppies and fried catfish, 206–207

Ice cream, three-fruit, 301–303
Improved Housewife, The (Webster), 277, 296, 308

Indian:
  blue cornbread, 31
  corn roast, 21–22
  cress salad, 299
  popped corn, 20
  slapjacks, 267–69
  squash and green chili, 57
Indian Fishing: Early Methods on the Northwest Coast (Stewart), 431–32, 448
Ingredients, 19

Jambalaya ala everything, 109–11
Jellied veal, 368–69
Jerky, homemade beef or venison, 462
Jerusalem artichoke pickles, 220–21
Jícama salad, 74
Johnnycakes, 263–64
Jonnycake Journal, 260
Josselyn, John, xxxii, 291, 295–96, 303
Joy of Cooking, The (Rombauer and Becker), 341–42, 389, 397

Kaa T'eix's Cookbook (Pelayo), 446
Kander, Lizzie Black, 341, 349, 351–52, 353, 360, 370, 381, 388–90, 393, 395, 399–401, 403–404
Kartoffelkloese, 390–91
Kavasch, Barrie, 70
Kavena, Juanita Tiger, 23, 28
Kitchen Companion (Parloa), 293–94
Kitchiner, Dr. William, 226
Kiwi and papaya salad, warm, 473
Koenigsberger klops, 354–55
Kush-kush, 149

La Cuisine (Saint-Ange), 294
La Cuisine Creole (Hearn), 99
Lamb and chili stew with blue balls, 30–31
Leberkloese, 389–90
Lee, Mrs. N. K. M., 226, 296
Lemon:
  butter, 130–31
  candied, slices, 154

Southern syllabub, 236–37
Soy:
    sauce, Carolina, 218–19
    -tomato barbecue sauce, 184–85
Spaetzle, 398–99
"Sparrow" dumplings, 398–99
Spinach and strawberry salad, 472
Spoon bread, fresh corn and pecan, 230–31
Sprouted wheat:
    flour, preparation of, 79
    pudding, 80
Squab with figs and olives, 467–68
Squash:
    deep-fried, blossoms, 55
    Indian, and green chili, 57
Squeezer's okra fritters, 212–13
Stew:
    chicken booyah, 387
    lamb and chili, with blue balls, 30–31
    pine bark, 207–208
    pork and hominy, 32–33
    pumpkin shell, 58–59
    tripe and hominy, 33–34
    venison and corn, 61–62
    wild mushroom ragout, 464–65
Stewart, Hilary, 431–32, 448
Stir-fry:
    Chinese tsap sui, 487–89
    nectarine-chayote, 495–96
Strawberry and spinach salad, 472
Stuffed soft-shell crabs with Creolaise sauce, 125–27
Succotash, Zuni summer, 56–57
Sülze, 368–69
Summer succotash, Zuni, 56–57
Sunflower and piñon cakes, 70
Sushi, homemade cocktail, 492–93
Swedish-Astoria crayfish, 497
Sweet and sour Christmas fish, 352–53
Sweet potato:
    cornbread, 215–16
    pone, 153–54
Syllabub, Southern, 236–37

Tabasco sauce, 100–101
Tamale pie, X-LNT, 49–50
Tamales, 47–49
Tart:
    coconut praline, 153
    Marlborough apple-cream, 315–16
    pecan praline, 152–53
Taste of Country Cooking, The (Lewis), 168
Thirded bread, 266–67
Thoreau, Henry David, 5, 245, 247–48, 262, 271, 295, 317
Three-fruit ice cream, 301–303
Tofu, grilled, with miso sauce, 493–95
Tomato:
    chili sauce with, 41
    -cinnamon church soup, 280–81
    sauce, 44–45
    -soy barbecue sauce, 184–85
Tongue with raspberry vinegar, 365–66
Torte:
    chocolate-almond, with apricot cream, 482–83
    poppyseed, 403–404
    raspberry "pinch pie," 404–405
Tortillas, fresh corn-dough, 24–26
Tostados, 27
    blue chips, 29
Towle, Dorothy, 311
Traditional Navajo Foods and Cooking, 12, 21
Tramp Abroad, A (Twain), xxvii
Treatise on Domestic Economy, A (Beecher), xxxvi
Trifle, a grand, 237–38
Tripe and hominy, 33–34
Tsap sui, Chinese, 487–89
Tuna, marinated, 442
Turkey with chili and bitter chocolate, 65–66
Turnip roots, yellow and white, 191–92
Turtle soup, green, 128–29
Tuthill, Mrs. Louisa C., 251
Twain, Mark, xxiii, xxvii
Two Hundred Years of Charleston Cooking (Rhett), 166, 200, 207, 209, 211, 215

Tyree, Marion Cabell, 188, 192–93, 196, 197, 200, 232–33

Ude, Louis Eustache, 180–81, 214–15, 272
U.S. Regional Cookbook, The (Berolzheimer), 369

Veal:
  balls, herbed, 354–55
  jellied, 368–69
  paprika cream, 355–57
Vegetable Garden, The (Vilmorin-Andrieux), 189
Venison:
  and corn stew, 61–62
  homemade, or beef jerky, 462
  pepper steaks with cranberry glaze, 381–82
Vilmorin-Andrieux et Cie, 189
Vinegar, fruit, 473
Virginia Cookery-book, The (Smith), 227
Virginia Housewife, The (Randolph), 180, 181, 185, 188–89, 224, 228, 320
Virginia's barbecued pork, 182–84
Vollstandiges Kochbuch für die Deutsch-Amerikanische Kuche, 341, 365

Wafers, salted benne, 216–17
Wakame, 445
Walden, or, Life in the Woods (Thoreau), 245, 295, 317
Walking (Thoreau), 5
Walnut pita, Croatian, 499–501

Walnuts and chèvre, grilled halibut with, 449–50
Washington, Martha, 191, 228, 254, 272, 300, 302, 324
Waters, Alice, 424, 428
Weaver, William Woys, 348, 362
Webster, Mrs. A. L., 277, 291, 296, 308, 316, 323
West Coast Cook Book (Brown), 50, 439, 442, 450, 490
Wet milling, 15
Wheels of Fortune (Seufert), 433
Whitefish with whitefish liver, planked, 349
White poppyseed soup, 386
White sauce, 355
Wild berry jam cake, 468–69
Wild duck with plums, 466–67
Wild mushroom ragout, 464–65
Wild rice with blueberries and morels, 383–84
Wilson, Anne, 291, 306
Winthrop, John, 250
Wisconsin Style Cooking, 350

X-LNT tamale pie, 49–50

Yam yeast bread, 147–48
Yankee nut cakes, 269–71
Yellow and white turnip roots, 191–92
Young Lady's Home, The (Tuthill), 251

Zuni Breadstuff (Cushing), 11–12, 18, 30, 56
Zuni summer succotash, 56–57
Zweiback, 395–96

FOR THE BEST IN PAPERBACKS, LOOK FOR THE